Wireless Futures

Technicities

Series Editors: Ryan Bishop, Winchester School of Art, University of Southampton and Jussi Parikka, Aarhus University and FAMU, Prague

The philosophy of technicities: exploring how technology mediates art, frames design and augments the mediated collective perception of everyday life.

Technicities will publish the latest philosophical thinking about our increasingly immaterial technocultural conditions, with a unique focus on the context of art, design and media.

Published

Lyotard and the Inhuman Condition: Reflections on Nihilism, Information and Art
Ashley Woodward

Critical Luxury Studies: Art, Design, Media
Edited by John Armitage and Joanne Roberts

Cold War Legacies: Systems, Theory, Aesthetics
Edited by John Beck and Ryan Bishop

Fashion and Materialism
Ulrich Lehmann

Queering Digital India: Activisms, Identities, Subjectivities
Edited by Rohit K. Dasgupta and Debanuj DasGupta

Zero Degree Seeing: Barthes/Burgin and Political Aesthetics
Edited by Ryan Bishop and Sunil Manghani

Rhythm and Critique: Technics, Modalities, Practices
Edited by Paola Crespi and Sunil Manghani

Photography Off the Scale: Technologies and Theories of the Mass Image
Edited by Tomáš Dvořák and Jussi Parikka

The Informational Logic of Human Rights: Network Imaginaries in the Cybernetic Age
Josh Bowsher

Art and Technology in Maurice Blanchot
Holly Langstaff

China and the Wireless Undertow: Media as Wave Philosophy
Anna Greenspan

Reconfiguring the Portrait
Edited by Abraham Geil and Tomáš Jirsa

Robotic Vision and Virtual Interfacings: Seeing, Sensing, Shaping
Edited by Luci Eldridge and Nina Trivedi

Probabilistic Aesthetics of the Avant-Garde: Predictive Arts
Konrad Wojnowski

Wireless Futures: Speculative Media and German Modernity
Erik Born

www.edinburghuniversitypress.com/series/TECH

Wireless Futures

Speculative Media and German Modernity

Erik Born

EDINBURGH
University Press

Edinburgh University Press is one of the leading university presses in the UK. Publishing new research in the arts and humanities, EUP connects people and ideas to inspire creative thinking, open new perspectives and shape the world we live in. For more information, visit www.edinburghuniversitypress.com.

Grateful acknowledgement is made to the sources listed in the List of Illustrations for permission to reproduce material previously published elsewhere. Every effort has been made to trace the copyright holders, but if any have been inadvertently overlooked, the publisher will be pleased to make the necessary arrangements at the first opportunity.

Edinburgh University Press Ltd
13 Infirmary Street, Edinburgh EH1 1LT

Typeset in 11/13 Adobe Sabon by
IDSUK (DataConnection) Ltd, and
Printed and bound in the UK using 100% renewable electricity by
CPI Group (UK) Ltd

A CIP record for this book is available from the British Library

ISBN 978 1 3995 5359 9 (hardback)
ISBN 978 1 3995 5357 5 (webready PDF)
ISBN 978 1 3995 5358 2 (epub)

EU Authorised Representative:
Easy Access System Europe
Mustamäe tee 50, 10621 Tallinn, Estonia
gpsr.requests@easproject.com

MIX
Paper | Supporting responsible forestry
FSC® C013604
www.fsc.org

This book is printed using paper from well-managed forests, recycling and other controlled sources

Contents

Figures

Acknowledgements

For Reanna

Wireless thinking involves making unexpected connections. Credit for the book cover and part of the inspiration for this media-philosophical project goes to the now-defunct Palais des Beaux Arts Wien. During a research stay in Vienna, supported by the Fulbright Program, I met Bernhard Garnicnig, a local artist who was attending an academic lecture at the International Research Center for Cultural Studies (Internationales Forschungszentrum Kulturwissenschaften, IFK). He was interested in wireless and happened to have access to an art space, named the 'Palais des Beaux Arts Wien' after its famous counterpart in Paris and with its own venerable history. However, there was a catch: the public was not allowed to enter the building. To create exhibitions, Bernhard thus brilliantly set up a Wi-Fi network that visitors could use to experience the collection. Unlike many virtual collections, it could only be accessed on site through the local network, which led us to think and talk about the origins and futures of wireless sign(al)s. After reading my essay, which has now been revised and expanded into the Preface to this book, the next artist-in-residence, Karin Ferrari, continued the process of pattern recognition as part of artistic research on decoding, occultism, and conspiracy theories. I am grateful to Bernhard, Karin (and for the book cover image!), Alexandra Mogyoros, and Linda Glaser for conversations about what has been my favourite part of this project in thinking through wireless.

The research and years-long revisions of this book would not have been possible without the support of several institutions and the labour of the individuals of which they are composed. I would like to express my deep gratitude to the Department of German Studies at the University of California, Berkeley, for supporting my dissertation, 'Sparks to Signals: Literature, Science, and Wireless Technology, 1800–1930', which provided the foundation for this book. Thank you to the Max Kade Foundation for providing research travel fellowships and to the Fulbright Scholars Program and the IFK for sponsoring an extended research stay in Vienna. For access to archival materials, I am grateful to Jörg Schmalfuß at the Deutsches Technikmuseum in Berlin and Wolf Harranth at the Dokumentationsarchiv Funk in Vienna. Thank you Günter Hack of the Österreichische Rundfunk and Ernst Schmiederer of the Austrian edition of *Die Zeit*, for publicising my research.

The idea for the antenna chapter materialised during a meeting of BTWH: The Emergence of Modernity, an international research network that provides a wonderful space for developing research projects. Birgit Nemec, Joachim Schätz, and Marie-Noelle Yazdanpanah are not only great interlocutors but also great people. As my intellectual role models, I particularly wish to acknowledge Ingo Zechner and to preserve the memory of Siegfried Mattl. For their criticisms, suggestions, and support of an unorthodox research project, I am grateful to my dissertation advisors, Mary Ann Doane, Anton Kaes, and Niklaus Largier, without whom this project would never have been completed. I owe my sense of the possibilities for this project and research in general to Niklaus, whose *Möglichkeitssinn* seems to know no bounds. I am also thankful for many inspiring conversations about this project with Yael Almog, Kurt Beals, Paul Dobryden, Kenneth Fockele, Sebastian Haselbeck, Tara Hottman, Jennifer Ingalls, Sabrina Rahman, Sasha Rossman, Eric Savoth, Matthew Stoltz, and Dagmar Theison.

Portions of various chapters were presented at conferences and summer schools at the Humboldt University of Berlin, the University of Vienna, and the Bauhaus University, Weimar. I am particularly grateful to Jocelyn Holland, Gabriel Trop, Leif Weatherby, and the participants at the GSA Seminar Series on 'Technologien' and 'Kulturtechniken'. Additional revisions were undertaken while I was a postdoctoral fellow at Cornell's Society for the Humanities. For feedback on the antenna chapter, I am particularly grateful to Gloria Kim, Daniel Smyth, Alicia Imperiale, Rahul Mukherjee, and Timothy Murray. The DAAD Summer School in Media Studies organised by Patrizia C. McBride on 'Literature, Media, Form' introduced me to other early career scholars in German media studies and pushed my methodology further. Thank you Josh Alvizu, Carl Gelderloos, Julie Johnson, Brandon Pelcher, Felix Twerase, Tyler Whitney, and Katrina Nousek, for discussing my work in progress. A dedicated Zoom manuscript workshop with Timothy C. Campbell, Florian Sprenger, and Wolf Kittler made for an incredible discussion and propelled the book towards its final form. The Introduction benefited greatly from being workshopped with a multidisciplinary group of scholars at Cornell's Media Studies Colloquium. I am grateful to Sophia König for hosting a collaborative workshop on waves and rays in literature under the title 'Unheimliche Allianzen', supported by the Dahlem Humanities Center (DHC) at the Freie Universität, Berlin, as the project entered its final stretch. For research and proofreading work, I would like to thank my tireless, generous, and detail-oriented student research assistant, Nicholas Sola.

For their ongoing feedback and support, I am grateful to my colleagues at Cornell University in the Department of German Studies and across campus. Thank you Jeremy Braddock, Andrew Campana, Paul Fleming, Patrizia McBride, Tim Murray, Natasha Raheja, and Elke Siegel for sharing all your ideas about wireless and for your publishing advice. Thank you Jussi Parikka and Ryan Bishop for making a home for this project in the Technicities series. I am grateful to the two anonymous readers for appreciating the book's two main ambitions in theorising wireless transmission and revitalising speculative media theory, and for their generative feedback on refining statements of the book's main argument and focus. Thank you Amanda Speake for your expertise in preparing the index. Thanks, too, to Carol Macdonald, Souhaila Jouhar, Grace Balfour-Harle, and everyone at Edinburgh University Press for shepherding this book through production.

I am grateful to the Hull Memorial Publication Fund of Cornell University for awarding this publication a production subvention.

For their constant inspiration and unflagging encouragement, I am forever grateful to my friends and family. Thank you Cari and Judy, for all your support throughout this project. Even though they are not yet old enough to read this manuscript, Georgia and Mae make me hopeful for better futures – wireless or otherwise. Thank you, Reanna, for always being my first and last reader.

Unless otherwise noted, all translations are my own.

Series Editors' Preface

Technological transformation has profound and frequently unforeseen influences on art, design and media. At times technology emancipates art and enriches the quality of design. Occasionally it causes acute individual and collective problems of mediated perception. Time after time technological change accomplishes both simultaneously. This new book series explores and reflects philosophically on what new and emerging *technicities* do to our everyday lives and increasingly immaterial technocultural conditions. Moving beyond traditional conceptions of the philosophy of technology and of techne, the series presents new philosophical thinking on how technology constantly alters the essential conditions of beauty, invention and communication. From novel understandings of the world of technicity to new interpretations of aesthetic value, graphics and information, Technicities focuses on the relationships between critical theory and representation, the arts, broadcasting, print, technological genealogies/histories, material culture and digital technologies and our philosophical views of the world of art, design and media.

The series foregrounds contemporary work in art, design and media while remaining inclusive, in terms of both philosophical perspectives on technology and interdisciplinary contributions. For a philosophy of technicities is crucial to extant debates over the artistic, inventive and informational aspects of technology. The books in the Technicities series concentrate on present-day and evolving technological advances, but visual, design-led and mass-mediated questions are emphasised to further our knowledge of their often-combined means of digital transformation.

The editors of Technicities welcome proposals for monographs and well-considered edited collections that establish new paths of investigation.

Ryan Bishop and Jussi Parikka

Preface: Signs, Signals, Speculations

What does it mean to be wireless? To pose this question for our current situation, there is no better figure of thought than the ubiquitous sign that also features on this book's cover, a vernacular representation of wireless signals (Fig. P.1). In stylised form, the dot represents an antenna, and the curved lines radiating out from it symbolise the physical transmission medium, radio waves. Wireless signals may be found everywhere, but human beings cannot sense them anywhere. Signs point the way to signals.

Like the signals it signifies, the wireless sign can be found nearly everywhere, from public spaces to private devices. The ubiquity of

Figure P.1 Vernacular symbol for wireless signals, especially WLANs (aka Wi-Fi). It remediates the iconography of national radio and television broadcasting, wireless telegraphy and telephony, and the physical transmission medium of electromagnetic radiation. Source: WikiMedia Commons.

wireless sign(al)s reinforces diagnoses of the present as a wireless age, a transitional period moving away from traditional borders, gatekeeping systems, and material constraints towards universal access, ubiquitous coverage, and unlimited circulation. Going wireless, to cite the industry's teleological rhetoric, reduces the complex and contested process of media change to the more easily marketable rhetoric of incremental and inevitable progress. Being wireless implies not only freedom and mobility but also having privileged access to the future. Wireless simply seems to be a sign of the times, expressed in concepts of ubiquitous computing, ambient intelligence, seamless connectivity, perpetual contact, the always-on society, or, in a word, wirelessness.

While the wireless sign crystallises many aspects of this contemporary discourse, which tends to frame wires as things of the past and wireless as a sign of the future, it also suggests a radically different way of thinking through medium specificity and media change. As an unofficial, non-standard, vernacular image of unknowable authorship and indeterminable origins, the wireless sign exhibits a different logic than organisational certification marks such as Wi-Fi and corporate brands such as Bluetooth or Qi, which usually attract the attention of media studies.[1] Instead of evoking pre-modern mythologies about the unification of polarised forces or metaphysical concepts related to spiritual energies, the wireless sign refers to something non-human, imperceptible, and yet very much real: electromagnetic radiation, the physical medium that makes wireless transmissions possible. Complementing its semi-technical functions in signifying imperceptible radio waves, indicating the strength and quality of network reception, and providing an invitation – or an imperative – to connect, the wireless sign also serves to connect user expectations of the new, strange, or mysterious to the old, familiar, and understandable. Presenting an elegant visual solution to the challenges posed by wireless signals, as an imperceptible form of electromagnetic radiation, to discourse, imagination, representation, and the articulation of knowledge, the wireless sign registers speculative connections across multiple generations of technology – or, more precisely, transhistorical 'genres of communication, genres of information', from wireless telegraphy and telephony through radio and radar to walkie talkies, Wi-Fi, and whatever the future may hold.[2]

The wireless sign's meaning has remained relatively stable for the past twenty-five years, ever since its popularisation as a sign for wireless local area networks (WLANs, aka 'Wi-Fi').[3] However, it is hardly future-proof, as evident in its semiotic fluctuations over the previous 250 years. To late twentieth-century observers, our wireless sign would have been an ambiguous figure. Coupled with an antenna tower, it could have been a sign for radio or TV, but with a telephone, loudspeaker, or ray gun, one for radio waves, sound waves, or 'death rays'. To mid-twentieth-century observers, our wireless sign would have seemed like a truncated version of the iconography for national broadcasting, a quadrant sliced out of a circle. To early twentieth-century observers, it would have had nothing to do with these so-called mass media but rather the then-new medium of wireless telegraphy. To nineteenth-, eighteenth-, or seventeenth-century observers who lived before the scientific verification of electromagnetic radiation but were still surrounded by this naturally occurring phenomenon, our wireless sign would have been more commonly found in elementary physics textbooks or scholarly treatises with diagrams of fluid motion (Fig. P.2). Why it took so long for mimetic images of waves in nature to make it into the European scientific tradition remains an open question, which is bound up with the history and theory of telegraphy and of the sciences of electricity and magnetism. It would be absurd to speculate that early modern diagrams of mechanical fluid motion (Fig. P.2) were the direct source for our wireless sign (Fig. P.1), despite their close formal resemblances. Yet they clearly resonate with each other.[4]

As a critical study in the spirit of speculative media philosophy, *Wireless Futures* unpacks the media question for the case of German modernism and modernity, challenges outmoded assumptions about medium specificity and media change, and presents a new way of thinking through wireless at the nexus of media, aesthetics, and philosophy. In communications and mass media studies, wireless has been traditionally equated with the communications media of telegraphy and telephony or the mass media of radio and television, despite other important applications in radar and radioastronomy; and the wireless age said to have started around 1900 is assumed to continue into the present. *Wireless Futures* presents a different way of thinking through the medial order of things, from wireless as synonymous with individual media; through wirelessness as a condition of possibility enabling experiments with electromagnetic radiation across the radio frequency spectrum; to wirelessing as a cultural technique bound up with speculative media and technologies of future-making. Although this book's primary objects of study are historical, its theoretical touchstones are contemporary, providing an innovative approach to rethinking relations between old media and new media. In reading across the perceived analogue/digital divide, *Wireless Futures* aims to rewire contemporary media discourses through their historical antecedents. Far from an antiquarian study, this media-philosophical

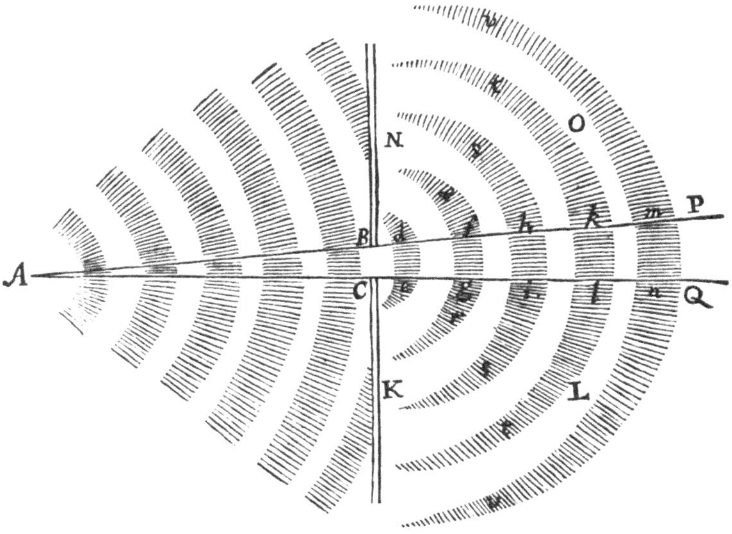

Figure P.2 Early modern physics treatises established the iconography of fluid motion that would subsequently inform representations of the transmission or propagation of electromagnetic radiation in modern physics. In a physical 'medium', waves flow from source (A) through a hole (B–C), thereby creating refraction at subsequent points (d–e, f–g and so on). Source: Isaac Newton, *Principia* (1687), 355.

project mobilises the critical urgency of wireless for a recursive perspective, whereby our present situation reveals new facets of the past and insights into the future.

Thinking through media, writing in a critical conditional mode, and exploring unexpected resonances across space and time – the media-philosophical approach introduced here and developed further throughout this book is what I term 'speculative media studies'. Speculation simultaneously describes the book's main object of analysis (that is, wireless as a medium of intellectual and financial speculation) and a way of reading, writing, and thinking about it (that is, doing speculative research). For a study that explores connections across speculative philosophy, financial speculation, speculative fiction, and related forms of scientific forecasting, it seems only fitting to experiment with reading, writing, and thinking in a speculative mode. However, this book's critical approach must be distinguished at the outset from common associations of speculation with idleness, paranoia, gambling, and armchair philosophy. 'Speculative media theory' was one of the earliest labels for what came to be known as

'German media theory' (GMT), an influential 'academic discourse network' associated with the name of Friedrich A. Kittler and entangled with ongoing scholarly debates about media archaeology, media anthropology, and media philosophy.[5] Themes of aesthetics, materiality, and limit-thinking that are central to this body of scholarship are also addressed in speculative realism and object-oriented ontology, and yet these approaches are not as relevant to this present study, due to their categorical dismissals of history and aesthetics.[6] Science fiction studies presents a more complementary framework for analysing modernist visions of wireless futures, provided that 'SF' is understood not only in the sense of the modernist genres of science fiction, speculative fiction, fantasy, horror, alternative history, or utopias and dystopias, but also as an entire way of thinking or being in an 'as-if' mode. 'As a mode of narrative and a form of knowledge', SF is distinguished not by 'its capacity to keep the future alive, even in imagination' but by 'its deepest vocation [. . .] to demonstrate and to dramatize our incapacity to imagine the future'.[7] For a provisional definition, speculating can thus be understood as a cultural technique of future-making, a means of projecting the past into the future, or vice versa, thereby creating the social, economic, and affective investments necessary for undertaking unprecedented projects in the present. Beyond the book title's immediate connotations, underscoring the plurality of modernist visions, *Wireless Futures* can be understood in the sense of futures trading or futures contracts, a reminder not only of how every medium affects both space and time, but particularly of how 'the telegraph shifts speculation into another dimension [. . .] from space to time, from arbitrage to futures'.[8]

This critical speculative approach differs from uncritical speculations about being wireless, going wireless, and the wireless age, insofar as they posit non-existent ontological identities and elide important technical and conceptual differences among distinct genres of technology. What if there are no wireless media per se, as most other studies assume, but rather only historically contingent cultural techniques that escalate into media technologies and thereby become wireless at certain times and under certain conditions? What if the word 'wireless' only makes sense in its adjectival and adverbial but not its nominal forms, only as a relational term or an action verb connecting subjects and objects, and not an isolated entity? What if there are no wireless beings, but perhaps only 'radio beasts', 'the new species' that 'feeds on the etheric (quint)essences of the new noosphere, electromagnetic waves [. . .] and in oscillating circuits and feedback loops [. . .] spits these essences out again, broadcasting radio'?[9] What if wireless cultures, despite all their rhetoric of freedom and mobility, remain subject to the same structures of power and control established by their supposedly obsolescent wired precursors? What if there is neither a wireless revolution, nor a wireless age, only ongoing negotiations across the historical timeline? What if 'contemporariness', besides a colloquial synonym for the present, describes 'a singular relationship with one's own time, which adheres to it and, at the same keep, keeps a distance from it [. . .] *through a disjunction and an anachronism*'?[10]

This book is about the sociotechnical imagination of wireless futures. However, it is not primarily about the possible futures of wireless at present, but rather the resonance of our current situation with wireless futures past. Before 'wireless' became synonymous with laptops, smartphones, and local area networks, it was associated for over half a century with national radio broadcasting (aka 'the wireless'). Before wireless became an institution, even before the first successful experimental trials in wireless telegraphy, it was already a central object of financial and theoretical speculation. Uncritical studies of wireless normally begin by recounting breathtaking numbers about media usage and presenting statistical models that only ever predict future market growth.[11] We need to question the ideological purpose behind such rhetorical strategies committed to upholding the status quo. Thinking not about user numbers and potential returns on investment but about wireless signs, signals, and speculations ultimately supplies this 'untimely mediation' with a 'time-critical' edge.[12] Although it is unlikely that a historically informed media philosophical study will prevent the repetition of the past, it can provide an important corrective to both the 'accidental amnesia' of contemporary media studies and the 'chronocentricity' of contemporary media cultures, 'the egotism that one's own generation is poised on the very cusp of history'.[13]

As will be shown in this book, speculation, conjecture, prediction, forecasting, risk-taking, and gambling played crucial roles in the media history and theory of wireless. Speculations about the possibility of long-distance signalling without wires date back to classical antiquity, albeit usually in the form of predetermined optical or acoustic systems. In the early modern period, scientists experimenting with electricity and magnetism started to detect a previously unknown phenomenon, though they continued to dismiss what would eventually become known as electromagnetic radiation as a limit case of induction. In 1865 James Clerk Maxwell predicted the existence of oscillating electric and magnetic fields that travel through empty space at the finite speed of light.[14] In 1888 Heinrich Hertz scientifically verified the existence of such waves within the radiofrequency spectrum with his epochal laboratory experiments.[15] And Guglielmo Marconi gambled on the mode's commercial application for telegraphy, wirelessing the first messages across the Bristol Channel in 1897, the English Channel in 1899, and the Atlantic Ocean in 1901.[16] Early wireless media empires such as the Marconi Company in England or the Telefunken Company in Germany were the objects of massive financial speculation. In his 1912 'Technical Manifesto of Futurist Literature', F. T. Marinetti speculated about the emergence of a literary 'wireless imagination' (*l'immaginazione senza fili*).[17] And authors of genre fiction increasingly exploited wireless for SF stories about interplanetary communication, future warfare, and the limits of commercialisation. Across vernacular modernisms, wireless fuelled speculations about what kinds of messages noisy signals might contain; what wireless might have in common with magic, telepathy, hypnotism, occultism, action at a distance, and communication with the dead; and what kinds of wireless-enabled devices might eventually materialise to exploit the medium's multiple affordances.

Although such wireless imaginations might seem limitless and although wireless transmissions themselves ignore sociopolitical borders, wireless studies have largely tended to replicate the traditional divisions of modern universities. In the Anglophone world, Guglielmo Marconi and the British Empire remain the dominant site for thinking through wireless, though recent studies have generated further insights through comparison with Ireland, Italy, and the United States.[18] Given the transnational trajectory of contemporary radio studies, this book's focus on the 'German' case might seem paradoxical or simply outmoded, and yet it is precisely the overdetermination of German radio, German media theory, and German media philosophy that makes it an important interface for 'the global wireless'.[19] German modernism and modernity presents a crucial site for thinking through wireless not only for the distinctive concept of *Funken* (wireless/sparks) connected to radio (*Rundfunk*) and cellular (*Funk*); for influential radio theories composed by Theodor W. Adorno, Rudolf Arnheim, Walter Benjamin, Bertolt Brecht, and many lesser-known media theorists *avant la lettre*; and for the problematic legacy of National Socialist radio politics for mass media studies. Though long neglected in favour of the standard period for theorising wireless, the periods bracketing the emergence of national radio broadcasting in the 1920s and its perceived decline since the 1980s are worthy of equal attention. As a contribution to media philosophy, *Wireless Futures* expands the traditional canon of speculative thinking from Immanuel Kant through Martin Heidegger to include a wide range of vernacular media thinkers.

In exploring resonances across space and time, this book's temporal scope is primarily delimited by the transitional period from radiotelegraphy and -telephony to radio, traditionally known as the pre-history of national broadcasting (c. 1880–1930); and secondarily by media scholars engaging with the contested legacy of mass media and making predictions about media convergence during the digital transition (c. 1980–present). My analysis addresses the sociotechnical imagination of wireless futures during the period from the 'discovery' of electromagnetic radiation through the 'invention' of wireless telegraphy to the 'institutionalisation' of national radio broadcasting. However, I argue that the meaning of media change only becomes apparent retrospectively, which demands the secondary period of analysis. By bracketing broadcasting and pursuing new connections between the mode's pre-history and post-history, *Wireless Futures* challenges the dominant narrative in communications and mass media studies of wireless telegraphy as the logical extension of wired telegraphy and national radio broadcasting as the endpoint of perfect communication. In Anglophone media studies, the radio is traditionally assumed to be a mass medium associated with democracy and the public sphere, and the period from the 1920s to the 1950s is colloquially known – because of the rapid growth in consumer adoption rates, the governmental regulation of the radio spectrum, and the consolidation of multiple radio stations capable of simultaneously broadcasting the same content into powerful broadcasting networks – as the 'Golden Age of Radio'. While this standard developmental narrative might make sense for England or the United States, it is untenable for the simultaneous history of 'German radio', a term coined in the Weimar Republic, appropriated in Nazi Germany, and subsequently critiqued by scholars working in radio studies, media studies, and cultural studies.[20]

This book's geographical scope is focused primarily on modern Germany – particularly, the German Empire (1871–1918) and the Weimar Republic (1918–33) – though it also considers Austria, Switzerland, and other parts of the German-speaking world, along with further resonances across 'vernacular modernism'.[21] Questions of futurity are crucial for rethinking familiar stories about the mode's apparent destiny as an instrument of domination and control. *Wireless Futures* reimagines the seemingly linear trajectory from radiotelegraphy in Imperial Germany through radio broadcasting in the Weimar Republic to radar, encryption, and mass propaganda in Nazi Germany. Deeply invested in techniques of future-making while also committed to the idea that the future remains open, opaque, and unknowable, German modernity was occupied with deep-seated crises of representation and attempts to come to terms with rapid technological change.[22] By analogy with Tom Standage's concept of 'the Victorian Internet', I propose to call this book's main archive,

Wilhelmine wireless.[23] If the fascist-authoritarian model of mid-twentieth-century German radio, which immediately conjures up images of mass audiences susceptible to ideology, propaganda, and disinformation, once seemed key for unlocking the medium's essence, the capitalist-imperialist model of Wilhelmine wireless, though also not a model to be imitated, creates different resonances with our current situation, as media empires emerge through speculation and speculatively claim to represent the world's interests.

Rather than an essentialising theory or a universalising chronological account, 1880–2020, *Wireless Futures* presents a historically informed, media-philosophical study of select resonances among the epistemic markers, 1900/2000/2100.[24] *Wireless Futures* thus brackets the period traditionally associated with 'the wireless', and instead explores new connections between its pre-history and post-history. To connect the past to the future, the book's introduction and conclusion describe the two 'discourse networks' of wireless futures. The chapters present a means of thinking through wireless with interrelated case studies, which challenge familiar stories about the seemingly inevitable linear trajectory from experimental radiotelegraphy to mainstream radio broadcasting. Individual chapters examine the difference between wired and wireless transmission; the physics of electromagnetic media; speculations about the wireless age; literary and philosophical questions about wireless infrastructure; applications of radio beyond broadcasting; and the antenna as a media object.

Each medium exhibits its own 'techno-logics' and creates its own periodisation, which do not necessarily coincide with those established for the study of literature, culture, politics, philosophy, or other disciplines.[25] Hence, the method informing this media-philosophical study is necessarily transdisciplinary, the perspective is transhistorical, and the order of the following chapters is not strictly chronological, but rather topical and, in some cases, recursive.[26] The book's structure thereby enacts my contention that there is no absolute zero point from which to answer questions of medium specificity or media change once and for all.

The present continuously generates new resonances between the past and the future.

Notes

1. See Mackenzie, *Wirelessness*, 2–3; Greenspan, *China and the Wireless Undertow*, 23–5.
2. Hacking, 'Genres of Communication'.

3. See Lemstra et al., *The Innovation Journey of Wi-Fi*; Schaefer, 'Dematerialized Infrastructures'.
4. For further analysis of the wireless sign, see Born, 'A Little History of the Wireless Icon'; Born, 'Sparks to Signals'; Born, 'Wi-Fi Signal Icon'.
5. Lovink, 'Essay on Speculative Media Theory', 22–9.
6. See Harman, 'Speculation'.
7. Jameson, 'Progress versus Utopia', 153.
8. Carey, 'Technology and Ideology', 168.
9. Ernst, 'Das Radiotier', 331.
10. Agamben, *What is an Apparatus?*, 39.
11. See Katz and Aakhus, *Perpetual Contact*; Nyíri, *Mobile Understanding*; Castells, *Mobile Communication and Society*; Turkle, 'Always-On/Always-On-You'.
12. Geoghegan, 'Untimely Mediations'; Volmar, *Zeitkritische Medien*.
13. Lacey, 'Up in the Air?'; Standage, *The Victorian Internet*, 213.
14. Maxwell, 'Dynamic Theory of the Electric Field'.
15. Hertz, 'On the Action of a Rectilinear Electrical Oscillation'.
16. Marconi, 'Wireless Telegraphic Communication', 196–222.
17. Marinetti, 'Destruction of Syntax', 95.
18. See Cohen et al., *Broadcasting Modernism*; Campbell, *Wireless Writing*; Bloom, *The Wireless Past*.
19. Rikitianskaia, *The Global Wireless*.
20. For critical approaches to 'German radio', especially Weimar radio, see among others, Lacey, *Feminine Frequencies*; Gilfillan, *Pieces of Sound*.
21. On 'vernacular modernism', see Hansen, 'Mass Production of the Senses'.
22. See Adelson, 'Futurity Now'.
23. Standage, *The Victorian Internet*.
24. The slashes pay homage to Kittler, *Discourse Networks*.
25. Dotzler and Roesler-Keilholz, *Mediengeschichte als historische Technologie*, 113–39.
26. See Winthrop-Young, 'Siren Recursions'; Ofak and Hilgers, *Rekursionen*; Kittler, 'Observations on Public Reception', 79–80.

Introduction

Wireless Futures, 1900/2000

> I can think of no other means than historical inquiry to prepare us for the future.
>
> —Friedrich Kittler[1]

The future is wireless. At least this much seemed certain to anyone speculating on media change at the turn of the century.

'Everything that we can now send and reach through the wire', whether words, images, sounds, or numbers, 'we can also send and reach in a wireless way.'[2] Despite some technical difficulties, 'as soon the field of wireless is cleared up as expected, everyone will have their own pocket telephone through which they can be connected to anyone, regardless of where they are'.[3] Complementing commercial applications, other predicted scientific, industrial, and medicinal applications included wireless power transmission, weather control, extraterrestrial communication, and interplanetary exploration. Just imagine the possibilities: 'there is nothing you won't be able to do'.[4] Wireless makes it possible to 'participate [. . .] in every event' and 'travel the whole world comfortably from one's own room'.[5] In the 'wireless century', 'the whole world will just be one single place we live in. Space will no longer divide us. We will be everywhere, assuming that we are still around at all.'[6] Even after the extinction of humanity, according to this classic SF topos of post-apocalyptic radio, an unattended wireless device will keep broadcasting the same message in the future. 'In short, all these wonders of *wireless telegraphy* will make the coming age' – namely, *Die Welt in hundert Jahren* (The World in 100 Years), as imagined over a hundred years ago – 'into a wonderful, unbelievable one.'[7]

Speculations about the future usually reveal more about the present, even or especially if they now belong to the past. This is true in two senses for this modernist vision of 'Das drahtlose Jahrhundert' (The wireless century), attributed to an American journalist named Robert Thompson Sloss and published in 1910 in the earliest German-language futuristic anthology. It is undeniable that Sloss's techno-utopian vision still resonates with the present, as evident in its widespread quotation in recent years.[8] However, it seems short-sighted to conclude that 'one century before the iPhone was launched, Sloss rightly predicted the advent of a "wireless century" marked by the availability of "pocket phones"'.[9] To dispel the magic of such wildly speculative 'media archaeology', it usually suffices to consult the original source(s).[10] Rather than predicting the emergence of a singular, multi-function precursor to the smartphone, Sloss imagined the continued development of multiple, single-function wireless technologies, each dedicated to the respective transmission of words, images, and sounds. Revealingly, 'The Wireless Century' would still include the 'wireless telephone', the 'spoken newspaper', and the 'image telegraph'. There is one conspicuous absence in Sloss's vision – namely, a mode of one-to-many transmission that would supply regular entertainment programmes in the sense of national radio broadcasting. It would be generous to call Sloss's vernacular way of thinking through media 'philosophy', despite his imagination that in the future 'perhaps a new Marconi will be listening and talking to the philosophers of Mars',[11] and yet it is representative of modernist media theory *avant la lettre*.

Is the future wireless? Will wired and wireless systems ever fully converge in an exclusively wireless mode? What role does speculation play in envisioning applications of media technologies and negotiating competing visions of the future? How might the *fin-de-siècle* imagination of the 1880s–1920s relate to that of the 1980s–2020s? In this book, I will argue that meaningful answers to these questions depend not only on markets and technical limits but on sociotechnical imaginaries of medium specificity and media change. Modernist media thinkers imagined the wireless age in singular, totalising, and universalising terms, which obliterated the differences not only across a wide range of cultural techniques and media technologies but also across markers of identity and identification. In many of the modernist visions examined in this book, everyone was imagined to be connected, energised, located, or controlled. Every transmission to be live, synchronised, ambient, or ubiquitous. Every message received from the void or addressed to the unknown. In retrospect, modernist predictions about apparent precursors to mobile phones, smart devices, and wireless networks might generate a strange sort of vertigo, were it not for our certainty and security that much of the future remains unknowable in its entirety – as does the past. Based on the foundational assumption that the future remains opaque, inaccessible, and unpredictable, studying wireless futures might seem like an exercise in groundless speculation. However, the very contingency of speculation presents an opportunity to ground our thinking in second-order observations about '*how future media are imagined*'.[12]

Wireless Imaginations

A major goal of this book is to recover imaginations of wireless futures beyond 'the wireless' and thereby to complicate the apparent destinies of radiotelegraphy and -telephony to become the mass medium known as national radio broadcasting. To describe apparent precursors to new media in the mid- to late nineteenth-century British Empire, Tom Standage once coined the deliberate anachronism: 'the Victorian Internet'.[13] By analogy, the counter-project undertaken in the late nineteenth to early twentieth-century German Empire can be called Wilhelmine wireless. 'Today the Internet is often described as an information superhighway', Standage observed. 'Its nineteenth-century precursor, the electric telegraph, was dubbed the "highway of thought".'[14] Although the Victorian Internet included both optical and electrical telegraphy, Standage's account ended before the emergence of wireless telegraphy and consequently overlooked potential connections with wireless data networks. Today, I would add, wireless is often described as a means of connecting the world, and its modernist precursors were called worldwide wireless networks. In Standage's symptomatic reading, 'the hype, scepticism, and bewilderment associated with the Internet [. . .] mirror the hopes, fears, and misunderstandings inspired by the telegraph. Indeed, they are only to be expected. They are the direct consequences of human nature, rather than technology.'[15] In exploring resonances between old media and new media, Standage's journalistic account participates in a rich scholarly tradition of comparing the emergence of analogue mediums for storing, transmitting, and processing information in the years leading up to World War I to that of digital systems in the years after World War II.[16] Rather than attributing the imagination of media change exclusively to people or technology in a monocausal explanation, *Wireless Futures* follows this scholarship in exploring the dialectics of media change.

Wireless Futures contributes to the study of 'wireless imaginations', a period term originally derived from the modernist Futurist movement, subsequently reactivated in an influential study of the European avant-garde, and currently a description of the burgeoning subfield of 'literary and cultural radio studies'.[17] While the title of Douglas Kahn and Gregory Whitehead's edited collection, *Wireless Imagination: Sound, Radio, and the Avant-Garde*, referenced F. T.

Marinetti's seminal essay, 'Destruction of Syntax – Wireless Imagination – Words-in-Freedom', its contents focused not on radiotelegraphy, which had informed Marinetti's 'wireless imagination', but rather on the terms in the subtitle, as in a chapter by Mark E. Cory on 'German radio art'.[18] Just as art historians examining the impact of electromagnetism on modernist art have expanded the discipline's traditional objects of analysis,[19] literary and cultural radio studies have productively expanded the traditional focus of radio studies beyond the medium-specific format of the 'radio play' (*Hörspiel*) to include representations of radio in novels, films, plays, and poems. Other contributions to literary and cultural radio studies have continued this trend, illuminating contexts related to early radio cultures with a focus on English literature, the BBC or the Marconi Company, and the Anglophone world.[20] In recent years, comparable studies engaging with German media theories have provided insights into how the avant-garde used wireless transmission to test out the limits of experience, the economy of language, and reconfigurations of the senses.[21] By connecting questions raised in these studies about modern subjectivity and aesthetics to German media theories and philosophies, this study aims 'to interweave aspects of the political, the cultural, the technical, and the social – to conduct, in other words, *interdiscursive* analyses'.[22]

As a media system connecting the post office, war offices, and commercial interests, Wilhelmine wireless needs to be understood as one of the period's 'world projects', which tested out the limits of imperial ideologies, national resources, and international cooperation.[23] At the time, the British viewed communications technologies as 'instruments to stabilize an international status quo favourable to their nation, while Germans viewed products of engineering as tools to transform the international environment that stifled their political ambitions'.[24] In direct response to the British Empire's All Red Line, Imperial Germany constructed its own 'worldwide wireless network' (*Weltfunknetz*), an imperial and colonial megaproject that failed to materialise during World War I.[25] Neither empire's approach turned out to be sustainable, and Wilhelmine wireless presents a negative lesson in what historian Heidi Tworek calls 'How Not to Build a World Wireless Network'.[26] Engaging with the work of Tworek and other media historians, this study goes on to introduce the Telefunken Company, the world's second-largest wireless corporation around 1900, to Anglophone audiences more familiar with the Marconi Company.[27] While traditional radio historiography describes a linear trajectory from the local to the global in the sense of 'globalisation', this trajectory is better understood following Maria Rikitianskaia's study of *The Global Wireless* as that from imperial wireless telegraphy through transnational radiotelegraphy to national radio broadcasting.[28]

Wilhelmine wireless not only presents a different model for understanding wireless cultures but also challenges long-standing assumptions about 'German radio', a term that is still synonymous for some historians with only one moment out of a much longer and more complex media history – namely, Nazi radio, c. 1933–45.[29] While the main difference between European and American radio is usually taken to be that between the political economy of subscription-supported versus advertising-supported models, Wolfgang Hagen and other media philosophers have argued that such differences can be traced back further to two contrasting technical and epistemic models.[30] Whereas the media-epistemological background for understanding radio in the United States was based on extending the technical logic of radiotelephony to mass media, radio was not primarily seen as a participatory mass medium in Europe but rather as a 'medium of socialisation', an instrument for switching the population into state controls.[31] Despite the medium's attempts to reinvent itself in terms of presence and actuality, the experience and imagination of German radio remains 'deeply rooted to this day in an imperialist and thoroughly misogynistic war economy'.[32] To separate the Weimar model from both the Nazi and the Wilhelminian model, classic post-WWII German radio studies presented the history of radio up to that point according to a three-stage model, overlooking its silent pre-history (1897–1922): the 'pioneer period' (1923–33); the period of 'abuse [*Mißbrauchs*] as the instrument of internal standardisation [*Gleichschaltung*] and uncontrolled external propaganda' (1933–45); and the period of 'renewal on a federal basis' (post-1945).[33] When Friedrich Kittler notoriously described British and American 'rock music', and not Nazi radio, as an 'abuse [*Mißbrauch*] of military equipment', he was ironically parroting this narrative.[34]

In exploring resonances between the pre-history and post-history of wireless as a mass medium, *Wireless Futures* follows recent arguments for a revised periodisation based on the mode's different implementations in the two periods bracketing broadcasting.[35] In the 1920s–1980s, wireless was primarily implemented as a mass medium, and radio waves involved the structured, macrotemporal flow of programming, entertainment, and advertising. In the 1880s–1920s and the 1980s–present, wireless constitutes an epistemological entity capable of generating knowledge about the nature of electromagnetic radiation at frequencies oscillating in the 'time-critical' range of physics.[36] As a distribution model, broadcasting describes mass media systems such as radio and television that exhibit a centralising tendency because their connections are one-to-many, rather than one-to-one or many-to-many.[37] Hence, its main characteristics are monologic rather than dialogic speech; an orientation to the mass market instead of a small elite; and centralised control over content, programming, and systems of address. By the mid-twentieth century, broadcasting was deployed in a series of national, colonial, and imperial projects with the aim of disciplining subjects and consolidating power.[38] In media studies, some have speculated that the broadcasting model will prove to be the historical exception, only prominent in the mid-twentieth century and primarily in industrialised countries.[39] The changing meaning of radio in the analogue/digital transition, catalysed alternately by rhetoric about the death of broadcasting and celebrations of a hundred years of radio, has also provided an opportunity for reflecting on the meaning of such milestones and for reconfiguring radio studies. For most of the past century, radio was synonymous with mass culture, national publics, and the commercialisation of audiences into media markets.[40] But if we take national broadcasting to mark the end rather than the beginning of wireless technology as a producer of media knowledge, then we might consider wireless telegraphy, telephony, and other early applications as more than merely inevitable precursors to mass media.

As a series of 'roads not taken', the sociotechnical imagination of wireless futures represents a nexus of competing interests, from those concerned with transmitting audiovisual content to those experimenting with electromagnetic radiation at frequencies outside the perceivable spectrum. Rather than abandoning scholarship on broadcasting, radio studies can expand and sharpen its contours by comparing the mass medium to radar, radiography, radiotelegraphy, radiotelephony, and other applications across the radio spectrum.[41] Contributing to scholarship on this expanded sense of radio, this book highlights a wide range of wireless applications beyond entertainment and communication, including information (news, weather, time signals), science (radio astronomy), navigation (radio determination), coordination (emergency services), and infrastructure (wireless power). Expanding our perspective on radio beyond radio also requires the challenging of corresponding assumptions about the analogue/digital divide, insofar as early analogue radiotelegraphy was closer to today's digital code than the more recent developments of analogue radiotelegraphy and radio broadcasting.[42]

Connected to this book's extended critique of German radio history, *Wireless Futures* challenges familiar accounts of German radio theory and German radio philosophy. While critical studies of radio have expanded our understanding of identity, power, and society, they have simultaneously tended to restrict the possibilities of thinking through wireless to questions of markets, masses, and medium specificity.[43] Credit for formulating the earliest critical theories of radio is traditionally attributed to Bertolt Brecht, Walter Benjamin, Rudolf Arnheim, Theodor W. Adorno, and others who experienced the emergence of the 'new medium' in the Weimar Republic.[44] Even if none of these thinkers except Arnheim attempted to formulate a unified 'radio theory' in the sense of a systematic description of the medium, early radio theories *avant la lettre* can be resituated within the period's vernacular 'debate about radio'.[45] As in the better-known 'debate about cinema', media thinkers were enraptured by the ontological question, manifested in attempts to differentiate radio from other media, such as film, newspapers, and literature, while also critiquing the status quo and envisioning alternative futures. In retrospect, their prognoses and normative demands often seem speculative, as with Brecht's utopian call to transform the radio from a distribution apparatus into a communications apparatus.[46] Expanding this archive of early critical thinking about radio, recent studies have highlighted the important literary, cultural, and philosophical writings of Fritz Walter Bischoff, Hans Flesch, Ludwig Kapeller, Richard Kolb, Rudolf Leonhard, Fritz Kunze, Hans Reichenbach, and Ernst Schoen.[47] To expand this archive further along the historical timeline, this study introduces key figures involved in Wilhelmine wireless, including Heinrich Hertz, Adolf Slaby, Karl Ferdinand Braun, Hans Bredow, Georg von Arco, Christian Hülsmeyer, and Paul Nipkow.[48] While Hedy Lamarr has received some attention in recent years for co-patenting a wireless protocol seen as a precursor to Wi-Fi,[49] there is still much work to be done on rethinking the archive beyond the historiographical tradition exemplified by Sigfrid von Weiher's *Männer der Funktechnik*.[50]

In exploring connections across media, aesthetics, and philosophy, *Wireless Futures* reveals a large intermedial archive of previously untapped sources. As a mode of transmission rather than storage or processing, wireless offers a notoriously challenging archive. 'Radio's history is not, in essence, a material history', as Emily Bloom observes.[51] This observation applies even more radically to radiotelegraphy, radiotelephony, radionavigation, and other applications of radio waves beyond broadcasting. While radio broadcasts were not recorded before the late 1920s, radiotelegraphic and radiotelephonic messages were almost never recorded in acoustic form and only occasionally in written form. Because early observers of experimental wireless demonstrations were often sceptical regarding what one operator claimed to hear through their headphones, coded messages were often recorded by hand or printed on inker tape, and yet these kinds of first-hand documents are exceptionally rare. Radiograms and telegrams probably once outnumbered movie ticket stubs, QSL cards, or other paraphernalia associated with any mass medium. However, there are only a few popular academic outreach books that collect telegrams, and one sourcebook devoted to the radiograms associated with the RMS *Titanic*.[52] Telegraphy makes an ideal case study for the 'imagined uses' of technology following Simone Müller and Heidi Tworek's framework for expanding the traditional focus on media usage. While the mode's pricing structure limited its potential users to a small number and most of the world's population never personally sent a telegram, telegraphs reached a greater number of people, and an even greater number of people who never sent or received a telegram still imagined it.[53]

Reconstructing Wilhelmine wireless thus requires a wide range of literary, cultural, technical, and philosophical sources, including patents, trade magazines, technical journals, company publications, lecture notes, scientific treatises, laboratory diaries, and various forms of functional and speculative literature. For early German radio culture, there are several critical sourcebooks collecting historical, cultural, and literary sources in Red Vienna and the Weimar Republic.[54] However, there is nothing comparable for applications of radio beyond broadcasting, nor for the German Empire, the Austro-Hungarian Empire, or modern Switzerland. One sourcebook with critical apparatus, *Medientheorien, 1888–1933*, presents an invaluable selection of the kinds of short-form literary, cultural, and philosophical essays that constitute media theory *avant la lettre*, including speculations on 'Radioitis', 'TV at Home', 'Work Rhythms as Mode Code', 'The Human Body as a Transmitter', and 'Future Electrophysiological Problems'.[55] As indicated by these titles, the sociotechnical imagination of wireless cut across a wide range of discourses, narrative forms, and literary formats.

One of the major scholarly assumptions corrected by reconsidering this wider range of sources is that the pre-history of national radio broadcasting can only be written as a technical and not an intellectual history. Besides scientific articles on electromagnetic radiation in the *Annalen der Physik*, historical articles in the *Beiträge zur Geschichte der Technik*, and articles devoted to wireless technology in the *Jahrbuch der drahtlosen Telegraphie und Telephonie*, there were popular scientific outreach essays on wireless in journals such as *Prometheus* and satirical essays in ones such as the *Fliegende Blätter*. One of the first trade journals dedicated to wireless technology, *Telefunken-Zeitung*, occasionally published short fictional narratives alongside its technical articles, a strategy continued by the earliest science-fiction journals.[56] Beyond genre fiction, the speculative approach adopted in this book suggests new readings of canonical literature, examining the aesthetics of invention in literary naturalism, the desire for telepresence in early Expressionism, and the televisual imaginary in avant-garde experiments. If there had been a state poet of Wilhelmine wireless, it probably would have been the reactionary engineer, science journalist, and co-founder of 'German SF', Hans Dominik. Nevertheless, the literary imagination of what Bernd Flessner calls 'cyberspace in the German Empire' (*Cyberspace im Kaisserreich*) exceeds that of any individual author.[57]

Unpacking the speculative media question for wireless transmission in contingent sites, objects, and practices contributes to our understanding of the lived experience of wireless cultures and of the way the present connects the past and future. Rooted in German studies, this media-philosophical study underscores transnational resonances, including 'broadcasting modernism', 'vibratory modernism', 'energetic modernism', and other vernacular 'wireless imaginations'.[58] While Marshall McLuhan famously called radio 'that aboriginal mass medium, the vernacular tongue',[59] I use the term 'vernacular' more in Miriam Hansen's sense of 'vernacular modernism', which 'combines the dimension of the quotidian, of everyday usage, with connotations of discourse, idiom, and dialect, with circulation, promiscuity, and translatability'; instead of a 'universal narrative idiom', it suggests a global sensory vernacular.[60] Thinking both about and beyond German modernity, *Wireless Futures* has broader implications for the transnational engagement with German media studies from the Frankfurt School through the Kittler network and beyond.[61]

Speculative Media Studies

By engaging critically with contemporary media theories and philosophies, this book not only proposes a new reading of wireless as a medium of theoretical and financial speculation but also salvages speculation as a critical concept and methodological framework. It is beyond the scope of the present study to adjudicate competing readings of 'German media theory' (GMT), an explosive label coined in the early 2000s, declared obsolete in the late 2010s, but perhaps relevant for an updated approach to doing 'German media studies'.[62] Nevertheless, it will be helpful to outline where recent debates about *Medienwissenschaft*, the controversial term for this new 'media science', intersect with those about *Medienphilosophie*, a deceptively simple term that can be translated only naively, reductively, or ironically as '(German) media philosophy'.[63] Despite sceptical predictions that media philosophy would remain 'a temporary thing', it has established itself as an increasingly differentiated area of teaching and research.[64]

For a provisional heuristic, it is tempting to classify recent scholarship, much of which has not yet been translated,[65] into two main categories according to which of the two terms they emphasise in the compound noun.[66] To differentiate their philosophical approach from media theory, those who emphasise media *philosophy* have argued for disciplining the field through more rigorous conceptual work – above all, on the central concept of the medium.[67] To sharpen disciplinary contours and develop a 'systematic media philosophy', Mike Sandbothe, Ludwig Nagl, and other media philosophers have developed a triadic systems-theoretical model for studying connections among three main systems: 'sensory perception media' (for example, space, time, the senses), 'semiotic information and communication media' (for example, the body, speech, writing, images, music, dance, theatre) and 'technical distribution and storage media' (for example, the voice, print, photography, telephony, film, radio, television, computer, the Internet, virtual reality).[68] From this systematising perspective, media philosophy is largely a hermeneutic and philological project, which involves re-reading and re-processing relatively canonical works of critical theory and cultural studies. That the lines between philosophy and theory are often blurred, however, is evident in that a recent 'Media Philosophy of Radio' was simultaneously published without significant changes as a 'Media Theory of Radio' and that both versions of the essay omitted any thinking about wireless beyond mass media.[69]

Those who emphasise *media* philosophy, on the other hand, have underscored the radical potentials of transdisciplinary inquiry and the difficulties of constructing a unified or systemic theory of media beyond contingent situations. This second main variant, with which this book is more closely aligned, can also proceed from a historical perspective but it tends to work less on individual authors than on the history of concepts, metaphors, and ideas. To the extent that the first variant can help in studying the formation of media concepts in canonical texts of philosophy, the second variant stresses the need to pay attention to things that once did not count as media but would now. 'Where and how', Lorenz Engell asks, 'following the questions posed by this kind of media philosophy, were media conceptually considered and included in philosophical discourses, even if an explicit concept of media had not yet been attempted? In other words, how did the medium become thinkable in very different philosophies?'[70] Following Engell, the difference between the history of concepts and that of epistemes is that the former tends to proceed in the abstract and conceptual and to ground claims in definitions, whereas the latter examines material bodies, gestures, and concrete procedures of generating and using knowledge.[71]

Despite the potential utility of this provisional heuristic, imagining media philosophy as a spectrum with media at one end and philosophy at the other ultimately reinforces the problematic assumption that these are diametrical opposites or mutually exclusive terms. In fact, the notion that media have essentially been ignored by philosophy, or that 'the media debate reached philosophy late',[72] has itself been a central polemic in media philosophy. If media and philosophy are taken instead to mutually inform each other, inter- or transdisciplinary media philosophy can explore connections across philosophy, literary studies, film studies, theatre studies, book studies, new media studies, and other related disciplines.[73] If literature remains a privileged site of imagination, literary studies is particularly well poised to examine the construction of reality and the medial dimensions of philosophical work.[74]

One of the central but not yet fully articulated issues in these ongoing disciplinary and methodological debates concerns the status of speculation, its implied opposites, and corresponding assumptions about the relations among media history, theory, and practice. When Geert Lovink coined the term 'speculative media theory' in 1996/2002, he was attempting to describe the convergence of two main scholarly traditions.[75] On the one hand, there was 'hermeneutics, the essay or theory as such, which can easily be used to speculative [*sic*] about the future possibilities of new media, built on historical references, combining etymology with technological forecasts'.[76] On the other hand, there was the anti-, post-, or non-hermeneutic field of 'media archaeology', which Lovink originally associated with Kittler, Christoph Asendorf, Werner Künzel, Avital Ronell, Paul Virilio, and Siegfried Zielinski – a list that would now include Jussi Parikka, Erkki Huhtamo, Thomas Elsaesser, Wolfgang Ernst, and many others.[77] In Lovink's analysis, these two traditions intersected in the 1980s, 'when the Western societies went through a narcotic period of intense speculation – in bonds and currencies, real estate, painting, and . . . theory'.[78] For Lovink, the common denominator for speculative media theorists – besides perhaps their strong belief in a future market for their own scholarship – was their 'strong emphasis on style', 'strong affection for art and aesthetics', 'strong relationship to literature and philosophy', and strong argument that there are no media in general, 'there are only particular media'.[79] This claim remains central to the subsequent generation that came to be labelled too quickly and restrictively as 'new German media theory'. Following Eva Horn's cunning speculative description of this 'new media theory', it is important to stress that this loosely connected network does not offer a theory of new media but a new kind of media theory that is not necessarily new, nor German, nor media theory.[80]

In an unlikely success story, 'speculative media theory' was rebranded 'German media theory', which proved to be such a marketable export for the English-speaking world over the past few decades that the main thinker associated with the term is no longer Theodor W. Adorno but Friedrich A. Kittler. Critical transnational engagement with this distributed body of scholarship, taking the form of translations, commentaries, and original studies, produced some persistent stereotypes about 'hardware fetishism', 'utopian empiricism', and 'technological determinism'. However, it also revealed new directions for updating German media studies and, in a departure from Kittler's universalising model, for posing the media question within situated, disciplinary traditions.[81] Calling attention to the philological spirit of German media philosophy, Liam Young corroborates the view that its distinguishing feature consists in using 'methods from disciplines other than History to think about the past. Its primary texts are literary rather than archival.'[82] Preserving traces of media change, 'literary texts document these changes in motion; they do not simply *represent* these shifts, but they *are themselves* evidence of them'.[83] According to Kittler's preferred idiom for nonlinear, transhistorical narration, 'we are left only with reminiscences, that is to say, with stories [*Erzählungen*]'. In a period characterised by apocalyptic rhetoric about the death of the book, Kittler remained hopeful: 'How that which is written in no book came to pass may still be for books to record. Pushed to their margins even obsolete media become sensitive enough to register the signs and clues of a situation.'[84]

While it is unclear whether 'speculative media theory' was originally a specific synonym for German-language media theories at the turn of the century or a general diagnosis of scholarship speculating on the future currency of media concepts, Lovink generalised a similar critique in a subsequent exchange with Frank Hartmann about media philosophy: 'The whole debate, if you may call it one, revolves around the occupation of a term that antagonists guess may have some importance in the near future. It's dotcom for philosophers.'[85] Rather than a harsh critique of academic opportunism, Lovink's intervention highlighted the way media environments necessarily set limits on thinking. 'Once caught in a real-time regime, living in the constant fear of missing out, all we can do is speculate about the future value of concepts.'[86] Lovink's critique thus complicates the standard view of 'the media philosophical gesture' as 'turn[ing] one's back to the future and the present and reflect[ing] on the past in order to uncover the structures for experience'.[87] As scholars of media studies, we cannot not speculate. And yet speculating critically demands grounding such thinking within contingent situations.

Chapter Overviews

What is (not) wireless? What differentiates this seemingly impossible modern technology from pre-modern techniques of speaking, shouting, or signalling at a distance? Is wireless telegraphy better understood as a sociocultural response to ancient dreams of long-distance signalling or as a modern solution to technical engineering problems inherent in wired telegraphy? What are the mode's origins, if radio waves seem to exist outside of space and time, and in what respects might they determine its historical and theoretical ends? These speculative questions preoccupied modernist thinkers coming to terms with medium specificity and media change.

Chapter 1, 'Ends of the Wire: Thinking Through Wireless, Reimagining Media Change', reframes and grounds such questions through second-order observations about the origins of questions about the beginnings and ends of wireless. Before the wire, everything was in a sense 'wireless', and yet this fundamentally negational and relational definition only makes sense after the emergence of wired telegraphy in the mid-nineteenth century. Rather than the opposite of wired transmission or its inevitable replacement, I argue that wireless is better understood through the Kittlerian/Derridean framework of media supplementarity. Allegedly secondary, a latter medium supplements a former's primary, original, or natural connotations in the twofold sense of remedying its perceived faults and extending its latent potentialities. Despite the modernist rhetoric that attempted to differentiate wireless from wired transmissions in terms of openness, mobility, crossing borders, creating communities, and overcoming space and time, the so-called unguided medium ultimately remains entangled with guided mediums. Connecting Kittler's philosophical reflections on *Leitungen* (literally, wireless lines; figuratively, leadership or control) and *Verkabelung* (cabling, optical fibre networks, making connections) to recent media theories of the 'ends of the wire', this chapter relates questions about the materiality of transmission to those of conceptual, historical, and disciplinary limits.[88] Examining historical speculations on media convergence, it ultimately aims to reconsider the media anthropology of wireless in the early philosophy of technology (Friedrich Dessauer, Hans Reichenbach), philosophical anthropology (Aby Warburg, Helmut Plessner), and political theology (Carl Schmitt). In the 'deep time of the media',[89] as these thinkers reflected on it, cultural techniques of wirelessing were initially based on optical and acoustic channels, then escalated into modern media technologies based on a different model of signals intelligence. However, media change followed a different trajectory than the linear one suggested by recent catchphrases such as 'going wireless', consisting more of loops, recursions, or eternal returns of the same.

Wireless means not only the elimination of wires but also the production of electromagnetic radiation, the physical medium that enables the technical operations, such as tuning, modulation, and amplification, required for transforming energy into an information channel. Chapter 2, 'Etheric Speculations: Science, Fiction, and the Power of Prediction', unpacks the conceptual stakes behind claims to the 'discovery' of electromagnetic radiation as a precondition for the 'invention' of wireless telegraphy. To challenge the persistent narrative in telecommunications historiography about the emergence of modern technology as either a form of applied science or the realisation of ancient human desires, I engage with a contrasting media-philosophical approach to the 'physics of media', developed independently by Kittler, Wolfgang Hagen, Walter Seitter, and others.[90] From this perspective, the affordances of wireless transmission exceed communications and mass media and encompass a wider range of applications. We now tend to take for granted the continuity of the electromagnetic spectrum, the finite range of all the possible frequencies and wavelengths enabling such applications. However, speculation – across science, literature, philosophy, and other discourses – made up the spectrum as we now know it. Even with the emergence of field theory and special relativity, the concept of the ether survived larger epistemic shifts and inspired modernist philosophers, artists, and authors of SF. This chapter tracks the core concept of 'action at a distance' across modernist science – with a focus on Heinrich Hertz and Albert Einstein – and speculative fiction – with a focus on Kurd Lasswitz, Hans Dominik, and Carl Grunert – concluding with the concept's spectral afterlives for avant-garde experiments. Reading across science and fiction, this chapter aims to explain how radio-based wireless transmission became an 'epistemic thing', or a unified object of scientific research questions and laboratory apparatus.[91] What future possibilities were already included or excluded in the modernist physics of media?

Extending this critical reassessment of the 'discovery' of electromagnetic radiation to corresponding debates about the 'invention' of wireless telegraphy, Chapter 3, 'The Wireless Age: From Imaginary Media to Speculative Infrastructure', examines the explosion of 'imaginary media' predicted for a future wireless age and circulated in both the technical and popular press in the years around 1900.[92] Frequently used as a foil for a vanishing 'wired age', the impending 'wireless age' promised to revolutionise not only communications but also business, romance, politics, economics, and many aspects of everyday life. To deflate such media hype, I reconsider the modernist rhetoric of novelty, inventiveness, and actuality through the articulation and repetition of traditional themes, formulas, or what Huhtamo calls 'topoi in media culture'.[93] Encapsulating the notion of wireless as modern Europe's realisation of an ancient dream of perfect communication, the primal scene of wireless communication often featured two friends overcoming some obstacle to make contact at a distance. Crystallised in the imaginary medium known as 'pocket wireless', this scene was crucial for selling potential audiences on the future of the untested medium. Speculations about an impending wireless age might seem universal, but they were usually rooted in contingent contexts and only subsequently uprooted and mobilised by powerful officials to drum up investments in their own megaprojects and to create the very future they promised their investors, as evident from the wealth of seemingly visionary statements attributed to Marconi, Bredow, and David Sarnoff. Speculation can be a means of suspending revolutionary change in a bourgeois state of unlimited possibilities.

Wireless transmission was not only a privileged object of imagination, commentary, and representation in German modernism and modernity but also a condition of possibility for their transmission. Chapter 4, 'Patent Fiction: Wireless Writing in Worldwide Networks', interrogates the possibilities for combining wireless, language, and literature beyond what others have presumed to be a unique modernist literary invention created by the avant-garde and called the 'telegram style'.[94] Although the economy of language demanded by the telegraph clearly informed modernist poetics, it has long remained unclear what difference, if any, wireless telegraphy made for this discourse. While other chapters in this book examine multiple examples of short-form speculative fiction, this chapter revolves around a close reading of one bestselling historical realist novel: *Der tönende Erdkreis* (The Resounding World, 1951), one of Rudolf Brunngraber's 'thing biographies'. Composed at the height of National Socialist radio politics but only published after World War II, Brunngraber's *roman à clef* presents a complex story about the emergence of the German wireless industry following characters based on actual wireless pioneers including Braun, Bredow, Slaby, and Jonathan Zenneck. At the heart of the socialist narrative are the corporate patent disputes over wireless telegraphy that pitted the Marconi Company against the Telefunken Company. In Wilhelmine wireless, patents not only served strategic purposes tied to military-industrial complexes but also remain significant for media history and modernist fiction. More than either a straightforward reaction to or symptom of these historical developments, Brunngraber's anti-speculative and documentary realism serves to clarify the potentials of 'wireless writing' as both the object and subject of mediation.

Considering rampant speculation about wireless futures, the emergence of national radio broadcasting was met not only with enthusiasm or anticipation but also with disappointment, incredulity, and existential boredom. Chapter 5, 'Beyond Broadcasting: Programming, Forecasting, and "Radio for All"', unpacks the horizon of expectations for broadcasting that had previously been established by radiography, emergency alert systems, synchronised time signals, and radio direction finding. Long before radio programmes, these less-known wireless applications engaged with cultural and political debates about universal space, common time, and processes of synchronisation and standardisation.[95] In response to a notorious event known as the *Funkerspuk*, in which German revolutionaries occupied radiotelegraph stations and transmitted their own version of Lenin's famous message 'To All', authorities in the Weimar Republic provided airtight regulations, which permitted only receiving without transmitting and sought to transform the domestic medium into a public space for bourgeois education modelled on the cinema. Encapsulated in Bredow's catchphrase, 'radio for all', these problematic appeals to universality and inclusivity attempted to differentiate the mass medium from its perceived competitors. National broadcasting not only provided medium-specific allegories in the form of radio dramas negotiating the trauma of warfare, the maritime origins of radiotelegraphy, and the contingencies of studio productions and 'live' transmissions. It also exhibited intermedial connections with the radically different futures promised by wireless energy transmission. Thinking through wireless beyond broadcasting can help clarify our understanding of the emergence of media critiques and the epistemic potential of wireless transmission beyond education or entertainment.

Capping the book's contributions to speculative media studies, Chapter 6, 'The Antenna: At the Limits of Wireless Imaginations', presents an extended analysis of this now-easily overlooked but once-celebrated element of every wireless system. An indispensable technical component, the antenna remains understudied in media theory and cultural history, despite having attracted the attention of many poets, artists, architects, and philosophers. The main objects of analysis in this chapter, the Nauen Transmitter Station and the Berlin Radio Tower, are representative of the important historical shift from mobile and ephemeral wireless stations to semi-permanent broadcasting houses with their own dedicated and highly symbolic transmission towers. In German modernity, the antenna generated speculations not only about overcoming the limits of terrestrial architecture but also about the ideal receptivity, sensitivity, and tuning embodied by 'antenna people'.[96] To the extent that experimental wireless stations once provided aesthetic models of openness, aeriality, and attunement with one's surroundings, radio towers and broadcasting houses came to represent a closed, bunker aesthetic that would eventually be epitomised by radar stations and flak towers. If antennas once inspired heterotopias about mobility, decentralisation, and universality, they have been seen cynically ever since the early satellite era as the only visible components of invisible surveillance networks.

Wireless Futures concludes by exploring resonances between the discourse networks of wireless futures, 1900/2000/2100. Tying together the book's main arguments, I propose that speculative media studies, if conducted in a critical and not merely an idle mode, can help counter paranoia and conspiracy theories catalysed around the ongoing rollout of 5G networks. To counter the tech industry's mobilisation of the past as part of hype cycles and strategies of endless deferral, we might mobilise the critical concept of the 'promise machine'.[97] If wireless always seem to fall short of society's visions, speculations about wireless futures indicate the lasting power of the symbolic and the imaginary. The conclusion suggests how speculative media studies can engage critically with both modernity and futurity, and it offers new directions for future interdiscursive research in transhistorical media philosophy.

Neither a thing of the past nor a sign of the future, wireless always brings us back to the present. Cautious of the presentist fallacy, this media-philosophical study aims to avoid exploiting hindsight to make the present appear fated, destined, or the logical and necessary outcome of complex processes that were not necessarily transparent to actors in the moment. Speculative media studies demands not only critical thinking in the 'as-if' mode but also an awareness of contingency and conditionality. Rather than rehearsing what seems as though it had to have happened, this study aims to uncover what could, would, or, from some observers' perspectives, should have happened. If the wireless futures examined in the following pages still resonate with one's present situation, then what new insights might we now have into the past, and how might these resonances inform our thinking about the future?

Coming to Terms with Wirelessness

The resonance of wireless futures across space and time, combined with the capaciousness, flexibility, and indeterminacy of wireless concepts, present an obstacle and an opportunity for thinking through media from a conceptually rigorous and historically informed perspective. In polarising two main discourse networks, 1900/2000, this media-philosophical study negotiates the conceptual baggage of wireless and its German-language counterpart, *funken*, during the transitional periods bracketing broadcasting, separated by the span of a century, but connected by a certain *fin-de-siècle* imagination.[98] To start sorting things out, I would like to briefly review the key terms that will be developed further throughout this study. For a provisional definition, wirelessing describes a mode, not a medium, of transmission, and a genre, not a generation, of communication.

While 'electromagnetic radiation' is now the stable scientific designation for what Hertz verified in the late 1880s, and 'wireless telegraphy' (or 'radiotelegraphy') is now the conventional technical nomenclature for what Marconi commercialised in the late 1890s, the standardised terminology for these milestones emerged only retrospectively through negotiations of competing claims to 'invention' and 'discovery' with economic, social, and cultural implications.[99] From the 1890s–1910s, 'wireless' became the dominant international term for describing the imperial model of the point-to-point, long-wave transmission of Morse code, exemplified by the Marconi Company, the Telefunken Company, and the Société Française Radio-Électrique. However, national variants such as *Funken* (sparks) and *Funkentelegraphie* (spark telegraphy) remained the central object of language politics.[100] In the 1910s–1920s, 'radiotelegraphy' became the standardised international term for describing the transnational model of many-to-many, long- and short-wave transmissions of both Morse Code and voice/music, exemplified by transnational collaborations such as early time signal networks or the Deutsche Betriebsgesellschaft für drahtlose Telegrafie mbH (Debeg). With the rise of broadcasting in the 1920s, the terms 'wireless telegraphy' and 'telephony' (or 'radiotelegraphy' and '-telephony') initially remained interchangeable with 'radio' for describing the national model of the one-to-many long- and short-wave transmission of voice/music, exemplified by the BBC, Radio Paris, and the Reichs-Rundfunk-Gesellschaft (RRG). With the ascendancy of 'radio' by the mid-twentieth century, 'wireless' gradually fell out of usage, though it was preserved into the 1960s in the British term, 'the wireless'. When the terms 'wireless' and *funken* were revived in the 1980s, they served once again to differentiate a new, radio-based mode of transmission from an old, wire-based mode of transmission, only this time in the context of the analogue/digital transition and referring to cordless phones, cellular networks, and early computer data networks.

At first glance, the most fitting media-philosophical concept for understanding such a wide range of applications from a transhistorical perspective might appear to be 'wirelessness', a modernist term unintentionally revived in contemporary media philosophy.[101] Following Adrian Mackenzie, 'wirelessness' describes a contemporary 'state, condition, or mode of existence', 'an experience trending toward entanglements with things, objects, gadgets, infrastructures, and services, and imbued with indistinct sensations and practices of network-associated change'.[102] Though aware of the historical origins of the term 'wireless' and the important historical connections between radio and information networks,[103] Mackenzie overlooked that wirelessness was also a colloquial modernist term. For modernists, as Douglas Kahn observes, 'wirelessness immediately meant great distances, thus all the references to the expanses of the oceans, to crowds, to other lands, and to the otherness of the unexplored globe'.[104] For instance, early English-language press reports on radiotelegraphy were often headlined 'wirelessness'; and 'a couple of wirelessnesses' (*Drahtlosigkeiten*) provided the amusing subtitle for an early collection of 'radio humour'.[105] The mystifications of wirelessness are exemplified in Hermann Hesse's *Steppenwolf*, which introduces the landlady's nephew, a radio amateur who eventually edits and publishes the middle-aged protagonist's story, as a 'diligent young man [. . .] captivated by the idea of wirelessness [*Drahtlosigkeit*], bowing down on his pious knees before the god of technology who, after millennia, had managed to discover and most imperfectly represent things that every thinker has always known and put to wiser use'.[106] Modernist media thinkers were often wary of reproducing the mystifying properties attributed to modern technology in such a singular chronocentric concept.

Around 1900, 'wireless telegraphy' was only one of many proposed names that aimed to distinguish this new, radio-based mode from the old, wire-based mode of transmission. The exasperated title of one article, 'Spark, Space, Wireless, Etheric, Hertzian Wave or

Cableless Telegraphy – Which?', indicates the controversy over multiple terms in circulation for competing national systems.[107] 'In the distant future', its author predicted,

> when all wire systems, both telegraph and telephone, have been superseded by the so-called *wireless*, there will be no confusing qualifying adjectives, for there will be no dual systems requiring qualification, and *wireless telegraphy* and *telephony* will be spoken of as simply *telegraphy* and *telephony*. Should one recall the old, out-of-date systems connected with miles of wire strung on unsightly poles, the word *wire* will be necessary to make clear the meaning.[108]

Despite imagining a future where wireless becomes the only option, the author imagined the continuation and extension of telegraphy and telephony rather than the emergence of the Internet. In this book, I occasionally use 'wireless' as a stand-alone adjective where context allows, though this is not intended to imply that current applications will exist in the future, nor that the term makes sense in isolation or detached from specific technologies.

Is 'wirelessing' anything more than a tautology for 'signalling without wires?' In modern European languages, the vernacular terminology for wireless transmission (for example, Eng. *wireless telegraphy*, Ger. *drahtlose Telegraphie*, Fr. *télégraphie sans fil*, It. *telegrafia senza fili*) has tended to rely on definitional negations of wired telegraphy, grafting expectations about the old medium on to the new one.[109] Today, 'wireless' is often taken to be a misnomer, since wireless systems still require wires. However, this pedantic objection dates back to the 1850s, forty years before the mode's commercialisation, and only intensified in the 1890s.[110] One of the mode's earliest histories reflected that a 'better name would be *telegraphy without connecting wires*, but it is too cumbrous – an awkward mouthful',[111] especially since *wireless telegraphy* already implied *telegraphy without connecting wires*.[112] To Slaby, the English word 'wireless' appeared to be a misnomer for a different reason. The experimental trials he witnessed Marconi conduct in 1897 involved proto-antennas, and 'since these wires are the essence of Marconi's discovery, the term "telegraphy without wires" is really erroneous; more correctly should it be called "telegraphy by sparks", in opposition to the term used hitherto, "telegraphy by circuit"'.[113] Well into the early entertainment broadcasting period, there would still be complaints, especially in German-speaking countries, that wireless technology would only deserve its name once wireless devices came to use fewer wires.[114]

Like the term 'radio', 'wireless' presents a spatial metaphor for a time-based mode of transmission. Local, regional, and national variations of wireless terminology reflected the difficulty of coming up with an emphatic description that would appeal to the senses more directly than 'wireless'. In the German-speaking world, two alternative terms gained the most traction: 'wave telegraphy' (*Wellentelegraphie*), proposed by Braun, evoked the propagation characteristics of electromagnetic radiation; 'spark telegraphy' (*Funkentelegraphie*), preferred by Slaby, evoked the tangible effects of early spark-gap transmitters. In 1906 the term 'radiotelegraphy' was adopted as a universal standard at the Berlin-based Radiotelegraph Convention, and by 1910 communicating with electromagnetic waves was widely referred to as 'radio'. As an adjectival and relational term, wireless refers not only to the elimination of wires but also the production of electromagnetic radiation, as in the official German-language verb for 'sending a message wirelessly' (*funken*, literally, 'to spark'). If the English 'wireless' was always underdetermined, the German *funken* was overdetermined by a combination of older and newer meanings.[115] Although sparks were an object of literature, philosophy, and theology throughout the Middle Ages and the early modern period, they would only be fully articulated in science and technology during the eighteenth and nineteenth centuries.[116] By 1900 the connotations of *Funken* had shifted from the elemental senses of 'fire' and the 'divine spark' to the banality of wireless telegrams and the language politics of the German Empire.[117] In Wilhelmine Germany, sparks informed the official term for wireless telegraphy (*Funkentelegraphie*), and, in the Weimar Republic, that for radio (*Rundfunk*),[118] though the debate about using 'foreign words' for wireless technology continued well into the broadcasting period.[119]

The German term for radio, *Rundfunk*, was reportedly coined by Bredow, a former wireless operator and business manager who became the influential superintendent of national radio broadcasting, in the same breath as his programme of *Rundfunk für alle* ('radio for all').[120] While the term *Funk* was supported by official definitions from the Post Office, there was no standard terminology until a 1928 law codified the umbrella term 'telecommunications stations' (*Fernmeldeanlagen*).[121] To standardise previous regulations, the law defined telecommunications stations as 'electrical transmission and reception equipment in which the sending or receiving of messages, signs, images, or sounds can take place without connecting lines [*Verbindungsleitungen*] or with the use of electrical vibrations guided along a conductor [*Leiter*]'.[122] Wireless remains haunted by such thinking about lines, conductors, and other forms of guided control. Today, the word *funken* serves as a reminder that wireless transmissions were once generated through a rapid sequence of electrical discharges, a method rendered obsolete by the vacuum tube. Already in the early twentieth century, *Funkentelegraphie* meant what Braun called *Funken ohne Funken* (sparks without sparks).[123]

Like Timothy Campbell and Wolfgang König, I consider the English term 'wireless(ing)' to be more robust, if not more emphatic, than the German *funken*. The latter term applies primarily to one early generation of radiotelegraphy, whereas the former connects similar modes of transmission over an extended transhistorical period and with many applications beyond communications.[124] However, the German *funken* presents important implications for media philosophy and the history of knowledge.[125] To define media in their collected volume, *Medien vor den Medien* (Media before the media), Ana Ofak, Susane Holl, and Friedrich Kittler refer not only to 'the topographical placement in the middle, that is, in the in-between of things, that lends the "intermediate materials" (*Zwischenstoffen*) medial qualities' but also to 'the way in which they "spark" in between (*dazwischen "funken"*) and modify perception through this intermittency'.[126] A medium, in this sense, is neither a language, nor a container, nor an environment, but a dynamic and oscillating intermediate substance, whose emergence can be understood by analogy with the formation of a channel in spark-based wireless telegraphy. Wireless exhibits a unique relation to other media channels in that the physical 'medium' is not a material substance, like cables or wires, but rather electromagnetic radiation, which can propagate even in the absence of a medium. The act of wirelessing creates the information channel medially.

Notes

1. Kittler, 'Universities', 244.
2. Sloss, 'Das drahtlose Jahrhundert', 34.
3. Sloss, 'Das drahtlose Jahrhundert', 35.
4. Sloss, 'Das drahtlose Jahrhundert', 44.
5. Sloss, 'Das drahtlose Jahrhundert', 45.
6. Sloss, 'Das drahtlose Jahrhundert', 45.
7. Sloss, 'Das drahtlose Jahrhundert', 48 (emphasis added).
8. See Mattern, *Die Informatisierung des Alltags*, 356; Jäckel, 'Ein Ausblick in die Medienzukunft', 154; Snickars and Vonderau, *Moving Data*, 5; Fraunholz et al., 'Hochmoderne Visionen und Utopien', 11.
9. Snickars and Vonderau, *Moving Data*, 5.
10. Sloss, 'Sight Magic and Sound Magic'. A closely related article, presumably also authored by Sloss, appears to have been misattributed

to another author in the same issue and published as Lopez, 'The Wireless Future'.

11. Sloss, 'Das drahtlose Jahrhundert', 48.
12. Ernst and Schröter, *Media Futures*, 2 (emphasis in original).
13. Standage, *The Victorian Internet*.
14. Standage, *The Victorian Internet*, viii.
15. Standage, *The Victorian Internet*, 212.
16. See, among others, Briggs, 'Prediction and Control'; Marvin, *When Old Technologies Were New*; Gitelman, *Always Already New*.
17. Marinetti, 'Destruction of Syntax'; Kahn and Whitehead, *Wireless Imagination*; Cohen, 'Wireless Imaginations', 334–50.
18. Kahn and Whitehead, *Wireless Imagination*, 331–72.
19. See, among others, Asendorf, *Ströme und Strahlen*; Daniels, *Kunst als Sendung*; Clarke and Henderson, *From Energy to Information*.
20. See, among others, Campbell, *Wireless Writing*; Menke, *Telegraphic Realism*.
21. Beals, *Wireless Dada*; Ma, *The Stone and the Wireless*.
22. Zielinski, *Variations on Media Thinking*, xvii.
23. See Krajewski, *World Projects*.
24. Tworek, *News from Germany*, 14.
25. See Tworek, *News from Germany*, 45–69; Friedewald, *Die 'Tönenden Funken'*; Friedewald, 'Beginnings of Radio Communication in Germany'.
26. Tworek, 'How Not to Build a World Wireless Network'.
27. Scholl, 'Marconi versus Telefunken'.
28. Rikitianskaia, *The Global Wireless*.
29. See, for example, Potter et al., *The Wireless World*.
30. Hagen, *Das Radio*; Hagen, 'Alternating Currents and Ether'; Dotzler and Roesler-Keilholz, 'Radio'.
31. Schrage, 'Subjektivierung durch Normalisierung', 84.
32. Bromley, 'On the Air', 180–94.
33. For this periodisation, see Fischer, *Dokumente*, 4; cf. Dussel, *Deutsche Rundfunkgeschichte*.
34. Kittler, 'Rock Music', 152–64; cf. Pias, 'Friedrich Kittler'.
35. Ernst, 'Distory'; Fisher, 'Radio'; Rikitianskaia and Balbi, 'Radio Studies Beyond Broadcasting'; Winn and Brinson, *Transmitting the Past*.
36. Ernst, 'Distory'.
37. Winkler, 'Tauschen, Austauschen, Kommunizeren'.
38. Cohen et al., *Broadcasting Modernism*.
39. Bessire and Fisher, 'Anthropology of Radio Fields'; Fisher, 'Radio'.
40. Fisher, 'Radio'.
41. Rikitianskaia and Balbi, 'Radio Studies beyond Broadcasting'.
42. Ernst, 'Distory', 163.
43. On 'German radio theory', see Schätzlein, 'Theorien', 37–62; Föllmer and Wagner, 'Radio', 303–5; Mowitt, *Radio*; Filk, 'Medienphilosophie des Radios', 299–314.

44. Brecht, 'Texts on Radio Broadcasting'; Benjamin, *Radio Benjamin*; Arnheim, *Radio*; Adorno, *Current of Music*.
45. See Kümmel, 'Innere Stimmen', 175–97.
46. Brecht, 'Radio as a Communications Apparatus', 41–6.
47. See Ottmann, *Im Anfang war das Experiment*; Richardson, 'Hans Reichenbach, Radio Philosopher'.
48. For the primary period examined in *Wireless Futures*, additional wireless pioneers include Manfred Ardenne, Abraham Esau, August Karolus, Robert von Lieben, Eugen Nesper, Ernst Ruhmer, Hans Vogt, Max Wien, and Jonathan Zenneck. For the secondary period, influential German radio theorists include Gerhard Eckert, Eugen Kurt Fischer, Helmut Jedele, Friedrich Kittler, Wolf Kittler, Friedrich Knilli, Hans Magnus Enzensberger, Oskar Negt and Alexander Kluge, Christoph Busch, Werner Faulstich, Jürgen Häusermann, Wolfgang Hagen, and Heidi Grundmann.
49. See Barton, *Hedy Lamarr*, 113–25; Rothman, 'Random Paths to Frequency Hopping'.
50. Weiher, *Männer der Funktechnik*.
51. Bloom, *The Wireless Past*, 22.
52. Rosenkrantz, *Telegram!*; Hughes, *Titanic Calling*; Meier zu Eissen, *Telegraphie des Deutschen Reichs*.
53. Müller and Tworek, 'Imagined Use', 106.
54. Fischer, *Dokumente*; Schneider, ed., *Radio-Kultur in der Weimarer Republik*; Kaes et al., 'New Mass Media', 594–616; Kaes, *Weimarer Republik*; Born and Lambert, 'Newspapers and Radio'.
55. Kümmel and Löffler, *Medientheorie*, 433–7, 138–55, 177–209, 233–7, 281–4, 454–61.
56. See Wythoff, *Perversity of Things*.
57. Flessner, 'Cyberspace im Kaiserreich'.
58. Kahn and Whitehead, *Wireless Imagination*; Clarke and Henderson, *From Energy to Information*; Cohen et al., *Broadcasting Modernism*; Enns and Trower, *Vibratory Modernism*; Cohen, 'Wireless Imaginations', 334–50.
59. McLuhan, 'Radio: The Tribal Drum', 140; cf. McLuhan, *Understanding Media*, 302.
60. Hansen, 'Mass Production of the Senses', 59, 72.
61. On 'German media studies', see Geisler and Mattson, 'Special Issue on German Media Studies'; Born, 'German Media Studies'.
62. On 'German media theory' (often abbreviated GMT), see, among others, Lovink, 'Essay on Speculative Media Theory'; Horn, '"There Are No Media"'; Geoghegan, 'After Kittler'; Siegert, 'Cultural Techniques'; Pias, 'What's German About German Media Theory?'; Winthrop-Young, 'The Kittler Effect'; Born, 'German Media Studies'.
63. For English-language introductions to 'German media philosophy', see Engell, 'Ontogenetic Machinery'; Groys, 'What Is German Media Philosophy?'; Parikka, 'To Media Study'.

64. Seel, 'Eine vorübergehende Sache', 10–15.
65. For German-language introductions to 'German media philosophy', see Sandbothe and Nagl, *Systematische Medienphilosophie*; Engell and Siegert, 'Schwerpunkt Medienphilosophie'; Ernst et al., *Perspektiven interdisziplinärer Medienphilosophie*; Sandbothe and Burkhardt, 'Medienphilosophie'; Schweppenhäuser, *Handbuch der Medienphilosophie*.
66. For a similar two-part model, see Schweppenhäuser, *Handbuch der Medienphilosophie*, 11; for a four-part model, cf. Engell and Siegert, 'Schwerpunkt Medienphilosophie', 5.
67. See Münker et al., *Medienphilosophie*.
68. Sandbothe, introduction to Sandbothe and Nagl, *Systematische Medienphilosophie*, xv.
69. Filk, 'Medienphilosophie des Radios'; Filk, 'Medientheorie des Radios'.
70. Engell and Siegert, 'Schwerpunkt Medienphilosophie', 6.
71. Engell and Siegert, 'Schwerpunkt Medienphilosophie', 6.
72. Krämer, *Medium, Messenger, Transmission*, 28; cf. Kittler, 'Medien der Philosophie, Philosophie der Medien'.
73. Ernst et al., *Perspektiven interdisziplinärer Medienphilosophie*.
74. Gropp, 'Literaturwissenschaft'.
75. Lovink, 'Essay on Speculative Media Theory'. The now-standard term 'German media theory' appears only in the 2002 book version, whereas Lovink referred to 'emerging media theory in Germany' in his original lecture, 'From Speculative Media to Net Criticism', NTT InterCommunication Center (ICC), Tokyo, Japan, 12 December 1996.
76. Lovink, 'Essay on Speculative Media Theory', 28.
77. Parikka and Huhtamo, *Media Archaeology*; Parikka, *What Is Media Archaeology?*
78. Lovink, 'Essay on Speculative Media Theory', 28 (ellipses in original).
79. Lovink, 'Essay on Speculative Media Theory', 22.
80. Horn, 'Editor's Introduction: "There Are No Media"', 7.
81. Pias, 'What's German About German Media Theory?'; Born, 'German Media Studies'.
82. Young, 'Imagination and Literary Media Theory', 22.
83. Young, 'Imagination and Literary Media Theory', 25 (emphasis in original).
84. Kittler, *Gramophone, Film, Typewriter*, xl.
85. Lovink, 'Discipline Design', n.p.
86. Lovink and Rossiter, *Organization After Social Media*, 155.
87. Barker, *Against Transmission*, 18.
88. Gethmann and Sprenger, *Die Enden des Kabels*; Sprenger, 'Between the Ends of a Wire'; Starosielski, 'Ends of Media Studies', 305–11.
89. Zielinski, *Deep Time of the Media*.
90. Hagen, *Das Radio*; Seitter, *Physik der Medien*.
91. Rheinberger and Herrgott, *Experimentalsysteme und epistemische Dinge*.

92. See Kluitenberg, *Book of Imaginary Media*; Kluitenberg, 'On the Archaeology of Imaginary Media'; Natale and Balbi, 'Media and the Imaginary in History'.
93. Huhtamo, 'Dismantling the Fairy Engine', 34.
94. Beals, *Wireless Dada*; Kittler, 'Im Telegrammstil', 358–71; Segeberg, 'Technische Konkurrenzen', 430–6.
95. Balbi, 'Wireless's "Critical Flaw"'.
96. Sloterdijk, 'A Plug for Higher Energies', 232–9.
97. Appadurai and Alexander, *Failure*, 30–45.
98. Briggs and Snowman, *Fins de Siècle*.
99. On this terminology, see Haus, 'Radiogerede'; Lerg, *Die Entstehung des Rundfunks in Deutschland*, 19–23; Knörr, 'Funken', 268–87.
100. For this framework differentiating the historiographies of wireless telegraphy, radiotelegraphy, and radiobroadcasting, see Rikitianskaia, *The Global Wireless*.
101. Mackenzie, *Wirelessness*; Greenspan, *China and the Wireless Undertow*.
102. Mackenzie, *Wirelessness*, 5.
103. Mackenzie, *Wirelessness*, 4, 61.
104. Kahn, introduction to *Wireless Imagination*, 21; cf. Ronell, *The Telephone Book*, 418 n. 21.
105. Roellinghoff, 'Radio im Humor', 80–7.
106. Hesse, *The Steppenwolf*, 121.
107. Collins, 'Spark, Space, Wireless', 119.
108. Collins, 'Spark, Space, Wireless', 119. Other creative proposals such as 'atmography' (a portmanteau of 'atmosphere' and 'telegraphy') never caught on. See Dietz, 'What Shall We Call It?', 670.
109. In French, *télégraphie sans fils* means not only 'wireless telegraphy' but also 'telegraphy without a son', as evident in Ernst Picabia's poem of that name.
110. 'Telegraphic Progress. – Telegraphing without Wires!', qtd. in Fahie, *History of Wireless Telegraphy*, ix.
111. Fahie, *History of Wireless Telegraphy*, ix (italics replacing capitalisation).
112. Fahie, *History of Wireless Telegraphy*, ix; see further Preece, 'Electric Signalling without Wires'.
113. Slaby, 'The New Telegraphy', 871.
114. Fürst, *Im Bannkreis von Nauen*, 86.
115. On the medial history of Funken, see Hagen, '"Stürmische Plötzlichkeiten"', 99–138.
116. For the following, see Thibault, 'Bolts and Waves'; Schaal, 'Bild und Ikonographie der Elektrizität', 33–55.
117. Sarrazin, 'Sprachliches zur "Drahtlosen Telegraphie"', 194–9.
118. Lerg, *Die Entstehung des Rundfunks in Deutschland*, 19; Haus, 'Radiogerede', 14–17; Knörr, 'Funken'.
119. See Germanicus, '"Fremdwörter" in der Technik'; Ein Humanist, 'Fremdwörter in der Technik', 452.

120. For a critical take on this mythology, see Lerg, *Die Entstehung des Rundfunks in Deutschland*, 20.
121. Dotzler and Roesler-Keilholz, 'Radio', 113–39.
122. Lerg, *Die Entstehung des Rundfunks in Deutschland*, 19–20.
123. See Knörr, 'Funken', 280.
124. See König, 'Telegraphie, Telefonie, Funk', 56–70.
125. See Knörr, 'Funken'.
126. Ofak and Kittler, *Medien vor den Medien*, 11; cf. Knörr, *Funken*, 16.

Chapter 1

Ends of the Wire: Thinking Through Wireless, Reimagining Media Change

'Radio runs as easily as water from a tap [*Leitung*]', Friedrich Kittler once noted in a foundational media-philosophical lecture. 'And the same state that, since 1870 systematically imposed upon its populations the obligation to wash, brought radio to the Europeans.'[1] Exploring connections across media, aesthetics, and philosophy, Kittler's radically speculative 'Observations on Public Reception' questioned the standard way of thinking about radio as a mass medium, the way media systematically prevent users from thinking about them, and the way any medium simultaneously enables and delimits critical thinking. Like any new medium, the radio is suddenly just there, discouraging people from thinking about its origins. Once switched on, the stream of contents ceaselessly flows, preventing audiences from thinking about its sources. However, it is no coincidence, in Kittler's speculative analysis, that national broadcasting, though presented as an essential public service, originated out of the same imperial order that was responsible for regulating public water supplies. No coincidence, to repeat his favourite figure of thought,[2] that radio waves enable everything from radar to radio astronomy, and yet their public applications have been restricted ever since World War I to a relatively small and tightly controlled slice of the electromagnetic spectrum. Nor can it be a coincidence that Kittler's lecture on the radio was not broadcast on the radio but channelled through 'a two-way stereo wire [*Leitung*]' connecting the dispersed audiences at a symposium on the theory and practice of electromagnetic media and radio art.[3] Kittler's 'Observations on Public Reception' thus provide an untimely reminder not only of the self-reflexivity that distinguishes theory from philosophy but also of the mutual entanglements between wired and wireless systems.

Engaging critically with Kittler's speculative media philosophy, this chapter unpacks the theoretical differences between wired and wireless systems and interrogates assumptions in media historiography that the nineteenth-century wired age was linearly followed by the twentieth-century wireless age. Commonly opposed to wires, cables, and cords, as though each system belongs to its own epoch or expresses a different essence of technology, wireless remains entangled with the wire.[4] To nuance common-sense views of media change, I argue that wireless is better understood through the Kittlerian/Derridean 'logic of supplementarity', which describes how a 'new' medium supplements an 'old' medium's primary, original, or natural connotations in the twofold sense of remedying its perceived faults and extending its latent potentialities. That wireless necessarily involves many-to-many transmissions across an open, insecure, and shared channel that is prone to interference, eavesdropping, and other perceived disturbances was the notorious 'problem' that was simultaneously exploited and resolved for the creation of broadcasting. Despite the modernist rhetoric that attempted to differentiate wireless from wired transmissions in terms of openness, mobility, crossing borders, creating communities, and overcoming space and time, the so-called unguided medium remains entangled with its guided counterparts, a point captured in Kittler's philosophical reflections on the multivalent concepts of *Leitungen* ('wireless lines', 'leadership', 'control'), *Verkabelung* ('cabling', 'fibre-optic networks', 'hooking things up', 'making connections'), and *Volksempfang* ('public reception', though immediately evoking the *Volksempfänger*).

Originally titled '*Anmerkungen zum Volksempfang*', Kittler's characteristically provocative, self-reflexive, performative, and often infuriating lecture presented one of the most stereotypically Germanic accounts of the medium imaginable to the audiences at an Austrian symposium, organised by Heidi Grundmann, on 'The Geometry of Silence'.[5] In a typical tour de force, Kittler frenetically commented in six loosely connected sections on the radio's military-industrial origins; the priority of technical standards and formats over aesthetic contents; early radio dramas expressing the discourse on discourse channel conditions; the conceptual turn from media phenomenology to the physics of media; the technical grounds of Heidegger's '*Kehre*' in the materiality of radio; and possible futures for wireless transmission after the ends of commercial markets for national entertainment broadcasting. Challenging traditional narratives of invention and discovery, Kittler implied that there were important parallels between the post-history of national radio broadcasting and its pre-history in imperial radiotelegraphy and radiotelephony. In an equally speculative conclusion, Kittler suggested that there might be a future for radio even after another medium takes over radio's once-dominant function in broadcasting entertainment to the masses. For Kittler, wireless futures depended on the 'point of intersection [or interface, *Schnittstelle*]' between three mutually dependent systems: 'radio as a "fabrication of science"', an unattributed phrase that presumably references Karin Knorr-Cetina's contemporaneous study of epistemology and social constructivism; 'radio as cosmic electronics', a technical engineering phrase for radio astronomy and spacecraft equipment; and radio as national broadcasting, or 'public reception [*Volksempfang*]', an ambiguous, explosive, and untranslatable term that remains unexplained and appears only in the lecture's title and final sentence.[6] While *Volksempfang* might sound like typical *Kittlerdeutsch*, the term for his idiosyncratic style coined by analogy with *Adornodeutsch*, it derives from another node in the Kittler network, a literary study of Heidegger's relation to radio.[7] Twisted around, *Volksempfang* critiques the 'common-sense' restriction of wireless possibilities to those of a seemingly democratic mass medium that was deeply implicated with imperialism and fascism.

While other German philosophers are notorious for speculating on etymologies, limit cases, and often much worse, Kittler developed a different mode of critical speculation, grounding controversial conjectures in non-controversial literary, technical, and cultural sources through a radical process of 'close writing'.[8] To support his risky hypothesis about the conditions of possibility for national broadcasting, Kittler merely added two minor discourse operators,[9] a date and an exclamation point, to a historical *Meyer's Encyclopaedia* entry on 'water pipes' (*Wasserleitungen*). While the encyclopaedia had innocently described how clean water supplies promote public health and improve the population's living standards, Kittler added an exclamation point to the entry's speculative conclusion: 'At the same time, arrangements have been made that aim at increasing water consumption in all classes of the population!'[10] One can easily draw one's own paranoid conclusions about the *raisons d'état* behind supplying national radio broadcasting. By radicalising the hermeneutics of suspicion and pushing them to the limits of plausibility, Kittler's method was simultaneously analytical and speculative. There is no evidence that would definitively prove or disprove the correctness of his hypothesis about the emergence of mass media consumption out of the spirit of imperial hygiene regiments. The resonance between 'water pipes' and 'tap water' makes it plausible while also insinuating that national radio broadcasting and other wireless applications remain entangled with the wired counterparts they claimed to have made obsolescent and left behind.

Kittler's cryptic, suspicious, paranoid, or simply speculative readings are partly responsible for the controversies in his early Anglophone reception, and yet they deserve closer inspection for their resonances with our speculative media environment. Because Kittler's publications appeared in translation only piecemeal and with significant time delays, it is understandable why literary and cultural radio studies assumed that he ignored transmission in favour of inscription, despite his career-long emphasis on the information-theoretical triad of storage, transmission, and processing.[11] In *Gramophone, Film, Typewriter*, Kittler not only deconstructed these three dominant modern media storage technologies but also reflected on the transmission systems connecting them.[12] Furthermore, he wrote a handful of essays about radio, radar, and other wireless applications, appeared in dozens of radio lectures on German-language radio stations, and collaborated on experimental radio programmes with national broadcasting industries.[13]

Although Kittler's 'Observations on Public Reception' has been widely cited in both radio studies and sound studies, informing foundational definitions and encyclopaedia articles in those fields, this overwrought lecture is available only in a poor English translation that has been misconstrued and taken out of context by scholars overlooking its intricate intertextuality and its self-reflexive medial forms and formats.[14] In a cursory and ungenerous reading, Kittler might appear to be no different from media gurus who failed to foresee 'future commercial applications', who 'cannot imagine alternatives', and for whom 'extension seems only natural'.[15] However, this was precisely what Kittler was arguing against – 'the untenability of a philosophy that tried to explain media as extensions of man and thus attempted to humanize them' – and not what he was arguing for.[16] Kittler's perceived 'technological determinism' and his corresponding polemics against bourgeois humanism might take on new urgency for critiques of a contemporary technology industry that simultaneously celebrates and debases its so-called users.[17] To describe 'the Kittler effect', Geoffrey Winthrop-Young departs from traditional models of theory reception and underscores the 'North American engagement with Kittler [. . .] in the broadcast sense, from the marital to the martial'.[18] Instead of declaring Kittler's contributions to media studies obsolete, we can engage with them historically, theoretically, and heterogeneously to evaluate them in a new manner and reactivate their core impulses.[19]

To test out and ground Kittler's speculative theories, this chapter explores his references to the modern German philosophical tradition and reconnects his media philosophy of wireless to the modernist thinkers he cited who were themselves coming to terms with medium specificity and media change. As Kittler noted only in passing, German philosophers have occasionally commented on the medium ever since the mid-1920s; but for Kittler, 'the one-and-only Heidegger possibly succeeded, at whatever price, to grasp, as such, the circuitry between equipment and people'.[20] Best-known as a form of 'media ontology', Kittler's unsystematic and widely dispersed reflections on radio, wireless, and other modes of transmission reveal a lesser-known facet of his media-philosophical project, which Jussi Parikka describes as 'a media anthropology without the Man'.[21] Reading across the early philosophy of technology (Ernst Kapp, Friedrich Dessauer, Hans Reichenbach, Martin Heidegger), philosophical anthropology (Aby Warburg, Helmut Plessner), and political theology (Carl Schmitt), this chapter aims to address how and why 'radio, at the time not yet five years old in Europe, had already reached the rank of a philosophical category', as Kittler asserted.[22] How and why did wireless become an object not only of scientific research and commercial investments but also of philosophical thinking about space, time, materiality, and anthropology?

Wired Wireless

To think critically about wireless, it is necessary to start at the point most studies overlook – thinking about wires. The central passage in Kittler's 'Observations on Public Reception' hinges on wordplay about the perceived differences between wired and wireless that has been entirely lost in translation:

> Media that have reached their levels of saturation are hard to write about. They disappear at the juncture of high technology and triviality. They reach your ear from neighbouring yards as only the nightingale once did and, in the best-case scenario, just like the bird of all poetry, they spark Gottfried Benn's poems. The normal scenario however (to quote the engineers) is that transmission is constant although, or just because, it is wireless [*Im Normalfall dagegen steht (mit den Ingenieuren gesprochen) die Leitung, obwohl oder gerade weil sie drahtlos ist*]. Due especially to being the first electronic medium to programme day and night, radio has become a Platonic substantiality that causes it to vanish irresistibly as a technological medium.[23]

Like 'discourse networks' (*Aufschreibesysteme*), the 'abuse of military equipment' (*Mißbrauch vom Heeresgerät*), 'time-axis manipulation'

(*Zeitachsenmanipulation*), and other apparent Kittlerian coinages that turn out to have been ironic quotations of historical discourses,[24] *Leitung* is impossible to translate with a single word, since it contains both historical resonances and a new twist in Kittlerdeutsch. In German, *Leitung* is both the literal term for 'pipes', 'cables', 'wiring', 'lines', or 'leads', and the figurative term for 'leadership', 'management', 'guidance', 'direction', or 'being in charge'. By evoking these multiple meanings, Kittler was exploring the limits around the vanishing experience of wireless transmission: in the worst-case scenario, he finds it impossible to escape the sounds of radios echoing from neighbouring courtyards; in the best-case scenario, the medium can still inspire poetry; in the 'normal case', however, nothing is left up to chance.

In its literal sense, Kittler's thesis could be taken to mean that the engineering imagination of wireless transmission remains fundamentally wire-based, or based on waveguides.[25] Entire histories of telecommunications are routinely structured around this basic technical engineering distinction between 'guided' and 'unguided' mediums, or 'line-based' and 'radio-based' systems.[26] The technical sense of *Leitungen* is evident in the historical engineering terms *Luftleiter* (aerial conductor) and *Freileitungen* (overhead power lines); and Karl Ferdinand Braun's crucial wireless patent was for a 'Telegraph System without Directly Connected Wire [*Leitung*]'.[27] In the late nineteenth century, wireless was often associated with a crisis of the imagination and described as a technical, physical, or logical impossibility. 'There is something astonishing about telegraphing without a connection through electrically conducting wires [*leitende Drähte*] from one place to another', reflected German physicist and philosopher of technology Friedrich Dessauer, 'because it is not obvious to our powers of imagination to think of the propagation of electrical power independently of so-called conductors [*Leiter*].'[28] In its figurative sense, *Leitung* evokes a different kind of control. 'Sociologically', Christoph Asendorf explains in his seminal study of the impact of electromagnetism on modernist art, 'leads or leaders [*Leitung oder Leiter*] are hallmarks of hierarchical forms of organization; the flow of directives is organized from this point'.[29] Kittler's thesis thus also suggests that wireless, despite all the associated rhetoric about freedom and mobility, remains subject to control.

While commercial systems of wired telegraphy and telephony predate their wireless counterparts, the true meaning of the wired world only appeared to observers after the emergence of wireless transmission with attempts to control and manage the proliferation of wires. By 1900 wired telegraphy had existed for half a century, and despite occasional complaints, the expanding cable network did not seem particularly remarkable until after wireless telegraphy seemed possible. In the United States, most telegraph and electrical lines were installed above ground, making them subject to comparisons with industrial pollution. However, there was a time in the mid- to late nineteenth century when the future looked different, and 'going wireless' was construed differently than it is today. As Ghislain Thibault observes, 'wireless' applied to a wide range of cases in the late nineteenth century, from the strict sense of signalling via radio waves to the loose sense of getting rid of visible wires in public places, as when one municipal government touted 'more wireless streets' after merely clearing away telegraph poles.[30]

Around 1900, images of the wired world centred on the telegraph pole, the physical support for a dense communications network branching out towards multiple destinations, as depicted in a striking engraving attributed to French illustrator E. Tournois (Fig. 1.1). Under a web of wires, a crowd appears to be forming, if only for a moment, in collective observation of the usually unnoticed infrastructure. While the wires remain orderly, thanks to the artist's skill at cross-hatching, the telegraph pole with over thirty crossbeams supporting five to ten wires each makes visible the strains on wired infrastructure. Without support, the cables would collapse into a tangled mess. As a symbol of organisation and modernisation, telegraph lines assembled into a rectilinear grid attested to planning and foresight. By consolidating wires, telegraph poles allowed easier service access, as demonstrated by the figure who has climbed to the third rung of the pole and may represent a technician or an eavesdropper. 'What other tree can you climb where the birds' twitter, / Unscrambled is English?' asks John Updike in a poem dedicated to telephone poles.[31] Beneath the pole in Tournois's etching, several pedestrians, including two businesspeople and a costermonger with her clients, can be seen taking a break from their daily routines, absorbed by the scene. Gazing up at the cables, they embody Updike's description of the alternately stupefying and electrifying experience of wired infrastructure:

> Our eyes, washed clean of belief,
> Lift incredulous to their fearsome crowns of bolts, trusses, struts,
>   nuts, insulators, and such
> Barnacles as compose
> These weathered encrustations of electrical debris –
> Each a Gorgon's head, which, seized right,
> Could stun us to stone.[32]

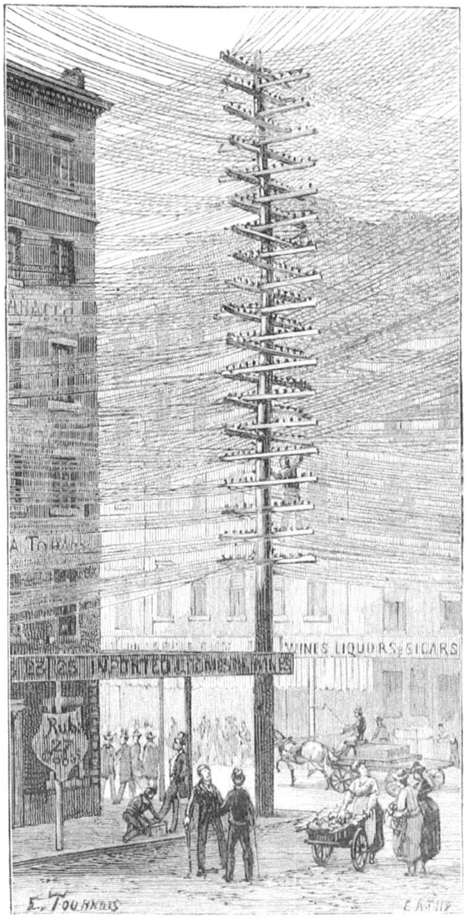

Figure 1.1 Satirical image of excessive wiring on Fulton Street, New York, drawn by E. Tournois, who produced many woodcut engravings for illustrated journals in the nineteenth century. Source: B. Abdank Abakanowicz, 'L'électricité en Amérique: La télégraphie', *La lumière électrique*, 11 July 1885: 491; cf. Kittler, *Gramophone, Film, Typewriter*, 6.

If grasping the wire directly is out of the question, and if cutting it, like a Gordian knot, would only make a dozen more appear in its place, then we might entertain more indirect strategies of reflection, such as Perseus's shield. A century after its composition, Tournois's satirical engraving of the wired city would be reprinted, albeit unattributed, in Kittler's cult classic monograph that will be examined in greater detail at the end of this chapter.

In German, there is a beautiful vernacular term for cables that have become so tied, twisted, and intertwined that the prospects of disentangling them are as unthinkable as unmixing a salad: *Kabelsalat* (cable salad) crystallises the problems of an old mode of transmission to which a new one was thought to provide the answers. There are already too many wires, and yet still not enough connections. Wireless transmission promised to clean up the mess technicians had made in the past, freeing future generations from getting tangled up in or having to think about technology. Capturing the point when it becomes impossible to make another connection without literally first unplugging and disentangling material cables,[33] *Kabelsalat* is something that cannot be undone without finding the figurative ends of wires, networks, infrastructures, perhaps even technology. Yet there is also something human about dealing with *Kabelsalat*. An elementary cultural technique informing weaving and storytelling, tying knots involves intertwining threads into compact, flexible, and sustainable forms.[34] Cabling techniques exhibit an equal amount of complexity, though they are often said to be simpler than wireless techniques. In the German signal corps, there was a long-standing hierarchy of 'wireless operators' (*Funker*) over the 'cable apes' (*Kabelaffen*) responsible for running wires across dangerous terrain. In civil society, *Kabelsalat* is perceived to be equally undesirable, a sign of poor housekeeping or a symptom of greater disorder, and is thus made to disappear inside cable ducts, behind walls, or above dropped ceilings. Only when cables run counter to the functional order of technology do they become visible in symbolic forms of disorder. When written with a dash, *Kabel-Salat* makes visible this rupture between the symbolic and functional orders of technology.[35] As an epistemological breakdown between these orders, *Kabelsalat* presents a figure of extreme disorder, of technology developing out of control.

To impose order on disorderly processes of media change, convergence narratives pit wires against wireless, as though each mode of transmission belongs to a distinct historical period. However, media convergence is itself a widespread topos in transitional periods when an established medium seems threatened by another one capable of performing similar functions. One of the earliest attempts to rethink the seemingly linear trajectory from old media to new media, which would later become known as the 'law of media complementarity', can be found in a 1913 dissertation on communication in classical antiquity written by Wolfgang Riepl, the journalist and chief editor of the *Nürnberger Zeitung*. Challenging modernist commonplaces about media competition, Riepl's law describes how, despite a 'quantitative and qualitative [. . .] escalation process', a new medium never completely renders an old one obsolete. To support this hypothesis, Riepl compared what he called the 'progress of human culture from simple social relations of primeval times to the height of civilisation' – implicitly, in Western Europe. On the one hand, Riepl was struck by the sheer survival of elementary communication techniques among 'primitive peoples' (*Naturvölkern*), among whom he counted not only pre-modern non-Romans but also then-contemporary Indigenous Peoples.

> On the other hand, there is a foundational law for the development of communications [*Grundgesetz der Entwicklung des Nachrichtenwesens*], so to speak, that the simplest means, forms, and methods, once established and found useful, can never again be completely and permanently suppressed or made obsolete, even by the most highly developed peoples; rather, they are conserved, only now forced to seek other tasks and areas for commercial exploitation.[36]

Following Riepl, early media historians speculating on Europe's wireless futures concluded that the new mode would not inevitably replace the old one, while also implying that Europe was the only civilisation capable of preserving historical traditions or re-commercialising obsolete technologies.[37] Mentioning none of this context, Kittler expressed Riepl's law with an oft-quoted soundbite: 'New media do not make old media obsolete; they assign them other places in the system.'[38]

Rather than the opposite of wired transmission or its inevitable replacement, wireless is thus better understood – building on Riepl's law and Kittler's multivalent concept of *Leitungen* – through the Derridean logic of supplementarity. Allegedly secondary, the latter term supplements the former's primary, original, or natural connotations in the twofold sense of remedying its perceived faults and extending its latent potentialities. To concretise this abstract point, it is helpful to recall two oxymoronic terms: a 'wireless wire' (*Funkendraht*), referring not to antennas but to the air as an information channel; and 'wired wireless' (*Drahtfunk*), a system of carrier-wave telephony using electrical power cables rather than standard telephone lines.[39] In both cases, wireless completes the wire by supplying something that was missing, and it adds something that the wire could have done without. According to the recursive logic of supplementarity, moreover, the thing being supplemented (that is, the wire) only seems to require supplementation because it has the same qualities originally assumed to have characterised the supplement (that is, wireless).

Wireless Before Wireless

Understood as a supplement, wireless occupies a pivotal position in media history and theory. Before the wire, all communication was 'wireless', and yet there was no such thing as 'wireless communication'. There was only communication, itself not yet even named as such.[40] Speculations about a potential means of signalling without wires can be traced back to classical antiquity, and pre-modern optical and acoustic techniques, such as beacon fires and tribal drums, remain in use today.[41] However, 'wireless telegraphy' only makes sense after the emergence of wired telegraphy in the long nineteenth century.[42] Ever since, the media histories and theories of wired and wireless transmission have remained entangled for European modernity, despite attempts to separate them in modernist historiography. Looking backward from the moment around 1900, wireless telegraphy and telephony are usually understood as the culmination of historical developments in telecommunication or the realisation of ancient fantasies about long-distance communication. Looking forward, they are said to anticipate radio and television as mass media by creating regular programmes, consolidating audiences into target markets, and broadcasting information and entertainment day and night.

For provisional orientation to these entanglements, Daniel Gethmann and Florian Springer's media-philosophical study *At the Ends of the Cable* provides a useful heuristic with three main phrases corresponding roughly to 1700/1800/1900.[43] Before there were networks, relays, or contents to be transmitted (c. 1700), early modern researchers started investigating the properties of cables.[44] In the second phase (c. 1800), relays and switches made cables into carriers of energy and information, and the act of networking cables generated a new 'address space' that enabled complex network topologies.[45] In the third phase (c. 1900), wireless networks extended the number of potential addresses, previously limited to the physical ends of the cable, to a theoretically unlimited number of unknown and potentially mobile stations.[46] By leaving behind the material cable, wireless decoupled its address system from concrete places, which fuelled the rhetoric around wireless transmissions being addressed 'to all'.[47] While the materiality of wired transmission limits access to the cable's physical ends, wireless extends the space of transmission and the possibility of being addressed to everyone – even those with no access to wireless technology. Throughout these epistemic shifts, the presence or absence of wires continuously redefined the meaning of distance, proximity, and the 'here and now'.[48]

While this brief account might create the impression that the wired age, c. 1700–1900, was superseded by the wireless age, c. 1900–present, there is more to the story. Although it exceeds the scope of *Wireless Futures*, optical telegraphy (c. 1800) is now widely recognised as the first modern system of 'wireless' transmission, a fast and reliable tool for governments to coordinate large-scale military manoeuvres and administrative operations. While optical telegraphy remains in use in some limit cases, it was largely superseded by electrical telegraphy, and by the 1880s there were underwater electrical cables connecting Europe to every other continent.[49] In its first phase (c. 1900), wireless was received primarily as a competitor to wired telegraphy with one essential advantage – extending services to locations that could not possibly be connected by wire. While wired and wireless telegraphy spread rapidly and dynamically, with worldwide networks arising over a span of decades, wired and wireless telephony spread only slowly, taking an entire century, due largely to technical differences.[50] According to Bernhard J. Dotzler and Silke Roesler-Keilholz's media genealogy, the now-familiar 'radio-logics of connectivity and personalisation' emerged with radiotelegraphy (c. 1900), but those of 'mobility and portability', which came to be a hallmark of walkie-talkies and two-way radios, came only in the second phase with the emergence of the transistor (c. 1950).[51] Whereas the analogue/digital transition starting in the 1980s spelled the end of some media, it gave the telegraph and telephone new life. The year after Kittler's 'Observations on Public Reception', Germany opened its first digital mobile phone network (*D-Netz*).

Though presented in chronological order, this short retrospective should not be taken to be another version of modernity's typical, forward-looking story about the triumphant realisation of an ancient dream of communication by a few heroic physicists and engineers. Historically removed from these narratives, media philosophers can make time-critical, second-order observations about the ontological and epistemological implications of the modernist search for the origins and essences of technology.

Like other 'engineering philosophers of technology',[52] Hans Reichenbach was inspired by the emergence of broadcasting to look beyond the present and peer into the deep time of the media:

> Telegraphy is as old as humanity. The prehistoric man, who raised his arm to wave to his comrade, telegraphed, because he was doing so to transmit a message to a distance, and this is exactly what is called telegraphy. Yes, he even telegraphed wirelessly [*drahtlos*]. Light rays transmitted the image of his arm to his comrade's eye – with no

> connecting line, truly 'wirelessly' [*drahtlos*]. And we now know that this simple type of telegraphy is the same as our modern radiotelegraphy. For physics has taught us that light rays are electric waves of the same kind as the electric waves of radio traffic; only that the latter take longer strides, so to speak, when they are rushing across space.[53]

Once again, media reveal aspects of unmediated communication only in retrospect. By downplaying the experiential differences between waving and telegraphing and playing up their identical physical medium, Reichenbach's transhistorical speculations made the two modes of electromagnetic transmission appear to differ not in kind but in degree. This assertion made it possible to rewrite the history of technology as one of progress from 'simple' to 'complex' societies. Like Reichenbach, other modernist thinkers (re)discovered premodern and indigenous techniques of signalling at a distance without wires, associated them with non-modern, non-European communication, and relegated them to the distant past, even though many of these techniques were still in use at the time – and remain in use today.

In German modernity, there were two main interpretative traditions of wireless history, which continue to inform its reductive, binary treatment to this day. To historians, wireless telegraphy appeared to realise the ancient dream of perfect communication. To engineers, it appeared to present a solution to recent problems of wired telegraphy. Both interpretations relied on a shared inventory of historical events but differed in their narrative forms and literary techniques. As a result, the same Eurocentric origin stories circulated in different forms that cut across the dividing line separating one interpretative tradition from the other, and nearly every modernist account of wireless transmission ended with a speculative conclusion. To construct the modernity of wireless transmission, modernist histories of wireless thus deployed speculation in two different senses: mobilising visionary statements about the medium's future and reconstructing its pre-history stretching back into the distant past.[54]

In this Eurocentric historiographical tradition, techniques for signalling at a distance without wires were usually traced back to three main historical moments. In the first case, optical techniques such as fire signals were said to originate in classical Greek and Roman antiquity, whereas acoustic techniques such as drum signals were said to be derived from ancient Africa and China. Although many of these optical and acoustic techniques remained known throughout the so-called Dark Ages, they were only said to have been (re)discovered during the late Middle Ages and the early modern period, which forms the second major moment in the mode's longer history. Techniques of signalling at a distance now assumed a new significance with the (re)discovery of magnetism, thought to enable sympathetic communication among interlocutors who had touched the same material with a compass needle. In developing these systems, early modern codes referred to the pre-modern order of communication with spirits, exploiting the ambiguity between symbolic codes and emerging practices of technical encryption. When optical telegraphy developed into Europe's first large-scale communications infrastructure around 1800, it challenged the established order of the postal service with a new kind of sign, giving rise to the third major moment of wireless history that was said to continue to the present.

According to the alternative genealogy prominent among physicists and engineers, wireless telegraphy was not a pre-modern but a quintessentially modern innovation. 'Attempts to create wireless telegraphy are only slightly more recent than the invention of practical wired telegraphy itself', as Karl Ferdinand Braun humorously put it in the scant 'historical introduction' to a seminal lecture he delivered in 1900. 'Having only barely accomplished transmission via the wire, people started looking for ways to get rid of it again.'[55] Understood as an internal solution to a perceived problem in media history, wireless transmission was taken to resolve issues of efficiency and optimisation, first reducing the number of connecting wires and then doing away with them. In his influential 1905 account of *Wireless Telegraphy*, engineer Eugen Nesper observed that

> nearly every historical introduction to an account of wireless telegraphy begins with the optical and acoustic sign transmissions of ancient civilisations [*alter Kulturvölker*], although these elementary and, by the standards of the time, ingenious devices have nothing more in common with electromagnetic wave telegraphy than that messages were transmitted from one place to another without a direct metallic line.[56]

For Nesper, none of these pre-modern systems qualified as 'distant writing' (*Fernschrift*) in the sense of Greek *telegraphia*, and yet 'one would be wrong to assume that wireless telegraphy is of very recent origin, although it must be admitted that the scientific clarification of the basic phenomena and their practical utilisation for transport only took place in the last decade or so'.[57]

Whether told by engineers or historians, modernist origin stories about signalling at a distance without connecting wires served multiple functions beyond straightforward publicity. In addition to these accounts of capitalism, imperialism, and colonialism, other origin stories emphasised the mutual interactions among science, industry, and military complexes.[58] As for many then-new media, origin stories invented an entire Eurocentric tradition in which wireless telegraphy represented the inevitable culmination of technical progress and an age-old desire for democratic communication. On the other hand, origin stories supported competing European claims to 'firstness' with future implications for actual and symbolic capital. As an unstudied but integral aspect of modernism, origin stories can provide insights into contingent attitudes towards space and time. Though centred on the question of beginnings, every origin story also conveys assumptions about the present and expectations about the future.

From Origins to Origin Stories

While there are a handful of stories in circulation that speculate on the origins of wireless connectivity, Kittler's memorable soundbite about the birth of mass media out of the spirit of tap water merely repackaged the one origin story that is better known than all the others. According to the standard tale, the 'discovery' of electromagnetic radiation can be traced back to the German Empire, but the 'invention' of wireless telegraphy only to the British Empire. The dominant narrative, which is not coincidentally the one that has been promoted by the industry and the press ever since the years around World War I, presents one young upstart, Guglielmo Marconi, who had the courage to defy the period's received scientific wisdom. While Heinrich Hertz famously pronounced that electromagnetic radiation would make an unviable medium for commercial applications, Marconi transmitted signals at ranges beyond what anyone predicted or imagined. On 12 December 1901 the letter 'S' zipped across the Atlantic and eventually landed as an oversized capital letter on the first page of James Joyce's *Ulysses*, announcing the alliance of modernist literature and media technology. Of course, this is only one version of why wireless transmission emerged at a particular place and time. By contrast, other origin stories, especially in the German-speaking world, viewed the British Empire's speculative investments in the Marconi Company as an attempt to extend its monopoly over wired transmission, and their authors critiqued the press for doctoring reports on experimental trials to make Marconi into a celebrity and an overnight success story.

As is well known, modern inventions are rarely the products of singular geniuses, and discoveries require months or years, thus making them difficult to reduce to any single moment or linear sequence.[59]

Nevertheless, origin stories about wireless telegraphy have tended to highlight a few key individuals. While Hertz is universally accepted as the foundational figure, Hans Christian Ørsted, Michael Faraday, and James Clerk Maxwell are frequently cited as his predecessors. Contenders for the inventor of wireless telegraphy today include, but are not limited to, Marconi and Oliver Lodge in England; Nikola Tesla and many others in the United States; Alexander Popov in Russia; Édouard Branly in France; Jagadish Chandra Bose in India; and either Braun or the team of Adolf Slaby and Georg von Arco in Germany.[60] While each of these figures made foundational contributions to the development of wireless technology, what remains contested are their claims to the priority of invention, which provide cultural capital and have implications for the administration of patent rights. By claiming that the Germans – or, more precisely, the 'same [German] state' whose emergence he dates to 1870 – 'brought radio [or, gifted it, *bescheren*] to the Europeans', Kittler was intervening polemically in these debates, thinking beyond individuals and connecting aesthetic and technical discourses.[61]

The search for an originator of wireless technology long tended to polarise media historians into two main camps: those who claimed that practice and tinkering played the dominant role in processes of invention; and those who claimed that wireless would not have been possible without abstract theory and scientific discoveries. However, Patrice Flichy argued that 'neither of these two contradictory analyses is entirely correct, for there is no unilinear model of the articulation between science and technology. More significantly, the sequence of different stages in the history of the wireless was not a foregone conclusion.'[62] What today appears natural, such as the once-dominant modality of broadcasting or the composition of the wireless spectrum, is only the result of complex negotiations whose outcomes remained unknowable to participants in the moment.

Consider the difference between the following two origin stories that were written about the same event and around the same time, one by a literary author interested in wireless technology, the other by two engineers interested in literature, history, and culture.

For the first annual German Radio Exhibition, engineers Franz Maria Feldhaus and Walther H. Fitze collaborated on a comprehensive chronology of wireless telegraphy and telephony, comprising around a thousand entries dating from 1500 BCE to 2 August 1924.[63] As the justification for their unorthodox collection, the co-authors reflected that 'rapid development has not yet made it possible to critically determine the historical data in a calm collection, much less to go beyond well-known events and to collect all the inventions and discoveries that more or less contributed to bringing wireless technology up to its current heights'.[64] However, Feldhaus and Fitze appeared unaware of the way their primary aim – to compile 'all data about information transmission with the end goal of wireless communication' – determined their project's teleology.[65] In Markus Krajewski's analysis, 'it is no wonder Feldhaus views himself not only as a chronicler of *everything* but to a certain extent as a radio announcer, as moderator of his own lifelong program of technological-historical data'.[66] However, it is not necessarily the case, as Krajewski suggests, that 'what emerges is nothing but bare facts'.[67] Even without a synthesising narrative voice, every chronology implies a narrative through its selection and ordering of significant events that belies the neutrality and objectivity of 'bare facts'.

Like most chronologies, Feldhaus and Fitze's far-reaching timeline prioritises events taken to represent significant 'firsts' – primarily on the modern European continent. Described as the 'first' megaproject of its kind, their chronology documents the dates of birth of wireless pioneers, along with dates of invention for the 'first magnet-detector', the 'first electromagnetic telegraph for military purposes', and the 'first German steamer equipped with wireless apparatus'. While the timeline's first entry is dedicated to debunking 'fairy tales' (*Märchen*) told by early modern scientists who attempted to rationalise the biblical episode of the Burning Bush as an electrical accident, the second entry, dated 1184 BCE, reads as follows in its entirety:

> The Greeks signal the Fall of Troy from Asia Minor to Greece. The linear distance measures 454km. They set up nine stations with fire signals, resulting in a total distance of 518km. One cannot yet speak of telegraphy here because they sent signals at a distance regarding an event that they could have long foreseen. There are no reports that they could also have signalled about an unforeseen event (Aeschylus, *Agamemnon*, verse 273–309; A. Poppe, *Antike Telegraphie*, 1867, p. 9).[68]

Such 'wireless' systems have frequently been said to represent the origins of modern technical media, insofar as they mathematised information into binary units and achieved speeds exceeding human dimensions by exploiting the properties of electromagnetic radiation. Whereas visual techniques, such as beacon fires, smoke signals, hydraulic telegraphs, ship flags, and semaphore lines, exploited the speed of light, acoustic techniques, such as 'bush telegraphs', calling chains, church bells, or war trumpets, exploited the speed of sound. In another respect, however, pre-modern cultural techniques of wirelessing differ from modern media technologies in that they only transmitted a single bit of information and required advance agreement about which signal would correspond to a message such as 'Troy has fallen'.

Alfred Döblin related the same origin story through a different narrative mode in *Berlin Alexanderplatz*. In an extended aside, the narrator compares pre-modern beacon chains to modern wireless telegraphy and comes to an unexpected conclusion that undermines the perceived superiority of modern technology. After an unforgettable description of the fall of Troy, the narrator exclaims, 'How splendid, be it said in passing, this flaming message from Troy to Greece! How great it is, this march of fire across the sea, this is light, heart, soul, happiness, rejoicing!'[69] At the kairotic moment, one watchman lights a torch; another watchman sees it and lights another torch; then a third watchman and a fourth . . . The established chain of communication stretches not only along the coastline, but all the way from the historical site of the battle to the modern hermeneutic scene, as 'this outcry continues, this madness, which you [that is, the reader] see, flaming red: Agamemnon is coming!'[70] To capture this symbolic, epoch-making message, Döblin presents a litany of elemental, anthropomorphic verbs, uniting the contents of the message, the technique for relaying it, and the experience of the event: 'it burns, it blazes, it speaks, it feels, at every moment, in each place, and the joy is general: Agamemnon is coming!'[71] Arriving in the present, the narrator concludes: 'We can't compare ourselves with this way of doing things. Here again we're *inferior*.'[72]

To most readers, modern wireless technology would have seemed quantitatively superior to anything that came before it. What makes modern technology appear 'inferior' (*zurückstehen*, literally, getting 'left behind') are three main qualitative differences between pre-modern cultural techniques and modern media technologies. First, the contents of modern telegrams (for example, MICHELMANN KOMMT) or telephone calls (for example, WATSON, COME HERE) appear trivial next to those of ancient signals (for example, AGAMEMNON IS COMING). Second, Döblin's narrator understands and appreciates the complexity of wireless technology but struggles to relate it to any foundational narrative or literary style. While there is an entire mythology surrounding the ancient Greek cultural technique, documented in the first play of Aeschylus's *Oresteia* trilogy, the only points the narrator can recall about the origins of modern wireless technology are scrambled technical details and trivial cultural gossip:

> To send a message, we make use of a few results from the experiments of Heinrich Hertz, who lived in Karlsruhe, died at an early age,

> and who, at least in the photo of the Munich Graphic Collection, wore a full beard.
>
> We telegraph by wireless. We produce high frequency alternating currents through transmitters in big stations. We produce electric waves by oscillations of a vibrating circle.
>
> The vibrations spread out spherically, as it were. And then there is also an electron-tube of glass and a microphone the disk of which vibrates in alternating degrees, thus reproducing tones, precisely as when they entered the machine, and that is astonishing, clever, tricky.
>
> It's hard to get enthusiastic about all this; it functions, and that's all.[73]

To simplify the technical process described here, which is Telefunken's system of *Tönende Funken* (singing sparks), what goes into the transmitter at point A is quantitatively the same as what comes out of the receiver at points B, C, or D – but with a qualitative twist. Whereas sending a message using sound and light keeps it accessible to the human senses throughout the entire transmission, electromagnetic media require multiple conversions, whereby information is encoded and decoded in a machine-readable format that bypasses human sensory limits.

This qualitative difference has repercussions for the relation of literature to technology. To describe the ecstatic fire signal, Döblin adopts a telegraphic expressionist style, whereas the description of modern wireless technology is narrated in the cool idiom of New Objectivity. Döblin's choice to make the narrative style mirror the two wireless systems demonstrates the potential of literature to produce media knowledge. If an elementary fire signal once seemed to lead a symbolic life intertwined with the fates of heroes ('it burns, it blazes, it speaks, it feels'), the wireless telegraph leads only a functional existence, a life of its own ('it functions, and that's all'). As much as modern subjects might insist that 'we make use of a few results from the experiments of Heinrich Hertz', 'we telegraph by wireless', 'we produce high frequency alternating currents through transmitters in big stations', and 'we produce electric waves', technology remains indifferent – and yet 'we' are the only ones capable of telling this story.[74]

Media, Philosophy, Anthropology

At the end of origin stories, there is always a trade-off, as Aby Warburg recognised in his celebrated and problematic 'Lecture on Serpent Ritual'.[75] Originally delivered at the sanatorium where he was recovering from 'shell shock' after World War I, Warburg's lecture outlined 'the evolution from primitive paganism, through the highly-developed pagan culture of classical antiquity, down to modern civilized man'.[76] Having observed the Native American Pueblo peoples on a trip in 1896, Warburg spent most of the lecture detailing their rainmaking rituals in which a serpent symbolises lightning. At the end of the lecture, he contrasted this description with a photograph he took in San Francisco of 'the type of man who overthrew the cult of the serpent and overcame the fear of lightning – the descendant of the indigenous race and of the gold-diggers who expelled the Indians: Uncle Sam in his tall hat'.[77] In his apophenic reading of the photograph, Warburg identified one innocuous background detail that remains illegible in the photographic reproduction: 'And away above his top hat runs the electric wire. In this copper-snake, invented by Edison, he has wrested the lightning from nature.'[78] From this detail, Warburg derived massive implications:

> The American of today no longer worships the rattlesnake. Extermination (and whisky) is his answer to it. Electricity enslaved, the lightning held captive in the wire, has produced a civilization which has no use for heathen poetry. But what does it put in its place? The forces of nature are no longer seen in anthropomorphic shapes; they are conceived as an endless succession of waves, obedient to the touch of a man's hand.[79]

The American in the photograph whom Warburg paranoidly imagined to be Uncle Sam operating some sort of pocket wireless device was thus said to exemplify a new human type. Technological rationalism, so this story goes, dispensed with rituals, cults, and fears of nature. 'With these waves', Warburg concluded, 'the civilization of the mechanical age is destroying what natural science, itself emerging out of myth, had won with such vast effort – the sanctuary of devotion, the remoteness needed for contemplation.'[80]

Affected by a chronic illness, cerebral sclerosis, that caused increasingly long-lasting delusions, one notorious jurist, political theorist, and member of the Nazi Party who had long shown paranoid tendencies now felt as though he was being followed by voices and other invisible waves. Near the end of his life, Carl Schmitt is reported to have revised his concept of the 'state of exception', which describes the sovereign's ability to ignore the rule of law during unforeseeable emergencies: 'After World War I, I said: "Sovereign is he who determines the state of exception." After World War II, in the face of my death, I now say: "Sovereign is he who commands the waves of space."'[81] Taking a cue from Schmitt's last words, Kittler argued that modern media and warfare no longer operate according to an additive, incremental, or combinatorial logic but rather one of acceleration, escalation, and strategic one-upmanship:

> With James Clerk Maxwell, control over the waves in space was a problem of theoretical physics, and with Heinrich Hertz it was an experimental one. Beginning with Guglielmo Marconi and Karl Ferdinand Braun, Reginald Fessenden, and Oliver Lodge, however, high-frequency research is predicated on its strategic usefulness.

The epistemic shift diagnosed by Kittler from theory-building and experimentation to competition and strategy describes not only the mode's connections to the emergent military-industrial complex. It also challenges understandings of wireless in the early philosophy of technology and philosophical anthropology, highlighting the withdrawal of media rather than any potential revelation.

'Going wireless' involves not only the elimination of wires, but also the production of electromagnetic waves, which demands a new way of imagining media change. The main argument at the heart of the next chapter is based on a similar observation made by philosophical anthropologist Helmuth Plessner in a 1924 essay titled 'The Utopia in the Machine'. In the year of Germany's first national entertainment broadcasts, Plessner was already able to view a wireless future in the deep time of the media:

> We think that after the radio and the aeroplane things will soon stoop, humanity will have had enough and put the toys of accelerated tempo in the museums of the nineteenth, of the twentieth century [. . .] everything will one day have an end, the human being already having been driven too far away from his essential centre.[82]

While Warburg viewed industrialisation, rationalisation, and mechanisation with nostalgia, Plessner sought another potential exit. Only two paths seemed possible: 'the grandiose destruction of the machine' or the 'development of its inner principles of work into qualitatively higher types of machines, which will set more people free precisely because they will replace them, and leave the rest of people to greater oversight and responsibility for their operation'.[83] Though limited to certain classes, Plessner's 'Utopia in the Machine' would thus put an end to alienated labour through a regenerative form exemplified by electromagnetic radiation in contrast to the exploitation of other natural energy reserves.

For Plessner, wireless transmission served as a sign not of overcoming space and time, nor of uniting vernacular modernisms into a worldwide network, but of the mutual entanglement of humanity and technology:

> Technology is steadily intensifying in that it passes over to an ever-purer penetration of the natural cycle of energy with the human cycle, to the ever-greater release of man from unused expenses of energy, to the ever-more regular accompaniment of man through nature. In this way, for example, *wires are disappearing, and in their place, electric waves provide for the transmission of energy themselves*. The bourgeois ideology of progress is only very limitedly prepared for this utopia in the machines, this driving self-production of an always new, eternal future, since naturally it affects the private capitalistic basis of their existence.[84]

To prepare for this technological utopia – exemplified by the energy universally available in electromagnetic radiation – the task then set by Plessner, as in many early twentieth-century socialist utopias, was to pave the way for the new human being (*der neue Mensch*). There is no way to escape from machines and return to the fields, as Plessner recognised: 'They are not letting us go, and we are not letting them go. With mysterious violence, they are in us, we are in them.'[85]

Like Warburg, Schmitt, and Plessner, Martin Heidegger considered the relation between wireless and philosophy in the deep time of the media, though in Kittler's speculative reading, the media-technological a priori of Nazi radio circumscribed Heidegger's thinking and informed his famous 'Kehre'. In a much-analysed aside in *Being and Time*, Heidegger engaged with the vernacular modernist discourse of media as means of overcoming space and time, providing a new twist to the concept of 'distance' (*Entfernung*) by adding a minor discourse operator that turned it into its opposite, 'de-distanciation' (*Ent-fernung*):

> *An essential tendency toward nearness lies in Dasein*. All kinds of increasing speed which we are more or less compelled to go along with today push for overcoming distance [*Entfernung*]. With the 'radio', for example, Da-sein is bringing about today de-distancing [*Ent-fernung*] of the 'world', which is unforeseeable in its meaning for Da-sein, by way of expanding and destroying the everyday surrounding world.[86]

As Christopher Busch has shown, Kittler repeatedly misquoted this passage from an older edition of *Being and Time*, which described 'an expansion of the everyday environment' (*Erweiterung der alltäglichen Umwelt*), and he ignored the later edition with 'an expansion *and destruction* of the everyday environment' (*Erweiterung und Zerstörung der alltäglichen Umwelt*).[87]

In 'The Age of the World Picture', Heidegger commented differently on radio – and, in Kittler's reading, Heidegger reversed his main premises, now describing technology without reference to subjectivity:

> [E]verywhere and in the most varied disguises gigantic things appear. At the same time this gigantism also materializes in the direction of getting smaller and smaller. We need only think of the figures in nuclear physics. The gigantic aspect pushes to the forefront in a form that seemingly makes it disappear: in the annihilation of large distances by the airplane, in the random presentation, produced by a flick of the wrist, of strange and remote worlds as an everyday occurrence of radio.[88]

While Kittler is routinely described as a (pseudo-)Heideggerian and occasionally accused of flirting with fascism, Kittler in this very lecture shamed the 'radio consumer or Black Forest inhabitant' for being unwilling to think about radio from a technological perspective.[89] Radicalising the hardware side of Kittler's project, Wolfgang Ernst has sought to determine the nature of Heidegger's radio.[90] Based on information provided by Hermann Heidegger, the exact model was likely a Grundig Musikgerät Type 88, a short-wave, high-frequency, long-distance radio brought with the family to their cabin to monitor breaking news about the Cuban missile crisis and speculations about a potential global nuclear apocalypse. In a late essay, 'Towards an Ontology of Media', Kittler reprocessed his 'Observations on Public Reception', revisiting his earlier reading of Heidegger's seminal claim that radio was 'a recent invention by whose means man's existential tendency to "de-distanciate" [*Ent-fernung*], to diminish distances, has been historically implemented'. 'This conclusion is obviously mistaken', Kittler stated. 'I do not mean that Heidegger should have attributed the invention of radio to Heinrich Hertz and Guglielmo Marconi; he simply should not have attributed it to man.'[91] In the next chapter, I will continue to unpack this speculative, post-human media-anthropological account of the 'discovery' of electromagnetic radiation and the 'invention' of wireless telegraphy. To tie up the remaining loose threads in this chapter, however, it is necessary to revisit the historical context of Kittler's 'Observations' in the changing media environment of the 1980s–1990s.

Reimagining Media Change

Unlike most academic monographs, Kittler's media-philosophical magnum opus, *Gramophone, Film, Typewriter,* begins and ends, more like a modernist novel, with the same multivalent word, *Verkabelung*, which can be translated depending on context as 'cabling', 'networking', 'hooking up', 'making connections', or 'optical fibre networks'. The term resonates with this cult book's central theme, which was topical at its time of publication but has been lost in translation and theory transfer over the years.[92] Ostensibly a historical study of modernity's three dominant storage media, *Gramophone, Film, Typewriter* presented a formal critique of the medium of the book and a speculative theory about other possibilities for transmitting knowledge in the future.

In the book's introduction, the spectre of West Germany's controversial, nationwide cabling project informs Kittler's apocalyptic, Cold War narrative about the last-minute actions for emergency preparedness in anticipation of the Doomsday Clock striking midnight:

> *Optical fiber networks* [*Verkabelung*]. People will be hooked to an information channel that can be used for any medium – for the first time in history, or for its end. Once movies and music, phone calls and texts reach households via optical fiber cables [*Glaserfaserkabel*], the formerly distinct media of television, radio, telephone, and mail converge, standardized by transmission frequencies and bit format.[93]

At the end of the last chapter, the spectre of *Verkabelung* returns in a polemical, geopolitical opposition, which contrasts the rapid diffusion of compulsory cabling by the United States Department of Defense with the slow adoption of computers among West German intellectuals:

> And while professors are still reluctantly trading in their typewriters for word processors, the NSA is preparing for the future: from nursery school mathematics, which continues to be fully sufficient for books, to charge-coupled devices, surface-wave filters, digital signal processors including the four basic forms of computation. Trenches, flashes of lightning, stars – storage, transmission, *the laying of cables* [*Verkabelung*].[94]

Connecting the analogue to the digital, Kittler completes the circuit of *Verkabelung* in multiple senses: its linguistic repetition exposes the structural conditions of the printed book; and its pictorial resonance with Tournois's image of *Kabelsalat* discussed above and reprinted in *Gramophone, Film, Typewriter* underscores the perceived ends of that medium.

Although the word *Verkabelung* seldom occurs in the rest of *Gramophone, Film, Typewriter*, it functions as the master figure for

Kittler's project. More than a flippant response to Marshall McLuhan's comments on the electric lightbulb as the key to *Understanding Media*, *Verkabelung* functions as a metaphor for making connections across media systems, an autobiographical reminder of Kittler's project of hardwiring a DIY synthesiser, and a sociopolitical symbol in the West German discourse of media change. As a pendant to the radiant electric lightbulb, which McLuhan took to be 'pure information [. . .] a medium without a message',[95] the shielded electromagnetic cable that Geert Lovink would later dub 'dark fibre' presents a provocative challenge to the dominant hermeneutics of media critique. For Kittler, the switch from copper wires to fibre-optic cables signals the end of media history as we can possibly know it. The defining characteristics of fibre-optic cables are their opacity, self-enclosure, and resistance to transparency, as Wendy Hui Kyong Chun observed when reimagining and rewriting parts of Kittler's book word-for-word into a critical feminist idiom.[96] If, as Kittler claims, film, radio, telegraph, telephone, and post offices once depended on distinct information channels, they have now been standardised into a form of information that can be transmitted over the same closed channel, which appears to be shielded against both electromagnetic warfare and (Frankfurt School) media critique. More than the transparent synonym for fibre-optic cables that the early Kittler reception took it to be, *Verkabelung* referred to Kittler's highly ambiguous and fundamentally indeterminate attempts to short circuit technical, cultural, literary, and philosophical history.

In the German language, there is no antonym for *Verkabelung*, no such thing as *Entkabelung*, much as there is no antonym in English for 'going wireless' – and even if there were, it would probably not be 'going wired'. Despite the vast sociological literature on networking and making connections, there is still no corresponding theory of 'unmaking connections', as Urs Stäheli has observed and argued to remedy this situation.[97] While the hypothesis of linguistic relativity remains debatable, as does Kittler's notorious claim that 'media determine our situation, which – in spite of or because of it – deserves a description',[98] any medium or mode can be said, in a variant of this Foucauldian thesis, to circumscribe our sense of possibilities and shape our imagination. Wireless media inform, constrict, or expand our sense of what connections are possible, as evident in a manipulated image of Goethe speaking on the telephone that is reprinted on the back cover of the German edition of Kittler's *Discourse Networks*. To complement the study of connectivity, contemporary media studies also needs to study the possibilities of *Entkabelung*, of disconnection, withdrawal, and unmaking connections.

In the end, the SF story, retold by Kittler and many others, about a future media environment in which everyone is 'totally wired' into all-encompassing networks of power and control never came to pass in this exact form. In fact, West Germany went in the opposite direction, having difficulties with laying cables that continue to cause problems for those seeking high-speed Internet access to this day. Totally but invisibly connected, our current media environment may appear to present an even more apocalyptic scenario than the ones that appeared in the 1980s or the 1880s. Emphasising that digital signals are not ideally compatible with the 'so-called ether', insofar as they require comparatively large bandwidths, Kittler once predicted that 'wireless telephony, as radio was called in the days of its military infancy, will likely continue to remain the domain for all that cannot be cached and, hence, manipulated through digital signal processing, that is to say, for randomness, for unpredictability, for danger'.[99] While digital telephony has become standard in the interim, analogue telephony continues to be reserved for current military operations. Yet, according to the interpretative logic governing these two mutually contingent systems, the present always determines the kinds of stories we find significant in the past, and these stories determine the kinds of predictions that can be made about the future. Each situation thus opens a space for new work on wireless futures past, providing further incentive to reconfigure the traditional relations between media and philosophy, open new perspectives on literature and culture, and dig *into* (rather than *dig in* to) the *Kabelsalat*.

Notes

1. Kittler, 'Observations on Public Reception', 75.
2. See Kümmel-Schnur, 'Patente als Agenten von Mediengeschichte', 53–76; Lethen, 'Amsterdam 1964'.
3. This contextual information appears only in the original lecture typescript: Kittler, 'Anmerkungen zum Volksempfang'.
4. For media-philosophical overviews of these differences between wired and wireless transmission, see Bexte, 'Kabel im Denkraum'; Gethmann and Sprenger, *Die Enden des Kabels*.
5. *Anmerkungen* refers to 'notes', 'comments', or 'annotations' – typically footnotes, endnotes, marginalia, or private and peripheral writings. Out of Heidegger's thirty-four *Black Books*, diaries kept on his bedside table and only published in recent years, nine were labelled 'Anmerkungen', the ones for the years 1942–51. *Volksempfang* literally describes a 'ceremonial reception by the people', in the sense of Goebbels' claims about

the 'big turnouts' at Hitler's rallies, and contains further connotations of mass manipulation, Nazi radio politics, and the radio receiver known as the *Volksempfänger*.

6. Kittler, 'Observations on Public Reception', 84; Knorr-Cetina, *The Manufacture of Knowledge*.
7. Pornschlegel, 'Verkehrter Volksempfang'. Kittler mentions Pornschegel in the acknowledgements in *Gramophone, Film, Typewriter*.
8. On Kittler's synthetic writing method, see Niebisch, 'Close Writing'; on its relation to Kittler's synth, see Born, 'What was Time Axis Manipulation?'
9. On Kittlerian discourse operators, see Winthrop-Young, 'Recursive Innovation'.
10. Kittler, 'Observations on Public Reception', 84, n. 1; *Meyers Grosses Konversations-Lexikon*.
11. Kahn, *Earth Sound, Earth Signal*, 21.
12. Kittler, *Gramophone, Film, Typewriter*, 95–8, 195, 251–7.
13. See, among others, Kittler, 'Observations on Public Reception'; Kittler, 'Rock Music'; Kittler, 'Im Telegrammstil'; Kittler, 'The Last Radio Broadcast'; Kittler, 'Von der optischen Telegrafie zur Photonentechnik'; Kittler, 'Playback'.
14. See, among others, Mowitt, *Radio*, 14, 40; Sterne, *MP3*, 131; Fisher, 'Radio', 151–64.
15. Sterne, *MP3*, 131.
16. Kittler, 'Observations on Public Reception', 81.
17. See Peters, '"You Mean My Whole Fallacy Is Wrong"', 22.
18. Winthrop-Young, 'The Kittler Effect', 205.
19. See Schröter and Heilmann, *Friedrich Kittler*.
20. Kittler, 'Observations on Public Reception', 81.
21. Parikka, 'Friedrich Kittler', n.p.
22. Kittler, 'Observations on Public Reception', 81.
23. Kittler, 'Observations on Public Reception', 75.
24. See Kittler, *Discourse Networks*, xii; Pias, 'Friedrich Kittler und der "Mißbrauch von Heeresgerät"'; Born, 'What was Time Axis Manipulation?'
25. Balanis, *Antenna Theory*, 1.
26. Huurdeman, *Worldwide History of Telecommunications*.
27. Braun, Telegraphiesystem ohne fortlaufende Leitung.
28. Dessauer, 'Die Drahtlose Telegraphie', 205.
29. Asendorf, *Ströme und Strahlen*, 58.
30. Thibault, 'Wireless Pasts and Wired Futures', 90.
31. Updike, 'Telephone Poles', 43.
32. Updike, 'Telephone Poles', 43.
33. See Bexte, 'Kabel im Denkraum', 18.
34. Vogel, 'Verstrickungskünste – Lösungskünste'.
35. See Bexte, 'Kabel im Denkraum', 18.
36. Riepl, *Das Nachrichtenwesen des Altertums*, 96.

37. See, among others, Fischer, *Die drahtlose Telegraphie und Telephonie*, 104; Riemenschneider, *Drahtlose Telegraphie und Telephonie*, 293; Bronk, *Über die geographische Bedingtheit*, 11.
38. Kittler, 'History of Communication Media', n.p.
39. See Patnode, 'Path Not Taken'.
40. On the question of 'media' before 'the media', see Ofak and Kittler, *Medien vor den Medien*; Born, 'Media Archaeology'.
41. On the prehistory of wireless communications, which largely remains to be written, see Hacking, 'Genres of Communication'; Völker, *Mobile Medien*.
42. Rikitianskaia et al., 'The Mediatization of the Air', 758–79.
43. Gethmann and Sprenger, *Die Enden des Kabels*, 11.
44. Gethmann and Sprenger, *Die Enden des Kabels*, 14–15.
45. Gethmann and Sprenger, *Die Enden des Kabels*, 18.
46. Gethmann and Sprenger, *Die Enden des Kabels*, 22–4.
47. Gethmann and Sprenger, *Die Enden des Kabels*, 22.
48. Gethmann and Sprenger, *Die Enden des Kabels*, 25.
49. König, 'Telegraphie, Telefonie, Funk', 56–70.
50. König, 'Telegraphie, Telefonie, Funk'.
51. Dotzler and Roesler-Keilholz, 'Radio'.
52. On the 'engineering philosophy of technology', a heuristic for describing Ernst Kapp, Peter Engelmeier, and Friedrich Dessauer, see Mitcham, *Thinking through Technology*, 19–38.
53. Reichenbach and Noack, *Was ist Radio?*, 3; cf. Dotzler and Roesler-Keilholz, 'Radio', 119–20.
54. See, among others, Sterne, 'Alte Ahnungen der drahtlosen Telegraphie'; Hennig, *Die älteste Entwicklung der Telegraphie und Telephonie*; Feldhaus and Fitze, *Geschichtszahlen der drahtlosen Telegraphie und Telephonie*.
55. Braun, *Drahtlose Telegraphie durch Wasser und Luft*, 5.
56. Nesper, *Die drahtlose Telegraphie*, 9.
57. Nesper, *Die drahtlose Telegraphie*, 9.
58. Hagen, *Das Radio*; Klein-Arendt, *Kamina ruft Nauen!*; Mantei, *Von der Sandbüchse zum Post- und Telegraphenland*.
59. Lee, *The Design of CMOS Radio-Frequency Integrated Circuits*, 39.
60. See Flichy, *Dynamics of Modern Communication*, 99.
61. Kittler, 'Observations on Public Reception', 75.
62. See Flichy, *Dynamics of Modern Communication*, 99.
63. Feldhaus and Fitze, *Geschichtszahlen der drahtlosen Telegraphie und Telephonie*.
64. Feldhaus and Fitze, *Geschichtszahlen der drahtlosen Telegraphie und Telephonie*, 3.
65. Feldhaus and Fitze, *Geschichtszahlen der drahtlosen Telegraphie und Telephonie*, 3.
66. Krajewski, *World Projects*, 101.
67. Krajewski, *World Projects*, 135.

68. Feldhaus and Fitze, *Geschichtszahlen der drahtlosen Telegraphie und Telephonie*, 5.
69. Döblin, *Berlin Alexanderplatz*, 75.
70. Döblin, *Berlin Alexanderplatz*, 75.
71. Döblin, *Berlin Alexanderplatz*, 76.
72. Döblin, *Berlin Alexanderplatz*, 75–6 (emphasis added).
73. Döblin, *Berlin Alexanderplatz*, 76 (translation modified).
74. Döblin, *Berlin Alexanderplatz*, 126.
75. Warburg, 'A Lecture on Serpent Ritual', 292. Warburg's lecture was originally titled 'Reminiscences from a Journey to the Pueblo Indians'.
76. Warburg, 'A Lecture on Serpent Ritual', 277.
77. Warburg, 'A Lecture on Serpent Ritual', 292.
78. Warburg, 'A Lecture on Serpent Ritual', 292.
79. Warburg, 'A Lecture on Serpent Ritual', 292.
80. Warburg, 'A Lecture on Serpent Ritual', 292.
81. Quoted in Kittler, 'Playback', 93.
82. Plessner, 'Die Utopie der Maschinen', 31.
83. Plessner, 'Die Utopie der Maschinen', 36–7.
84. Plessner, 'Die Utopie der Maschinen', 37–8.
85. Plessner, 'Die Utopie der Maschinen', 38.
86. Heidegger, *Being and Time*, 98.
87. Busch, 'Strategische Zitate'. Kittler's (mis)quotation of Heidegger circulates widely in English-language scholarship; see, for example, Mowitt, *Radio*, 40.
88. Heidegger, 'Age of the World Picture'.
89. Kittler, 'Observations on Public Reception', 82.
90. Ernst, 'Das Radiotier', 331.
91. Kittler, 'Towards an Ontology of Media', 29.
92. See Kirschenbaum, *Mechanisms*, 6; Chun, *Control and Freedom*, 300; cf. Winthrop-Young, *Kittler and the Media*.
93. Kittler, *Gramophone, Film, Typewriter*, 1.
94. Kittler, *Gramophone, Film, Typewriter*, 263. Although *Verkabelung* is the first and last word of Kittler's book, it is translated as 'optical fiber networks' at the start of the English translation and as 'the laying of cables' at the end – without the word's figurative sense of 'making connections' – which explains why most readers of the English translation overlook the connection.
95. McLuhan, *Understanding Media*, 8.
96. Chun, *Control and Freedom*, 299–300.
97. Stäheli, 'Undoing Networks', 1–30.
98. Kittler, *Gramophone, Film, Typewriter*, xxxix.
99. Kittler, 'Playback', 109.

Chapter 2

Etheric Speculations: Science, Fiction, and the Power of Prediction

Wireless transmission involves not only the elimination of wires but also the production of electromagnetic radiation, the physical medium supporting applications from wireless telegraphy to Wi-Fi. As argued in the previous chapter, it is tempting to tell the story of wireless transmission as a linear narrative of invention and discovery, but the historical timeline contains too many false starts, dead ends, leaps, and jumps. Nevertheless, electromagnetic radiation represents a plausible caesura, or epistemic break, around which to organise other points on the historical timeline. A naturally occurring resource only 'discovered' – or, more precisely, scientifically verified – in the late nineteenth century, electromagnetic radiation has been said to constitute a decisive 'turning-point' in media history, 'whose significance is probably equalled only by the invention of writing'.[1]

To make sense of this dilemma, this chapter introduces a methodology for studying the 'physics of media' and connects it to two related approaches, 'elemental media' and the 'materialities of communication'. Wrongly associated with technological determinism for positing a 'media technological a priori', German media philosophy reactivates the expansive pre-modern understanding of media as physical substances, intermediaries, or go-betweens. While electromagnetic radiation hardly determined the affordances of wirelessing, the imagination of an all-pervading substance known as the ether influenced modernists' understanding of the mode's possibilities to such a great extent that it warrants closer analysis. To address outdated but still widespread assumptions in modernism and modernity studies about the presumed epoch-making conceptual shifts from the ether to the electromagnetic spectrum, this chapter examines literary and philosophical reflections on the changing concepts of action at a distance and the short-range interactions of electromagnetic fields.

Ubiquitous, imperceptible, and yet very much real, electromagnetic radiation makes an ideal case for studying the 'materialities of communication'. In the mid-1980s Hans Ulrich Gumbrecht and Karl Ludwig Pfeiffer coined this term for a counterprogramme of post-structuralist, German-language scholarship responding to French-language theories of the 'immateriality of information'.[2] While the materialities of communication put parentheses around the philosophical concept of transcendental subjectivity, which might lead one to conclude that modern media fulfilled a transhistorical, universal desire to extend elementary human powers, it remains unclear where the materialities of wireless communication would then be located. At either end of any 'wireless line' there are transmitters and receivers that modulate and demodulate electromagnetic radiation into information, but these technical objects account only for the terminals and not the connecting channel.

Before the scientific verification of electromagnetic radiation in the 1880s, the channel was presumed to be a *material* substrate, and thus the very notion of 'wireless telegraphy' appeared to be a contradiction in terms. Having quickly become habituated to the materiality of cables, nineteenth-century observers remained rooted in Aristotelian and Newtonian physics. By this logic, any technical or artistic medium remains inseparable from its material supports, and 'telegraphy without wires' sounds like nothing more than an impossible solution to a non-existent problem. In 1879 the satirical magazine *Kladderadatsch* joined the press chorus in mocking a proposal from American physicist and dentist Mahlon Loomis for 'telegraphy without wires', claiming that it would be just as unthinkable as inventing 'photography without light, lithography without stone, xylography without wood, metallography without colour, and copper engraving without plates'.[3] By the end of the 1880s the scientific verification of electromagnetic radiation had challenged assumptions about the limits of human perception, the materiality of natural phenomena, and the nature of scientific knowledge production.

Following recent studies of the physics of media, the history and theory of media objects exceeds the conventional limits established by communication and mass media studies in terms of the thresholds of sense perception. For wireless transmission, this suggests turning from studying the experience of wirelessness to the impossibility of experiencing radio waves. In Friedrich Kittler's polemical formulation, 'No phenomenology of perception would have ever given us the least idea of them [that is, radio waves]. Media as extensions of science are obviously not, as McLuhan states, extensions of the human being.'[4] While Kittler only briefly remarked on the physics of media, the concept informed the work of Wolfgang Hagen, Bernhard Siegert, and others associated with the Kittler network; Walter Seitter and others independently developed the approach in other systematic directions.[5] John Durham Peters' related approach to 'elemental media' is well-known in English-language media studies, but its mischaracterisation as a 'return to nature' overlooks its resonance with the physics of media and the search for the most elemental units of media.[6] Though a naturally occurring phenomenon, electromagnetic radiation needs to be artificially manipulated to carry information. Many physicists conducting laboratory experiments that led to the verification of the physical medium's existence did not intend to invent wireless transmission, but to provide empirical evidence that might resolve a scientific dispute about wave-based phenomena and the speed of light. Operational techniques, such as amplification, modulation, and interference, only gradually developed into a system that would make it possible for wireless signals to contain information.

While electromagnetic radiation could have been 'discovered' and wireless telegraphy 'invented' outside of European modernity, other cultures do not appear to have needed a mode of transmission that can operate day and night across a threshold that remains imperceptible to human operators. Traditionally treated as two distinct phenomena, electricity and magnetism only came to be systematically related in European science during the long nineteenth century, as electromagnetism solidified into what Hans-Jörg Rheinberger might call an 'epistemic thing'. While physicists were already observing the inexplicable effects of electromagnetic radiation on their laboratory apparatus in the early 1800s, it was only in the 1860s that James Clerk Maxwell predicted the existence of a continuous spectrum of electromagnetic phenomena, and only in the 1880s that Heinrich Hertz provided empirical evidence that verified earlier speculations. Building on research by Michael Faraday, Carl Friedrich Gauss, and André-Marie Ampère, Maxwell speculated that electricity, magnetism, and light are manifestations of the same phenomenon, which he termed the 'electromagnetic field'. Challenging the traditional paradigm of 'action at a distance' (*actio in distans*), Maxwell modelled local interactions between electricity and magnetism with four partial differential equations now known as 'Maxwell's equations'. Describing how electric currents generate magnetic fields and vice versa, Maxwell's equations provided a mathematical model for wireless transmission, but they did not lead directly to any commercial wireless applications. Hertz once denied the possibility of any such applications, and taken out of context, this statement informed the foundational mythology about how supposedly 'progressive' engineers and entrepreneurs such as Marconi outpaced 'conservative' physicists and scholars,[7] a compelling but reductive narrative that is difficult to square with Marconi's involvement in Italian fascism or Telefunken's entanglements with Nazi radio.

If electromagnetic radiation exists beyond language and experience, as modernist physicists repeatedly affirmed, then how can it be hypostatised? To address this question, this chapter supplements the physics of media with literary representations of wireless transmission by the 'father of German science fiction', Kurd Lasswitz, his former student, Hans Dominik, and their contemporary, Carl Grunert, who, together with Oskar Hoffmann, make up the early German SF canon.[8] Though early speculative fiction is best-known for long-form, world-building novels à la Jules Verne, these three interconnected authors excelled at short-form literary compositions, seeking to update the literary form known as a *Kunstmärchen* (artistic fairy tale) into what Lasswitz called a *wissenschaftliches Märchen* (scientific fairy tale), Dominik a *technisches Märchen* (technical fairy tale), and Grunert a *Zukunfts-Novelle* (futuristic novella). If literary realism populates fictional worlds with the author's imagination of the so-called real world, speculative fiction is uniquely capable of imagining media technologies that eventually become real. Science fiction studies have shown that certain applications of wireless transmission, such as ray guns and wristwatch communicators, were ripped from the pages of pulp SF magazines.[9] In reading across literature and science, my approach here builds on Gillian Beer's claim that modern physics was just as 'modernist' as literary fiction, and the term *modernism* applies not only to literature but also to science, especially popular physics and philosophy.[10] Whenever there was an epistemic gap in the scientific discourse, the literary imagination tested out various possibilities for addressing these aporia. Even after the concepts of field theory and special relativity developed to fill this epistemic gap, the ether and the spectrum continued to inspire artists, poets, philosophers, and other media thinkers well into the twentieth century.

One potential objection to my insistence on examining multiple discourses and representations of wireless transmission might concern the purpose of approaching the physical medium in this indirect manner, rather than taking radio waves as they are 'in reality'. Even if concepts such as frequencies and wavelengths are discursive constructs, what else would electromagnetic radiation look like if not the now-familiar waveform? My claim is not that the construction of scientific knowledge is arbitrary or divorced from physical reality. Even if physicists cannot know for certain what an electromagnetic wave looks like beyond the purview of their measuring instruments, they still have good reason to believe in the extra-linguistic reality of electromagnetic radiation. To produce any knowledge, however, electromagnetic radiation needs to be converted, translated, or transformed through processes that can be described by Bruno Latour's concept of articulation.[11] Rather than evaluating knowledge in terms of absolute correspondence to the natural world (that is, 'true' or 'false'), Latour proposes considering gradual degrees of field-specific knowledge articulated through social, technical, and discursive operations (that is, 'more articulated' or 'less articulated').

Literary, cultural, and media studies have sketched out the general articulation of electromagnetic radiation in four main categories: 1) fields, currents, flows;[12] 2) rays, beams, auras;[13] 3) sparks, flashes, bolts;[14] and 4) waves, vibrations, oscillations.[15] Of these categories, the last two were the most articulated in German modernism and the ones most immediately relevant to the physics of media, since they provided both a metonym for the physical substrate that enabled wireless connections and a metaphor for its cultural imaginary. By connecting these studies to German media philosophy, this chapter aims to ground thinking about the metaphysics of wireless in the physics of media.

The Physics of Wireless Media

To introduce the differences between the physics of wireless media and its metaphysics, there is no better case study than Albert Einstein. Like many members of the post-Edisonian generation, Einstein's work as a theoretical physicist was suffused with the experience of electromagnetic media. After his father's electricity company went bankrupt, Einstein worked as a patent examiner and then served as an expert witness in wireless patent litigations in the 1910s–1920s. As Jimena Canales has shown, telegraphy informed Einstein's experimental set-ups and provided concepts such as 'signals' and 'messages' for describing the emergent special theory of relativity. Following Canales, 'Einstein's revolutionary interpretation of time, space, and the universe was, at its core, a media revolution', but Einstein's popularisers effaced the materiality and mediality of theoretical physics, as when Hans Reichenbach associated Einstein's work with dubious metaphysics and used it as a foil for logical positivism.[16] In a short bilingual preface for Upton Sinclair's *Mental Radio*, dated 23 May 1930, Einstein attempted to redirect the study's bogus claims towards the medial discourse of mass suggestion while also warding off accusations of occultism against his own speculative theories: 'If somehow the facts set forth rest not upon telepathy, but upon some unconscious hypnotic influence from person to person, this also would be of high psychological interest.'[17]

Three months later, Einstein again challenged the metaphysics of media in his opening address at Germany's Seventh Annual Radio Exhibition.[18] Delivered at the foot of the iconic Berlin Radio Tower on the exhibition fairgrounds and simultaneously broadcast on the RRG's radio station, Einstein's speech began by addressing the mediated rhetorical situation. Instead of the formulaic greeting, *Vereherte Anwesende* (Esteemed guests present today), Einstein began with the reflexive salutation, *Verehrte An- und Abwesende* (Esteemed guests present and absent). 'Whenever you listen to the radio', he said, 'remember how this wonderful communication tool came into our possession. The original source of all technical achievements lies as much in the divine curiosity and the ludic drive of researchers [*Forscher*] tinkering and ruminating, as in the constructive fantasy of the technical inventor [*Erfinder*].'[19] By elevating hands-on research to the status of intellectual speculation, Einstein's speech must have appealed to its intended audiences. Employing the classic nineteenth-century media topos of consumption, Einstein further admonished: 'Those who thoughtlessly accept the wonders of science and technology should be ashamed, for they do not understand science and technology any more than a cow understands the botany of the plants it eats complacently.'[20]

Like Einstein's speech, popular scientific lectures and outreach publications presented the physics of wireless, but unlike Einstein they often relied on uncritical concepts of the ether and action at a distance. 'In his theory of relativity, Einstein arrived at a concept of the world that denied the existence of the ether', Artur Fürst explained in his popular scientific outreach book on the Nauen Wireless Station. 'Nevertheless, we may continue to use it for the discussion of the technical processes to be described here, since it enables a convenient explanation of all phenomena. The assertion that there is a world ether [*Weltäther*] may be an auxiliary hypothesis, but it is a very useful one.'[21] What the hypothetical medium allowed Fürst and others to describe were the intangible connections between any two points along a transmission line represented by a tangible wire. Because the ether was taken to transmit energy, it helped popular physics explain the long-distance effects of wireless transmission. The ether's mythological associations with air enabled further connections with 'environments' and 'outer space'. Hence, Fürst's mixed metaphor: 'We human beings do not reside in a space that is filled exclusively with the world ether; rather, we live in a part of the world where there is also air with its impurities.'[22] Since nobody had ever seen or experienced the ether, it provoked dazzling proofs and thought experiments from Immanuel Kant to Hendrik Lorentz.[23] By 1900 this discourse was so rife with contradictions, as media historian Wolfgang Hagen has observed, that 'the physical properties of ether must have seemed almost crazy [. . .] a totally transparent substance, finer than any structure as yet known, all-pervading and invisible [. . .] and yet hard as diamond?'[24] Unpacking the modernist concept of the ether and understanding its persistence and longevity requires examining how it intersected with an earlier conceptual history of action at a distance.

Action at a Distance

In their media study of *Action at a Distance*, John Durham Peters, Florian Sprenger, and Christina Vagt examine how this classic scientific and philosophical concept informs the 'materiality of communication' and the 'mediality of transmission'. Action at a distance raises what Peters calls the 'media question concerning modern physics: How is it possible that objects interact with each other from a distance, without touching?'[25] In the first half of the nineteenth century, wired telegraphy popularised a concept of the ether derived from the sciences of electricity through the concept of the instantaneous transmission of electric action. Investigating the speed of electricity, researchers were haunted by 'phantasms of instantaneity, immediate transmission, and *actio in distans*'.[26] In the second half of the nineteenth century, there came to be two main schools for explaining electrodynamics: based on the work of Weber and Ampère, the theory of long-range effects, or *Fernwirkungstheorie*, proposed a model of action at a distance; the close-range theory, or *Nahwirkungstheorie*, represented by Faraday and Maxwell, posited only short-range effects requiring the immediate proximity of overlapping 'fields'.

Can an object at point A cause an effect at point B even if those two points are separated in space or time? Following the central axioms of early modern Newtonian mechanics, nineteenth-century scientists agreed that the two points would need to be connected spatially by some physical medium such as the ether. However, they continued to debate whether the effect would be instantaneous or time-delayed until the late 1880s, when Hertz's experiments demonstrated conclusively that the upper limit for any transmission is set by the finite speed of light. Taking up this scientific discourse, modernist philosophers inflected the question of action at a distance through further ethical, political, and cultural concerns. Friedrich Nietzsche decried 'women and their action at a distance', asserting that 'the magic and the most powerful effect of women is, to speak the language of the philosophers, action at a distance, *actio in distans*: but that requires, first and foremost – *distance*!'[27] By contrast, my mobilisation of the concept here is based more on what Hans Blumenberg would later term *actio per distans*, the human tendency to entertain and undertake pre-emptive actions even in the absence of the particular objects being acted upon.[28]

If an individual at point A can cause an effect on another individual at point B, does it matter whether the cause is intentional or inadvertent and whether the effect is benevolent or detrimental? If modern media were enabling liberal citizens of the interconnected world to undertake various forms of metaphorical 'action at a distance', whether new forms of charity, hospitality, or witnessing, then to what extent might one nation's engagements with distant others end up helping or harming them? These are the central questions explored in Kurd Lasswitz's speculative literary and philosophical treatments of the 'telelyte' (Gr. *tele-*, 'distant' + *luein*, 'to loosen, dissolve', in the sense of 'chemical disintegration at a distance'), an imaginary wireless medium that today remains known reductively as the world's first ray gun.[29] In Lasswitz's seminal two-volume 1897 novel *Auf zwei Planeten* (*On Two Planets*), the telelyte features not only as a portable, handheld SF blaster but as the weaponisation of nineteenth-century communications technologies.[30] In the first volume, the telelyte functions as a hostile military technology, a sort of miracle weapon that extraterrestrials deploy to threaten the inhabitants of Earth with extinction. In the second, the Earthlings counter the Martian technology with two other imaginary wireless energy devices known as the 'repulsite' and the 'nihilite'.[31]

Several years prior to its appearance in Lasswitz's 996-page SF novel, the telelyte first appeared in one of his little-known, short-form, seven-page typescripts. Composed under the title 'Telelyte', this fictionalised newspaper report was published anonymously on 20 August 1892 as 'To Chicago: A Prize Competition', and republished several weeks later, with additional pseudo-editorial comments, under the new title 'What Should She Do?'[32] In these earlier versions, the telelyte informed an equally dramatic but intraterrestrial conflict, reflecting Verne's fears, in *The Begum's Fortune*, about a French-made weapon of mass destruction falling into German hands. While Lasswitz remains best known as the 'German Jules Verne' and his short-form speculative fiction might seem like thinly veiled allegories for his trials and tribulations as a teacher at a preparatory high school, it is important to recall that he was also a respected philosopher, mathematician, and all-around polymath.[33] As a well-informed and highly connected intellectual, Lasswitz composed an influential history of atomism, edited part of the critical edition of Kant's collected works, and corresponded with many of the day's other leading literary and scientific luminaries, including Dominik and Grunert, along with Svante Arrhenius, Wilhelm Bölsche, Martin Buber, Georg Cantor, Hermann Cohen, Max Dessoir, Wilhelm Dilthey, Rudolf Goldscheid, Wilhelm Ostwald, Bertha von Suttner, Ferdinand Tönnies, and Wilhelm Wundt.

Engaging with actual scientific research in chemistry, Lasswitz's account of the imaginary scientific phenomenon of 'telelysis' and the invention of the 'telelyte' takes the form of a fictionalised newspaper report deploying multiple voices, literary registers, and documentary modes. Framed by comments written in a collective editorial voice, an embedded letter to the editor adopts the voice of a certain Miss Alice Barnot, a young French German émigré to the United States who has practically assimilated but remains spiritually connected to mainland Germany. The inventor is said to be her father, Charles Barnot, 'French by birth, stemming from Mühlhausen in the Alsace region and a chemist by trade'. On his deathbed, the father makes his daughter promise never to reveal the device's secret, especially not to Germans, having 'turned his back on his homeland after it became a German possession, until, as he liked to say, the Alsace would become French again'.[34]

How might the telelyte work? Alluding to then cutting-edge research instigated by Hertz's studies of ultraviolet light and the photoelectric effect,[35] Alice reasons that 'modifying a beam of light [. . .] could be used to carry out action at a distance in place of a connecting wire'.[36] Modelled on the scientific instruments used in Hertz's experiments and differing from the simplified ray gun in Lasswitz's later treatment, the telelyte is said to consist of two main components with an electrical connection: a chemical chamber and a standard astronomical telescope. 'The real secret lies in the composition and construction of the telelyte', the narrator hints, using the term *telelyte* here not for the device but for a secret 'substance' – presumably, quartz – 'that, depending on the chemical materials that are brought into contact with it, makes the ether waves of light change so that they transmit chemical energy from the experimental object to any distance that can be recorded via light waves'.[37] The telelyte enables an object at point A to exert a chemical effect on an object at point B, provided that the two are connected by a direct line-of-sight. After explaining the device's operation, Alice recounts the fateful day when she accidentally activated it, triggering a distant explosion and inadvertently condemning the innocent man falsely accused of causing it to death. In a metaphorical sense, one individual's actions at point A set off an inadvertent chain of effects at point B. Significantly, the only evidence that would subtend the sequence of cause and effect would be to reveal the secret behind the imaginary scientific device, which she claims would be unethical for reasons explained in her dramatic letter to the editors.

Presented as several nested newspaper reports, Lasswitz's narrative deploys an elaborate editorial fiction (*Herausgeberfiktion*), which serves to legitimate the contents of a fantastical-sounding story through multiple layers of authentication. It will be helpful to unpack each of the five layers. On 8 September 1892, the (real) editors of *Das Echo*, a weekly magazine published in Germany with news about Germans abroad, republished another magazine article, 'To Chicago: A Prize Competition', dated 20 August 1892, from the (real) *Schorers Familienblatt*, under the new title, 'What Should She Do?' The editors of the *Familienblatt* claimed to have been reprinting a mysterious letter to the editors from one of their readers, addressed from the 'Barnot's home, Breadstown [*sic*], Illinois, 22 July 1892'. Alice Barnot's (fictional) letter to the editors excerpts another (fictional) news item, modelled on the familiar tradition of *faits divers* or telegraphic news dispatches about sensational local events. Dated 10 July 1892, the (fictional) news report claims to have been published in what Barnot calls the '*Illinois-Abendpost*', presumably a reference to the (real) German-language newspaper, the *Abendpost* (1889–1950), the Midwest's most widely circulated foreign-language daily paper.[38] There is a neat symmetry in the frame: Whereas the outer layer is a real publication from mainland Germany with news about Germans in the United States, the inner layer purports to be a real publication from the United States with news about mainland Germany; the connective layers conceal the story's fictionality.

The embedded fictionalised newspaper report details the incident that culminated in the arrest of a 58-year-old Black man named Oliver, 'in the service of the widow Mrs Barnot, on suspicion of arson'.[39] Despite multiple levels of fictionality, the charge – destroying two miles of property along the Illinois River belonging to the 'Croked [*sic*] Creek Company' – reflects actual charges of alleged barn burning documented in Ida B. Wells-Barnett's *The Red Record: Tabulated*

Statistics and Alleged Causes of Lynching in the United States. At his trial, Oliver claims that he was napping in the shade, without any fire starter, when he heard a loud noise and 'simultaneously, the wooden wall next to him went up in flames'.[40] Alice suddenly declares that she was responsible for starting the fire by accidentally triggering the telelyte. However, the other parties suspect that she is lying to protect the accused and ask her either to repeat the experiment or explain the device's secret workings in court, lest her entire testimony be rendered invalid. The fictionalised newspaper report concludes by calling for the telelyte's secret to be revealed, not only to exonerate the innocent, but in the interests of commerce and public knowledge, since a private 'company has formed that wants to buy the secret from Miss Barnot for a million dollars; underwritten by C.F. Hix & Co'.[41] Hence, Alice's dilemma: to keep her promise to her father not to reveal the secret workings of the telelyte, sell it to a private company, and make a tidy profit, but condemn an innocent man to death; or to make the secret public and exonerate the wrongly accused, but make no profits and break the promise. 'Nobody can advise me here', she laments to mainland Germany, 'because nobody understands that I don't care about the millions I could earn because I already have more than I need. Nobody understands that the fate of an old [N-Word] is a sacred matter of conscience to me, nobody knows–'. With the dash hinting at a different secret, much like the ellipsis in Kleist's novella *The Marquise von O . . .*, Alice appeals with great pathos to those in her 'motherland' for advice on 'how Germans, who understand how to feel with me, would advise me on my decision'.[42]

To any readers who could solve this fictional but seemingly real puzzle and advise Miss Barnot on her dilemma, the editors of the *Familienblatt* offered a real, but seemingly fictional prize – a trip to the World's Fair in Chicago – which had to be redeemed by 1 March 1893, accompanied by 'proof of subscription' to their journal. Astonishingly, the editors appear to have awarded the prize to one submission from a certain teacher from Merseburg named 'Fr. Wendenburg', though they did not provide any further details on the contents of the solution.

Although it is over a century too late for me to submit my own solution to the prize competition, any solution to these alleged problems is irrelevant, seeing as the telelyte, the Barnots, the servant Oliver, and the other characters invented in the story never existed, even if they are based on contemporary figures and stereotypes. For the simplest and most elegant solution to the puzzle, the original readers would have only needed to observe that there was never any Sunday 10 July 1892 issue of the *Abendpost*, which was only published that week on Saturday 9 July and Monday 11 July, and they would have thus seen through the fiction.[43] If that context-dependent solution is unsatisfying, given the unlikelihood of any readers in mainland Germany subscribing to a German-language newspaper published in the United States with news about Germany for émigrés living abroad, the point is that the speculative story was designed to engender further speculation. Regardless of the proposed solution, Lasswitz's story remains significant not only as a literary imagination of the consequences of untested technologies and a philosophical reflection on the classic problem of *actio in distans*. It also mobilises the ethical sense of *actio per distans* to explore competing ideas about charity and witnessing, as well as patent laws and the ideology of making inventions public knowledge.

Lasswitz's story can be understood further in relation to his scientific and philosophical writings on action at a distance, which combined empirical science and the theory of knowledge into a critical form then known as *Erkenntniskritik*. As a neo-Kantian and co-editor of Kant's pre-critical writings, Lasswitz would have been well acquainted with Kant's *Magisterarbeit*, a 'Concise Outline of Some Reflections on Fire'.[44] In his celebrated history of atomism, Lasswitz used Kantian epistemology to historicise the scientific knowledge of matter and elementary particles, tracking the interconnected conceptual histories of 'space', 'ether', and the 'world soul' from classical antiquity through to the early modern period.[45] For Lasswitz, the concept of action at a distance signalled a decisive turn in the history of atomism from a kinetic model of corpuscles to a dynamic theory of matter, culminating in Newton's law of gravity, which Lasswitz viewed as an attempt to smuggle the concept of action at a distance back into modern science.[46] Despite apparent scientific progress, Lasswitz argued in an essay on 'Newton and Action at a Distance', the increase of knowledge applied only to theory-formation and not its conditions of possibility.

> The big question that remains is the following: How is it *possible* and through what means can it be explained that bodies separated in space and at a distance from each other mutually influence each other's states in such a manner that they approach each other? Or, in short, how is action at a distance possible?[47]

While the referent for Lasswitz's Alsatian inventor, 'Charles Barnot', could be any number of scientists who attempted to harness electromagnetic radiation and other forces in the years before Marconi, Lasswitz's main source on action at a distance paraphrased a seminal lecture delivered by Heinrich Hertz.[48] When summarising his epoch-making series of experiments, which had confirmed Faraday's suppositions, Hertz concluded that electromagnetic waves require time to travel from point A to point B; and thus electricity is not a force acting at a distance, but one that propagates from one ethereal particle to the next. Still, Hertz also maintained that there remained several interrelated open questions for modern physics: 'the question of direct actions-at-a distance'; 'the more definite question of the nature of electric and magnetic forces in space'; and 'the great problem of the nature and properties of the ether'.[49]

Epistemic Things

Although we are surrounded by electromagnetic radiation, visible light was the only known part of the electromagnetic spectrum for most of recorded history. Over the course of the long nineteenth century, electromagnetic radiation emerged as an 'epistemic thing', a unified object of scientific research questions and laboratory experiments.[50] Though credited with this 'discovery', Hertz was neither the first to generate electromagnetic waves in the radio frequency spectrum, nor the first to detect them in a laboratory.[51] Starting around 1800, scientific researchers had increasingly observed that some unknown phenomenon was causing inexplicable results in their laboratory experiments with electricity and magnetism, but dismissed these occurrences as limit cases of induction.[52] By the 1860s many scientists observed that sparks were drawn from distant objects in their lecture rooms whenever they were operating electrical machines or (dis)charging Leyden batteries, but again dismissed these phenomena as cases of induction. By the 1880s it was known that electrical discharges from a coil that is interrupted by a gap will create electrical vibrations and thus show electrical sparks at the 'spark gap'. When Hertz was examining sparks during his own experiments, he accidentally discovered that a second coil, even if not electrically charged, would exhibit similar sparks when it was brought near the first one. The sparks seemed to leap across the gap, appearing in a space where there should not have been anything at all.[53]

In its completed form, Hertz's experimental apparatus resembled the transmitting and receiving devices that would come to be used in the early days of wireless telegraphy. Driven by an induction coil, the spark-gap transmitter, or 'Hertzian oscillator', emitted electromagnetic radiation within the radio spectrum to a corresponding receiver, or 'detector'. From c. 1887 to 1916, transmitters continued to use an electric spark gap, and they were implemented in competing systems of wireless telegraphy until they came to be supplanted by the vacuum tube during World War I and were fully phased out by World War II. The spark-gap transmitter's use of high-voltage electrical currents with open spark gaps created not only an electric arc of light but also a lot of noise. An inefficient system, the spark-gap transmitter was 'inherently a dirty radiator, polluting the spectrum with radiation that was unnecessary, wasteful of energy, and damaging to the interests of other users'.[54] Another drawback was that the energy it produced, a form of damped or attenuated vibration, would dissipate rapidly. As a result, experimenters worked to develop undamped or continuous-wave transmitters, whose signals occupied only a single frequency. These could transmit audio signals, making possible the radio. Despite this apparent lineage, it remains problematic to consider Hertz's work as the direct precursor to radio and wireless telegraphy. As Vivian J. Philipps has shown, the early development of radio was a matter of investigating a new phenomenon in the laboratory, and the very word 'detect', as in Hertz's 'detector', means 'to find out or discover the existence or presence or nature or identity' of something.[55]

Because Hertz's detector was another coil, the signal had to be strong enough to induce a visible spark. In summarising his experiments, Hertz reflected on the importance of this visual evidence: 'In carrying them out we are decidedly working in the region of optics [. . .] Starting with purely electrical phenomena we have gone on step by step until we find ourselves in the region of purely optical phenomena.'[56] Following this line of inquiry, a group of British Maxwellians devoted their work first to optical media and only later to communications media. Even after the existence of electromagnetic radiation had been verified, scientific experiments followed along the track established by Hertz and remained focused on low-frequency waves, which created difficulties for wireless telegraphy. Foundational research in high-frequency physics would have to wait until the 1910s and would not be applied to communications and entertainment media for another two decades.[57] In this respect, the ontological and epistemological implications of Hertz's experiments are more significant than their debatable contribution to wireless technology.

While Hertz is rightly celebrated for detecting electromagnetic radiation, his experiments are not the absolute origin of radio, television, or wireless telegraphy.[58] Hertz's intentions are difficult to square with the emergence of communications and mass media, seeing as he once denied the possibility of such applications. Asked in December 1889 whether his newly detected waves could transmit *telephone calls* (and not *telegrams*, as is often reported), Hertz replied in the negative. According to the conventional wisdom of the time, very low frequencies would be too slow and their corresponding wavelengths too large to transmit and replicate the human voice. As Hertz put it, 'If you could build a concave mirror the size of a continent, then you could conduct such experiments, though this is hardly practical, and you won't get anywhere using normal concave mirrors', like those used in his own experiments.[59] Although Hertz was only answering a technical question, this widely circulated story about the 'founding father' denying the possibility of commercial applications deterred further research.[60] One of Hertz's contemporaries reflected: 'As epoch-making and foundational as Hertz's investigations are, his research method requires an apparatus of significant dimensions [. . .] so that repeating the experiments involves a great deal of trouble.'[61] Although Hertz suspected that the sparks could be detected at greater distances, he showed no interest in taking the experiment out of the laboratory and conducting field tests, having already settled on an ideal range of roughly 6–10 metres.[62] Hence, Hertz's experiments did not represent the absolute origin of wireless transmission but the endpoint of gradual developments in physics.[63]

For vernacular modernisms, the epistemological implications of Hertz's experiments were even greater than their contribution to the discipline of physics. On 20 September 1889 Hertz delivered an eloquent and accessible keynote address, 'On the Relations Between Light and Electricity', which would become the most quoted of his oeuvre. Near the start of the lecture, Hertz made a striking epistemological statement about our speculative knowledge of electromagnetic radiation:

> I must confess that it is not easy to speak of these matters in a way at once intelligible and accurate. It is in empty space, in the free ether, that the processes which we have to describe take place. They cannot be felt with the hand, heard by the ear, or seen by the eye. They appeal to our intuition and conception, scarcely to our senses. Hence we shall try to make use, as far as possible, of the intuitions and conceptions which we already possess.[64]

If everything that 'cannot be felt with the hand, heard by the ear, or seen by the eye' had traditionally been banished from physics to metaphysics, then it might seem impossible to base modern physical sciences on the study of imperceptible, non-observable phenomena.

Hertz's provisional solution to this problem consisted in proceeding from 'intuitions', 'conceptions', and 'mental images'. Based on his first-hand experience with the difficulty of producing visible evidence of invisible phenomena, Hertz made the surprising turn from experimental physics to theoretical mechanics, and formulated what came to be known as his *Scheinbild(er)theorem* (theorem of apparent image[s]).[65] In a radical gesture, Hertz ruled out perception as the primary source of knowledge, and synthesised the methods of perception into a process of completing mental images:

> We form for ourselves [mental] images [*innere Scheinbilder*] or symbols of external objects; and the form which we give them is such that the necessary consequents of the images in thought are always the images of the necessary consequents in nature of the things pictured.[66]

For science to have any purchase, however, 'there must be a certain conformity between nature and our thought. Experience teaches us that the requirement can be satisfied, and hence that such a conformity does in fact exist.'[67] With these three sentences, Hertz laid the epistemological foundations for modern physics.

To convey the epistemological difficulties of producing evidence of electromagnetic radiation, Hertz presented the metaphor of the 'mountain summit' (*Passhöhe*) to describe the point from which the surrounding regions of empirical experimentation and scientific theory become equally visible.[68] From this lofty vantage point, optics appears 'as a small appendage to the great domain of electricity', or what we would today call the electromagnetic spectrum:

> We perceive electricity in a thousand places where we had no proof of its existence before [. . .] Thus the domain of electricity extends over the whole of nature. It even affects ourselves closely: we perceive that we actually possess an electrical organ – the eye. These are the things that we see when we look downwards from our high standpoint. Not less attractive is the view when we look upwards towards the lofty peaks, the highest pinnacles of science. We are at once confronted with the question of direct actions-at-a-distance.[69]

Convinced that his discovery was only the first in a series extending into the future, Hertz imagined electromagnetic radiation leading not to wireless applications but to resolving the fundamental conceptual tension between the ether and action at a distance. As he put it, 'Take away from the world electricity, and light disappears; remove from the world the luminiferous ether, and electric and magnetic actions can no longer traverse space.'[70]

Ether Stories

The ether was the topic of extensive debate across vernacular modernisms. It continued to be an attractive object of analysis for subsequent work on the history of science, philosophy, and physics, where it was taken to epitomise scientific change.[71] The typical story, based on Karl Popper's account, was that the rejection of the ether after Michelson and Morley's experiments exemplified the generational struggle, based on Thomas Kuhn's concept of paradigm changes, between older and more conservative physicists and younger and more progressive relativists, quantum physicists, and electrical engineers. In recent years, however, social historians of science and technology have shifted from studying such categories of 'belief' and 'unbelief' to examining the technical and pedagogical 'uses' of scientific concepts. Instead of being eliminated, the singular concept of the ether exploded and fragmented into that of multiple ethers, and the concept's persistence in the modernist imagination can be attributed to its adaptability and connectability.[72] For media studies, the ether is of particular interest as a physical medium, intermediary, or go-between.[73] Even after Einstein's revolutionary 1905 essay 'On the Electrodynamics of Moving Bodies' pronounced the concept to be obsolete for relativity theory, the ether proved to be an extremely resilient concept in physics and remained a popular concept well into the 1930s. As Linda Dalrymple Henderson has shown, the ether informed modernist aesthetic debates about the existence of a 'fourth dimension' – usually, time.[74] While there are many valuable studies of the ether's impact on occultism, abstract modernism, and what Joe Milutis calls the 'ethereal avant-garde', there are still few studies of the vernacular conception of the ether in more prosaic compositions.[75]

Writing both technical articles and speculative fiction, Hans Dominik explored the ether, wireless communication, and energy transfer throughout his career, most notably in his bestselling 1922 novel, *The Power of Three*, about the implications of finding a radically new energy source. Published in 1902, Dominik's first short story, 'Ätherwellen' (Ether waves), presented a technical fairy tale about the wireless station on the coast of Cuxhaven, Germany, drawing on his professional experience as an employee for Siemens & Halske operating the navigation equipment at this historic site where the Elbe River meets the North Sea.[76] Narrated like many of Lasswitz's scientific fairy tales by non-human things, Dominik's 'Ether Waves' situates wireless communication between the poetic tradition that associated the lyric with birdsong and the engineering discourse that associated the new mode of transmission with interplanetary communication.[77] In a polyvocal conversation, a flock of birds attempts to identify a strange new object that does not resemble the site's renowned 'navigation beacon' (*Kugelbake*). Suddenly, the wind interjects, identifying the object, a piece of wire, and causing it to speak up for itself:

> Who am I, you want to know – I am one of modernity's most important inventions and am entitled to expect to replace and suppress all other wires, beacons, and other means of communicating and signalling. I am a transmission rod [*Gebergestänge*] and belong to wireless telegraphy. The albatross already saw my brothers in Heligoland, in England, and in America. We transmit people's communication and exchange of ideas. We bring their messages securely across the sea and faster than on land.[78]

In a variation on Aesop's fable of 'The Belly and the Members', the voices of the other technical components of the 'transmitter station' (*Geberstation*) chime in, as a battery, a transformer, and a capacitor bicker about which one is truly indispensable, until their conversation suddenly gets interrupted by news of a task requiring their cooperation. The Cuxhaven station receives a mysterious message, simultaneously received by other wireless stations but whose contents remain a riddle. While some claim that the message results from a meteorological disturbance, others, like the narrator, take it to be a message from extraterrestrials. What seemed to have been a prophecy for the future is thus revealed to be one for the present. In similar fashion, what seemed to be a description of futuristic technology turns out to be a description of one cutting-edge wireless system already in existence.

Giving voice to Dominik's reactionary politics, the quarrelsome technical components in 'Ether Waves' provide a political allegory for the division of labour in late Imperial Germany. The battery, transformer, and capacitor generally shared the 'transmitter wire's self-confident attitude', but 'they sometimes disagreed with each other. After all, each component already had its own prehistory and personal merits.'[79] Familiar from the history of electrical lighting and power transmission, the massive and stinking 'lead-acid battery' stands in for the democratic working class.[80] Though later the default battery in portable, mobile, low-voltage systems, 'it was the true son of high-voltage technology, always had to do the roughest, most difficult work and probably as a result [. . .] had something clumsy and servant-like in its manners, which could easily repulse the superficial observer'.[81] Next, there is the 'Ruhmkorff induction coil', an electrical transformer first used in medical experiments and then in X-rays, arc lights, electrotherapy, and spark-gap radio transmitters.[82]

Unlike the power source, the transformer never experienced a 'raw fight for its own existence', and 'its character and its political attitude among the electrical apparatuses was somewhat wavering. If one could call the battery a "democrat", then the induction coil tried to mediate between it and the pure high-voltage apparatus.'[83] The third and last component, a 'Leyden jar' (or 'Kleist jar'), was an early capacitor (or 'condenser'), which stored high-voltage charges between electrical conductors on the inside and outside of a glass jar. Its 'age and lineage exceeded the other two significantly',[84] being named after its independent and simultaneous invention in 1745 by German cleric Ewald Georg von Kleist and Dutch scientist Pieter van Musschenbroek of the town of Leyden in the Netherlands. In Dominik's political allegory, the capacitor represents a 'thoroughly conservative character [. . .] averse to any changes'; resisting any attempts to improve it, 'it represented the standpoint that one had to take it as it is'.[85]

Modelling typical forms of political behaviour, the technical components 'got along with each other alternately well and poorly', arguing loudly but civilly about which one deserved the most credit for doing the most important work. However, as soon as the station's Morse device switches on, 'the other machines went silent, for as much as they liked to argue with each other when off duty, they worked just as promptly and precisely when in operation'.[86] As Jens Tismar argues, Goethe's *Märchen* aim at staging harmonious social gatherings, whereas Dominik's technical *Märchen* aim at frictionless operation.[87] In my analysis, Dominik's political allegory resonates not only with Georg Simmel's contemporaneous observations about 'the functional specialization of man and his work', which 'makes one individual incomparable to another, and each of them indispensable to the highest possible extent'.[88] The infighting components also reflect the situation of competing systems for wireless telegraphy in the German Empire during the months before the forced merger of the two companies that would form Telefunken on 27 May 1903. Dominik promotes the widespread (German) view that Marconi's wireless system merely combined well-known components from 'physical apparatuses' or 'instruments of high-voltage technology'.[89]

At the end of Dominik's story, the wireless station in Cuxhaven receives a 'strange message' consisting of individual words written in Morse code:

> The English '*well*' and the French '*reçu*' [received] were written next to the German '*sofort*' [at once], but the overall content of the telegram made no real sense and gave the impression of a conglomerate

of individual chunks picked up from different conversations in different languages.[90]

Since the message remains indecipherable, the other components express doubts about the coherer's ability to receive it properly,[91] until successive reports of the same message arrive from the nearby station in Heligoland, Germany, and from further wireless stations across the sea in Blåvandshuk, Denmark; the Lizard, Great Britain; Avalon, Canada; and a Nantucket-based light-vessel near New York. In the end, 'one was faced with a riddle'. While some scholars in the story attribute the indecipherable message to atmospheric conditions, others believe, as does the narrator, 'that on that memorable day in Cuxhaven, the first messages [or messengers, *Botschaften*] came to us from extraterrestrial beings, and that we owe them an answer'.[92] Though this conclusion might sound like science fiction, it mirrors contemporary press reports about Marconi, Tesla, and other wireless technicians then speculating on the origins of indecipherable wireless signals, which the press sensationalised into accounts of conversing with Martians.[93] For a more local source, Dominik may have drawn on Slaby's or Braun's accounts of the Cuxhaven experiments, which also mentioned a mysterious message that was attributed to cosmic noise, or on Lasswitz's philosophical essay on 'Mars Fantasies'.[94]

In his 1913 short story 'Ein Experiment' (An experiment), Dominik again explored the sociotechnical challenges of interplanetary communication, but from the human perspective of venture capitalists who make financial speculations on the future of wireless television a century later. To construct a gigantic wireless station, modelled implicitly on the one in Lasswitz's *On Two Planets*, the German engineer Rudolf Kaempf requires a $20,000 capital investment from German-born American industrialist John Braun (formerly Hans Braun). One day, their signals are answered by Martians, whose mysterious return signal is deciphered by Indian philosopher Soma Atma to contain a message using mathematics as a universal language. Encoded in Pythagorean numbers, the zero, the decimal system, and basic arithmetic are extraterrestrial plans for using coordinate geometry to transmit images. At the end of the story, the Martians telegraph a portrait that is decoded to reveal a 'quite human-like face, the forehead a little higher, the eyes a little larger than is normal on earth, the mouth and chin remarkably small, but otherwise absolutely the same as human beings'.[95] The encounter confirms Kaempf's 'theory of the universality of all life forms [. . .] the dominant form here and on Mars is the one that best fulfils its function, and that is doubtless the well-known human form'.[96] Wireless signals are exchanged for another half-year until the distance between the two planets becomes too great to maintain the connection. However, the American investor writes another cheque for $1,000,000 to continue the experiments and try to make contact again – a century later.[97] In Roland Innerhofer's analysis, Dominik's attention to technical details corresponded to a lack of literary imagination and an inability to imagine biological differences.[98] While 'An Experiment' might be the earliest story to combine the theme of interplanetary contact with the principles of television transmission, it was hardly the first, last, or only one to develop the trope of the 'heroic engineer' responsible for constructing gigantic technical projects.

Among early speculative fiction imagining interplanetary contact, H. G. Wells's *The First Men in the Moon* (translated into German in 1905) stands out for establishing the trope of receiving coded wireless signals from Mars. Combining elements of cryptography and the detective story, Wells made the story plausible by referring to advances in wireless telegraphy and reports of atmospheric disturbances, which leave the messages 'damaged, broken, and partly effaced'.[99] In his 1907 short story 'Feinde im Weltall?' (Enemies in Space?), Carl Grunert provided a new twist to this topos by imagining why extraterrestrials would transmit coded signals: 'With all the scientific means at its disposal, the planetary government has set up a fully equipped surveillance system for citizens who feel unsafe, with the result that the government needed to exercise the greatest caution whenever sending a warning telegram.'[100] In Grunert's story, the inventor Justus Stark suddenly receives a repeating coded signal from outer space on his highly sensitive receiver for wireless telegraphy: 'HERSTERNEV DEI INGENDEMONI ENEMI ELANGIS? NUGAE REMPO! INDEDEF HENNA!' After several failed attempts, he cracks the code, which involves simple anagrams: 'VERSTEHEN DIE EINMONDIGEN MEINE SIGNALE? AUGEN EMPOR! FEINDE NAHEN!' (DO YOU ONE-MOONERS UNDERSTAND MY SIGNALS? HEADS UP! ENEMIES APPROACHING!) Once ridiculed by the imperial authorities and the scholarly community, the inventor is finally vindicated, and the story ends with mass mobilisation in preparation for the alien invasion.

In a 1913 essay speculating on 'The Colonies in 100 Years', Carl Peters imagined another first contact scenario using 'electrical pulses' transmitted from 'wireless stations' located at the poles and deciphered with a 'code book'.[101] In Peters's colonialist vision, the interplanetary wireless system succeeds in exchanging 'astronomical observations', 'but as soon as it was a question of history, customs, and folk life [*Völkerleben*], the communication apparatus failed completely'.[102]

Reflecting his biases about subaltern alterity, Peters concluded that aliens must be a totally different species, incapable of communicating with human beings. Elsewhere in the same essay, published only five years after the attempt to wipe out the Herero in German Southwest Africa, Peters predicted an apartheid system in which German colonists would live in a permanently airborne Zeppelin fleet, with Black servants on the ground providing the necessary labour to support them.[103] Speculations about extraterrestrial communication always reflect terrestrial realities.

Spectres of the Wireless Spectrum

If Kittler's thesis about media as 'extensions of science' is correct, then it should apply not only to Hertzian heroism and the triumphant physics of electromagnetism, but also to what he would have called the 'dark side of the moon'. Indeed, Maxwell's equations led not only to scientific proofs of the existence of radio waves in 1886, X-rays in 1895, and gamma waves in 1910. They also inspired debunked and now-forgotten parascientific discoveries, such as René Blondlot's 'N-rays' and Karl von Reichenbach's 'Od-rays', both of which were first accepted by the international scientific community but then revealed to be erroneous.

Furthermore, the formation of the electromagnetic spectrum produced 'abject' figures, including Friedrich Krauss and, most famously, Daniel Paul Schreber, the respected German judge who documented the onset of mid-life psychosis in his book *Memoirs of My Nervous Illness*, a key case later interpreted by Sigmund Freud.[104] After waking up one morning and thinking that it would be pleasant to experience sexual intercourse as a woman, Schreber hypothesised that his doctors had implemented this thought in his mind by hypnosis or telepathy. Schreber was convinced that his primary psychiatrist, Paul Flechsig, was controlling him using an imperceptible 'nerve-language'. As his psychosis progressed, Schreber believed that God was transforming him into a woman by sending men to torture him and by emitting 'thought rays' that would enact 'miracles'. 'It is presumably a phenomenon like telephoning', Schreber reasoned.

> The filaments of rays spun out towards my head act like telephone wires; the weak sound of the cries for help coming from an apparently vast distance is received *only by me* in the same way as telephonic communication can only be heard by a person who is on the telephone, but not by a third person who is somewhere between the giving and the receiving end.[105]

Although the two main sciences informing wireless transmission are physics and mathematics, the mode has been connected historically to other scientific disciplines including biology, chemistry, psychiatry, psychotechnics, and 'electrophysiology', Stefan Jellinek's term for the discipline he helped found around 1900 that would later develop into a subfield of neurology.[106] In some experiments, the human nervous system was inserted quite prosaically as a substitute for wireless relay components. In others, the human senses were said to function by analogy with wireless devices, in that they can analyse complex electromagnetic signals into their sine-wave components (Fig. 2.1).

Figure 2.1 Fritz Kahn's pedagogical visualisation of the human body as a wireless system. Depicting the central nervous system by analogy with a radio receiver, cells correspond to the antenna (labelled 1), neurons to wires (2), the nervous centre in the brainstem to a transducer (3), and conscious activity in the cortical cells to listening via headphones (4). Source: Fritz Kahn, *Das Leben des Menschen: Eine volkstümliche Anatomie, Biologie, Physiologie und Entwicklungsgeschichte des Menschen*, 4 vols (Stuttgart: Kosmos, 1924–29), vol. 4, plate VII.

In search of a suitable detector for electromagnetic radiation, experimental physiologists revived Luigi Galvani's classic experiment, which involved making a frog's leg twitch in response to an electrical stimulus.[107] One of the earliest and most sensational experimental trials with transforming organic bodies into wireless stations was conducted by American wireless amateur Archie Frederick Collins, whose research involved turning feline and human cadavers into electrical coherers. Not intended for wireless telegraphy, according to Collins,

> the purpose of arranging these tests was to verify, if possible, the casual observations long since made that approaching electrical storms manifested their presence in persons afflicted with certain forms of nervousness and other pathological conditions, though the storm influencing them might be many miles beyond, or even below the horizon.[108]

Although other scientists were unable to duplicate Collins's experimental trials, Charles Lefeuvre, Professor of Philosophy at the University of Rennes, succeeded in 1913 in creating a frog's leg receiver sensitive enough to receive time signals sent from Paris.[109] 'While many cold-blooded animals can be used for this experiment', Berlin-based physiologist Alfred Gradenwitz commented on Lefeuvre's experimental set-up, 'the muscles of frogs' legs are particularly well adapted for the purpose, on account of the regularity of their form, the long duration of their excitability and the special ease with which they can be separated from the body'.[110] As Gradenwitz also noted, however, the sciatic nerve spliced out of the frog's leg and into a receiver's output terminal would quickly lose its sensitivity, thereby rendering commercial applications unrealistic.

Undeterred, one radio engineer writing under the name of A. K. Fiala was still proposing to manufacture wireless biotech around 1924–25 with a frog's leg transmitter and an earthworm amplifier.[111] However, it is difficult to determine whether this proposal was made in earnest or in order to satirise popular media topoi about 'psychic television'.[112] Of mind control, for instance, Fiala incoherently asserted that

> this kind of suggestive influence would only be the most fabulous and effective if [. . .] it is possible to transmit commands, wishes or instructions of any kind by a purely mechanical means 'wirelessly' – in this case, that is, without the use of electrodes – just as the hypnotist can also do without any linguistic, that is, acoustic communication with his medium but remains in constant spiritual contact and forces it to carry out his wishes – not said aloud but only

> thought of and thus transmitted and communicated to the medium in a tuned manner.[113]

In a rambling continuation of this one-off project, Fiala racialised electropathology and attributed people's susceptibility to hypnosis and suggestion to miscegenation, claiming that 'there is doubtless an intrinsic connection between the number and strength of the electrical and ether waves and the individual's strength of will and – racial purity'.[114]

Early speculative literature was filled with extraterrestrials, superhuman types, and hyper-sensitive characters said to be attuned to imperceptible frequencies – perhaps none more poignantly than in Carl Grunert's last published short story, 'Der Ätherseelenmensch' (The ether-soul-man).[115] Injured during a flight test when a propeller slices off the top of his skull without damaging his brain, the adventurous Nordic pilot Hjalmar Ätherström is unable to wear anything metal, and instead dons a straw hat to insulate his exposed mind from direct contact with the 'world ether'. Assuming that 'all of our spiritual and intellectual functions are the manifestations of tension, waves, or vibrations in the world ether, just like light and electricity in the inanimate world',[116] Ätherstrom reasons that his direct contact with the ether makes him experience thoughts and feelings more intensely than others. When the narrator's friend objects that this is self-deception, the narrator underscores Ätherstrom's powers of attraction by recounting how he once influenced the effects of specific gravity with his bare hands. Even more astonishing is the pilot's ability to travel through the ether, where he visits a distant planet and encounters a flower creature named Saivula, modelled on Lasswitz's last book, an ode to his lifelong love interest. After one last instance of astral projection, 'Hjalmar Ätherström did not wake up.'[117]

Paradoxically, the ether lent itself well to metaphysical speculation, while also presenting any such speculation as being grounded in everyday experience and empirical research.[118] As J. J. Thomson put it, 'The ether is not a fantastic creation of the speculative philosopher; it is as essential to us as the air we breathe [. . .] The study of this all-pervading substance is perhaps the most fascinating duty of the physicist.'[119] In *Das Radio*, Hagen illuminates the roots of radio physics in occultism and spiritualism and argues that electromagnetism was just as much of a construct: Hertz had already departed from the ontology of physics to speak of *Scheinbilder*, used to unlock unobservable but still measurable phenomena; and Crookes, who coined the term *radio*, believed in thought transference, as did Schreber and many others. In England, the Society for Physical Research, frequented by Crookes and Lodge, played a key role in the vernacular imagination of wireless connectivity, as evident in Kipling's allusions to it in his short story 'Wireless'. A further study might explore parallels in Germany, where wireless pioneer Georg von Arco was the chair of the German Monist League from 1921 to 1922, and was in contact with prominent figures such as Wilhelm Ostwald.[120] However, the mobilisation of the ether was hardly limited to the political left, as is evident from Dominik's ether stories. The so-called Aryan physics developed by Hertz's former assistant, Philipp Lenard, sought to discredit Einstein by treating the ether as a para-occult phenomenon.[121] Richard Kolb combined the metaphysical with the physiological: 'Electrical waves hit people, pass through them, and it would not be absurd to think that people may have nerves that receive these waves directly and bring them to the brain.'[122]

Between the triviality of invertebrate biotech and the delirium of mind control, other contemporary psychotechnicians worked on therapeutic applications of electromagnetic radiation, which resonated strongly with the avant-garde's programme of retraining the senses. One of the most successful entrepreneurs in early European radiotherapy was Georges Lakhovsky, whose work on 'cosmic waves' and 'vital vibrations' as the 'secret of life' proved to be an international bestseller that would exert a strong influence on international constructivists who were then searching for the elementary units of artistic construction. In a special issue of the avant-garde magazine *G: Materials for Elemental Form-Creation*, the editors reprinted a 1926 newspaper clipping, excerpted from the mainstream *Vossische Zeitung*, about Lakhovsky's 'research on the origin of life' under the title 'Shortwave Life'.[123] While the excerpt omitted the details of Lakhovsky's research, it highlighted his conclusion: 'The basis of organic existence is infinitely shortwaves at infinitely high frequency. The combination of an immense number of waves of various shortness – voilà, that is life.'[124] According to Lakhovsky and other early electrophysiologists, each cell functions by analogy with a wireless station, receiving and transmitting various signals. Accordingly, apparent differences between organisms such as birds and human beings are only the result of their *Abstimmung*, a word used in the sense of 'tuning', as one might rotate a radio dial to lock in on a radio station amid the static. Depending on whether an organism is tuned correctly or incorrectly, according to Lakhovsky, it could be said to be healthy (a signal) or diseased (a noise). While Lakhovsky's most notorious invention, a medical device developed in collaboration with Nikola Tesla called a 'multi-wave oscillator', was advertised to cure cancer with electromagnetic radiation, his research interests in the mid-1920s still focused on electromagnetic radiation in the animal kingdom, as did those of many of his contemporaries. Just as a migratory bird can orient itself with the help of a 'goniometric apparatus', claimed Lakhovsky, all that remains for people is 'to build an apparatus with which one would be able to receive these infinitely short waves'.[125] With the help of this machine, one was supposed to be able to orient oneself in the world like a homing pigeon.

The appearance of the news report on 'Shortwave Life' in a special issue of the avant-garde magazine *G* on 'Film' suggests a means of rethinking film's habitual classification as a *visual* medium. Well beyond the international constructivists, one main strand of the European avant-garde understood film, photography, and television not in terms of our contemporary opposition between visual studies and sound studies, supported by the division of the human senses, but as *optical* media, meaning physical media operating along a common electromagnetic spectrum.[126] The report on 'Shortwave Life', for example, was situated in a suggestive constellation of different texts: Marcel Duchamp's hypnotic spirals, Lakhovsky's organic orientation apparatus, Viking Eggeling's rhythmicisation of a natural object, and Man Ray's photograph of a pile of film strips as a mountain range. Taken together, these multisensory physical experiments can hardly be understood as so-called visual music. Corresponding more to the principle of 'vibratory modernism',[127] this suggestive constellation is not about the usual relationships among the arts, but rather the concept of *Gestaltung* (forming, shaping, designing) as an intervention into the relationship between nature and technology.

Figurations of Electromagnetism

Cultivating a true 'sense' for wireless transmission requires more than a sense organ capable of perceiving radio waves. It demands an understanding of the physics of media and the epistemology of electromagnetic radiation. Over the course of the long nineteenth century, radio waves, X-rays, and other electromagnetic phenomena gradually came to be mapped on to the same continuous spectrum. Understanding different physical phenomena as part of the same continuous spectrum provided a condition of possibility for artistic experiments in converting light waves into sound waves and vice versa. If light and sound are understood as part of the same spectrum, then any differences between them appear to be nothing more than those in frequency or wavelength, even though sound is a mechanical wave that propagates only in a physical medium and light an electromagnetic one that propagates even in a vacuum. The emergence of the spectrum as a modern reconfiguration of the ether created an epistemic gap frequently explored in speculative thinking: the unification of a continuous electromagnetic spectrum consisting of visible and invisible phenomena created a sense of continuity; but the separation of the senses through physical and physiological research created a sense of discontinuity.

Speculation – across science, literature, philosophy, and many other discourses – made up the spectrum as we now know it. The next chapter will look at how speculators drummed up affective investments in an imminent 'wireless age', while the wireless spectrum was being divided up for public consumption, sliced into various bandwidths, and sold to the highest bidder. Today, the concept of the ether is preserved only in the name 'Ethernet', coined in direct reference to modernist thinking about *wireless* transmission but used, counterintuitively, to describe *wired* local area networks.[128] Once seen as an inexhaustible natural resource, the spectrum has long been an economic and political resource, as any 'Einstein' who has ever considered opening their black-boxed routers and wondered why our contemporary Wi-Fi networks are restricted to 2.4 and 5.0 GHz (or where the nomenclature of Giga*hertz* came from) will understand. 'After all, you do not have to understand electricity to use it [. . .] Media need not be understood to be used. This is both their degree of freedom and their bane.'[129] In the end, it is easier to recognise concepts such as *radio*, *telecommunications*, and *broadcasting* as interpretative constructs than it is to recognise *waves*, *frequencies*, or *spectrums* as figurations of electromagnetism. While communication and mass media studies once attempted to predetermine what electromagnetic waves could do – making them appear destined for one-to-one telecommunication, one-to-many information dissemination, or many-to-many data transfer – the physics of wireless media contain other possibilities, which connect distinct epistemes across space and time.

Notes

1. Kittler, 'History of Communication Media', n.p.
2. Gumbrecht and Pfeiffer, *Materialities of Communication*.
3. 'Neueste Nachrichten aus beiden Hemisphären', 110.
4. Although Kittler does not provide a source for his critique of 'Merleau-Ponty's phenomenology of perception' ('Observations on Public Reception', 80), see the remarks on physics and 'sense experience' in Merleau-Ponty, *Phenomenology of Perception*, 51–5, 207–42.

5. See Kittler, 'Observations on Public Reception'; Siegert, 'Cacography or Communication'; Seitter, *Physik der Medien*; Hagen, *Das Radio*; Seitter, 'The Meta-Physics of Media'; Ernst, 'Distory'; Krämer, *Medium, Messenger, Transmission*, 31–6.
6. Starosielski, 'The Ends of Media Studies'.
7. See Süsskind, 'Hertz and the Technological Significance'.
8. On Lasswitz and Dominik, see Fischer, *The Empire Strikes Out*; cf. Innerhofer, *Deutsche Science Fiction*. Grunert corresponded with Lasswitz and included a dedicatory poem to Lasswitz at the start of his first short story collection, *Im Irdischen Jenseits*. See Innerhofer, *Deutsche Science Fiction*, 278–9.
9. See Wythoff, *Perversity of Things*.
10. Beer, 'Wave Theory', 295.
11. Latour, *Pandora's Hope*, 142–3.
12. On fields, currents, and flows, see Hagen, 'Alternating Currents and Ether', 53–62; Ofak, '"Where voices and currents flow . . ."'; Thibault, 'Streaming'; Gethmann, *Feld*.
13. On rays, beams, and auras, see Asendorf, *Ströme und Strahlen*; Haupt, 'Strahlenmagie'; Natale, 'Cosmology of Invisible Fluids'.
14. On sparks, flashes, and bolts, see Hagen, '"Stürmische Plötzlichkeiten"'; Thibault, 'Bolts and Waves'.
15. On 'figures of vibration, inscription, and transmission', see Kahn, introduction to *Wireless Imagination*, 14; cf. Enns and Trower, *Vibratory Modernism*.
16. See Canales, 'The Media of Relativity', 611–12; Canales, *The Physicist and the Philosopher*, 262–72.
17. Sinclair, *Mental Radio*, viii–ix.
18. Einstein, 'Rede', 240.
19. Einstein, 'Rede', 240.
20. Einstein, 'Rede', 240.
21. Fürst, *Im Bannkreis von Nauen*, 14.
22. Fürst, *Im Bannkreis von Nauen*, 14.
23. See Peters et al., *Action at a Distance*.
24. Hagen, 'Alternating Currents and Ether', 61.
25. Peters et al., *Action at a Distance*, xl.
26. Peters et al., *Action at a Distance*, xlii.
27. Nietzsche, *The Gay Science*, 71.
28. See Vagt, 'Physics and Aesthetics'.
29. Schlobinski and Siebold, *Wörterbuch der Science-Fiction*, 126.
30. Lasswitz, *Auf zwei Planeten*, vol. 1, 411. For an overview of the imaginary science and technology in the novel, see Fischer, *The Empire Strikes Out*, 142–6.
31. Lasswitz, *Auf zwei Planeten*, vol. 2, 360, 519.
32. In the Lasswitz archive, his typescript is dated 3 August 1892. It was originally published as Anonymous, 'Nach Chicago (Eine Preiskonkurrenz)', *Unsere Zeit: Scherers Familienblatt (Salon-Ausgabe)* 8, no. 1 (1892/93): 101–6. Unable to access this version, I am using a recent

edition (Lasswitz, *Gedichte und Erzählungen*, 261–8), which reprints a different version, 'Was soll sie thun?', *Das Echo* 11, no. 523 (8 September 1892): 1139–42. The same reprint can also be found as the titular story in Lasswitz, *Telelyt*.

33. On Lasswitz's multifaceted biography, see Fischer, *The Empire Strikes Out*; cf. Willmann, 'Leibniz's Metaphysics'.
34. Lasswitz, 'Nach Chicago', 267.
35. Hertz, 'Ueber einen Einfluss des ultravioletten Lichtes'. Hertz's research led to further studies by Hallwachs and Lenard, Hoor, Righi, and Stoletov.
36. Lasswitz, 'Nach Chicago', 263.
37. Lasswitz, 'Nach Chicago', 263–4.
38. The *Abendpost* should not be confused with the *Abendblatt der Illinois Staats-Zeitung* (1891–94).
39. Lasswitz, 'Nach Chicago', 262.
40. Lasswitz, 'Nach Chicago', 262.
41. Lasswitz, 'Nach Chicago', 263.
42. Lasswitz, 'Nach Chicago', 267.
43. I am grateful to Nicholas Sola for this observation.
44. Lasswitz co-edited Kant's pre-critical writings, including an updated version of Kant's Latin *Magisterarbeit*, 'Meditationum quarundam de igne succincta delineatio' (Concise Outline of Some Reflections on Fire), vol. 1, 371–84.
45. Lasswitz, *Geschichte der Atomistik*, vol. 1, 267–8.
46. Lasswitz, *Geschichte der Atomistik*, vol. 2, 238–42, 298–300.
47. Lasswitz, 'Newton und die Fernwirkung', 490–2.
48. Lasswitz cites Gerstmann, 'Elektrische Wellen'.
49. Hertz, 'On the Relations Between Light and Electricity', 326.
50. Rheinberger and Herrgott, *Experimentalsysteme und epistemische Dinge*.
51. See Thomson, 'Curious Effects of Hertzian Waves'; Süsskind, 'Hertz and the Technological Significance'; Aitken, *Syntony and Spark*, 49.
52. See Fahie, *History of Wireless Telegraphy*, 204, cited in Phillips, *Early Radio Wave Detectors*, 1.
53. See Hagen, *Das Radio*.
54. Aitken, *Syntony and Spark*, 73.
55. Phillips, *Early Radio Wave Detectors*, 5.
56. Hertz, 'On the Relations Between Light and Electricity', 325.
57. Schreier, *Die Entstehung der Funktechnik*, 26.
58. Völker, *Mobile Medien*, 163; Hagen, *Das Radio*, 7; Ernst, 'Experimenting with Media Temporality', 186–9.
59. Letter from Heinrich Rudolf Huber to Heinrich Hertz, 3 December 1889, qtd. and trans. in Süsskind, 'Hertz and the Technological Significance of Electromagnetic Waves', 344.
60. See, for instance, Braun, *Drahtlose Telegraphie durch Wasser und Luft*, 15.

61. Weilenmann, *Die elektrischen Wellen*, 7.
62. Hertz 'On Electric Radiation', 176.
63. See Hong, *Wireless*, 7.
64. Hertz, 'On the Relations Between Light and Electricity', 314.
65. Hertz, *The Principles of Mechanics*; cf. Mulligan, 'The Aether', 144; Gethmann, 'Innere Scheinbilder', 125–61.
66. Hertz, *The Principles of Mechanics*, 67.
67. Hertz, *The Principles of Mechanics*, 67.
68. Hertz, 'On the Relations Between Light and Electricity', 324–5.
69. Hertz, 'On the Relations Between Light and Electricity', 326.
70. Hertz, 'On the Relations Between Light and Electricity', 311.
71. Navarro, *Ether and Modernity*.
72. Badino and Navarro, introduction to Navarro, *Ether and Modernity*, 12.
73. For an overview, see Schaffner, *Nineteenth-Century Aether Theories*; and, for case studies, see Hagen, 'Alternating Currents versus Ether'; Hagen, 'Medienäther – Äthermedien'; Kümmel-Schnur and Schröter, *Äther*.
74. Henderson, 'Cubism, Futurism, and Ether Physics', 451–2.
75. Milutis, *Ether*, 80.
76. Dominik, 'Ätherwellen', 9–23. This reprinted version drops the subtitle, 'technical chat', from the original publication, 'Ätherwellen: Technische Plauderei', *Berliner Tageblatt*, 9 February 1902. Developing Lasswitz's notion of the scientific and technical 'chat' (*Plauderei*, or 'salon/parlour conversation'), Dominik referred to his feuilletons, published 1902–04, as 'Phantastische Plaudereien', and published another collection of the non-narrative pieces under the title *Wissenschaftliche Plaudereien* in 1903.
77. Dominik developed this trope of talking cables and chatty wires in other stories including 'The Vagabonds', 'The Test Run', and 'What the Overhead Wire Told Itself'. These three stories were also published in the *Berliner Tageblatt* in 1902 and then reprinted in the collection of Dominik's *Technische Märchen*.
78. Dominik, 'Ätherwellen', 10.
79. Dominik, 'Ätherwellen', 16.
80. Dominik, 'Ätherwellen', 16.
81. Dominik, 'Ätherwellen', 17.
82. Dominik, 'Ätherwellen', 17.
83. Dominik, 'Ätherwellen', 17.
84. Dominik, 'Ätherwellen', 17.
85. Dominik, 'Ätherwellen', 18.
86. Dominik, 'Ätherwellen', 21.
87. Tismar, *Das deutsche Kunstmärchen*, 25–6.
88. Simmel, 'The Metropolis and Mental Life', 409.
89. Dominik, 'Ätherwellen', 16.
90. Dominik, 'Ätherwellen', 22.
91. A coherer was an early type of radio signal detector.

92. Dominik, 'Ätherwellen', 23.
93. See, for instance, Tesla, 'Talking with Planets', 4–5.
94. Lasswitz, 'Marsphantasien'.
95. Dominik, 'Ein Experiment', 94.
96. Dominik, 'Ein Experiment', 94.
97. Dominik, 'Ein Experiment', 94.
98. Innerhofer, *Deutsche Science Fiction*.
99. Wells, *The First Men in the Moon*, 276.
100. Grunert, *Feinde im Weltall?*; Grunert, 'Enemies in Space', 182–92.
101. Peters, 'Die Kolonien in 100 Jahren', 112.
102. Peters, 'Die Kolonien in 100 Jahren', 112.
103. For a pulp fiction story about interplanetary wireless communication written by a Telefunken engineer, see Frerichs, 'Hier Mars, Hier Erde'.
104. See Rieger, 'Psychopaths Electrified'; Chun, *Control and Freedom*, 31–5, 266–70, 299–301; Peters, 'Broadcasting and Schizophrenia'.
105. Schreber, *Memoirs of My Nervous Illness*, 277.
106. See Jellinek, *Elektro-Pathologie*; Jellinek, 'Stefan Jellinek'.
107. On Galvani's experiment, see Phillips, *Early Radio Wave Detectors*, 198–204.
108. Collins, 'Effect of Electric Waves on the Human Brain'; cf. McIntosh and Graham-Willmore, 'Effect of Electric Waves on the Human Brain'.
109. See Phillips, *Early Radio Wave Detectors*, 198–204.
110. Gradenwitz, 'Frogs' Muscles as Wireless Detectors', 830.
111. Fiala, 'Elektrophysiologische Zukunftsprobleme'.
112. Andriopoulos, 'Psychic Television'.
113. Fiala, 'Elektrophysiologische Zukunftsprobleme', 154.
114. Fiala, 'Elektrophysiologische Zukunftsprobleme', 191–5.
115. Grunert, 'Der Ätherseelenmensch'; cf. Grunert, 'Auf den Schwingungen des Weltäthers'.
116. Grunert, 'Der Ätherseelenmensch', 190.
117. Grunert, 'Der Ätherseelenmensch', 195.
118. See Hagen, *Das Radio*, 73.
119. Thomson, 'Address to the British Association', 335.
120. See Fuchs, *Georg von Arco*.
121. Lenard, 'Über Äther und Materie'; cf. Schirrmacher, 'Lenard's Ether'.
122. Kolb, *Das Horoskop des Hörspiels*, 53.
123. 'Shortwave Life', reprinted in Mertins and Jennings, *G*, 218.
124. 'Shortwave Life', 218 (translation modified).
125. 'Shortwave Life', 218.
126. See Kittler, *Optical Media*.
127. See Enns and Trower, *Vibratory Modernism*.
128. See Schaefer, 'Dematerialized Infrastructures'.
129. Hagen, 'Alternating Currents and Ether', 61–2.

Chapter 3

The Wireless Age: From Imaginary Media to Speculative Infrastructure

What won't be possible in the wireless age?! In a cartoon drawn by Ferdinand Barlog, one of the most popular illustrators of the interwar period, the vanishing wires are not telegraph, telephone, or electrical cables but a dogcatcher's leash, the wires on a mousetrap, the bars on a birdcage, the strings on a harp and a cello, and a barbed-wire fence (Fig. 3.1).[1] Ironically captioned 'In the wireless age!', Barlog's satirical image ridicules the media hype around the 'wireless concert', and suggests that as much as media may change, society often remains the same. The last image in the series, captioned 'completely wireless' (*ganz drahtlos*), depicts a down-and-out person with empty pockets, in the sense of not having been 'wired' money and thus being socially 'disconnected'. For all its cynicism, Barlog's critical imagination of media change participates in a rich experimental culture of speculations on possible applications for new technologies.

If words, images, and sounds can all be transmitted wirelessly, vernacular media thinkers reasoned, then wireless might also be suitable for more innovative and unorthodox applications. A telephone could be used for ringing up the dead, a gramophone for playing back an author's voice, or a radio for picking up historical broadcasts.[2] In the deep time of media, one finds remarkable contraptions, such as an electrolytic telegraph that would signal by producing water bubbles corresponding to each letter of the alphabet, or a proposed method for signalling at a distance across any given obstacle, which appeared to consist of incantations for summoning spirits but turned out to be the first modern treatise on steganography.[3] In the early twentieth century, mass-marketed wireless devices included a doll containing a hidden recorder, programmes for learning languages in one's sleep, and miniature receivers intended to be attached to one's hat, teeth, or undergarments. National broadcasting sparked a variety of further designs for portable radio sets, including wallet radios, purse radios, and pinkie ring radios.[4]

Figure 3.1 Satirical cartoon by Ferdinand Barlog, captioned 'In the wireless age!' Source: Roellinghoff, 'Radio im Humor', 87.

This chapter contributes to the media-philosophical study of 'imaginary media', examining their relation to the modernist 'experimental spirit' known in German as the *Erfindergeist*.[5] Around 1900 this technical and humanistic imagination still crossed any perceived 'two cultures' divide, as evident in a collection of engineering humour titled '*Made in Germany*'.[6] To ease the burden of standing while lecturing, one 'important invention' was imagined to be a pulley system with loops passing under a lecturer's armpits; another satirical illustration depicted the 'newest invention', a perpetual motion machine running on railway tracks and powered by an airhorn; other cartoons showed a 'novel fountain' using live monkeys to spit out the water and a mechanism for dispensing beer through a garden-style tap on the side of a building.[7] Elsewhere, one satirical W. Heath Robinson contraption consisted of an elaborate system of levers and pulleys whose simple function was to elevate a bucket of water to the height where brushes could clean one's antenna (Fig. 3.2).

Figure 3.2 Satirical drawing captioned, 'For the coming spring cleaning: apparatus for cleaning the antenna', and credited to W. Heath Robinson. Source: Roellinghoff, 'Radio im Humor', 85.

As literary figures embodying this experimental spirit, Christian Morgenstern presented the travelling companions Palmström and Korf throughout his cycles of modernist nonsense poetry. Indefatigable in searching for novelty, their literary-scientific inventions explored the gamut of imaginary media – the *untimely*, the *conceptual*, and the *impossible*, to borrow Siegfried Zielinski's useful schema.[8] The first category, *untimely media*, are 'devised and designed either much too late or much too early, realised in technical and media practice either centuries before or centuries after being invented', as with Palmström's 'olfactory organ' (*Geruchsorgel*) and Korf's 'aroma machine' (*Aromat*).[9] While untimely media eventually materialise, *conceptual media* are 'artefacts that were only ever sketched as models or drafted as concrete ideas on paper, but never actually built'.[10] Here the '*Korfsche Uhr*', a clock with two hands crossing forwards and backwards, and '*Palmströms Uhr*', a watch whose speed adapts to the user's wishes, exhibit parallels with devices for which patents were registered but that were never constructed. At the furthest remove from reality, *impossible media* are 'imaginary media in the true sense [. . .] hermetic and hermeneutic machines, that is, machines that signify something, but where the initial design or sketch makes clear that they cannot actually be built, and whose implied meanings nonetheless have an impact on the factual world of media'.[11] In this category, Korf's 'day-night lamp' turns the day into night; a special form of 'eyeglasses' focuses on the essential aspects of books; a 'mid-day newspaper digest' (*Mittagszeitung*) makes one full through reading; and a certain 'type of joke' only takes effect a few hours later. In 1938, the same year in which three poems were censured and excised from the new edition of Morgenstern's still-popular poetry volume, Otto Sroka composed an occasional poem for the NSDAP Presseball under the title 'The TV-Newspaper: Recipe following Palmström-Korff'.[12] Aping Morgenstern's sing-song rhythm, Sroka ridiculed a hypercapitalistic future in which TV news would become customised and tailored for each subscriber. This is a fourth category of imaginary media – speculations that materialise but only in a twisted form – for which there is still no good name.

Connecting this framework of 'imaginary media' to what the French sociologist of technology Patrice Flichy called the 'technological imaginary', this chapter analyses the modernist imagination of the 'wireless age'. As Flichy argues, ideas, dreams, visions, and utopias are 'an integral part of the development of a technical system', providing a crucial resource and reference point for designers, inventors, and engineers.[13] While some speculators imagined radically different wireless futures, most focused on finding new applications following established patterns and pathways. As a result, the same scenes and forecasts kept recurring around 1900, and they would return to the popular imagination around 2000. Looking forward from 1900 to the present, wireless futures challenge the discursive grounding for the dominant contemporary ideology of connectivity. Looking backward, the (an)archaeological approach to the deep time of the media developed in this chapter is allied with the study of origin stories and primal scenes, which differ from the concept of beginnings in that they exceed historiographical models based on progress, teleology, or developmental stages.[14] Rather than revolutionising society, the most successful wireless futures have obeyed the logic of expansion, resource concentration, and multiplying market connections. By focusing instead on historical 'losers', this chapter counters the 'success stories' often told in the history of technology, which tend to present creativity and connectivity as unassailable goods.

Modernity, Novelty, Media Topoi

Media scholars studying early wireless transmission have long been interested in questions of firsts, origins, and innovations. However, the modernist discourse of the wireless age is better understood through the articulation and repetition of traditional themes, formulas, or what Erkki Huhtamo calls media 'topoi'.[15] Instead of novelty, Huhtamo's approach to media archaeology relishes 'the clichéd, the commonplace, and "the tired". Media culture relies on the already known: the past lives on in the present, allowing us to detect novelties.'[16] The negative connotations of 'commonplaces' led the pioneering figure of topos study, medieval literary historian Ernst Robert Curtius, to adopt the term *topos*. While the topoi of interest to Curtius were literary commonplaces in the Latin rhetorical tradition, such as the *locus amoenus* or the 'book of nature', Huhtamo extended the approach to account for media tropes, such as the 'magic mirror', the ghost in the machine, or a society hypnotised by its own devices.[17] From this perspective, studying media change requires 'identifying topoi, analysing their trajectories and transformations, and explaining the cultural logics that condition their "wanderings" across time and space'.[18] Media topoi are preserved even after technological jumps and epistemic ruptures, revealing points of continuity in periods of apparent discontinuity. Examining the conventional aspects of media topoi should not only counterbalance the rhetoric of 'new media'; present changes to our media environment should also reveal new paths for historical study.[19]

In the late nineteenth and early twentieth century, media topoi included the consciousness of epochal change, an awareness of shifting space-time relations, and the possibility of creating a singular multisensory medium – the last representing a species of speculation known, based on the title of Richard Wagner's influential essay, as 'future music' (*Zukunftsmusik*). The two best-known wireless topoi refer to the radio as 'voices from the ether' and the television as a 'window to the world', to cite the title of Clas Dammann's cultural history of German broadcasting.[20] Further examples include 'perpetual contact', 'pocket wireless', and 'chaos on the airwaves', which reveal not only marketing clichés but also several 'roads not taken' in media history. While the main topoi examined by media archaeologists exhibit a dreamlike, forward-looking, or progressive quality, it is important to expand this corpus to account for its reactionary counterparts. For instance, the reactionary trope of 'reverse colonisation' mirrored the progressive tropes of internationalism and cosmopolitanism; and the 'window to the world' could be interpreted as a 'two-way mirror', with fantasies about seeing at a distance reflecting those of being seen and monitored. Media topoi are not neutral, and many were formulated by engineers, technicians, advertisers, and managerial insiders at the expense, and sometimes even deliberate exclusion, of their perceived others. As evident in a genre of 'educational anecdotes' about electrical telegraphy, modernist media topoi often expressed racist and classist biases against those deemed to be incapable of understanding media, and served to further differentiate the objects of ridicule from the authors of and audiences for the jokes, obfuscating responsibility for managing technological risks.[21]

One collection of 'radio humour', assembled from international sources and translated into German by Charlie K. Roellinghoff in 1923, indicates the bourgeois ideologies that informed early broadcasting.[22] Classist jokes ridicule the lower classes for using antennas like clotheslines, and those, like the speaker's 'cleaning lady' (*Portierfrau*), who mistake the term 'antenna' for the name of one's companion animal. There is a running gag about mutual interference and the threat of eavesdropping – real concerns for official programmes of attentive listening. One misogynistic joke describes a wireless repair technician who makes a house call to fix a man's radio set, only to learn that the source of the 'noises' and 'disturbances' is the voice of the man's wife. These wireless topoi are developed further in satirical illustrations culled from a variety of international sources: one cartoon reprinted from *The Sketch* shows 'the wireless widow', who sits by idly while her husband lovingly caresses his radio; another reprinted from the *Berliner Illustrierte* depicts an 'absent-minded doctor' unable to focus on listening to a woman patient's heartbeat because of the 'background noises' of wireless concerts; a drawing by Willibald Krain features two mortified older women, who, as the caption explains, 'wanted to hear a talk about "food preservation" but tuned in to the wrong wavelength and caught a lecture on the "sex life of primitive peoples"'. In the final punchline, the comedian who assembled the collection claims to have asked a friend whether they had heard a radio lecture he delivered, only to be told that the broadcast did not contain one 'spark' (*Funken*) of humour.

Like modernity, the study of media topoi remains an incomplete project that may never be completed. While my preliminary excavations of wireless topoi will need to be extended further, the study of media topoi will also need to keep sharpening its critical edge by relating the category of space to that of time. To become a viable research method for modernisation processes, Huhtamo's approach to media topoi, as spaces or places, needs to be complemented by an approach to media kairos, as propitious times or opportunities. 'When a place counts as a topos it also counts as a kairos', Bruno Latour argues. 'Deeper than time and space there is another question about who or what counts.'[23] In contrast to the concept of time as *chronos*, or duration, Latour develops the concept of time as *kairos*, an opportunity for action, asking 'which actants can interrupt, modify, interfere, interest which others, thus producing as many topoi-kairoi?'[24] Giorgio Agamben, Peter Sloterdijk, and other contemporary thinkers have generally discussed 'Kairology' (as opposed to chronology); Siegfried Zielinski views kairos as historical junctures in the deep time of media; and John Durham Peters proposes to think of 'syn-kair-ization as well as synchron-ization'.[25] Studying media topoi thus requires analysing the constitutive folding of past, present, and future into significant moments on the historical timeline. What, then, made the historical moment in Europe around 1900 seem 'destined' – as modernists would have it – for the birth of wireless? Why, if electromagnetic radiation has always existed, was it only first scientifically verified in Hertz's laboratory and commercially exploited in Marconi's field tests?

The Primal Scene of Wireless Communication

In 1897, the year Marconi was awarded his first patent for wireless telegraphy, it was still difficult to establish a wireless connection across a couple of kilometres. Yet technical periodicals and the illustrated press were already filled with predictions about the possibility of contacting anyone at any place and time.[26] Before delving into the kinds of futuristic visions provided by Albert Robida and other *belle époque* figures, it will be useful to reconsider a different kind of popular scientific outreach source, which articulated and circulated an imaginary 'primal scene' of wireless communication.

This *locus classicus* for the modernist wireless imagination is a lecture delivered by physicist and engineer William Edward Ayrton at the Imperial Institute in London on 15 February 1897.[27] Although Ayrton lectured on a historical topic, 'Sixty Years of Submarine Telegraphy', and the editors framed the transcript by noting that, apart from Ayrton, 'it would have gone hard with us to name a possible historian' of underwater telegraphy, its most quoted part turned out to be a brief pseudo-prediction made in the rhetorical conclusion:

> I have told you about the past, I have told you about the present. What about the future? Well, there is no doubt the day will come, maybe when you and I are forgotten, when copper wires, gutta-percha coverings and iron sheathings will be relegated to the museum of antiquities.
>
> Then when a person wants to telegraph to a friend, he knows not where, he will call in an electromagnetic voice, which will be heard loud by him who has the electromagnetic ear, but will be silent to everyone else, he will call, 'Where are you?' and the reply will come loud to the man with the electromagnetic ear, 'I am at the bottom of the coal mine, or crossing the Andes, or in the middle of the Pacific'. Or perhaps no voice will come at all, and he may then expect the friend is dead.[28]

Ayrton's primal scene encapsulates the fundamental tension between two main communicative forms, which John Durham Peters calls 'dialogue and dissemination', and Sybille Krämer calls 'the *personal* principle of understanding and the *postal* principle of transmission'.[29] As in dialogues, the interlocutors exchange greetings, though, in a testament to wireless mobility, their questions are not about the other's identity (Who are you?), nor disposition (How are you?), but position (Where are you?).[30] As in dissemination, their intimate conversation has the potential to reach a mass audience of unknown recipients, which requires selectivity and tuning.

Despite such transhistorical resonances, Ayrton's present circumscribed his vision of the future, as is evident in his assumption that the telegraph and telephone would remain the dominant media of interpersonal communication even after the obsolescence of wired technology. What usually gets omitted from quotations of Ayrton's prediction are two additional lines about its implications that follow the impactful statement equating radio silence with the presumed death of one's friend:

> Think what that will mean. Think of the calling which goes on from room to room, then think of that calling when it extends from pole to pole – a calling quite audible to him who wants to hear, absolutely silent to him who does not.[31]

As Ayrton's additional explanation makes evident, his prediction was not primarily about a wireless future but about the horizon of expectation established by wired telegraphy and telephony in the past.

Ayrton's prediction quickly became one of the most quoted in the popular scientific and philosophical literature on wireless technology. Originally published in *The Electrician*, it was popularised through a lecture summary in *Nature*,[32] and subsequently used in framing statements for technical handbooks and early media historiography.[33] In his influential *History of Wireless Telegraphy*, John Joseph Fahie quoted Ayrton's prediction as an example of how 'cautious men of science spoke, or should I not say dreamt thus'.[34] To Adolf Slaby, it revealed how 'the wonderful phenomena that nature has revealed to us in the mysterious play of electric sparks make many people into poets. Indeed, even so serious a scholar as Professor Ayrton cannot resist dreaming up an image of the future in his waking moments.'[35] Translated into German, Ayrton's remarks appeared in a wide range of contexts, from speculative fiction to the Dadaist Raoul Hausmann's work on a wireless device for converting between light and sound.[36] The appeal of Ayrton's prediction was twofold: framing modern science and technology as antidotes to vernacular astonishment, and presenting wireless as the solution to a universal dream of distant communication. In a gesture of one-upmanship, Marconi extended the scenario even further from information to energy transfer: 'If it should become possible to transmit waves right around the world, it may be found that the electrical energy travelling round all parts of the globe may be made to concentrate at the antipodes of the sending station.'[37] The dream of contacting a friend halfway around the world engenders that of wireless energy transmission, with one birth following the next.

In recent years, dating back at least to Arthur C. Clarke's *1984, Spring*, Ayrton's prediction has been quoted for its resonance with the discourse of ubiquitous connectivity.[38] Taken out of context, the prediction is often linked to an essentialist history of communication, as in the following prefatory remarks to Ayrton's comments in a technical handbook: 'Arguably, wireless communication between humans is as old as the human civilization itself, for as soon as the first humans started communicating with each other using their vocal cords, we had achieved wireless communication.'[39] Developing a more nuanced transhistorical account of communication, Imar de Vries mobilises Aytron's prediction as evidence of the universal dream of 'communicat[ing] without obstacles and without misunderstanding', whereby 'fear of miscommunication and restoration of the natural balance of our extended sense-organs [. . .] drives us to improve existing media'.[40] However, this approach presumes a stable anthropological constant and posits a singular narrative for media history: improving or perfecting interpersonal communication. Reflecting on the 'universalizing anthropology of *homo conexus*', Urs Stäheli critiques sociology and network studies for assuming that 'being human' means making connections, creating relationships, and communicating at a distance.[41] Likewise, media change is usually assumed to mean improving communication channels, increasing access, and eliminating barriers. Regardless of this story's validity, it remains difficult, if not impossible, to conceive of disconnectivity or non-communication. What makes Ayrton's prediction so quotable is not only its lack of technical details but also its encoded resonances: two (white male European) friends, separated at a distance, overcome some obstacle thanks to modern technology. Ayrton's pseudo-prophecy is thus better understood as a recursive media topos.

To complement the North American study of media topoi, German media philosophy presents the concept of *recursions*, a term for generating different results by repeatedly applying the same definition or procedure to each new output of a dataset.[42] Originating in mathematics and linguistics, then computer science and systems theory, the concept has been developed further in recent German media philosophy. According to Niklas Luhmann's systems theory, every concept is relational, a hinge between differences, and the complexity of systems derives from processing these differences recursively. 'We pay attention to the return of the same', Friedrich Kittler explained when adapting Luhmann's concept to media systems. 'We "run back" in time [. . .] but simultaneously we also run ahead, from the first beginning to its repetitive overcoming.'[43] More than a pleonasm, Kittler's notion of 'the first beginning' speaks to what Wolfgang Ernst – adapting Gilbert Simondon's related concept of 'recurrent causality' – terms *Gleichursprünglichkeit*, or the problem of multiple, simultaneous origins for technical media.[44] Reflecting on the technical history of wireless, Sungook Hong refers to the invention's 'unfaithful offspring'.[45] Describing the 'double birth of wireless', Gabriele Balbi and Simone Natale build on André Gaudreault and Philippe Marion's claim that 'media are always born at least twice' to argue that the mode's birth in point-to-point radiotelegraphy anticipated its second life in point-to-multipoint radio.[46] The conceptual difficulty in grasping wireless consists in adapting this binary logic from two to three to four *ad infinitum*, as many more switches were involved in a longer process of recursion.

As a recursive media topos, wireless telemedia appeared to fulfil the dream of contacting a distant friend, and each generation of wireless technology – from telegraphy through telephony to television – appeared to approach the ideal of unmediated communication – telepathy, teleportation, telepresence. Despite the apparent continuity established by the framework of telecommunications, the primal scene of wireless connectivity has changed significantly as media technologies have changed. In addition to the semantic and experiential differences between tele*graphy*, tele*phony*, and tele*vision*, there is a key technical difference between wired and wireless transmission, which is more evident in another pseudo-prediction. Five years before Ayrton's lecture, William Crookes described a future in which

> any two friends living within the radius of sensibility of their receiving instruments, having first decided on their special wavelength and attuned their respective instruments to mutual receptivity, could thus communicate as long and as often as they pleased by timing the impulses to produce long and short intervals on the ordinary Morse code.[47]

Crookes's description of the 'radius of sensibility' reflected a nascent awareness of the problem of tuning. In contrast to Ayrton's comments, the space connecting the two friends was imagined not to be a direct line-of-sight but a circle whose diameter was determined only by the sensitivity of wireless equipment. Like Ayrton, Crookes reassured readers of his authority to make this prediction, citing his early experiments and stating that

> this is no mere dream of a visionary philosopher. All the requisites needed to bring it within the grasp of daily life are well within the possibilities of discovery, and are so reasonable and so clearly in the path of researches which are now being actively prosecuted in every capital of Europe, that we may any day expect to hear that they have emerged from the realms of speculation into those of sober fact.[48]

As specious evidence, Crookes mentioned potential applications of wireless beyond telecommunications, such as brain waves, weather control, wireless lighting, electrophysiology, agriculture, and water sterilisation.

Whenever there was a technological jump, these same applications, primal scenes, and media topoi would be conjured up again and again. Although classical antiquity established the two dominant paradigms of dialogic communication and postal dissemination, the primal scene of two friends making contact across an insurmountable distance only first appeared in a fabricated reference to antiquity in an early modern steganographic treatise.[49] Up to around 1800, the scene typically involved two conversational partners from the same community but separated by the greatest imaginable distance, the 'antipodes'. Although the conversation partners in the primal scene were imagined to be acquaintances, none of their imagined conversations went further than the obligatory greeting. Around 1900 the topos of making contact expanded to include the possibility of speaking with the unknown, television and videotelephony, and an imaginary medium known as 'pocket wireless' – all of which would get looped back into descriptions of wireless connectivity a century later.

Telemedia and Telesthesia

From a deep-time perspective, the imagination of *speaking* and *hearing* at a distance was always intertwined with that of *seeing* at a distance. Fantasies about telecommunicating these so-called higher senses were augmented further by ones about the so-called lower senses – *smelling, tasting,* or *touching* at a distance. The structural parallels between telegraphy, telephony, and television tend to present media as the extensions of the human senses culminating in ubiquitous telepresence. However, visions of media change always need to be understood in their contingent social, cultural, and historical contexts.

Over the course of the long nineteenth century, an entire televisual paradigm emerged through the discursive construction of the desired medium as a 'window to the world'.[50] Disseminated in the popular press, this discourse of television came to signify immediacy, simultaneity, and ubiquity – what we might now call 'telepresence'. In the absence of a human body, the televisual machines present in its place were supposed to create a sense of real-time participation in remote events.[51] From this perspective, the history of television may again appear to be one of perfecting communication, instrumentalising science, or extending the human senses. However, television was not a foregone conclusion in the years around 1900. Until the end of the nineteenth century, the now-standard German noun for a television, *Fernseher*, still referred to the telescope; and the master patent for television, effectively a mechanical scanner that could analyse an image into pixels, was filed by Paul Nipkow under the rubric of an 'Elektrisches Teleskop'.[52] At the time, the German verb for watching television (*fernsehen*) still referred to the ability 'to see at a distance' in the competing senses of remote viewing practices and psychic visions of the future – which indicates the alliance between occultism and technology well into the twentieth century.[53]

The imagination of wireless distribution emerged during a period when there were few reliable distribution networks for moving images, making the wireless distribution of movies modelled on telegraph or telephone networks seem like a viable solution.[54] As a physical but often invisible step, distribution describes the problem formulated in Nipkow's patent, of how to make 'an object located at point "A" visible at any other point "B"'.[55] While this might seem a straightforward, linear path, George Méliès explored a potential detour in his celebrated 1908 short film *Long-Distance Wireless Photography*.[56] In the film, an older couple visits a 'telephotographer' (played by Méliès) hoping to have their portraits taken. While the massive televisual apparatus depicted in the film strikes other commentators as fanciful, it resembles several patented televisual systems. After the telephotographer switches the machine on, there are two experimental trials: transmitting one photograph of the Charites, who come to life; and another of a live model, whose copy flirts with the older man – and, by extension, the audience. With one image an animation and the other a double, the imagination of television speaks to two contrasting notions of 'liveness': *temporal simultaneity*, in the sense of 'live transmission'; and *spatial storage*, in that of 'living images'.[57] Despite the success of these initial trials, the experiment turns out differently with the wireless portrait of the older couple: the woman's face, presented in close-up, suddenly bursts out into contagious laughter; the man's face transforms into a grotesque monkey; and, upon discovering his alter ego, he destroys the machine in a fit of rage while simultaneously electrocuting himself. Against the popular image of scientific researchers as masterful figures in complete control of the outcome of experimental trials, *Long-Distance Wireless Photography* illustrates the potential of any laboratory experiment to spiral out of control.

In subsequent years a dramatic conflict between 'genius' inventors of televisual devices and a society with its own machinations continued to provide the plot device of short films including *Amour et science* (Love and science, 1912), *Il raggio meraviglioso* (The wonderful rays, 1913), and *Denn die Elemente hassen* (For the elements hate, 1913). The imaginary uses of television are particularly evident in *Die Welt ohne Maske* (The world without a mask, 1934), as competing inventors attempt to create the optimal TV apparatus for an international competition. As emphasised in the film, television is not only an entertainment medium but also a surveillance apparatus, as wireless signals penetrate walls, pass through rooms, and appear to give one access to someone else's home or their internal thoughts. If traditional theories of knowledge reduce the experiment to a matter of 'prediction' and 'testing', these films resonate with recent work in historical epistemology that challenges the tyranny of the subject and experimenters' presumed mastery over their experiments. As Hans-Jörg Rheinberger argues, 'the future is in the experiment, and experimenting is about handling and engaging'.[58] Testing out the limits of imagination, these and other vernacular experiments with wireless connectivity explored the borders of dream and reality, corporality and incorporeality, as well as the living and the dead.

In his 1898 short story 'The Resurrection Co.', Walther Rathenau radicalised the media topos of radiophonic communication as a form of speaking with the dead.[59] Designed and operated by Elihu Hannibal I.T. Gravemaker, 'the burial facilities in the city of Necropolis, Dakota are the best in the United States'. Equipped with an automated grave-digging apparatus and a sort of jukebox containing the greatest hits of funeral orations,[60] the state-of-the-art graveyard also features a modern communications system:

> Each buried coffin was [. . .] linked via electric cable with the administration building. Telephones and electric bells [. . .] connected up to the lines and each *customer* could not only report to the administration instantaneously if the occasion arose [for example, being buried alive], but could also give the necessary orders to his doctor, his banker, and his family.[61]

In imagining this wired system, 'The Resurrection Co.' draws on the modernist discourse of underground telegraphy, as two wires buried at a distance from each other were mistakenly assumed to establish a stable 'wireless' connection through the earth. The problem facing the enterprise, in the absurdist conclusion to Rathenau's story, is that the dead make extensive use of the system, overtaxing its resources. One subscriber rings the main office to complain that no one has visited his gravesite; another calls the switchboard operator and requests to chat with another burial plot; a third asks to be reburied so that she will not have to spend eternity next to her loathsome husband. 'The Resurrection Co.' ultimately proves to be a flawed business venture because of a surplus of demand.

In the early days of radio, the uncanny voices of broadcasters were compared, like those of (wireless) telephony, to conversations with the dead, and this media topos materialised in cartoons about the 'wireless widow', depicted knitting while her zombie-like husband operates a nearby radio set.[62] As Albert Kümmel-Schnur observes, the radio's media topoi and mythological origin stories have long privileged two-way communications and the uncanniness of the disembodied voice. However, this emphasis overdetermines the medium's occult, spiritualistic, and uncanny dimensions at the expense of its 'shocking' potential and its ability – often attributed to but never realised in the cinema – to incite an actual mass panic.[63] Although the *fin-de-siècle* imagination of wireless connectivity reflected on a wide range of potential applications for wireless transmission, it was usually within the established context of domestic news and entertainment, centring bourgeois concerns.

In his 1882 vision of *The Twentieth Century*, Albert Robida presented one of the most influential speculative treatments of a precursor to television with the 'telephonoscope – the word says it all – one can both see and hear'.[64] Robida's telephonoscope was imagined to allow for transmitting both real-time or recorded theatre performances and two-way conversations and surveillance, and its portable version, the 'pocket telephonoscope', was intended for roaming reporters to transmit live news, but both imaginary media were still envisioned as wired devices.[65] In *The End of the World*, Camille Flammarion reconfigured Robida's telephonoscope into a multisensory device: 'not only could one hear or see at a distance: the brainpower of man had even managed to transmit by cerebral influences the sensation of touch as well as that of the olfactory nerve'.[66] Developing the implications of the theme in a 1910 short story, Guillaume Apollinaire imagined the implications of 'research in wired and wireless telegraphy, the transmission of photographs, colour photography and photography in relief, cinematography, the phonograph, and so on'.[67] This research enables the experimenter, a film director and false messiah named Baron D'Ormesan, to transmit himself simultaneously to multiple locations around the globe, resulting in his untimely demise. Just as Apollinaire's short story connected discourses of telepresence, messianism, and media hype to those of Zionism, other authors of short-form modernist fiction connected them to those of nationalism and imperialism.

Writing under the pen name Mynona (the German word for 'anonymous' spelled backwards), Salomo Friedlaender took the notion of media as extensions of the physical senses *ad absurdum* in his short 1913 literary grotesque, 'Idea for a Telehaptor'.[68] Seeing as wireless transmission of audiovisual data involves imperceptible radio waves, Mynona reasons, then it should be possible for haptic vibrations to propagate like radio, light, or any other electromagnetic wave.

Imitating the prophetic voice of engineers, Mynona imagines tele-media developing into a future so perfect that it spills over into the present:

> Now then, we have the telegraph, the telephone, the television is as good as done and ready-to-go, and all that is left to wait for is tele-haptics, the telehaptor, the teletoucher. What use is the entire [oeuvre of H. G.] Wells, if he shrinks back from this idea? But the matter is much more miserable than one might suspect: we are *lost* if we do not learn how to telehapt. As long as our sense of touch is frozen as if in stone, and only its refinements, vision, smell, and hearing, are free to roam around in the world, we will remain pitiful prisoners. But there is no reason to weep! We need some words of encouragement. Some things are not found only because nobody ever has the idea to look for them. The thought of telehapting the sense of touch, once grasped, will have to be realised.[69]

Putting aside the questions of whether the telehaptor would be useful, desirable, or technically possible, Mynona proposes that the main reason nobody had invented it already is that nobody had grasped its conceptual implications.[70]

At several points in the text, this prophetic voice of the engineer, addressed to a universal future, is interrupted by a different, polemical voice, addressed to a cast of characters from Heinrich Zille's Berlin 'Milljöh' (milieux). As if in answer to the most frequently asked question in wireless communication (Where are you?), Mynona writes:

> I am not now in Bessarabia, I am here in the place where some people with a healthy digestive system always ask: 'What is the German's fatherland?' Take them . . .
>
> Yes, the cuckoo sometimes sings too prettily, Frau Werner – What I wanted to say just now: 'I am here! But I am not everywhere . . . apart from . . . apart from . . . apart from my little – touch?'[71]

Mynona not only transforms the locative question, 'Where are you?', into the temporal one, 'Where are you now?' By subverting the exotic locations usually provided in answer to these questions, he also critiques the heated nationalist discourse that existed on the eve of World War I, as is evident in his references to Bessarabia, Burma, and to Ernst Moritz Arndt's patriotic song, 'Of the German Fatherland'. Mynona thus makes a crucial point about the primal scene of wireless communication: 'When somebody asks me where I am, the implication is that he is really asking where I can be felt. For I could just as well be seen, heard, smelled somewhere else.'[72] In other words, there is a deictic dimension to the question, 'Where are you?', since it implies the respondent being 'Not here' – or, to put it in

Mynona's terms, 'Not where you could touch, taste, smell, or sense me.'[73] Among all the senses, 'this heavy and clumsy touch' remains the most resistant to technological instrumentalisation. 'We must pry it out, thaw it out, pull it through wires, and finally send it wirelessly [*drahtlose*, *sic*] into every distance. How easy!'[74]

A century later, in the wake of Smell-o-Vision, AromaRama, and Odorama, McKenzie Wark would revisit the less spectacular senses of 'telesthesia' in a postcolonial essay titled 'Telegram from Nowhere', addressing philosophical telegrams to 'Professor Foucault', 'Doctor Heidegger', and 'Guy Debord'. For Wark, 'telesthesia, or "perception at a distance"' refers more broadly than for Mynona to the 'tools that, for years now, make it possible to create reason without enclosure, to cause things to move and to monitor their movement. Telesthesia enables the monitoring of things moving even while they are moving.'[75] Reflecting on the implicit deixis in the discourse of telesthesia, which locates the Global North 'here' and the Global South 'there', the Australia-born media theorist upturns its implied antipodes:

> . . . Hello? Hello? Is anyone there? I'm calling here from there. I'm calling night from day. I'm calling summer from winter. I'm calling from the other side of the world. Here is how things look from here (there), looking at there (here). And of course, there is something that connects us, connects an us, in between.[76]

Wark's call reverses the usual trajectory of the communicative vector and challenges the dominant narrative of modernity opening out into globalisation, which recodes the expansion of colonial communications networks throughout the long nineteenth century.[77] From this transversal perspective, 'globalization is nothing new [. . .] All that has changed is the speed of globalization, but even that is an old story.'[78]

While the origin stories and primal scenes of wireless transmission examined in this study have come from the Global North, similar stories circulated in the Global South, and further studies will need to examine the precise differences among these inflections across vernacular modernism. At the same time, it must be underscored that different nations explored different visions of wireless futures, as evident in two seminal cases of speculative fiction that can only be briefly mentioned here. In 'The Story of the Missing One', scientist and wireless pioneer Jagadish Chandra Bose, also the president of the Academy of Bengali Literature, presented a speculative story about a cyclone that is predicted by meteorologists to destroy Calcutta but that never materialises. The reason for its disappearance, as explained in the second half of the story, is that a balding man in the middle of the cyclone dumps a miracle hair-growth product overboard, preventing the disaster. After the 1896 version won a competition organised by an Indian hair oil company, whose stipulation was that entries needed to reference the company's flagship miracle hair-growth product, Bose republished the story in 1921 under the title '*Palatak Toofan*' ('Runaway Cyclone'), and it remains remarkable for its critiques of the failures of Western approaches to science and prediction. In 'New Tales of Mr. Braggadacio', Xu Nianci, the distinguished translator regarded as the first author of Chinese science fiction, described a company that would extract and commodify brain electricity, drawing on European discourses of animal magnetism and critiquing Western approaches to science.[79] Inspired by Iwaya Sazanami's *Mr. Absurdity*, itself an adaptation of *The Wonderful Tales of Baron Münchhausen*, Xu's speculative fiction uses the trope of wireless energy transfer to present a rare Marxist critique of political economy in the late Qing dynasty. Further comparative studies are needed to correct such gaps and omissions.

The Wireless Century

Based on the principles of extension and expansion articulated in origin stories and primal scenes about Western Europe, the 'wireless age' was taken in German modernity to be synonymous with the European age, and the wireless world with the continental wired world. While German-language authors occasionally imagined radically different wireless futures, most speculations considered applications, extensions, and implications of current developments. In the popular American press, which supplied Germany with some of its most indelible images of the future, the coming century was depicted as one of scientific and technological progress, especially in physics, chemistry, and engineering. This was evident in the contributions to *The World in 100 Years*, a collection of 22 essays edited in 1909–10 by Arthur Brehmer and illustrated by Ernst Lübbert in a lavish colourised edition.[80] Credited as the earliest anthology of futuristic writing in the German language, *The World in 100 Years* contained translations of journalistic essays, original SF stories, and contributions combining journalism with speculative fiction in complex forms. Composed by such leading authorities as Hermann Bahr, Hudson Maxim, Karl Peters, and Bertha von Suttner, the contributions covered topics including art, literature, theatre, music, sport, medicine, pedagogy, women's rights, social mores, and international relations. When imagining means of solving perceived problems in these areas, several contributors conflated the radio-based medium with radioactivity, which was taken to provide a cure-all, much like electricity, for society's ailments. Contributors' visions of the wireless age included now uncanny applications, from virtual shopping and wireless energy transfer, through receiving opera broadcasts and contacting distant family members, to military command, death rays, and weather control. However, none of the imagined applications came close to national radio broadcasting, understood as distributing education and culture to domestic audiences.[81]

Complementing these discursive fantasies, Lübbert's fantastical illustrations rounded out the volume's imagination of wireless futures, as evident in an image made to accompany Robert Sloss's essay on 'The Wireless Century' (Fig. 3.3). Framed by bolts and waves rendered in the *fin-de-siècle* idiom for electricity and magnetism,[82] Lübbert's allegory of wireless telephony centres on a globe, itself centred on Germany, as

Figure 3.3 Titled 'Wireless Telephony: An Allegory', Ernst Lübbert's engraving depicts four Sirens encircling the globe and a Janus-faced figure that evokes spark-based transmission, suggesting the perceived promises and perils of global connectivity. Source: Sloss, 'Das drahtlose Jahrhundert', 41.

seen from outer space. In allusion to the Sirens, four feminine figures with their faces contorted in screams join hands, as if in an ecstatic round dance, to represent the wireless channel connecting the world. At the bottom of the image, Lübbert depicts a Janus-like figure, one of modernity's central figures for simultaneously looking backwards and forwards, which here further evokes omnidirectional broadcasting. With one hand raised as if calling to someone in the distance, the figure emits lightning bolts out of its three mouths, echoed by the Siren-like figures – a reminder of the binary gendering of media around 1900. Lübbert's allegorical engraving not only emphasises the perceived danger of an alluring new medium that seems to transcend both space and time. Like the text it illustrates, the image spatialises the time-based mode of wireless transmission and transforms the temporal construct of the wireless age into a spatial construct of a wireless world.

Interweaving science and fiction, Sloss's 'Wireless Century' crystallised the bourgeois imagination of technological change then circulating in the popular press.[83] Widely quoted for its perceived anticipation of 21st-century smartphones and ubiquitous connectivity,[84] it also exemplified the way journalistic speculations about wireless futures fed off each other and circulated out of control. Employing a combinatorial composition method, Sloss connected journalistic accounts of wireless technology to pastiches of science fiction adventure stories. In the original English-language version, the dramatic opening narrative describes an impending war between Great Britain and Russia over the occupation of Tibet, and follows one of the former's wireless-powered scout planes 'through a driving snowstorm [. . .] hurling through space, pulsating rhythmically like some huge bird of mythology'.[85] After making an emergency landing to await further orders from the British office in Bombay, the crew transmit a report that is then 'reproduced in exact *facsimile* in the distant wireless headquarters'.[86] To pass the time awaiting further orders, they attach a 'megaphone' to a 'radiophone', which plays both 'opera' and 'music halls', including '[Nellie] Melba singing *Aida* in Covent Garden'.[87] In the German-language version, the opening narrative follows the similar voyage of the 'Albatross' (*Sturmvogel*), an airship whose name deforms the original name '*HMS Roc*' and a related reference to 'some huge bird of mythology'.[88] Forced to make an emergency landing after the wireless power drive fails near the South Pole, the ship's captain passes the time with a wireless telephone call not to another military station, but to his wife; and at the end of the short narrative, they listen to a New York Opera broadcast of 'The Hero of the Air' by 'Redfer [?], the Wagner of our times'.[89]

The English and German versions both follow their dramatic narratives, like Crookes, Ayrton, and Mynona, with a laconic statement assuring readers that everything imagined in these stories has already been achieved by engineers: 'They are facts that are only waiting to be introduced into our practical life, just as the telegraph and telephone and phonograph have been.'[90] But whereas the original English-language story reinforced the distinction between science fiction and technological facts with a clear printer's break, the expanded German-language translation lets the fictional mode continuously erupt through journalistic descriptions of technological advancements, generating one imaginative scene after the next: 'Here, for example, is a scene that will play out every day in a hundred years or less', Sloss predicts, referring to the wireless circulation of a wanted profile that leads to the apprehension of a fleeing suspect.[91] Another 'scene: a jail, heaven knows where. Time: one hour before the execution of someone innocently condemned'; but the order is postponed through the wireless transmission of the 'Emperor's signature'.[92] 'Scene: An elegant boudoir on 5th Avenue in New York. A bride, the daughter of a multimillionaire, is completely beside herself and drowning in tears', having ruined her bridal gown. After being contacted 'teleautophonically', the designer, Jeanne Paquin, instantly delivers a replacement dress via 'wireless air motor'.[93] Centred on memorable incidents in which wireless technology is the *deus ex machina*, such dramatic scenes encouraged readers to envision concrete use cases for unproven technologies.

When Sloss narrativised the dramatic impacts of wireless transmission on future societies, he was again repackaging media topoi about the mode's implications for commerce, warfare, and social relations. While the English-language version makes no predictions about gender or sexuality, the German-language version predicts that 'the influence of wireless telegraphy will also be extraordinary for marriage and love. Lovers and married couples will never be separated from each other, even when they are hundreds and thousands of miles away.'[94] Such predictions could have been derived from Carl Grunert's 1904 short speculative story 'Die Fernehe' (Distant marriage), which imagines a 23rd-century society in which lovers are connected only by communications devices.[95] With one finger on the pulse of the news, the protagonist, a young telegraphist named Fritz Oldenburger, operates a Hughes apparatus and a 'double-keyed syphon recorder', receiving diplomatic telegrams about an escalating conflict between Venezuela and the German Empire.[96] Turning from military to civilian dispatches, Oldenburger continues to plan for his wedding but freezes upon reading the telegraphic announcement of a new law governing 'distant marriage' (*Fern-Ehe*). It stipulates that partners are no longer allowed to live in the same place and can only belong to each other 'spiritually' (*geistig*).[97] Oldenburger's friend and colleague Fritz Mohwecke consoles him, spelling out the apparent advantages of distant marriage over the traditional institution. Looking back on the previous centuries, they summarise epoch-making changes leading to the current legislation, including the emancipation of women, the decimation of the population by disease, and women withholding kisses for sanitary reasons.[98] Because a new synthetically created human being, *homo chemiae*, remakes citizens in the state's interest, marriage is no longer an institution based on inheritance and property.[99] Updating Romantic discourses of sympathy and animal magnetism, romantic partners communicate telepathically using the '*Fernfühler*', a hygienic telemedium said to have been invented by 'Paulmüller' (a reference to Palmström?); an upgraded model even stores these telepathic communications for future playback.[100] While distant marriage might appear to realise the dream of 'an ideal, purely spiritual community of the sexes', it turns out to be a nightmare – and Grunert underscores this moralising conclusion through the heavy-handed use of *A Christmas Carol* for the closing narrative frame.[101]

Considering other institutional and commercial applications of wireless transmission, Sloss's 'Wireless Century' imagined a precursor to virtual shopping and wireless delivery services.[102] In 'Das Warenhaus der Zukunft' (The department store of the future), Friedrich Thieme also entertained the possibility that, in the future, it would be possible to buy education and experience, just as one might buy food or clothing.[103] Written in 1908 and uncannily set in 1940, Thieme's short speculative fiction follows a Black character named Malo Basso, described with racial epithets and said to be from 'Kilemba in Urua', which was not necessarily a 'fictive homeland', as Hans Frey asserts, but more likely a historical term for the Luba Empire in central Africa.[104] Inverting European expectations about the *Bildungsroman* and the sub-genre of *Erfinderroman* while also reinforcing stereotypes about primitive accumulation, Thieme presents Basso as the potential heir to an African gold mine whose father decides that, before he can inherit the family business, he must first complete a finishing school offered by the 'Universal World Department Store' in Berlin.[105] Although the reception speaks every language – apart from Basso's dialect – they eventually communicate using a 'language machine' (*Sprachautomat*) and offer a package deal to transform Basso, within ten days and for a discounted cost of 10,000 marks, into a 'true [read: white European] gentleman'. The racist aspects of the story, as SF scholar Hans Frey notes, can be seen not only in the imagination of a Black man expressing the secret desire to become white. Using actual technologies then marketed as bleaching products, the 'medical department' (*medizinische Abteilung*) irradiates

Basso's skin to the point that its pigmentation is no longer black, and yet not entirely white, but that of a 'brown-coffee-colored Spaniard' (*kaffeebrauner Spanier*). After this drastic cure, Basso begins a hygienic regiment of bathing, getting a haircut, and dressing elegantly, as well as exercising his intellect at a sort of hypo-school, seeing as one of the department store's employees had determined, according to eugenic procedures, that 'his brain [is] that of a second-rate semi-talented person' (*sein Gehirn das eines Halbtalents zweiter Ordnung*).[106] Since the only things the 'true gentleman' now lacks are property and a wife, the department store happily supplies him, for 500,000 marks, with the 'loveliest blonde from a noble family, highly educated, witty, a gentle character but without any wealth'.[107] For Frey, the story uncannily presages the Internet as a total department store, demonstrating the implications of perfecting the capitalistic valuation process down to every detail: the consolidation and replacement of medical expertise, the property market, and activities traditionally administered by the Church or the state, such as getting an education or getting married. In my analysis, it also speaks to the legacies of what Cedric J. Robinson calls 'racial capitalism', describing the exploitative processes involved in extracting socio-economic value from people of colour.[108]

In terms of warfare, wireless was predicted to lead occasionally to world peace but more often to more efficient forms of military command and control. In Sloss's 'Wireless Century', characterised by ubiquitous commerce and communication,

> there will be no more commands that are misunderstood, and the commander will not have to wait for a report about the course of a battle. He will have an overview of the whole battlefield [. . .] His general's gaze alone will make the decision, since whether he is in his room or in his barracks, he will see everything, the movements of his armies, as well as those of the crowd of enemies.[109]

An omnipotent and omniscient figure, the wireless commander was imagined influencing distant events through gestures of remote control. Alfred Count von Schlieffen, chief of the Imperial German General Staff, and, in Kittler's words, 'creator of the new weapon called signal corps', predicted that warfare would be characterised by the retreat of military commanders to invisible surveillance positions:

> The Feldherr finds himself further back in a house with a spacious office, where telegraphs, telephones and signals apparatus are to hand [. . .] From there, he telephones stirring words. There, he receives reports from the army and the corps commanders, from the

observation balloons and from the dirigibles that observe the movement of the enemy along the whole line and that look behind the enemy's positions.[110]

This dream of increasing security while eliminating risk for those in command caused fantasies of remote control to remain popular throughout the 1920s, developing in tandem with early fantasies of television.[111] While media and cultural studies have long analysed resonances with entertainment 'command centres', it is important to account for those receiving such commands. One speculative illustration accompanying a military history of WWI imagines the 'future wireless operator' (Fig. 3.4) as a cavalry unit carrying a frame antenna, loudspeaker, and other wireless equipment; the operator turns a crank to self-power the cybernetic system.

The imaginary of televisual command and control also gave rise to visions of the remote-control police officer, a popular trope in the Weimar Republic thanks to translations and 'deformances' of an American journal article that was part science fiction, part science fact. Hugo Gernsback's 'Radio Police Automaton' imagined combining 'means available today' from the field of 'telemechanics': a loudspeaker would issue commands, relayed from the human operator

Figure 3.4 Drawing of the 'future wireless operator' (*Zukunftsfunker*) from a history of the German signal corps composed by their military commander during World War I. Source: Thiele, *Geschichte der Nachrichten-Truppe* (1925), 231.

driving in a car behind it, to the terrified masses; a 'telegraphone', or magnetic tape recorder, would provide instructions; and the automaton would itself be light-activated. The German reception of Gernsback's radio police automaton focused less on its feasibility than on its mannered anthropomorphism: 'Why put the machine on two legs, when it could roll much more safely on three wheels or on three little tanks?' one commentator reflected. 'We could build machines that would combine cold, infallible exactness with human rhythms and thus perform the services for which the radio policeman is intended'.[112] Considering the close associations between wirelessing and policing, it is perhaps no coincidence that the '2-way radio wristwatch', often taken to represent a precursor to the 'smartwatch', was popularised in comics by an American detective named Dick Tracy.

To what extent did any of these visions of the coming 'wireless age', whether of surveillance, commerce, or entertainment, predict our current situation? Wolfgang König draws a useful distinction between the difficulty of predicting the immediate and proximate effects of a new medium: 'Primary effects arise directly and predominantly from the new technology. Secondary effects have other causes and are only indirectly related to the new technology.'[113] Many late nineteenth-century observers predicted the primary political and economic effects of the transoceanic cable, albeit with 'divergent expectations'.[114] However, they failed to foresee its secondary effects, such as the way the telegraph would give greater significance to public opinion and thus make politics into a business based on media presence and forecasting, because such secondary effects were bound up with complex social processes beyond the immediate sphere of technology. In the case of wireless, many observers around 1900 predicted the primary effects of ubiquitous connectivity, on-demand access, and instant gratification. However, they remained oblivious to secondary effects that might now seem self-evident, such as the ubiquity of advertising, the monetisation of surveillance technologies, and the racialisation of media users.

Pocket Wireless

As a limit case of imaginary media, 'pocket wireless' – to use the period's terminology for miniature gadgets that seem like precursors to pagers and smartphones – warrants further analysis. Because of its complex relation to futurity, Grant Wythoff calls pocket wireless a 'speculative apparatus'.[115] If the study of imaginary media suggests a shift from the utilitarian to the fantastic, in Wythoff's analysis, 'gadgetry such as pocket wireless [. . .] seems to evoke a completely different set of questions about the liminality of the real and the imaginary, the material and the immaterial. What is at stake here is the feedback between technical interaction and speculation, between science and fiction.'[116] Whereas imaginary media, by definition, never materialise, 'pocket wireless succeeded in "materially popularizing" the new technology of wireless, not only as a *functional device* [. . .] but as a *fictional device* in novels and cinema'.[117] Even as pocket wireless started to materialise in portable telegraphic and telephonic devices, the actual state of technology is difficult to verify, ranging from vapourware to working prototypes.

Blurring the borders between science and fiction, a sub-section of Sloss's 'Wireless Century' on the 'telephone in the waistcoat pocket' (*Telephon in der Westentasche*) cited Ayrton's prediction and extended it from speaking and seeing at a distance to being spoken to and seen by miniature wireless receivers, 'affixed to one's hat or somewhere else', almost like pagers.[118] Using a 'voice indicator' (*Stimmzeiger*) that renders switchboard operators redundant, 'the man being called will instantly be able to hear his headset vibrating or giving a signal, and will be able to decide whether he wants to answer or break off the connection'. Anticipating the objection that operators would then need to carry around an additional wireless transmitter, seeing as the two remained separate devices, the author imagined '"transmission stations" on every ship, every airship, and every train [. . .] in any public place or at home'. Citing the Budapest wireless newspaper system, Sloss extrapolated the implications for receiving news and entertainment:

> On the way to and from work, you will no longer need to strain your eyes with newspapers, since you'll be in touch with a 'spoken newspaper' in the subway, or the railway, or on the bus, or whenever you're travelling just then, and even if you're walking on the street, you'll find out about all the events of the day, all the political events and all the markets that you want [. . .] or every theatre, every church, every lecture and concert hall [. . .] you'll be able to participate in performances, sermons, and symphonies.[119]

As much as it might seem to anticipate the Internet, this wireless future remains rooted in the European modernist imagination, as the author imagines Telharmoniums, or early electrical organs, connecting people to Paris, Vienna, London, and Berlin, as well as their hometowns.

Because potential operators would not necessarily have been familiar with telegraphic code, pocket wireless remained a telephonic and televisual fantasy. In 1907 Ernst Walter Ruhmer, a German physicist who found successful applications for his groundbreaking research on selenium in radiotelephony, experimental television, and optical sound-film recording, took stock of future developments by contrasting multiple predictions about the future of wireless telephony:

> While it is only a few months ago that the great inventor Edison rightly gave to the question, 'What is the outlook for wireless telephony?' the answer, 'It does not exist', we are already in the position to transmit speech wirelessly over several kilometres.[120]

As further evidence for realising the dream of Ayrton's prediction, Ruhmer referred to subsequent 'prophecies' from Lee de Forest and Nikola Tesla, quoting the latter from the *English Mechanic*: 'With proper apparatus telephonic communication will be carried on with ease and precision to the greatest terrestrial distances, and very soon it will be possible to speak across an ocean as clearly as across a table.'[121] Before the eventual failure of his Wardenclyffe Tower project – a prototype of wireless power distribution backed by J. Pierpont Morgan and other prominent investors – Tesla published many promotional pamphlets with outrageous claims about his proposed World (Wireless) System. In retrospect, Tesla's utopian vision highlights the function of speculation in obtaining investment capital for infrastructural megaprojects in untested markets.[122]

While Ayrton's and Crookes's predictions established the horizon of expectation for pocket wireless in the United States and the United Kingdom, they had a similar impact in German-speaking countries where expectations were filtered further through critical views of *Amerika*. 'The telephone in the waistcoat pocket is at once a beautiful and a terrible idea', wrote Artur Fürst, reflecting on the trade-off involved in enabling a ship's passengers to transmit private telegrams at the expense of being always reachable at sea.[123] Quoting Ayrton's prediction, one contributor to the *Deutsche Uhrmacher-Zeitung* expressed disappointment and scepticism about its feasibility:

> This enthusiastic dream of the future [*Zukunftsmusik*], which Prof. Ayrton started playing many years ago during the cradle of wireless telegraphy [*Funkentelegraphie*], has still not been realised to this day and it probably can never be realised in the literal sense of the imaginative depiction. Nevertheless, one is at least vividly reminded of this fantasy when one reviews the latest attempts and successes at creating a radiotelegraphic pocket watch.[124]

In particular, the author cited a pocket wireless device, weighing only 400g, that was developed in France for receiving time signals from the Eiffel Tower and was known as the Ondaphone.

Beyond timekeeping, the desired hand-held, pocket wireless device was associated with surveillance and police work, suggesting apparent precursors to dragnets, all-points-bulletins, and real-time coordination of the masses. In Erich Kästner's lyric formula, 'The net they catch thieves with today / is woven out of wire and called / the telephone network'.[125] One of the earliest filmic representations of wireless technology was appropriately called *Caught by Wireless* (1908), and the culprit in a highly publicised murder case in 1910 was apprehended after a wireless profile outpaced the ship on which he had taken flight across the Atlantic. In the detective film *Das Geheimnis der Telefunken* (The Secret of Telefunken, 1914), the director of a wireless telegraph station sets off in search of his daughter, who has mysteriously vanished, and locates her by decoding an incomprehensible wireless telegram.

While some observers reflected that wired telephony already made it impossible to avoid contact, others concluded that just as wireless telegraphy would make it possible to catch criminals, wireless telephony would make it possible to 'catch' anyone for a phone conversation.[126] In a satirical 1910 essay on the 'Pocket Telephone', Thomas Grimm imagined a 'Viennese monologue from the year 1925' characterised by constant interruptions and crossed wires. When the narrator decides to take a day trip alone, his wife commands him to take along an antenna, so that – in a twisted version of Ayrton's prediction –'whether you walk or stand or sit, whether on the train or in the clean Gumpoldskirchen Wirtshaus, I can control you a little'.[127] On the tram, the pocket telephone keeps buzzing with calls from home and the tax office, two signals that get crossed when his wife, who had been eavesdropping the entire time, jealously reproaches him for making a '*Termin*' (date/appointment). Loaded with *Wiener Schmäh*, Grimm's misogynistic story concludes with the narrator's assertion that he only became a 'free man' after being 'freed from' the modern invention.[128] In a 1922 essay 'On the Wonders and Blunders of Technology', German cultural critic Alexander Moszkowski imagined resisting ubiquitous wireless connectivity, which he worried would make it impossible to have an authentic experience of being alone, in similarly gendered terms: 'Technology, you sorceress [. . .] you won't catch me yet. Everybody may call wirelessly, but I won't listen wirelessly, since I've decided never to purchase this pocket ghost.'[129] Nevertheless, Moszkowski admits, 'I'm enmeshed in the vicious cycle, one person can't fight everyone, and so I, too, will fall into the wireless trap; into the workable foldable antenna together with overworked nerves. And my first wireless phone call will be: *bene "vixit, qui bene latuit"*', the maxim attributed to Ovid, Epicurus, Plutarch, and Horace ('he lives happily who lives in hiding').[130] In a 1922 essay on the 'Radiophone', by contrast, Joseph Roth observed that the very possibility of eavesdropping makes everyone 'modest' by obliterating the private sphere: 'There are no more secrets [. . .] no more secret conferences, no whispered consultations, no "seal of silence". The wireless telephone breaks it all open. Discretion has become loud, silence speaks, stillness cries.'[131]

In Huhtamo's analysis, the pocket telephone was also a crucial surveillance technology and 'its adoption by police departments was related with other developments such as the installation of street lighting in cities to eliminate dark spots where crimes could occur'.[132] While Huhtamo believes several US magazine reports about a pocket telephone network operating in Berlin around 1910, the ontological status of these devices was just as complex and convoluted as in other cases of pocket wireless. For instance, the Chicago-based magazine *Telephony* claimed that the German police, unlike its American counterpart, already 'carried [wireless telephones] in a pocket without inconvenience, or in a lady's hand bag', supporting this claim with a doctored photograph of a woman detective 'calling the patrol wagon'.[133] However, such reports referred to detachable telephone earpieces, described misleadingly as 'pocket wireless'. In one of the more reliable reports, Alfred Gradenwitz specified the details of the early surveillance network, designed for 'assisting the work of patrolling policemen by some means enabling them to communicate with headquarters from any point of their district'.[134] As a wired system, each emergency call box was 'connected together and with the nearest police station by cables protected against injury by iron pipes [. . .] In those suburban districts which have as yet no cables, overhead conductors are used, lead cables protected by iron pipes serving for connection with the contact boxes.'[135] Patrolling officers would connect their detachable telephone to the nearest call box, with multiple wired devices combining into a pseudo-wireless system.

At the heart of this dialectic of alienation and empowerment through pocket wireless was the equation of being modern with consumerism and the early adoption of unproven technology for the sake of its novelty alone.[136] A pair of satirical images drawn by Karl Arnold and published in *Simplicissimus* in 1926 contrasted a scene captioned, 'Berlin: Wireless Telephony', where a businessman on the street uses a pocket wireless device to coordinate a meeting, with 'Munich: Technological Progress', where a brewery introduces an automated 'conveyor

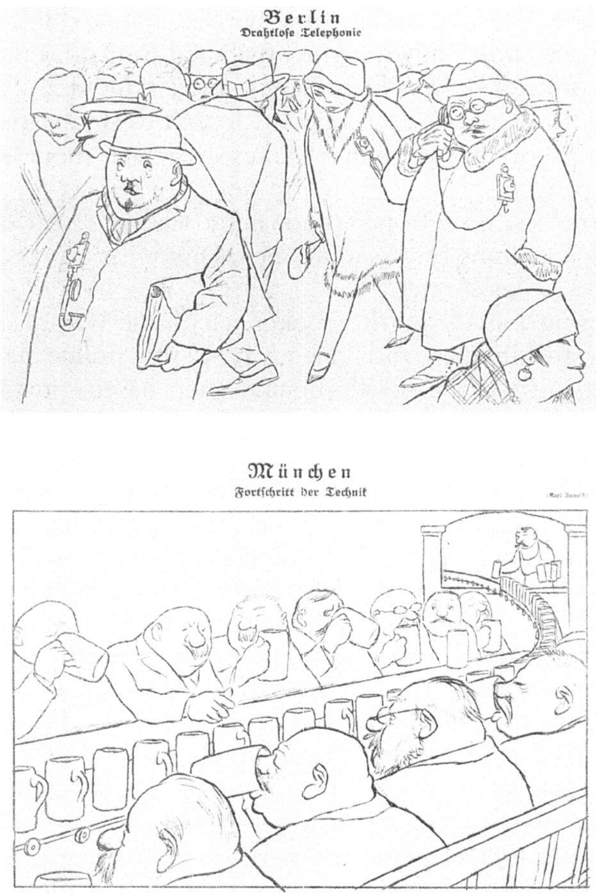

Figure 3.5a–b Satirical drawings of 'wireless telephony'. Drawn by Karl Arnold, the diptych contrasts urban business technology in Berlin (top) with an automated beer conveyor belt in Munich (bottom). Source: *Simplicissimus* 31 (1926).

belt' to deliver '10L of beer per hour', suggesting parallels between the two forms of consumption (Fig. 3.5). In the mid-1920s two of the most influential predictions about pocket wireless came from two former radiotelegraph operators turned broadcast executives, David Sarnoff and Hans Bredow, both of whom compared the imaginary medium to the pocket watch. Although they might sound like multi-function precursors to the smartwatch, the imaginary gadgets remained bound up with their own contested rollout of radio infrastructure, as is evident in Bredow's insistence that 'just like pocket watches, the transmitter and the receiver have to become people's constant companions'.[137]

Rather than a prescient statement about perpetual contact, ubiquitous connectivity, or a future generation of smartphone owners, Bredow's remark about constant companionship is better understood as part of the modernist discourse of consumption. In a cynical reading, his vision for mass ownership of wireless radio receivers – encapsulated by the slogan, *Rundfunk für alle* ('radio for all') – could be reduced to a shallow consumer appeal about the eager consumption of new gadgets. Have we arrived in this future?

Bredow is widely credited with coining the official term *Rundfunk* (radio), even if some of his claims do not hold up to scrutiny. As is less well known, he reportedly coined the term on 16 November 1919, four years before the inaugural national broadcast, during the same experimental lecture in which he coined the phrase *Rundfunk für alle* ('radio for all').[138] As the rationale for the lecture, delivered to representatives of science, industry, government, and the press assembled at the Urania-Haus in Berlin, Bredow disingenuously claimed that the 'significance of ether waves for popular applications was completely unknown before then'.[139] After outlining maritime applications for wireless transmission in the first part of the lecture, Bredow presented 'future possibilities of wireless', including the announcement that 'before long everyone will be able to listen to all kinds of performances in their homes via wireless'.[140] While Bredow strove to present an imaginative vision of this programme, he later recalled that 'it was only with difficulty that I was able to finish this part of the lecture, because I felt that I had increasingly lost contact with the audience, which had previously been very interested, and apparently I was not being taken very seriously'.[141] In retrospect, Bredow described the event as a failure: his predictions met with incredulity; his demo programme was too quiet to fill the small auditorium; and after a technician increased the amplification, the intended sounds were drowned out in noise. In attendance, however, were the Urania director and scientific outreach writer Artur Fürst, and science fiction author and technology reporter Hans Dominik. The next day, Dominik published a favourable account of Bredow's event in the *Berliner Lokalanzeiger*, omitting any technical difficulties.

> Although the lecturer remained strictly on the ground of objectivity, he was occasionally able to sketch future perspectives of Jules Verne's audacity, for example, the future political orator speaking into the wireless apparatus in one place and simultaneously heard by a million people in a thousand different halls all over Germany.[142]

Whose future was this?

Speculative Infrastructure

If pocket wireless was a 'speculative apparatus', as Wythoff argues, then it depended on an entire speculative infrastructure, by which I mean not only predicted communication networks but also the social, cultural, and political connections that enabled such speculations to circulate in the first place. While previous studies of the wireless imagination have made productive use of vernacular sources, they have tended to overlook the elite networks connecting scientists, publicists, and industrialists responsible for the so-called popular press. That many 'popular' predictions about a future wireless age analysed in this chapter were made by those with insider knowledge of nascent wireless companies connects the future-sense of speculation to that of capital investments. Early wireless companies received huge amounts of start-up capital: in 1897 Marconi's Wireless received 100,000 pounds in one-pound shares; in 1910 Emperor Wilhelm II provided 1,000,000 gold marks as capital for wireless stations at Eilvese and Tuckerton, used to form the company HOMAGES (Hochfrequenz-Maschinen GmbH); by comparison, the BBC received 10,000 pounds in 1922, still a hefty sum. It is perhaps no coincidence that the very phrase, 'the wireless age', was also the title of one of the earliest wireless trade magazines, a monthly journal (for which Sarnoff served as the contracts manager) published from 1913 to 1925 by the American arm of the Marconi Publishing Corporation. To complement 'strictly educational articles', *The Wireless Age* promised readers 'good fiction, well-illustrated, and narratives seething with human interest', as well as 'features of commercial wireless that are of absorbing interest to holders of wireless securities'.[143] Anticipating the objection that the company-sponsored journal was 'recording only the achievement of the Marconi system to the exclusion of all others', the editor appealed bluntly to its monopoly: 'there is only one commercial wireless company in the United States conducting a regular message traffic every day in the year [. . .] Marconi and wireless are synonymous words, and Marconi development is pre-eminent in wireless affairs.'[144] In an issue published the following month, the editor reiterated, 'Some may term us visionary. Wait and see. The magazine is here, and the period it antedates – *The Wireless Age* – is close behind.'[145]

Although I am not aware of any German-language journals that claimed such direct ownership of the wireless age, it is important to recognise that many visions of wireless futures in Imperial Germany and the Weimar Republic were presented by authorities first in the radiotelegraph and then in the radio industry. After working as a radiotelegraphist, Bredow's career took off as the executive director of the Telefunken Company, where media-savvy wireless pioneers mobilised the power of prediction for both publicity and counter-publicity. Just as the most successful visions of the wireless age were presented by Fürst, Dominik, and other technology reporters associated with the company, the predictions they routinely cited came from its official spokespeople, including Bredow, Slaby, Arco, and Carl Schapira.[146] The next chapter will continue to examine the problematics of such self-fulfilling predictions by focusing on one realist historical novel, a *roman à clef* about the Telefunken Company.

Based on previous scholarship on imaginary media, the expected conclusion for this chapter might have been that the real state of wireless technology always fails to live up to its ideals, or that the imagination always fails to materialise or exhibit real-world effects. Complicating such reductive binaries, however, the real state of wireless technology turns out to be the most imaginary, as the imaginary turns out to be the most real. Even if everyone seemed to agree that they wanted wireless, few agreed on what they wanted it for, as imagined applications ranged from the police and the military, through meteorology and medicine, to illustrated magazines and the cinema.[147] Rather than envisioning a direct precursor to national broadcasting, the wireless futures examined in this chapter spoke more to the promises of liveness, synchronisation, and telepresence, contained not only in telegraphy and telephony but also in lesser-known applications, such as direction finding, time signals, and energy transfer. In this respect, radio broadcasting was neither the inevitable extension of wireless telegraphy nor the culmination of progress in telecommunications. Rather, its very unlikely emergence spoke more to what Bertolt Brecht famously called 'inventions that have not been asked for'.[148]

For a final reminder of the liminal status of wireless futures, one need only consider the following patents granted in the late nineteenth and early twentieth centuries: a procedure for deriving electricity from the interplanetary ether; a wired electrical power supply for mobile airships; a coffin equipped with electric lighting for seeing whether someone has been buried alive; a remote control for activating musical instruments wirelessly; and a plan for replacing telegraph wires, not with electromagnetic radiation, but with a relay system of equally spaced, free-floating air balloons that would have suspended live wires precariously across the ocean.[149] While some of these patents were *untimely* and others *conceptual* or *impossible*, they all depended on the same speculative infrastructure, which sought to contain the experimental spirit by managing the boundaries separating imagination from reality.

Notes

1. Barlog's drawing was published in Roellinghoff, 'Radio im Humor', 87.
2. Hartenau, 'Die Resurrection Co.'; cf. Kluitenberg, 'Connection Machines', 157–85; Mynona, 'Idee vom Ferntaster'; Mynona, 'Goethe spricht in den Phonographen'.
3. Trithemius, *Steganographia*; on Weber's telegraph, see Gethmann, *Die Übertragung der Stimme*.
4. Huhtamo, 'Pockets of Plenty', 26.
5. On the concept of *Erfindergeist*, see Asserate, *Deutsche Tugenden*; Dienel, *Der Optimismus der Ingenieure*.
6. Seydel, *'Made in Germany'*. On the slogan, see Umbach, 'Made in Germany'.
7. Seydel, *'Made in Germany'*, 109, 116, 121, 133.
8. Zielinski, 'Modelling Media for Ignatius Loyola'; cf. Kluitenberg, 'On the Archaeology of Imaginary Media', 56.
9. Zielinski, 'Modelling Media for Ignatius Loyola', 30.
10. Zielinski, 'Modelling Media for Ignatius Loyola', 30.
11. Zielinski, 'Modelling Media for Ignatius Loyola', 30.
12. Sroka, 'Die Fernseh-Zeitung'.
13. Flichy, *The Internet Imaginaire*, 2.
14. On the multiple meanings of 'origin' (*Ursprung*) and 'primal scene' (*Urszene*), see Almog et al., 'Ursprung/Urszene'.
15. Huhtamo, 'Dismantling the Fairy Engine'; Huhtamo, 'Pockets of Plenty'.
16. Huhtamo and Parikka, introduction to *Media Archaeology*, 14.
17. Huhtamo, 'Magic Spectacles and Portable Boxes', 28.
18. Huhtamo, 'Dismantling the Fairy Engine', 28.
19. Huhtamo, 'Magic Spectacles and Portable Boxes'.
20. Dammann, *Stimme aus dem Äther*.
21. See Marvin, *When Old Technologies Were New*, 35.
22. Roellinghoff, 'Radio im Humor', 80.
23. Latour, 'Trains of Thought', 178.
24. Latour, 'Trains of Thought', 178.
25. Zielinski, *Deep Time of the Media*; on kairology, see Peters, *The Marvelous Clouds*, 242; Peters et al., *Action at a Distance*, 45.
26. See Marvin, *When Old Technologies Were New*, 154–7; de Vries, 'Mobile Telephony'.
27. Ayrton, 'Sixty Years of Submarine Telegraphy'. See the brief mentions of Ayrton in Marvin, *When Old Technologies Were New*, 157; Connor, 'Atmospherics', 159; Buschauer, *Mobile Räume*, 286; for longer analysis, cf. Hong, *Wireless*, 9–13; Gethmann, *Die Übertragung der Stimme*, 18–19, 90; Wythoff, 'Pocket Wireless', 54–6.
28. Ayrton, 'Sixty Years of Submarine Telegraphy', 548.
29. Peters, *Speaking Into the Air*, 33–6; Krämer, *Medium, Messenger, Transmission*, 22 (emphasis in the original).
30. See Ferraris, *Where Are You?*, 2.

31. Ayrton, 'Sixty Years of Submarine Telegraphy', 548.
32. For the lecture announcement, see *Nature* 55, no. 1423 (4 February 1897): 320; for the summary, see *Nature* 55, no. 1426 (25 February 1897): 403–4.
33. On the phrase 'pocket telephone', see, for instance, Gibson, *Wireless Telegraphy*, 140.
34. Fahie, *History of Wireless Telegraphy*, viii.
35. Slaby, 'Die neuesten Fortschritte', in Slaby, *Die Funkentelegraphie*, 119.
36. Slaby, *Die Funkentelegraphie*, 119; Jentsch, *Telegraphie und Telephonie ohne Draht*, 'Vorwort', n.p.; Ruhmer, *Drahtlose Telephonie*, 142; Hausmann, *Scharfrichter der bürgerlichen Seele*, 176; Lux, 'Rundschau', 197–8; Lodemann, 'Drahtlose Telephonie', 345–7; Lampl., 'Der radiotelegrafische Empfangsapparat in der Westentasche', 185; Dominik, 'Stimmen im Äther', 324; Arnheim, *Radio*, 274.
37. Marconi, 'Wireless Telegraphic Communication', 221.
38. Clarke, *1984, Spring*, 12.
39. Chandra, *Bulletproof Wireless Security*, xii, qtd. in Wythoff, 'Pocket Wireless'.
40. De Vries, *Tantalisingly Close*, 13; cf. Fullerton and Olsson, *Allegories of Communication*.
41. Stäheli, 'Undoing Networks', 7.
42. See Ofak and Hilgers, *Rekursionen*.
43. Kittler, *Musik und Mathematik*, vol. 1, 245.
44. Ernst, *Gleichursprünglichkeit*.
45. Hong, 'Unfaithful Offspring?'
46. Balbi and Natale, 'The Double Birth of Wireless'.
47. Crookes, 'Some Possibilities of Electricity', 13504. This lecture is an updated and expanded version of Crookes's 'Electricity in Relation to Space' (1891). On the influence of Crookes's articles throughout Europe, see Aitken, *Syntony and Spark*, 114; Hong, *Wireless*, 10–12.
48. Crookes, 'Some Possibilities of Electricity', 13505.
49. Trithemius, *Steganographia*.
50. See Dammann, *Stimme aus dem Äther*.
51. See Bergmann and Zielinski, '"Sehende Maschinen"'.
52. Nipkow, Elektrisches Teleskop; cf. Riedel, *Fernsehen*, 14.
53. See Andriopoulos, 'Psychic Television'.
54. See Strauven, 'The Imagination of Wireless Distribution', 296.
55. Nipkow, Elektrisches Teleskop.
56. See Strauven, 'The Imagination of Wireless Distribution'.
57. See Uricchio, 'Storage, Simultaneity, and the Media Technologies of Modernity'; Kern, *Culture of Time and Space*.
58. Rheinberger, 'Forming and Being Informed', 203.
59. Hartenau, 'Die Resurrection Co.', 63–9; cf. Kaplan, 'Walter Rathenau's Media Technological Turn'.
60. Hartenau, 'Die Resurrection Co.', 63.
61. Hartenau, 'Die Resurrection Co.', 65–6.

62. See, for instance, the cartoon captioned 'die drahtlose Witwe' (the wireless widow) and reprinted from *The Sketch* in Roellinghoff, 'Radio im Humor', 81.
63. Kümmel, 'Innere Stimmen', 175–97.
64. Robida, *The Twentieth Century*, 52.
65. Robida, *The Twentieth Century*, 55, 201.
66. Qtd. in Strauven, 'The Observer's Dilemma', 159.
67. Apollinaire, 'The False Amphion'; cf. Kern, *Culture of Time and Space*, 74–5.
68. Mynona, 'Idee vom Ferntaster'. Originally published in the Expressionist journal *Der Sturm*, Friedlaender's story was reprinted in his *Rosa, die schöne Schutzmannsfrau* and later incorporated into *Bank der Spötter* and *Graue Magie*.
69. Mynona, 'Idee vom Ferntaster', 66 (italics in original).
70. See, for example, Loos, 'Der technische Impresario', which decried the sensational reports about a purported American invention, 'wireless electric smelling' (*das elektrische Riechen ohne Draht*), and its uncritical reception in Austrian journals.
71. Mynona, 'Idee vom Ferntaster', 66.
72. Mynona, 'Idee vom Ferntaster', 67.
73. Mynona, 'Idee vom Ferntaster', 67.
74. Mynona, 'Idee vom Ferntaster', 67.
75. Wark, 'Telegram from Nowhere', 32.
76. Wark, 'Telegram from Nowhere', 31 (ellipses in original).
77. Wark, 'Telegram from Nowhere', 31.
78. Wark, 'Telegram from Nowhere', 31.
79. Cf. Ma, *The Stone and the Wireless*, 181–206.
80. Brehmer, *Die Welt in hundert Jahren*. For historical context and biographical details, see Forster, 'Die Welt in 100 Jahren'.
81. Sloss, 'Das drahtlose Jahrhundert', 31–2.
82. On this *fin-de-siècle* visual idiom, see Asendorf, *Ströme und Strahlen*.
83. Sloss, 'Das drahtlose Jahrhundert', 27–48.
84. See my Introduction, note 8.
85. Sloss, 'Sight Magic and Sound Magic', 300; Lopez, 'The Wireless Future', 424.
86. Sloss, 'Sight Magic and Sound Magic', 301; Lopez, 'The Wireless Future', 426.
87. Sloss, 'Sight Magic and Sound Magic', 301; Lopez, 'The Wireless Future', 426.
88. Sloss, 'Das drahtlose Jahrhundert', 27–32.
89. Sloss, 'Das drahtlose Jahrhundert', 31–2.
90. Sloss, 'Das drahtlose Jahrhundert', 32.
91. Sloss, 'Das drahtlose Jahrhundert', 38.
92. Sloss, 'Das drahtlose Jahrhundert', 42.
93. Sloss, 'Das drahtlose Jahrhundert', 46–7.
94. Sloss, 'Das drahtlose Jahrhundert', 47.
95. Grunert, 'Die Fernehe'; cf. Innerhofer, *Deutsche Science Fiction*, 410–11.

96. Grunert, 'Die Fernehe', 17.
97. Grunert, 'Die Fernehe', 18.
98. Grunert, 'Die Fernehe', 20.
99. Grunert, 'Die Fernehe', 21.
100. Grunert, 'Die Fernehe', 21–2.
101. Grunert, 'Die Fernehe', 22–3.
102. Sloss, 'Das drahtlose Jahrhundert', 46–7.
103. Thieme, 'Das Warenhaus der Zukunft'. For analysis, cf. Innerhofer, *Deutsche Science Fiction*, 421–2; Ritter, *Anno Utopia*, 279–86; Frey, *Fortschritt und Fiasko*, 292; Flessner, 'Cyberspace im Kaiserreich'.
104. Thieme, 'Das Warenhaus der Zukunft', 72; Frey, *Fortschritt und Fiasko*, 292.
105. Thieme, 'Das Warenhaus der Zukunft'.
106. As Innerhofer observes, the scene was hardly a literary fantasy (*Deutsche Science Fiction* 421 n. 59).
107. Thieme, 'Das Warenhaus der Zukunft', 79.
108. Robinson, *Cedric J. Robinson*.
109. Sloss, 'Das drahtlose Jahrhundert', 47–8.
110. Schlieffen, 'War Today', qtd. in Kittler, 'Playback', 97.
111. Gumbrecht, *In 1926*, 241.
112. F.H., 'Die Radio-Polizist-Maschine', 216.
113. König, 'Telegraphie, Telefonie, Funk', 69.
114. König, 'Telegraphie, Telefonie, Funk', 69.
115. Wythoff, 'Pocket Wireless', 42.
116. Wythoff, 'Pocket Wireless', 51.
117. Wythoff, 'Pocket Wireless', 42–3 (emphasis in original). As the concrete device, Wythoff proposes Evan Shelby's pocket telephone. For an overview of related military pocket wireless devices in Germany, see 'Eine Sensation der Wissenschaft'; Gesellschaft für drahtlose Telegraphie mBH, *Telefunken-Stationen und -Geräte*.
118. Sloss, 'Das drahtlose Jahrhundert', 35–8.
119. Sloss, 'Das drahtlose Jahrhundert', 37–8.
120. Ruhmer, *Wireless Telephony*, 196.
121. Ruhmer, *Wireless Telephony*, 196.
122. Tesla, *My Inventions*, 43; Tesla, 'When Woman is a Boss'.
123. Fürst, *Im Bannkreis von Nauen*, 8; cf. Fürst, 'Das drahtlose Telephon in Nauen'.
124. Lampl., 'Der radio-telegraphische Empfangsapparat in der Westentasche', 185.
125. Kästner, *Die verschwundene Miniatur*, qtd. in Dotzler and Roesler-Keilholz, *Mediengeschichte als historische Techno-logie*, 238 and book epigraph.
126. For English-language sources, see 'The Wireless 'Phone Will Get You', 487; Herbert, 'Modern Nuisances'.
127. Grimm, 'Das Taschentelephon', 33–4.
128. While Grimm's account may sound fantastical, it alludes to actual 1910 reports about Luigi Cerebotani's (1847–1928) telegraph patents.

129. Moszkowski, *Die Welt von der Kehrseite*, 114.
130. Moszkowski, *Die Welt von der Kehrseite*, 114.
131. Roth, 'Radiophon', 185–7.
132. Huhtamo, 'Magic Spectacles and Portable Boxes', 26.
133. 'The Pocket Telephone in Germany', 280; cf. Huhtamo, 'Magic Spectacles and Portable Boxes', 26.
134. Gradenwitz, 'A German Police Telephone', 61.
135. Gradenwitz, 'A German Police Telephone', 61.
136. See Scholz et al., 'Rhetorik des Neuen', 251.
137. Bredow, 'Eure Aufgaben im Rundfunk', 321.
138. See Bredow, *Im Banne der Ätherwellen*, vol. 2, 167–73; Lerg, *Die Entstehung des Rundfunks in Deutschland*, 94. The director of the Urania was the technical publicist Artur Fürst, who would later write *Im Bannkreis von Nauen*.
139. Bredow, *Im Banne der Ätherwellen*, vol. 2, 168.
140. Bredow, *Im Banne der Ätherwellen*, vol. 2, 168.
141. Bredow, *Im Banne der Ätherwellen*, vol. 2, 168.
142. Dominik, qtd. in Bredow, *Im Banne der Ätherwellen*, vol. 2, 169.
143. 'About Ourselves', 4.
144. 'About Ourselves', 4–5.
145. 'In Our Opinion', 89.
146. Fürst, 'Rundfunks Zukunft', 1–3; Arco, 'Wünsche und Wege im Rundfunk', 429–31; Schapira, 'Die Zukunft des deutschen Rundfunks', 417.
147. For period sources, see Friedel, *Elektrisches Fernsehen*; Lertes, *Fernbildtechnik und elektrisches Fernsehen*; Korn, *Elektrisches Fernsehen*.
148. Brecht, 'Radio as a Communications Apparatus', 41 (translation modified).
149. Koch, *Erfindergeist auf Abwegen*, 150, 85–6, 78–9, 86.

Chapter 4

Patent Fiction: Wireless Writing in Worldwide Networks

Media make things (im)possible. According to one of the central tenets of German media philosophy, each medium makes possible aesthetic forms and medial formats that would be impractical, illogical, or inconceivable in another medium. As previous chapters have shown, modernist writers, artists, and philosophers were occupied with thinking through wireless, whether imagining futuristic wireless-enabled devices, drawing inspiration for small-scale literary forms from telegrams and telephone calls, or exploring parallels between poetic inspiration and electrical induction. However, fewer large-scale literary projects engaged with wireless technology, and the only major exceptions from the canon of literary modernism might be James Joyce's *Finnegans Wake* and Thomas Pynchon's *Gravity's Rainbow*. While several of Franz Kafka's stories can be read as allegories for wireless transmission, and several of Bertolt Brecht's plays explored parallels between radio and theatre, there are only brief mentions of wireless transmission in Alfred Döblin's *Berlin Alexanderplatz*, Robert Musil's *The Man Without Qualities*, and other monuments of German modernism. However, there were two significant exceptions in interwar Austrian literature: Arnolt Bronnen's *Kampf im Äther* (Fight in the ether), which will not be analysed here because this notorious and much-analysed *roman à clef* focuses on broadcasting rather than the mode's pre- and post-histories;[1] and, this chapter's central object of close reading, Rudolf Brunngraber's *Der tönende Erdkreis: Roman der Funktechnik* (The resounding world: A novel of wireless technology).[2]

Composed after the Anschluss and at the height of National Socialist radio politics but only published after the end of World War II, Brunngraber's now-forgotten novel bypasses the history of national broadcasting and instead revels in its complex pre-history.[3] One of Brunngraber's *Tatsachenromane* (novels of facts) or *Dingbiographien* (biographies of a thing), this 575-page hybrid work of non-fiction and *roman à clef* was based on his detailed study of historical sources and empirical statistics,[4] as is evident from extended monologues about wireless technology delivered to apprentice technicians and surprisingly enraptured paramours. Interweaving documentary details about the functional order of broadcasting with the symbolic order of Heimat, *The Resounding World* explores tensions between the collective and the individual, embodied by a fictive technician, Eugen von Lorz, whose life story loosely parallels that of Jonathan Zenneck (1871–1959), a physicist, electrical engineer, Rector of the Technical University of Munich, and Director of the Deutsches Museum. Starting his career as a trainee for Siemens' telegraph division in Africa, the protagonist collaborates with Braun on the cathode-ray tube and ends up serving as one of Germany's representatives at the Paris Peace Conference following World War I. In the process, he overcomes both family drama – primarily, his stepmother having his child – and professional obstacles – primarily, an ongoing conflict over wireless patents. Despite this dramatic narrative, or perhaps because of it, the critical consensus is that the novel, unlike most of Brunngraber's other bestsellers, was a disappointment.[5] Nevertheless, *The Resounding World* not only provides a representative historical narrative of the patent wars conducted both in Germany and with Marconi in England and others in America. For negotiating the status of scientific facts about the history of wireless, it also sheds light on the mid-twentieth-century shift from the poetics of expressionism to those of realism, and it can thus help address the question of 'wireless writing'.[6]

Brunngraber's *Resounding World* divides the early history of wireless in the 1890s–1920s into three sections of the novel that focus, respectively, on science, engineering, and politics. The first part, 'Lifting a New World Veil [*Weltschleier*]', is set in 1897, a momentous year not only because of the first public wireless demonstrations, but also for the discovery of the electron, the formation of Freud's theory of the unconscious, Saussure's work with the medium Hèlene Smith, William Crookes's last speech as the president of the Society for Physical Research, and Daniel Paul Schreber's memoirs.[7] Restricting the events to this significant year allows Brunngraber to compare Marconi's work in England to Braun's in Germany. Set in the years 1898 to 1905, the second part, 'The Birth of a World Company [*Weltfirma*]', focuses on the meteoric rise of the Gesellschaft für drahtlose Telegraphie mbH, colloquially known after its telegraphic address as Telefunken.[8] During the period described in the novel, Telefunken was founded as a joint venture through the merger of Allgemeine-Elektricitäts-Gesellschaft (AEG) with Siemens & Halske, and yet during the novel's composition it was a sole subsidiary of the pro-Nazi AEG and is thus not named as such in the novel. Instead, the novel's title, *Der tönende Erdkreis*, alludes to the company's patented system of *Tönenden Funken*, which created a distinctive tone dubbed a 'singing spark'. The novel's third part, 'The Path to World Chaos [*Weltwirrnis*]', starts with the construction of Telefunken's first wireless station at Nauen in 1906 and concludes with contributions from its subsidiary, Transradio, to the first international broadcasts in 1921. Although Brunngraber planned to write a sequel 'on the radio itself, that is, the period from 1920 to the present', he attempted only this single volume 'on high-frequency technology', and 'each volume was to be a self-contained work'.[9]

At the outset of the period narrated in *The Resounding World*, there was still no such thing as wireless transmission in the strict sense. Even after Hertz verified the existence of electromagnetic radiation in his laboratory experiments of the late 1880s, commercial applications took at least another decade. During this period, the individual technical components required for wireless telegraphy arose simultaneously in several different countries not only across Europe but around the world. Nevertheless, the main news that started making the rounds in the German daily press by 1897 was that the Italian-born Marconi had invented a wireless system in England that would supplement the British Empire's 'All Red Line' cable network. At the time, three main groups of researchers in the German Empire were working on the scientific and technical development of wireless technology, each with different approaches, objectives, and institutional contexts. In 1903 a patent war broke out between two of these groups: AEG, with Slaby and Arco working to develop wireless technology for the Imperial German Navy; and Siemens & Halske, with Braun and others working to develop technology for the German Army. Through the intervention of Emperor Wilhelm II, the two companies were merged into the joint venture that came to be known as Telefunken, consolidating their patent holdings. In the first decade of the twentieth century, possession of these patents became critical, since competing systems of wireless telegraphy in the German Empire relied on at least four different transmission technologies: spark-gap, electric arc, high-frequency alternators, and vacuum tubes. Even after the 'invention' of wireless telegraphy, there was still no singular media system, only a multiplicity of competing ones.[10]

On the eve of World War I, several 'worldwide wireless networks', such as Telefunken's planned *Weltfunknetz*, were already under construction. Though the war delayed and altered their completion, it also gave a push to the research and development of wireless technology, due to its significance for military strategy. During the war, the first experimental radio broadcasts occurred, some of which could be heard on the fronts, and many German soldiers, including some prominent artists, physicists, philosophers, and future leaders of national broadcasting, were stationed in signal corps where they learned the principles of wireless transmission.[11] After the war, the potential audience for national broadcasting was greater than ever before, and the radio appeared to be ready, at least technologically, as a mass medium. Wireless transmission rapidly developed from a short-range, point-to-point communication system with limited access into a long-range, point-to-multipoint distribution system with broadcasts capable of addressing mass audiences. Throughout this transitional period, the main concern was increasing the *range* of wireless transmissions, and not providing *coverage*, as would only emerge with national broadcasting after World War I and cellular networks after World War II. Worldwide wireless networks expanded in linear and not radial directions, largely reinforcing pathways established by capitalism and colonialism.[12]

Following recent revisions of the former grand narrative of struggles for control over global communications, however, media historians need to examine not only international rivalry but also interdependence, especially in terms of investment patterns in wireless companies, and to consider the intersections between imperialism and capitalism.[13] As Brunngraber's novel repeatedly reminds readers, worldwide wireless networks are not self-enclosed worlds but networked environments in which collective destinies are shaped by systemic forces and chains of causality beyond any individual's control.

Range Tests

The first chapter of *The Resounding World*, 'In Togo, Land of the Apes', begins *in medias res* with a young German engineer convalescing in a colonial hospital. The setting in Togoland mobilises the media topos of the 'tribal drum' as a primal scene of wireless communication and presents a colonialist view of the German colony established in 1884 and surrendered to French and British troops in 1914 – but only after German forces destroyed the massive colonial wireless station near Kamina, east of Atakpamé. Having come down with an unknown illness, Lorz (that is, Zenneck) suffers from a feverish Heimatladen nightmare, hallucinating, 'Home again, after a month in the ape-land Togo, after a diarrheal month, an ape diarrhoea, back home from Togo, home in Germany.'[14] Mimicking Lorz's disorientation, the narrative switches between his perspective and that of another engineer, a 'blond and rosy-faced giant' named 'Laubinger' (probably Adolf Koepsel) who cannot understand the reasons for Lorz's fever dreams. 'This Lorz, who was a scientific type, a physicist, and only occasionally a technician', Laubinger reasons, 'could not be taken for a poser, neither a romantic-hysterical one nor a sentimental one.'[15] Repeatedly described as 'homeless', Lorz appears averse to life in the German colony and yet unwilling to return to mainland Germany. Only four chapters later is the reason for Lorz's fever dream and his 'flight' from his home(land) revealed to be that his stepmother, Katharina von Lorz, is pregnant with his child.[16]

Before learning the personal reason for Lorz's flight from Germany, readers find out the professional reason for his relocation to Africa: his employment as a 'trainee' [*Voluntär*] in the Siemens Company, 'lay[ing] a telegraph line from Aného to Topli'. While the rhetoric of wirelessness might create the false impression that this networking project aimed to provide continent-wide telecommunications coverage, the network was intended only to connect mainland Germany to its African colonies. Reflecting this colonial discourse, Brunngraber recycles media topoi and origin stories of wireless telegraphy, combining the European imagination of the African tribal drum with that of wired telegraphy. During the opening scene, the engineers are suddenly interrupted by a shout in the Ewe dialect of the Niger-Congo language spoken in southern Togo: 'Hometale? Hometale? / Hometale? Alletah! / Sron je ale? Deviale? / Ele! Ele! Alletah!'[17] However, this song was not composed by native speakers, the narrator explains, but by German colonists with their rudimentary knowledge of the language, and 'meant not much more than the question, "how it's going, at home and with everything," and the answer, "it's going well"'.[18] By the end of the first chapter, Lorz will embark on a new career in wireless telegraphy after hearing one of the Siemens employees, a 'mastodon peeled from the egg' named Maisenbach (perhaps Matthias Cantor), read aloud a Berlin-based newspaper report about wireless range tests being conducted in Europe. 'Without me', he brags, 'you would still be running around for all eternity through all the world's "ape lands", setting up your ridiculous telegraph poles and hanging dumb wires over them! But now you can leave them to the orangutans for tight-rope dancing.'[19] Framed as a step towards civilisation, the reported event referred to a wireless range test conducted by Marconi in the Bristol Channel and 'attended, at the request of the Emperor [Wilhelm II], by a lecturer at the Technical University of Berlin, Professor Dr Pallaban [that is, Adolf Slaby]'.[20]

Wilhelmine wireless only began in this roundabout way. It required a transnational transfer of knowledge, from Marconi's work in England to Slaby's promotion and replication of that work in Germany, as various components necessary for wireless telegraphy were developed contemporaneously throughout continental Europe.[21] International press reports, such as the one authored by Slaby about Marconi's Bristol Channel trials, were crucial for establishing the credibility of wireless telegraphy in the vernacular imagination.[22] As Aaron Toscano argues, a new medium can fail unless it is shown to be superior to already available media technology.[23] Instead of pitting unproven wireless transmissions against their proven wired counterparts, Marconi, Slaby, and others cleverly staged demonstrations that pitted each new generation of wireless telegraphy against the previous one, since each incremental increase in transmission distance could be accurately measured and easily reported.

As soon as Slaby and Arco had obtained usable results, they appear to have been granted permission to circumvent Marconi's patents, which were still pending in Germany. Slaby and Arco applied for five crucial patents from the Imperial Patent Office, primarily to differentiate their work from that of Marconi.[24] The system secured by these patents would be developed, together with AEG, through the support of the Imperial Marine Office. As Slaby recognised, the most important applications of wireless telegraphy were military: the army could use it in a siege or when encircling enemy troops; the navy could use captive balloons or modern kites on the high seas; and wireless telegraphy would be crucial for lighthouses and lightships. Yet, as Slaby also recognised, 'An undeniable weakness of spark telegraphy is this: every telegram is imparted to the whole world; every receiver can take it up.'[25] To secure the channel, Slaby advised creating new forms of cryptography and predicted that future wars would include battles not only over terrestrial space but also the virtual space of wireless transmissions.

Meanwhile, Braun had also started experimenting with wireless telegraphy on the other side of Germany, only a few months after Slaby. As an expert consultant for three citizens of Strasbourg, he was tasked with providing a scientific explanation of 'hydrotelegraphy'.[26] Braun was also occupied with electromagnetic waves and soon applied for a patent for his system of wireless telegraphy.[27] Since potential users tended to measure success almost exclusively by the obtained transmission range, Braun, like Marconi and Slaby, initially sought to fulfil this demand by using longer wavelengths and increasing transmission power. Quickly, however, Braun solved the problem in a radically different manner: coupling the antenna inductively on to a second closed oscillatory circuit, rather than merely consuming more and more power.[28] In summer 1899 Braun's assistants, Matthias Cantor and Jonathan Zenneck, successfully tested this new 'tuned spark transmitter'. For the commercial exploitation of Braun's patents, the project's backers established the Gesellschaft für drahtlose Telegraphie Professor Braun, and attempted to establish contracts with shipping and insurance companies. However, financial difficulties and Braun's desire to escape from commercial pressure and to concentrate on his own scientific research caused his wireless company to merge in 1901 with Siemens & Halske, with the latter having the upper hand technically and financially.

Part One of *The Resounding World* concludes in the same year it started, 1897, with a conversation between Braun (one of the few characters in the novel not presented under a pseudonym) and his assistants about an imminent patent war. 'We are getting drawn into a battle over wireless telegraphy', Braun warns Lorz after explaining his patent-pending wireless system. 'Perhaps, in the process, we will succeed in bringing back home the Hertzian waves, which were a German seed, and making them into a German harvest. And if we should then have a patent trial with Privy Councillor Pallaban [that is, Slaby], I will send you to Berlin.'[29] Following the conversation, there is an image of three circuit diagrams (Fig. 4.1) comparing Hertz's original laboratory apparatus (a spark gap and an induction coil), Marconi's modifications for long-distance transmission (a longer antenna and grounding the circuit), and Braun's distinctive resonating circuit (separating the antenna from the circuit and adding a capacitor).[30] Whereas Hertz's set-up is dated '1889' and Marconi's '1897', Braun's system is not dated: the narrative structure, with Part One focusing only on the year 1897, runs into the problem that Braun was not issued a patent until several years later. Part Two thus begins with Brunngraber copying the headings verbatim from the patent awarded to Braun for a 'Telegraphy System without Directly Connected Wire', filed on 13 July 1898, and issued on 7 November 1900.[31] In this respect, Brunngraber's novel demonstrates the power of literature to process events in a non-chronological manner, provocatively suggesting that even if Braun's patent is dated and numbered after the others, it comes before them in terms of significance.[32] Although Braun died during World War I and there is no research on his reception under National Socialism, one of the challenges for Brunngraber's novel appears to have been to rehabilitate Braun's image without reinforcing the Nazi framework of invention and discovery.

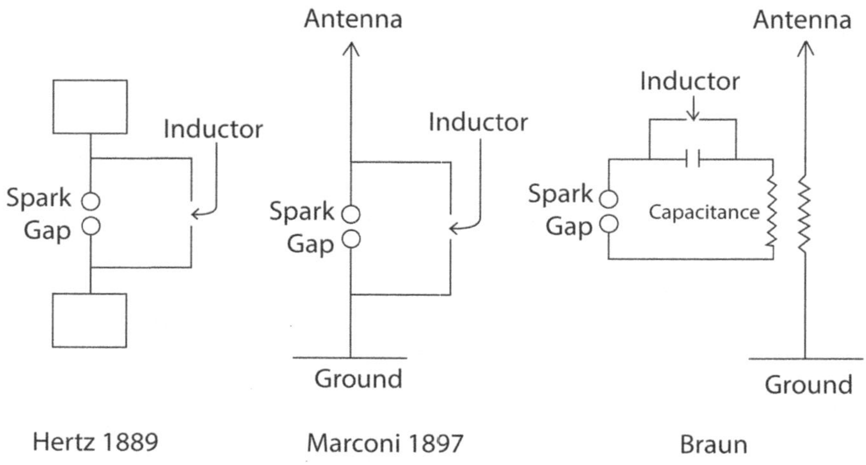

Figure 4.1 Rudolf Brunngraber's novel *The Resounding Earth* compares three crucial patents: Hertz's experimental laboratory apparatus (i.e., a spark gap and an induction coil); Marconi's addition to make the set-up capable of transmitting over long distances (i.e., adding a longer antenna and grounding the circuit); and Braun's resonating circuit (i.e., separating the antenna from the circuit and adding a capacitor). Source: Brunngraber, *Der tönende Erdkreis*, 141, recreated by Erik Born.

Brunngraber's negotiation of these challenges situates him in the middle of a developing spectrum of realism and debates about the facticity of inventions. While inventions are central to both literary and media history, there has been little reflection on the act of invention in literary, cultural, and media studies beyond the period around 1800. For the period around 1900, patents have served as a crucial source for media history, and citing them was a standard anti-hermeneutic gesture in German media theory, but their social, cultural, and medial aspects remain understudied.[33] As Stathis Arapostathis and Graeme Gooday show, Marconi did not merely patent an application of electromagnetic radiation; he radically changed the period's understanding of what was patentable, which kicked off a 'vicious circle of patenting'.[34] Because patent litigation seemed unprofitable or undesirable to many inventors, scientists, and company managers, Arapostathis and Gooday argue, 'the battles over ownership of patent rights were fought almost entirely without litigation. Instead, they played out in the press, the tribunal of public opinion'[35] – and, I would add, in historical writing and literary fiction.

National Systems

In recent years, historians of wireless telegraphy have routinely juxtaposed 'Marconi versus Telefunken' or 'Telefunken versus Marconi'.[36] The competition is also one of the main themes of Brunngraber's novel, though, according to the narrator's refrain, 'Wireless [*der Funk*] was not made for competing companies but for humanity.'[37] Near the start of the novel, Lorz negotiates questions of invention in a conversation with Michaela Pallaban, the daughter of Privy Councillor Pallaban (that is, Slaby) and Lorz's most recent love interest. Although Michaela admits that she 'understand[s] absolutely nothing of technical things', she knows 'that there is a dispute over the priority of this Italian inventor Marconi's achievement, or at least, the view that he only improved on what had been prepared by others'.[38] Wrinkling his brow, Lorz responds that calling it a 'priority dispute' (*Prioritätsstreit*) may be an overstatement, but 'in the invention, or the constructions of Marconi, much foreign preliminary work is hiding'.[39] During the course of the novel, Lorz is employed by Telefunken's subsidiary, Transradio, the first news agency to introduce duplex transmission, to review patent disputes with other wireless companies. Near the end of the novel, he compares Marconi's celebrated patent Nr. 7,777 and Braun's patent Nr. 111,578, and comes to the devastating realisation that neither of them can lay claim to the invention of wireless telegraphy: 'even if Marconi was the immortal centre of attention, wireless came about before, with, and after him as a collective work'.[40] While *The Resounding World* seeks to expose Marconi's contested claims to the priority of invention, it does not simply reassign the priority of invention to Braun, instead attempting to resolve the question of invention within a collective.

Not everyone was pleased with the spread of wireless telegraphy, or with Marconi's claims to the priority of invention. Those who had invested considerable sums of money in wired systems across Europe and the United States did not welcome the new competitor.[41] Technical critics of Marconi pointed to the necessity of creating undamped, continuous electromagnetic vibrations.[42] After Marconi's system had established itself on coastlines, there were complaints in France that Marconi stations rendered another company's stations partially ineffective, due to the Marconi Company's policy of non-communication with competing systems. In the United States, there were reports that a Marconi-equipped ship had refused to answer radioed queries about the position of a derelict vessel in the shipping lanes. In Austria and Germany, the reception of the celebrity inventor was particularly fraught with conflict.

By 1902 critiques of the media hype around wireless transmission were channelled towards the emergent professional figures responsible for organising and financing wireless experiments, whom Victor Loos bitingly called the 'technical impresario' and the 'wireless impresario'.[43] The problem, according to this cultural critic, was that the 'technical impresario' treats a 'gift' as a 'commodity, which helps its retailer make a handsome profit'.[44] To create a pseudo-scientific air around staged demonstrations, Loos observed, wireless technicians collaborated with the press and gave them privileged access, presumably in exchange for reporting only on successful trials and omitting failed or contested results. For Loos, the media's motivation for presenting the untested medium as an inevitable success ('overnight Marconi *must have* telegraphed wirelessly from America to Europe, whether he was able to or not!') was to put an end to competition and turn Marconi into a marketable celebrity: 'There we saw Marconi in the experiment room, Marconi engaged, Marconi as disloyal fiancé, Marconi dancing around the telegraph apparatus, Marconi informing the open hands of the reporters . . .'.[45] Rather than following the money, Loos followed his primary target – the language and editorial decisions of the commercial Viennese newspaper frequently targeted by Karl Krauss and *Die Fackel*:

> the millions that were mis-experimented with, the 'towering goal' that had been reached, the 'great Christmas present for all humanity', which, greased with Schiller and Heine verses, the *Neue Freie Presse* and the likeminded commercial press dished out to their subscribers, when the impresario connected Europe with America wirelessly.[46]

Sickened by the commercial newspaper's exploitation of the wireless topos of universal brotherhood to drum up investment capital, Loos overlooked the different institutional settings in England, where Marconi exploited his inherited whisky fortune and identified primarily as an entrepreneur, and Germany, where Slaby and Braun were physicists whose livelihood was secured by the Wilhelmine professorial system.

As a result of these developments, there was growing anxiety about the Marconi Company having a worldwide monopoly over wireless transmission, which would be tantamount to Great Britain having a monopoly over colonial communications, an anxiety felt not only in the German Empire but also by other imperial powers. Mobilising this discourse, Emperor Wilhelm II intervened in the company politics of the two competing research groups and expedited the founding of Telefunken. For historian Margot Fuchs, 'the foundation of this company was an early example, on the European market, of national cooperative management and a horizontal community of interests between two German groups of companies'.[47] From the perspective of scientific organisation, on the other hand, it could also be understood as a case of what Susan Leigh Starr calls 'cooperation without consensus'.[48] 'From high above came words elated / Let Telefunken be created', a veteran of the German signal corps later remembered.[49] Hans Bredow was named Telefunken's business director, the start of a career that would find him directing national radio broadcasting; and Slaby's former assistant, Arco, was appointed Telefunken's technical director.[50] Telefunken's patent politics played a key role in the company's success, registering 400 wireless patents during Arco's tenure alone, including several that would play a decisive role in international negotiations: a patent for a receiver with a high-frequency amplifier by Otto von Bronk, the director of Telefunken's patent division; another patent on feedback by Alexander Meissner; and the renowned vacuum tube patent by Robert von Lieben.[51]

Founded in 1903, Telefunken was given twenty years to focus on addressing technical problems and developing wireless components, while also specialising in constructing massive wireless stations. One of the organisation's first main tasks was to create a standard system out of the different transmitters and receivers used by the different groups; Braun's coupled transmitter was chosen for this purpose.[52] Next, to make wireless useful for military purposes, Telefunken focused on the military's requests for new features, including mobility, secrecy, eliminating interference, increasing transmission range, establishing connections faster, and providing a written record of received messages.[53] Each feature aimed at making wireless more secure by eliminating the element that would eventually enable broadcasting – omnidirectional propagation over an open, insecure channel. To increase security, Telefunken developed syntonic tuning principles with the result that unauthorised reception was only possible if a receiver knew the wireless transmission's exact frequency. The military accepted Telefunken's proposal for using a rapidly changing frequency along with a basic encryption system. Up to 1908, military stations accounted for about three-quarters of the company's business.[54] Developing organisational abilities at a rapid pace, Telefunken had c. 200 employees plus representatives stationed in 39 countries by the outbreak of World War I. By the end of the 1930s, when Brunngraber started writing *The Resounding World*, Telefunken counted c. 23,500 employees, and by the end of World War II, when he finished it, c. 40,000 employees, many forced workers and Ostarbeiter.

It is often forgotten that the 1909 Nobel Prize in Physics was awarded jointly to Marconi and Braun 'in recognition of their contributions to the development of wireless telegraphy'. In *The Resounding World*, their meeting is described in vivid detail from the perspective of Braun's assistant Lorz/Zenneck, as the narrator relishes reporting Marconi's statement that he planned to decline 'half a prize'.[55] In their acceptance speeches, Braun and Marconi both focused on the central problem of long-range transmission. But while Marconi's speech framed his contribution in terms of increasing transmission *range*, minutely listing each incremental distance obtained by each modification of the transmission system, Braun's speech framed his contribution in terms of increasing *efficiency*. This contrast appears most clearly at the end of their speeches. While Marconi's main strategy for increasing transmission range was to increase the transmitter's power, Braun's strategy was to increase its efficiency and safety through the development of resonant circuits, directional antennas, and *Funken ohne Funken* (sparkless telegraphy), which he would never see fully realised in his own lifetime. In this system, as Braun quipped, 'the spark which produces the waves also destroys them again as Saturn destroyed his own children'.[56] Whereas Marconi's speech came to the speculative conclusion that it would soon be possible to transmit wireless energy around the world, Braun's speech concluded with the sober reflection on sparkless telegraphy that 'we have come appreciably nearer to this target and have thereby made the coupled transmitter still more effective'.[57]

Based on Braun's and Max Wien's innovations, Telefunken's quenched-spark system (*Löschfunkensystem*) was a means of circumventing the patent disputes over a practical arc-lamp method developed by Danish engineer Valdemar Poulsen, whose patents for Germany and the European market were acquired by C. Lorenz AG. The competition in the still relatively small military and navy markets led from 1906–10 to developing and marketing Telefunken's new quenched-spark transmitter. In contrast to Marconi's system, which transmitted Morse characters with interruptions between them, Telefunken's generated electromagnetic waves at frequencies of 300–2,000 Hz, which therefore produced continuous sounds. While the strongly damped wideband transmitters used in Marconi's system produced c. 100 impulses per second and thus created noises that made it difficult for human or technical receivers to distinguish signals from atmospheric noise, Telefunken designed its system in direct response to army and navy demands for improved selectivity, greater ranges, more robustness, and smaller equipment sizes.

Using a weakly damped, quenched-spark transmitter, Telefunken's system created a musical tone in receivers that was easily distinguishable from noise, which is what gave rise to the term 'singing sparks'. Using this new system, the military was able to switch from printer-tape reception with a telegraph receiver to audio reception using a telephone receiver. Compared to the spark-gap transmitter and the arc-lamp transmitter, Telefunken's quenched-spark transmitter could achieve ranges up to a factor of three times greater with the same electrical performance. In late 1909 there were plans to equip all 90 German warships with the stations, as Telefunken also expanded its business to marine wireless and civilian trading vessels. From a technical perspective, Telefunken's wireless systems ended up representing dead ends in the development of wireless technology after the development of alternator transmitters in 1911 and vacuum tube transmitters in 1913. Although the only thing that remains from this original generation of *Funktechnik* is the word *Funk*, it left a lasting imprint on international regulations and world infrastructure projects.

International Regulations

Consider the *Titanic*. The sinking of the quintessentially modern passenger liner in April 1912 was the first international disaster to be broadcast wirelessly in 'real time'. While most people would only learn of the event from newspaper reports published the following morning, an international community of wireless telegraph operators telegraphically witnessed the event and attempted to coordinate a rescue operation. The British passenger liner was equipped with a state-of-the-art wireless apparatus, capable of transmitting over 550km, that had been supplied and staffed by the Marconi Company. As soon as the ship collided with the iceberg, the two wireless operators on board interrupted their regularly scheduled broadcasts of passenger telegrams and navigational messages to transmit distress signals. Significantly, they broadcast at least three different distress signals in Morse code. At first, the senior operator sent out the company standard CQD, a combination of 'calling all stations' (CQ) and 'distress' (D), which had proven successful in previous wireless rescue operations at sea. Shortly thereafter, the junior wireless operator suggested, with a sort of gallows' humour, that they might as well try an experimental signal proposed by the German government and ratified at the first International Radiotelegraph Convention, held in Berlin in 1906, since they might not ever have the chance to use it again – 'SOS'. In the end, the final wireless message received from the *Titanic* was a desperate transmission in the operators' native language ('WE ARE SINKING FAST'). Despite previous calls for the creation of a standard international distress signal, it took the spectacle of this international disaster for a standard protocol to be adopted at the second International Radiotelegraphic Convention, held only three months later in London.

One of the most successful attempts at standardising international wireless communications derived from a proposal made by the British government in 1909, then ratified at the second International Radiotelegraphic Convention in 1912. What came to be known as the 'Q code' was a collection of three-letter codewords standing in for frequently used phrases in wireless telegraphy. Each codeword started with the letter Q and could be inflected with a question mark at the end. One significant code pair is 'QSL?' (Do you confirm receipt of my transmission?) and 'QSL' (I do confirm receipt). In the early days of amateur radio, wireless enthusiasts started to exchange QSL cards, physical postcards sent through the mail by radio broadcasters to any listeners who submitted reports of having received a broadcast, as a final courtesy for long-distance reception. The Q code was the first brevity code, or non-secret system of abbreviations, to create an entirely virtual system of address, making it a potential precursor to today's Wi-Fi protocols. Out of the forty-five original Q codes, the first, QRA, established the identity of each wireless station; the next five, QRB–QRG, determined their mobile positions in relation to each other; and the remaining thirty-nine, QRH–QSX, served to optimise their shared communication channel through metadata reports about signal quality in each location. Thus, a conversation in Q code represented the masterful orchestration of many contingent factors affecting wireless transmission, in multiple locations, in 'real time'. The Q code proved to be an extremely resilient system, surviving multiple generations of amateur radio technology into the present.

At another International Radiotelegraphic Convention depicted in *The Resounding World*, Oberpostrat W. H. Worpspiller (that is, Bredow) conflates the global with the local aspects of a potential worldwide network in revealing terms, proposing 'the establishment of a world organisation and the creation of independent radio stations in all continents – in short, the creation of German worldwide wireless connections [*deutscher Weltfunkverbindungen*]'.[58] Instead of international cooperation, the main task was imagined to be 'to build a large transmitter' as 'the first big step towards a global wireless centre [*Weltfunkzentrale*]'.[59] Sensing the project's latent ideology, Lorz 'once again was overcome with vertigo', as at every such moment in the novel, and recognises that 'the ultimate goal would be to transform today's sporadic wireless traffic into a worldwide wireless network [*Weltfunknetz*]', and thereby make 'the entire earth into a sales area [*Absatzgebiet*] for wireless stations'.[60]

Worldwide Wireless Networks

The endpoint of the Imperial German Wireless Network, or *Weltfunknetz*, may seem to be *Der tönende Erdkreis*, as in the title of Brunngraber's novel, collapsing the image of a 'resonant earth' into the name for Telefunken's patented system. However, the Imperial German Wireless Network needs to be understood in relation to other modernist 'world projects', including not only the Imperial British Telegraph Network, but also Imperial German projects for universal currency, a global language, and a world brain, which all struggled to transcend their local origins. Markus Krajewski sums up these projects' central dilemma: 'No world format can function without a world that accepts it.'[61] Following Krajewski's media-philosophical study,

> global transit is the media-technological a priori of the global projects. It forms the *conditio sine qua non* of internationality as such. It is first the expansion, consolidation, and acceleration of transit that produces the global innovations in the world around 1900. Accelerated by railway networks, in the wake of steamship lines and brought to mind by telegraph wires, a notion develops that makes all such grand projects feasible.[62]

Beyond Imperial Germany, one of the most sensational projects was Nikola Tesla's World Wireless System, a plan for delivering messages and distributing power wirelessly around the world. By 1901 the project had already received enough funding to start the construction of Wardenclyffe Tower, a massive antenna station on Long Island, New York. However, the money ran out, the structure was never completed, and the spectacular failure became seen as a testament to the failure of Tesla's erroneous theories about electricity and magnetism – overestimating conductivity and underestimating power loss over significant transmission distances. Rather than realising ideals of global communication, worldwide wireless networks turned into national format wars.

As Heidi Tworek has shown in historical studies of Telefunken's networking project, the German imagination of the British Empire's communications prowess not only shaped investments in wireless technology.[63] The very possibility of wireless transmission also reshaped Germany's colonial imagination to the point where 'Paramaribo and Java could be more important than Poland and Japan. The world was no longer simply divided into land and sea. For Germans, the air had become the vital third dimension.'[64] As early as 1911 the German Empire was already concentrating on exploiting its overseas holdings for the creation of a new information network, intended not to replace but to supplement the existing sea cable. The position of the German colonies not only determined the structure of the network and its stages of construction, but also defined the central demands for future wireless technology.[65] Given the position of the German colonies, plans for a worldwide network would have needed to proceed in four main stages, as historian Michael Friedewald explains.[66] First, coastal stations would need to be constructed for the colonies to communicate with their own ships and to monitor foreign ships on the seaway to India and East Africa. Next, German colonies in Africa and the Pacific would need to be connected to each other using large wireless stations with a range of at least 4,000km. Only then could the African colonies be linked back up with the German Empire, using a transcontinental wireless station with a range of 6,000km. Lastly, the oceanic colonies were to be connected to the rest of the colonial network with further relay stations. At the start of World War I the first three stages of the plan had been mostly completed, but the fourth had not even started and would not be completed by the end of WWI.

As Telefunken's envisioned worldwide wireless network struggled to materialise, early network maps played an integral role in promoting it. While the scarce scholarship on network maps has tended to approach them as transparent representations of infrastructural politics,[67] analysing maps as mediums requires approaching them, as Bernhard Siegert argues, 'not as representations of space but as spaces of representation'.[68] In this respect, network maps reveal a sea change in the understanding of wireless transmission, from directional transmission to omnidirectional broadcasting. A map commissioned in 1913 by Telefunken Director Bredow shows the company's planned *Weltfunknetz* (Fig. 4.2). At the centre of the network is Nauen, the site of the world's largest and most powerful wireless station at the time, which was to be connected in linear fashion to every other continent through a series of relays. In the projected worldwide network, the representation of these connections remains linear: solid lines connect wireless stations, dashes represent German cables, and distances are given as the bird flies. The angularity of the worldwide communication network would be rounded off in subsequent maps, which depicted signals emanating from Nauen in concentric circles across the globe.

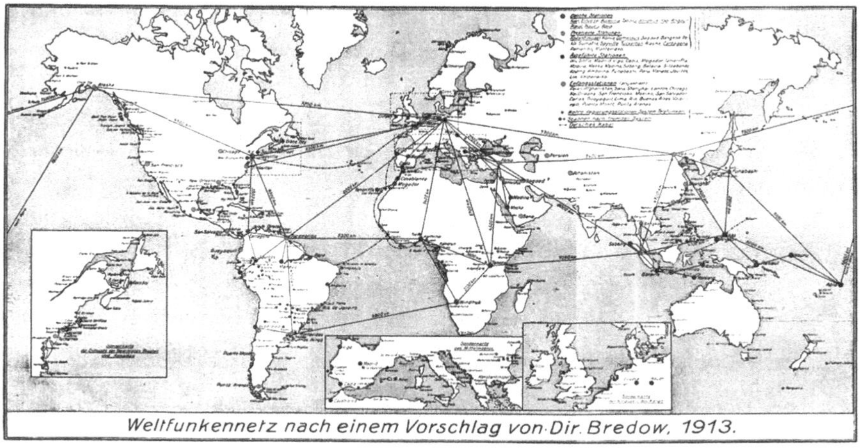

Figure 4.2 A map of the world wireless network according to Telefunken director Hans Bredow's proposal, centred on Nauen, with linear connections extending to every continent. Source: unknown, scan by Gorm Helt-Hansen, https://nshdpi.ca/is/radio30/radio-first-30yrs.html.

Since a single station could not cover the entire globe, multiple relay stations were necessary, as evident in a 1913 article published in Telefunken's company magazine comparing the 'radiotelegraphic world projects' (*Funkentelegraphische Weltprojekte*) of France, Germany, Great Britain, India, Italy, Japan, Norway, Portugal, Russia, and the USA.[69] The article, printed along with another map of Telefunken's *Weltfunknetz*, described the significance of wireless networks for colonial communications, while restating the prevailing military view of wireless insecurity:

> In these kinds of connections, the existing or planned cable connections are not usually taken into consideration, since radiotelegraphic connections are less in the interest of [civilian] traffic than primarily [. . .] in military and political interests, and they possess the advantage over the sea cable that they cannot be destroyed by enemies in the event of war.[70]

For the author of this article, it was unthinkable that wireless traffic could share civilian channels. During World War I, military wireless stations were destroyed, often by a nation's own troops, as happened with the stations in German colonies. Reflecting on film's potential as a storage medium to 'preserve [. . .] ancient traditions, which will be swept away by the advancing civilization', one nationalistic commentator observed that 'the construction of Telefunken's station in

Kamina has also been saved by us in moving pictures for future generations', even after 'this masterful example of pioneering technology [. . .] had to be detonated by our own troops so as not to fall into enemy hands'.[71] Though images of the station survive, the messages it transmitted do not, since wireless is primarily a present-oriented transmission medium.

Despite the media topos of global connectivity, early wireless network configurations hardly took into consideration the now familiar concept of area-wide *coverage*. In the German-speaking world, it was not until the 1930s–1940s, with the establishment of semi-permanent national broadcasting networks, that the terminology for *range* underwent an important semantic change. Rather than the measurement of a geographical distance between a transmitter and a receiver, the concept came to express the statistical probability with which a transmitted signal would be received within a given area. While the entry for *Reichweite* (range) in Hanns Günther's multilingual dictionary for radio amateurs still equated it with the term *Entfernung* (distance) in the mid-1920s, the same lemma was described in much greater detail in his monolingual German lexicon in the mid-1930s:

> Range. The distance from a transmitter at which the field strengths from this transmitter are so great that they exceed the field strength of the interference level by about an order of magnitude. Then the guarantee is given that the transmitter in question can still be recorded with a receiver.[72]

No longer a measure of physical distance, the term *range* came to mean a proportional value between the signal's received strength and that of interference sources, later known as the *signal-to-noise ratio* (SNR).

Counterintuitively, one of the main reasons for the slow epistemic change from notions of linear transmission range to omnidirectional coverage area was that wireless transmission was conceived as different in kind than wired transmission. Although the wired telegraph network was optimised by the end of the nineteenth century, the optimisation of wireless networks went largely unnoticed until the rapidly growing number of subscribers to national radio services made it necessary to ensure quality of service. The main reason for this delayed development was an oversight in the theory and practice of switching technology: wired and wireless networks were still viewed as radically different problems, which made it difficult to identify the equal dependence of wireless transmission on switches and relays. Thus, as late as 1927, radio engineer Lloyd Espenschied, who worked for Telefunken from 1909 to 1910 and then for the

American Telephone and Telegraph Company, where he contributed to the invention of the coaxial cable, could observe that 'in the case of radio broadcasting, the absence of a common control of the two ends makes this overall "systems" aspect less apparent than it is for wire systems'.[73] Whereas the common control in wired systems (that is, the wire) can be optimised through engineering and switching technology, wireless systems use two different controls (that is, the transmitter and the receiver), which made it less apparent that they belong to a common system and more difficult to optimise their shared information channel.

Signals Intelligence

Although Brunngraber's *Resounding World* is largely silent about wireless warfare, it is impossible to ignore the role of the military-industrial complex in shaping the sociotechnical imagination of wireless futures in Wilhelmine Germany and elsewhere.[74] With funding provided by corporations, governments, and militaries, the emerging field of 'signals intelligence' developed methods of monitoring, intercepting, and interpreting electromagnetic signals that greatly shaped consumer technologies. Due to the massive deployment of wireless telegraphy, World War I went down in history as the first war fought in the ether. Here it is worth retelling one of the most familiar origin stories from German media philosophy – that of the German signal corps, or *Nachrichtentruppe*. Having entered the war with 550 officers and 5,800 infantry, the German signal corps returned home with 4,382 officers and 185,000 infantry.[75] When, at the start of the war, British cable steamers cut the five cables connecting the German Empire to both its African colonies and then-neutral Spain and America, they fulfilled its fears of being cut off from the world.[76] Because of this 'cable blockade', Germany was unable to communicate directly with its diplomats and agents, and lost access to 'the New York money market and thereby the ability to sell securities to raise foreign currency'.[77]

Long before Kittler popularised this story through the ironic quotation of German World War I veterans, Marshall McLuhan was already telling a similar story about the ways wireless broadcasting developed in response to perceived threats of 'encirclement'.[78] In McLuhan's analysis, the rapid expansion of railway systems in neighbouring countries that would facilitate wartime mobilisation in the 1910s provided a 'highly visual image that had great novelty for this newly industrialized nation. In the 1930s, by contrast, the German obsession was with lebensraum', which McLuhan links to the radio and the 'tribal past'.[79] Debunking Kittler's and McLuhan's origin stories, media scholars have demonstrated that the German Empire also isolated itself by halting all outbound telegraph and telephone traffic at the border, and by issuing a moratorium on wireless traffic conducted for research and commerce. With its only remaining connections to the outside world at Nauen and Eilvese, Germany's transoceanic stations in neutral countries were given the task of transmitting news 'To All'. During the war, 'the Germans prided themselves that their military communiqués were being published almost simultaneously in the German and American press'.[80] Their Transatlantic Office supplied German messages further to the Latin American press, and even after attempts to censor the stream, Telefunken continued to build and operate wireless stations in Mexico, Peru, Brazil, and the Danish West Indies.[81]

Considering ongoing debates about the relation between warfare and media change, it remains safe to state that civilian wireless equipment converged with military equipment during World War I.[82] At the start of the war, wireless was used primarily by the High Command to coordinate divisions. 'Electrical channels were indispensable for bridging the never-ending deadly distance between the front line and the command centres', Wolf Kittler observes in a study of media wars.[83] The transition to trench warfare in 1915–16 led to the creation of many portable wireless devices for the troops at the front, but as the war dragged on, the intensifying wireless traffic made it increasingly difficult to transmit any signals.[84] The war also blurred the boundaries between military and civilian technology for decades to come. 'In the realm of electromagnetism', Bernhard Siegert argues, 'the borders blur between listening and eavesdropping, entertainment and command, interception and reception.'[85] With the onset of trench warfare, German troops recognised that their opponents were eavesdropping on them, because the Allied infantry would suddenly disappear into the trenches whenever the German infantry gave the command to fire through the telephone.[86] There were rumours that opposing troops were in possession of an eavesdropping apparatus, and patrols discovered wires leading to the opposing trenches. As a result, the German signal corps developed its own eavesdropping measures, on the one hand, and introduced deceptive countermeasures, on the other, both of which intersected in the then already century-old project for underground earth-based wireless telegraphy (*Erdtelegraphie*). To counter potential German attempts to jam Allied radio communications and to enable signals originating in the United States to be received only in France but not Germany, the eminent inventor Ernest F. W. Alexanderson tasked Harold H. Beverage with developing a 'barrage' device, an alternator transmitter system using two antennas that could be adjusted to neutralise interference, which were later revealed to be attached to kilometre-long wires.[87]

By the time the United States entered the war in April 1917, the American marines had already occupied Telefunken's stations in Sayville, New York (corresponding to Nauen) and Tuckerton, New Jersey (corresponding to Eilvese), which had been used to transmit encrypted orders to U-boat captains in the Atlantic. Although the US Navy had monitored, inspected, and censored every message passing through Telefunken's American stations, their focus on cryptography overlooked the possibility of steganography – that is, the possibility that 'covert messages could be hidden not within the content of a given message, but rather within the signalling itself', as Grant Wythoff demonstrates in a case study.[88] One of Telefunken's innovations was an automatic keyboard that enabled messages to be input faster than was possible by any manual operator. Incidentally, it also anonymised the telegrapher's unique cadence, rhythm, or signature, which cryptanalysts normally used to identify larger patterns.[89] After amateur telegraphist Charles E. Apgar cracked Telefunken's code by recording wireless telegraph signals on phonograph cylinders, the American government revoked Telefunken's licence for Sayville on 7 July 1915, and a force of naval engineers and sailors seized control of the station. However, the official statement failed to answer many questions and instead caused rampant speculation associating Germany's wireless communications systems with imaginary miracle weapons. In subsequent years, many militaries involved in the war took control of the local airwaves in a similar manner, determining which frequencies would be reserved for military and civilian uses, and they remained reluctant to relinquish this control over the electromagnetic spectrum in the early years of broadcasting.[90]

At the end of World War I, demobilisation left a surplus of wireless equipment, along with vast numbers of trained wireless operators, and these two factors were often cited by governments as arguments for restricting wireless services to reception without transmission. Hence, 'the entertainment industry', according to Friedrich Kittler's thesis associated with the origin story told above, 'is, in any conceivable sense of the word, an abuse of army equipment [or, a misuse of a military device, *Mißbrauch von Heeresgerät*]'.[91] Without the horrific events of World War I, to paraphrase Kittler's provocative claim, wireless telegraphy would have withered within the confines of European laboratories and never accelerated into the mass medium known globally as radio broadcasting. While this might now sound like a familiar story, Kittler's once-provocative thesis deconstructed foundational myths about the origins of national broadcasting, as the alliance of the gramophone industry and commercial radiotelegraphy, into martial stories about the connections between gramophone records (for issuing commands) and military-grade wireless devices (for receiving them).[92] Following Albert Kümmel-Schnür's insightful critique, Kittler's attempt to debunk foundational mythology unintentionally reinforced the medium's official origin story by ascribing to radio an inherent potential for insurrection, due to the incident known as the *Funkerspuk*, which national broadcasting operatives used to legitimise their claims to hegemony.[93] Furthermore, Kittler's phrase, *Mißbrauch von Heeresgerät*, was actually an ironic quotation, as Claus Pias has shown, and its contents are less significant than its rhetorical form.[94] Historically, radio administrators used the phrase 'abuse of army equipment' in reference to early wireless operators in the trenches who would neglect their duty to relay military commands in favour of broadcasting themselves playing music or reading newspaper articles. Historicising Kittler's thesis, Pias asks, 'How and why did someone in 1984 even come up with the idea of making the coupling of gramophone and radio into a radio station a central figure in media historiography?'[95]

We might ask a similar new-historicist question about Brunngraber's project: How and why did an author in 1940–44 come up with the idea of writing a novel about the world history of wireless telegraphy from a German perspective? And, given that Brunngraber's project was not completed and published until 1951, how could it possibly have been concluded in the aftermath of Auschwitz and Hiroshima? Omission and compression were key to Brunngraber's scant allusions to World War I, only hinting at Lorz's/Zenneck's internment in the United States and Braun's death in Brooklyn, New York.[96] A modern journeyman, the protagonist ends up switching companies one last time to work for Transradio, and appears at the end of the novel as a representative of Germany at the Versailles Peace Conference:

> Here he encountered Marconi once again, who was representing Italy, though not in matters of wireless, but in those of politics. Neither had any success: Lorz was not able to save Germany's cables, and Marconi was not able to get Italy's imperialistic demands accepted. But the actual work they had both served had by now grown to such a scale that it was no longer theirs and belonged to the world.[97]

No longer occupied with questions of invention, *The Resounding Worlds* ends – at least in the 1951 version – with this chapter on 'The Path of Service'.

During the celebratory inauguration of Transradio's international (German-language) news services, Lorz looks at Worpspiller, now 70 years old, who predicts that Lorz will soon take over the family company, and then Lorz starts reminiscing dreamily about his lost beloved Katharina. But 'he sank into thinking about the times [. . .] The whole continent was full of graves and groaning victims; was there now peace and had the problems that led to war been resolved?'[98] In an implied answer to this rhetorical question, which he simultaneously explored in essays on moral philosophy,[99] Brunngraber constellates world-historical events that all happened to occur around the same time: Oswald Spengler's remarks on 'the age of warring states' and the start of future wars; Ernest Rutherford's work on splitting the atom; and two British expeditions, one made to the coast of Africa, the other to the Brazilian Sobral, which confirmed Einstein's theory of spatial curvature.[100] The socialist Brunngraber concludes that the only path for the protagonist to follow is daily work, even if his hard-earned expertise had been rendered obsolete by a changing world:

> Even if [humanity], under the pale sun of peace, appeared to be on the pathway to hell, a man could do nothing other than his work. But doing that work, in a company that had lost nearly all its foreign possessions and a state that had lost all its cables, meant confronting a challenging mountain. And wireless, which was beginning its world domination also led those who had been put down into a new era.[101]

As much as the individual characters in the novel desire to control their fates, in the end 'it was not enmities that determined the course of things but the conquering science of the twentieth century'.[102]

As individual failures are offset by the characters' absorption into different collectives, *The Resounding World* ends with an allusion to the first international amateur radio transmissions across the Atlantic, instead of the official national broadcasts of the years to come:

> During the days of the Peace Conference, America legalised private radio broadcasting. Two years later, in summer 1921, Pittsburgh broadcast the first radio concerts, and radio amateurs using homemade equipment created a connection between the United States and England, the connection across the ocean.[103]

While these wireless transmissions established a link between the United States and England, they would never find their way to Germany, or perhaps only illicitly, given attempts to render the German amateur radio movement powerless. In the Weimar Republic, former Telefunken executive director and signal corps officer Bredow would become the chairman of the federation of broadcasting companies, suppress the amateur movement, and make wireless coverage into a problematic cultural agenda for national radio broadcasting that will be the subject of this book's next chapter. 'While foreign nations strive for a wider range', Bredow asserted, 'we strive for deepening [*Vertiefung*].'[104]

Wireless Writing Beyond the Telegram Style

To return to this chapter's central question about the relations between media technologies and literary modernism, wireless transmission is not only the object of representation, as is the case with Brunngraber's novel, but is also one of its conditions of possibility, as is clearer in other cases. If the *Hörspiel*, or radio drama, constitutes a medium-specific form, then the (wireless) telegram constitutes a medium-specific format. However, it is difficult to determine the difference, if any, that wireless made to literary content. With the emergence of wireless telegraphy, telegram forms in Imperial Germany merely added a line where the telegraphist was supposed to indicate whether the telegram was received 'wirelessly' (*drahtlos*), though only for calculating surcharges. Of course, this is not the only difference wireless transmission made to literary modernism, as evident in several insightful case studies, whose conclusions still provide unsatisfactory answers about the defining features of wireless literature. In modernism studies, Rudyard Kipling's short story 'Wireless' and F. T. Marinetti's 'Futurist Manifesto' have both been presented as exemplary cases of a wireless style, though Kipling's modelling of poetic inspiration on wireless tuning procedures could not be further removed from Marinetti's convoluted analogies between wireless transmission and the 'destruction of syntax'.[105] In *Wireless Dada*, Kurt Beals juxtaposes the *Telegrammstil* of German Dada and Expressionism with Italian Futurism and the French imagination of *télégraphie sans fils*, but it remains unclear what, if anything, differentiates a *wireless* telegram style from its wired counterpart.[106]

Characterised by clipping, abbreviations, and economical diction, the telegram style aims to pack the greatest amount of information into the smallest number of words or characters.[107] As yet another case of ironic quotation of a period term, what Kittler once termed the 'telegram style' (*Telegrammstil*) was also known historically as 'telegraphese' and related to 'cablese'. Said to be exemplified by Peter Altenberg, Ivan Goll, and August Stramm, it predates Dada,

Futurism, and Expressionism. Scholars adapting Kittler's apparent coinage have overlooked that he was explicitly quoting Luise Thon's literary typology of German impression,[108] and that before her literary study, the word *Telegrammstil* was primarily a pejorative term, as evident in Rudolf Leonhard's ridicule of Marinetti's 'wireless imagination'.[109] Unlike Thon, Kittler attributed the style's invention not to a poet but to a military commander, Alfred von Schlieffen, whose 'red pencil relentlessly crossed out redundant adjectives and redundant personal pronouns such as "I"'.[110] According to Kittler's speculative theory, the economies of pay-per-word telegraph services influenced the economy of telegraphic language in modernist poetry. Whereas the postal system traditionally calculated prices based on spatial distances, wired telegraphy charged based on the capacity of available electrical cables, and wireless telegraphy charged based on that of open frequencies or wavelengths. Once in the habit of paying per word, so this story goes, authors and publishers became obsessed with counting the words in their manuscripts. Likewise, the telegraph made newspaper correspondents avoid lexical and stylistic complications that could have been misunderstood by telegraphists, which further paralleled codes in literary modernism.

What, then, might constitute *wireless writing*? The contents of the wireless telegram, 'GNITEERG MORF ECNARF OT DNALGNE HGUORHT EHT REHTE', were less radical than they sound when quoted in avant-garde studies.[111] In this publicity stunt, each word was spelled backwards to increase the credibility of the message's reception: 'GREETING FROM FRANCE TO ENGLAND THROUGH THE ETHER'. In Germany, early radiotelegraphists in training would have been subjected to a slightly more Dadaistic exercise when practising how to transmit the following alphanumeric data, chosen because the letters and/or numbers in each group happened to have similar signs in Morse code:

> ei eis eisk si sie 5 he isis his esse hesse 55 sei heiss see siehe hihi 555 ehe heise hiess sieh hisse 5555 hehe es iss see heisse 55555
> to mot tom chot moch 0 motto otto ohm tot io 50 emme et so moos moses 05 messe miss hose tisch me 500 toi heim ost este home 505 stimme most hommes chemie meist 5005 motette mimi mio om 50505.[112]

While it is still possible to reverse-identify individual words corresponding to arbitrary code signs here – and perhaps even to recite them at the Cabaret Voltaire – the emergence of wireless cryptography in World War I marked the end of an era of 'cleartext'. Because any wireless signal can be intercepted, encrypted messages became entirely illegible, as evident in the following message, once thought to be uncrackable:

> FGAXA XAXFF FAFVA AVDFA GAXFX FAFAG DXGGX AGXFD XGAGX GAXGX AGXVF VXXAG XDDAX GGAAF DGGAF FXGGX XDFAX GXAXV AGXGG DFAGG GXVAX VFXGV FFGGA XDGAX FDVGG A

The cleartext, decoded from the ADFGVX cipher, reads, 'MUNITIONIERUNG BESCHLEUNIGEN PUNKT SOWEIT NICHT EINGESEHEN AUCH BEI TAG' (ACCELERATE AMUNITION STOP IF NOT SEEN DURING DAY TOO). With the end of cleartext, literature and technology part ways.

While previous studies of wireless writing have prioritised the avant-garde, we need to keep situating these literary experiments in relation to the kinds of literary realism examined in this chapter and the anti-realist SF analysed throughout this book. For the modernist tradition of aestheticism, the avant-garde tradition of wireless writing was relatively rare. While some modernist poets did write poems about the wireless, as was the case in the German-language context with Johannes R. Becher, Ivan Goll, Gerhart Hermann Mostar, and Alfred Vagts, among others, the intensity of lyrical expression and the loftiness of the rhetorical tradition situates the lyric form at a distance from the banality of wireless telegraphy and the everydayness of infrastructure. The focus in scholarship on the so-called avant-garde overlooks vernacular modernism, where wireless transmission had even greater impacts on literacy and literary form.

What, then, might constitute *wireless writing* beyond the wired telegram style? The *Funkspruch* (radiogram, or, to use the proprietary eponym, Marconigram) developed a unique format for transmitting messages to unknown addressees with various headers and message sections. By extension, the radio voice was taken to be a particular form of *Funkspruch* known as the *Rundspruch*, where information is transmitted blindly to multiple recipients with no expectation of receipt or acknowledgement of reception. Exemplarily, Alfons Paquet's poetic 'Funkspruch' extended

> Greetings to those who are ready to hear, with the elastic steel band over the hair on your head and the black shells on both ears – so that in the sudden silence you can catch the one voice that rushes toward you in space like a little ship riding its wave, straight to you but also to where there is no ear.[113]

In a Whitmanian litany of greetings, Paquet's radiogram addressed a wide range of imagined audiences:

> those who are snowed in [. . .] those who sit around little marble tables in packed coffeehouses [. . .] those who lie stretched out in narrow white hospital rooms [. . .] the boy who has stretched out some copper wires [. . .] the worker who has just returned home [. . .] the old woman who [. . .] peers out the window through a spyglass [. . .] the magician who takes the antenna on a walk [. . .] everyone, even if we don't know each other.[114]

If there is such a thing as wireless writing, it might be located not only in the economy of the telegram style but also in this virtual system of address uniquely found in wireless transmission. Just as writers now habitually count their words, so they address unknown audiences and attempt to predict, but can never fully determine, what will resonate.

Notes

1. Schelle-Noetzel [Bronnen], *Kampf im Aether*. For critical analysis, see Ketelsen, 'Der Rundfunk', 36–64.
2. Brunngraber, *Der tönende Erdkreis*. On the novel's history of composition and publication, see Schneider, 'Rudolf Brunngraber', 417–27.
3. For Brunngraber's interwar biography and relationship to literary realism, see Hughes, 'Facts and Fiction'.
4. On Brunngraber's self-identification as a 'poet-sociologist' (*Dichter-Soziologe*), see Hughes, 'Facts and Fiction', 207.
5. See Schneider, 'Rudolf Brunngraber', 417–27.
6. See, among others, Campbell, *Wireless Writing*; Beals, *Wireless Dada*.
7. On this constellation of events, see Hagen, *Radio Schreber*; cf. Kümmel-Schnur, 'Patente als Agenten von Mediengeschichte', 22.
8. On Telefunken, see Schröter et al., *25 Jahre Telefunken*; *50 Jahre Telefunken*; Malanowski, *The Race for Wireless*, 122–31; Thiele, *Telefunken nach 100 Jahren*; Winseck and Pike, *Communication and Empire*, 229.
9. In a January 1946 letter to his friend Hans Dostal, Brunngraber described these plans to write a second part to the novel. See Schneider, 'Rudolf Brunngraber', 417.
10. See Fuchs, 'Anfänge der drahtlosen Telegraphie'; Friedewald, *Die 'Tönenden Funken'*.
11. On prominent members of the German signal corps, including Hans Bredow, Karl Mehnert, and Wilhelm Runge, see Aschoff, *Geschichte der Nachrichtentechnik*, vol. 1, 8 n. 2. For a brief allusion to prominent physicists who were also members of signal corps, see

Canales, 'The Media of Relativity', 610–45. John Durham Peters claims that 'Harold Innis, László Moholy-Nagy, Norbert Wiener, and Ludwig Wittgenstein all worked artillery in World War I' (*Marvelous Clouds*, 243).

12. See Headrick, *The Tentacles of Progress*, 126–30; Anduaga, *Wireless and Empire*, 54–120; Winseck and Pike, *Communication and Empire*, 228–56.
13. Winseck and Pike, *Communication and Empire*, xv–xvii.
14. Brunngraber, *Der tönende Erdkreis*, 9.
15. Brunngraber, *Der tönende Erdkreis*, 9.
16. Brunngraber, *Der tönende Erdkreis*, 80.
17. Brunngraber, *Der tönende Erdkreis*, 9.
18. Brunngraber, *Der tönende Erdkreis*, 12.
19. Brunngraber, *Der tönende Erdkreis*, 17.
20. Brunngraber, *Der tönende Erdkreis*, 17–18.
21. See Hagen, *Das Radio*, 46.
22. Slaby, 'The New Telegraphy', 867–74.
23. Toscano, *Marconi's Wireless*, 69–70.
24. See Fuchs, 'Anfänge der drahtlosen Telegraphie', 117; Slaby and Arco, Schaltungsweise; Slaby and Arco, Sendeschleife; Slaby and Arco, Schaltung am Empfänger; Slaby and Arco, Empfangsapparat für Funkentelegraphie; Slaby and Arco, Empfangsapparat für Funkentelegraphie mit gemeinsamer Stromquelle.
25. Slaby, 'The New Telegraphy', 875.
26. Braun, *Drahtlose Telegraphie durch Wasser und Luft*.
27. See Fuchs, 'Anfänge der drahtlosen Telegraphie', 117–18. Braun, Telegraphirsystem [*sic*].
28. See Fuchs, 'Anfänge der drahtlosen Telegraphie', 118. Braun, Schaltungsweise; Braun, Schaltung für elektrische Funkentelegraphie.
29. Brunngraber, *Der tönende Erdkreis*, 140.
30. Brunngraber, *Der tönende Erdkreis*, 140.
31. Brunngraber, *Der tönende Erdkreis*, 145; cf. Huurdeman, *Worldwide History of Telecommunications*, 215; Braun, Telegraphirsystem [*sic*].
32. The presentation closely mirrors that in Zenneck's article, 'Die Zeit des Funkensenders', in *50 Jahre Telefunken*, 153.
33. See Kümmel-Schnur and Kassung, foreword to *Bildtelegraphie*, 7–12.
34. Arapostathis and Gooday, *Patently Contestable*, 172.
35. Arapostathis and Gooday, *Patently Contestable*, 165.
36. Scholl, 'Marconi versus Telefunken', 281; Friedewald, 'Telefunken vs. Marconi'; Tworek, 'How Not to Build a World Wireless Network'.
37. Brunngraber, *Der tönende Erdkreis*, 449.
38. Brunngraber, *Der tönende Erdkreis*, 40.
39. Brunngraber, *Der tönende Erdkreis*, 40. The patent discussed is Marconi, Improvements.
40. Brunngraber, *Der tönende Erdkreis*, 429–30.
41. See Lyall, *International Communications*.

42. See Aitken, *Syntony and Spark*, 28–33.
43. Loos, 'Der technische Impresario'; Loos, 'Der drahtlose Impresario'.
44. Loos, 'Der drahtlose Impresario', 12.
45. Loos, 'Der drahtlose Impresario', 12–13 (ellipses in original).
46. Loos, 'Der drahtlose Impresario', 12–13.
47. Fuchs, 'Anfänge der drahtlosen Telegraphie', 119.
48. See Star, 'Cooperation Without Consensus', 93–106.
49. Qtd. and trans. in Zielinski, *Variations on Media Thinking*, 207.
50. For Arco's biography, see Fuchs, *Georg von Arco*.
51. Gesellschaft für Drahtlose Telegraphie mbH, Empfangseinrichtung für drahtlose Telegraphie und Telephonie; Gesellschaft für Drahtlose Telegraphie mbH, Einrichtung zur Erzeugung elektrischer Schwingungen; Lieben, Kathodenstrahlenrelais.
52. Fuchs, 'Anfänge der drahtlosen Telegraphie', 120.
53. Friedewald, *Die 'Tönenden Funken'*, 29–30.
54. Fuchs, 'Anfänge der drahtlosen Telegraphie', 120.
55. Brunngraber, *Der tönende Erdkreis*, 401–2.
56. Marconi, 'Wireless Telegraphic Communication', 196–222; Braun, 'Electrical Oscillations and Wireless Telegraphy', 245.
57. Braun, 'Electrical Oscillations and Wireless Telegraphy', 245.
58. Brunngraber, *Der tönende Erdkreis*, 290.
59. Brunngraber, *Der tönende Erdkreis*, 290.
60. Brunngraber, *Der tönende Erdkreis*, 290.
61. Krajewski, *World Projects*, 66.
62. Krajewski, *World Projects*, 32.
63. See Tworek, 'How Not to Build a World Wireless Network', 182; Tworek, *News from Germany*, 45–69.
64. Tworek, *News from Germany*, 180.
65. See Friedewald, *Die 'Tönenden Funken'*; Friedewald, 'Telefunken vs. Marconi'; cf. Klein-Arendt, *Kamina ruft Nauen!*.
66. See Friedewald, *Die 'Tönenden Funken'*.
67. Parks, 'Earth Observation and Signal Territories'.
68. Siegert, 'The Map *Is* the Territory', 13.
69. 'Funkentelegraphische Weltprojekte', 134–40.
70. 'Funkentelegraphische Weltprojekte', 134.
71. Schomburgk, 'Africa and Film', qtd. and trans. in Korn, 'Why We Still Do Not Have Television', 590–2.
72. Günther, *Fünfsprachenwörterbuch für Radioamateure*; Günther and Richter, *Lexikon der Funktechnik*.
73. Espenschied, 'Radio Broadcast Coverage of City Areas', 117.
74. See, for instance, Siemens, *History of the House of Siemens*, vol. 1, 158, vol. 2, 256.
75. See Kittler, *Gramophone, Film, Typewriter*, 95; cf. Kümmel, 'Innere Stimmen', 175–97.
76. Fuchs, 'Anfänge der drahtlosen Telegraphie'.
77. Winseck and Pike, *Communication and Empire*, 243.

78. McLuhan, *Understanding Media*, 300–1; cf. McLuhan, *Take Today*, 152: 'World War I a railway war of centralization and encirclement. World War II a radio war of decentralization concluded by the Bomb. World War III a TV guerilla war with no divisions between civil and military fronts.'
79. McLuhan, *Understanding Media*, 300–1.
80. Winseck and Pike, *Communication and Empire*, 243.
81. Winseck and Pike, *Communication and Empire*, 243.
82. See Meier, 'Drahtlose Telegraphie im Schützengraben?'
83. Kittler, 'Grabenkrieg – Nervenkrieg – Medienkrieg', 303.
84. Bredow, *Im Banne der Ätherwellen*, vol. 1, 35–6.
85. Siegert, *Passage des Digitalen*, 394; cf. Siegert, 'Eskalation eines Mediums', 13–39.
86. Schäfer, 'Das Abhorchen von Ferngesprächen', 93–7.
87. Beverage and Crowswell, 'Some Notes on the History of Antenna Developments', 13–18.
88. Wythoff, 'Invention of Wireless Cryptography', n.p.
89. Wythoff, 'Invention of Wireless Cryptography'.
90. See Peters, *The Marvelous Clouds*, 243.
91. Kittler, *Gramophone, Film, Typewriter*, 96–7; for similar phrasing, cf. Kittler, *Gramophone, Film, Typewriter*, 110, 111, 253; Kittler, 'Rock Music'.
92. See Dotzler and Roesler-Keilholz, *Mediengeschichte als historische Techno-logie*, 113–39.
93. Kümmel, 'Innere Stimmen'.
94. Pias, 'Friedrich Kittler', 5.
95. Pias, 'Friedrich Kittler', 6.
96. Brunngraber, *Der tönende Erdkreis*, 510–12.
97. Brunngraber, *Der tönende Erdkreis*, 574–5.
98. Brunngraber, *Der tönende Erdkreis*, 573.
99. Brunngraber, *Wie es kam*; Brunngraber, *Was zu kommen hat.*
100. Brunngraber, *Der tönende Erdkreis*, 573.
101. Brunngraber, *Der tönende Erdkreis*, 574.
102. Brunngraber, *Der tönende Erdkreis*, 574.
103. Brunngraber, *Der tönende Erdkreis*, 575.
104. Bredow, 'Die Verwirklichung des Rundfunkgedankens', qtd. in Führer, 'A Medium of Modernity?', 728.
105. On Marinetti, see, among others, Campbell, *Wireless Writing*; Campbell, 'Marinetti, *Marconista*'; Fisher, 'Futurism and Radio'. On Kipling, see, among others, Menke, *Telegraphic Realism*, 217–48; Kittler, 'Abstimmung', 199–214.
106. Beals, *Wireless Dada*.
107. On the telegram style, see Kittler, 'Im Telegrammstil'; Segeberg, 'Technische Konkurrenzen'; Standage, *The Victorian Internet*, 105–26.
108. Kittler cites Luise Thon, *Die Sprache des deutschen Impressionismus*, 88.
109. See Beals, *Wireless Dada*, 49.

110. Kittler, 'Im Telegrammstil'.
111. Lewty, 'Syntonic Desire', 324.
112. Ohlsberg, *Handbuch für Funkentelegraphisten*, 31. The similar characters for the telegraphist to practice are as follows: 'e' (dot), 'i' (two dots), 's' (three dots), 'k' (four dots), '5' (five dots); 't' (dash), 'm' (two dashes), 'o' (three dashes), 'ch' (four dashes), and '0' (five dashes).
113. Paquet, 'Funkspruch', in Hay, *Literatur und Rundfunk*, 253.
114. Paquet, 'Funkspruch', 253–5.

Chapter 5

Beyond Broadcasting: Programming, Forecasting, and 'Radio for All'

When asked in 1926 to provide some words of wisdom for the next generation of wireless enthusiasts, Hans Bredow, a former executive director of the Telefunken Company whom the editors here called the 'creator of German radio' and compared further to Goethe, responded with a laundry list of speculations.[1] 'My dear girls, dear boys, the future of radio lies in your hands. What we have begun you will need to bring to completion', Bredow asserted, referring to his official programme of *Rundfunk für alle* ('radio for all'). 'Only with you will the secrets of electric waves become a natural, universal cultural heritage, and smiling you will look back on all the errors and mistakes in the evolution of wireless.'[2] According to Bredow's bourgeois ideology of media change, wireless history played out in terms of inevitable technological progress driving a perpetual search for harmony between nature and society (Fig. 5.1). With the first official entertainment programme broadcast on 29 October 1923, the new medium was said to inaugurate a 'new epoch of world and cultural history', comparable to that of the printing press.[3] Deploying these and other standard modernist media topoi, Bredow predicted that 'the time will come when there is no longer any separation between people. The concept of space, of distance, of being alone will have been overturned, and there will no longer be any borders, if you are mature enough, for friendship and brotherhood.'[4] In Bredow's techno-determinist vision, technological progress would inevitably lead to social progress, making the naturally occurring phenomenon of electromagnetic radiation into second nature. An expert speculator, Bredow repeatedly mobilised such timeworn visions of wireless futures not only to obtain financial support for his unprecedented and often unpopular megaproject of supplying 'radio for all', but also to deflect demands

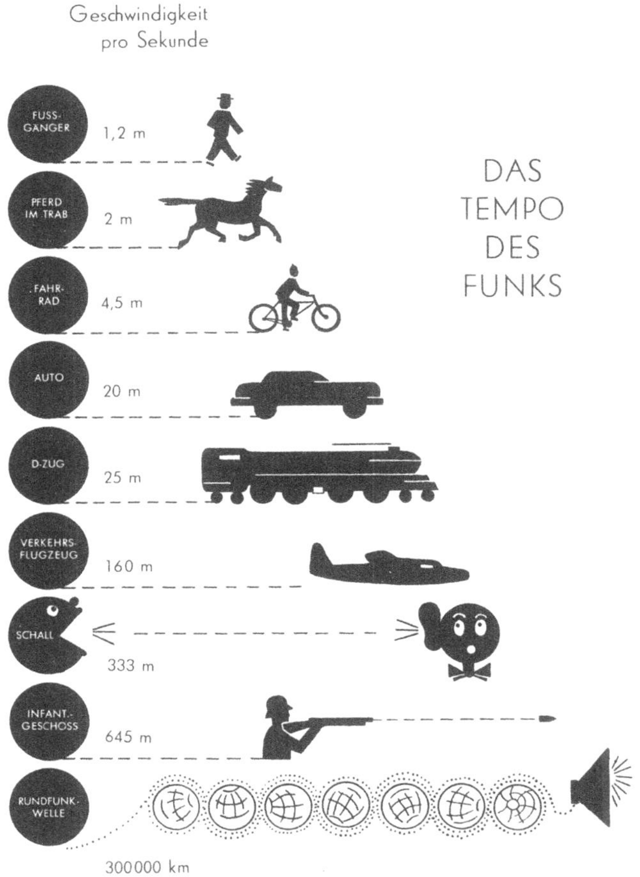

Figure 5.1 An infographic from the memoirs of the 'creator of German radio', Hans Bredow, showing the accelerating 'tempo of wireless': (from top to bottom), the speed in m/sec of a pedestrian, a galloping horse, a bicycle, a car, an express train, a commercial aeroplane, a sound wave, a bullet, and a radio wave. Source: Bredow, *Im Banne der Ätherwellen*, vol. 1, 32.

from the medium's users for immediate, systemic change and keep them suspended in a state of future possibilities.[5]

'Alongside sound and vision', Bredow predicted in his advice to wireless enthusiasts, 'the wireless transmission of light and power will have to appear. Only this will bring God's gift of Hertzian waves to completion and lead the radio to the highest height.'[6] At a time when the German wireless industry was developing plans for a wireless energy distribution system that never materialised, the omnidirectionality of wireless energy and information transfer challenged existing models of capitalistic circulation and governmental essential services, and instead seemed like a divine gift, equally and freely available to everyone. Inflecting this discourse through the European intellectual tradition, Bredow outlined not only his politics of nation-building through the creation of communities of radio listeners, but also his metaphysics of wireless transmission derived from the understanding of electricity and magnetism in German Romanticism as elemental, polarising forces. Drawing on Hermann von Helmholtz's seminal lecture on 'The Conservation of Energy', Bredow's laundry list of speculations concluded with the following prediction about the unifying force of electricity: 'Then the continuous universal element, which accompanies all material and atmospheric existence, the "world-soul", as Goethe calls electricity, will become the ruler of the world.'[7] Written in the future perfect, Bredow's concluding remarks presented a utopia of universal wireless energy transmission, which remains an object of intense speculation today. As an ideal, 'radio for all' may seem inevitable and perhaps even desirable, an impression that officials such as Bredow eagerly sought to naturalise. However, this chapter reveals the medium's universality, accessibility, and desirability to be laborious social and cultural constructs rather than inherent properties of media technologies.

Of the official programme of 'radio for all', Bredow reflected years later that 'only German radio was in the course of time able to satisfy German desires'.[8] To unlock the new medium's allegedly democratic potential, national radio broadcasting programmes in the Weimar Republic aimed to create a monolingual public sphere, centred on the urban bourgeois subject, and ideally free from conflict and dissent. Throughout the 1920s German radio was primarily under the jurisdiction of the Reich Postal Ministry, an institution in which Bredow was a civil servant and – as of the year of his address to future generations – the newly appointed Reichs-Rundfunk-Kommissar, or administrative chairman of the federation of broadcasting companies known as the Reichs-Rundfunk-Gesellschaft (RRG). While other officials were sceptical of the radio, treating it as a means of minimising the financial deficit created by the post office's telegraphic services, Bredow viewed it as a mass medium with democratic potential. According to Bredow's bourgeois vision, the radio was tasked with serving the nation's cultural interests and remedying its perceived educational deficits, rather than obeying the demands of investors, as he conceived of privatised broadcasting in the United States. On German radio, cultural programmes were supposed to educate, and thereby integrate, all levels of society, especially the lower classes, into a reinvigorated *Kulturnation*.[9] To implement these ambitious radio politics, Bredow and others planned to create communal assembly-hall radio listening spaces known as *Funkhalle* or *Funksäle*. However, there was an irresolvable tension in this conception of radio as a mass medium for the public sphere. On the one hand, radio was to provide something for everyone in terms of programme contents, which led the audience to be stereotyped into target groups, culminating in the formation of empirical audience research. On the other, everyone was to be connected to the radio through a fundamentally open, insecure channel, which made it possible for anyone not only to receive broadcasts but also to transmit them.

This chapter examines the extent to which the emergence of national broadcasting represents a continuation of or departure from previous modes of wireless transmission. Long relegated to playing the role of the pre-history of radio, wireless telegraphy and related applications for timekeeping, radio navigation, and weather forecasts are worthy of greater attention in their own right as forms of 'logistical media'.[10] Building on Maria Rikitianskaia, Gabriele Balbi, and Katharina Lobinger's recent work on the 'mediatization of the air', I examine how 'this transformation of the medium, often considered a rather sudden phenomenon that occurred in the 1920s, actually originated in the early twentieth century with the possibility of listening to contents floating in the air'.[11] To the extent that this communications model tends to evaluate the medium's success in terms of its ability to increase connections, however, I adopt a critical view of the connectivity paradigm by comparing wireless communications to the limit case of wireless energy distribution.[12]

This chapter answers Balbi and Rikitianskaia's further call to expand the purview of radio history beyond the traditional framework of national broadcasting.[13] To update and expand the field for the study of radio beyond radio, we need to account for at least five non-canonical examples of radio-based transmission, which are already objects of analysis in media and cultural studies and resonate more directly than national broadcasting with today's main wireless applications: radiography, or medical imaging; radiotelegraphy and radiotelephony; radar and satellites; radiophones, or mobile phones; and radio-based data networks such as Wi-Fi. Reflecting on this transhistorical constellation, Balbi and Rikitianskaia conclude that 'radio is not a medium but a family of different media, technologies, and meanings'.[14] From this transhistorical and intermedial perspective, we can rethink long-standing assumptions about medium specificity and the dominative narrative of historical events long thought to have determined the medium's future.

Radiodetermination

In the years leading up to the institutionalisation of national broadcasting in the Weimar Republic, one central event that occurred during the November Revolution appeared to reveal the new medium's possibilities while also determining its future course.[15] On 9 November 1918 the abdication of Emperor Wilhelm II ended the monarchy of the German Empire. Later that same afternoon two new forms of government were proclaimed: the Social Democratic Party (SPD) politician Philipp Scheidemann proclaimed a Democratic Republic from the balcony of the Reichstag, and the Independent Social Democratic Party (USPD) leader Karl Liebknecht proclaimed a Free Socialist German Republic from the roof of a car in front of Berlin Castle. As historian Heidi Tworek has shown, the competing news was highly mediated by wireless news services.[16] Shortly after these announcements, Wolff's Telegraph Bureau, the headquarters of the German press and part of a news agency cartel with British Reuters and French Havas, was occupied by envoys sent from the revolutionary Berlin-based Workers and Soldiers Council. Relaying their own version of Lenin's message 'To All', they pre-emptively broadcast, 'To All! Here the revolution has achieved a brilliant almost completely bloodless victory.' This event became remembered as the *Funkerspuk*, as the 'ghosts of wireless operators' and the spectre of a political revolution haunted the centrist authorities responsible for administering national broadcasting. By showing what was already possible in the present, the event shaped officials' imagination of what they deemed undesirable for the future.

Although wireless operators represented a minor threat to state authorities, the *Funkerspuk* inflamed officials' fears about the potential radicalisation of unmonitored receivers by unauthorised transmitters. This paranoid conservative rhetoric was then used to justify state controls permitting reception but prohibiting transmission. Critiquing this rhetoric, one reader observed that the official term, *Rundfunk*, did not actually 'mean that anyone who has the money to buy a radiotelephonic apparatus or anyone who builds one by virtue of their own skills, can radio around anywhere they want'.[17] While radiotelegraphy allowed for both transmission and reception, and the radio inherited these same affordances, the rhetoric of media change naturalised the official prohibition against transmission, further erasing recent memory. 'After all, it can't be any other way. Any reproaches made to the authorities for not dropping these restrictions are unfounded.'[18] Confronted not with an uncertain future but a highly contested one, the state officials responsible for administering the medium mobilised their own predictions about which futures would be the most desirable and turned to extensive planning to realise these objectives. In retrospect, Bredow described the concrete steps required for the 'liquidation of the "Funkerspuk"' in terms of three main technical and social controls: banning private transmission; requiring a subscription fee and a reception licence; and updating and safeguarding the German Empire's exclusive right to operate wireless transmitters. As in the United States and other countries, German radio was founded by former radiotelegraphists such as Bredow who rose to prominence after serving in wireless signal corps during World War I. Haunted by this wartime experience and its apparent culmination in the *Funkerspuk*, newly appointed state authorities then excluded the interests of their amateur counterparts and construed their unauthorised transmissions as an 'abuse of military equipment'.

Reflecting critically on this mythology around the *Funkerspuk*, Albert Kümmel-Schnur wonders whether the story about a failed revolution, which has often been used by other scholars to explain the differences between European and American broadcasting, is nothing more than a 'phantom pain'.[19] Repeating the story, Kümmel-Schnur argues, inadvertently confirms the postal ministry's official position, as is always a danger with reviewing stereotypes or foundational mythologies only to debunk them. Like the *Kinodebatte*, or debates about cinema's proper relation to literature, theatre, painting, and other established art forms, the period's lesser-known *Radiodebatte* sought ways of understanding, authorising, and legitimising the new medium in relation to old ones. Outlining the contours of this debate, Kümmel-Schnur highlights six main issues: the 'selection' of contents; 'participation' in distant events; 'externalisation' of the senses; integrating programming into the 'order of knowledge'; the 'storage' of ephemeral broadcasts; and navigating the tension between 'actuality and presence', on the one hand, and the conditions for attentive listening, on the other.[20] From this perspective, the medium was not fully determined by the authorities or by a singular historical event, but rather remained contested, negotiated, and in a state of becoming.

Based on the dominant model of national broadcasting, radio is usually assumed to be an acoustic medium, the alliance of gramophony (music) and telephony (voice), and its origins are located in early attempts to broadcast gramophone recordings or the human voice. However, this 'common-sense' categorisation overlooks the importance of radiotelegraphy (writing), which was responsible for creating the impression of a unique omnidirectional mode of wireless transmission known as the *Bannkreis*, or 'magic circle'. For Fritz

Walter Bischoff, the superintendent of the Schlesien Funk-Stunde and co-producer of the radio play *Hallo! Hier Welle Erdball!* (Hello! Here's channel earth!), the mission of broadcasting consisted in redemption from the 'Babylonian confusion of ideas' on the book market. For Bischoff, the radio provided a 'means for communication and understanding [. . .] so as to beat down the multiplicity, the confusion of voices and shouts in a magic circle [*Bannkreis*] radiated through waves, the periphery of which is unlimited, but the centre of which lies in the heart of listeners themselves'.[21] Hardly a novel proposal, Bischoff was repurposing an internationalist topos from popular scientific outreach narratives, composed by engineers and publicists including Hans Dominik, Artur Fürst, Walter de Haas (Hanns Günther), and Erich Lasswitz. For these Wilhelminian authors, the general public was defined by its perceived media illiteracy, and the proposed remedy for technophobia and anxiety about modernisation or globalisation was education in the 'art of technology'.[22] In the Weimar Republic, these Wilhelminian attempts to salvage the transformative potential of new technology in the disenchanted world of secular modernity were already being ridiculed across the political spectrum, even as they continued to be taken up and renewed by the authorities responsible for administering the medium colloquially described as the 'New Tower of Babylon'.[23]

What might be an alternative origin story of broadcasting? Before there were any regular radio programmes, early broadcasting experiments appeared to capture the Kittlerian 'discourse on discourse channel conditions'. Suggesting a medium's future *in nuce*, the discourse on discourse channel conditions retraces and re-performs otherwise invisible genealogies.[24] For instance, Katja Rothe examines the large corpus of early radio plays on maritime subjects, showing how they reprocessed the new medium's origins in maritime telegraphy and emergency rescue operations.[25] While early radio plays have often been read as allegories or metafictions, Kittler surprisingly located their discursive channel conditions not only in Orson Welles's *War of the Worlds* but also in Richard Wagner's *Nibelungen*, 'the zero series of all world wars'.[26] For Kittler, the Weimar Republic's radio dramas ostensibly captured the trauma of World War I and anxiety about the separation of voices from bodies, but 'behind such melodramatic panic [. . .] there was however the impossible realization of belonging to an era where the conditions of existence were and are characterized by applied mathematics'.[27] Extending Kittler's thesis about the medium's inability to reveal its conditions of possibility, Bernhard Siegert applies it to how post-WWII German radio repressed experimental sound culture in favour of the aesthetics of the spoken word.[28] Taking Kittler's speculations in another comparative direction, Bernhard J. Dotzler and Silke Roesler-Keilholz analyse the first radio European plays as multifaceted explorations of the medium's 'techno-logics' (*Techno-logie*): *A Comedy of Danger* explores the medium's invisibility; *Marémoto* (Seaquake) its actuality; and *Magic on the Air*, the contingency of live transmission.[29] The discourse on discourse channel conditions for early broadcasting experiments thus underscores the medium's multiple origins, alliances, and ontologies, rather than any essential medium specificity.

The medium's acoustic properties admittedly fuelled a search for a new medium-specific form, which would combine the spoken word with sound, music, and noise in a manner that came to be known as the *Hörspiel* (radio drama; literally, 'audible play'). However, the official programme of 'radio for all' started out with straightforward remediation of canonical literary and cultural contents. In a biting critique of the state of 'broadcast poetry' (*gefunkte Dichtung*) in 1924, Hans Natonek remarked that 'I will never forgive Marconi for an introductory lecture on Hölderlin delivered by a radio director who works around the clock [*rundfunktionierenden Rundfunkdirektors*].'[30] As Natonek recognised, one challenge that faced broadcasting literature was the competing programme offerings on different stations. 'What am I supposed to do with Adalbert Stifter', Natonek quipped, 'if the wavelengths get mixed up and it suddenly gets interrupted by a report about the beet market!'[31] Assuming that the audience desires 'hits, not intellectualism' (*Schlager, nicht Geistigkeit*), Natonek concluded that

> anyone who wants to spend time with Hölderlin does not need the mediation of radio. The great appeal of radio lies not in what it brings, but in the fact that that it comes wirelessly; it is the legitimate satisfaction of being able to take part in the popularisation of the greatest invention of the century.[32]

For Natonek and other early adopters, the sheer possibility of wirelessing exceeded any potential attractions of the medium's forms and contents.

'From the beginning', Brecht later reflected, 'the radio imitated practically every existing institution that had anything at all to do with the distribution of speech or song.'[33] Admittedly, broadcast literature in Germany started out with moderators reciting Goethe, Heine, Hölderlin, Stifter, and other standbys of the established literary canon. However, contemporary authors were already reading their own works on the radio as early as 1924, and the programme

Stunde der Lebenden, established in 1925, would introduce mass audiences to the works of 'living authors' such as Gottfried Benn, Marieluise Fleißer, and Hermann Kasack, who read their own works in their own voices.[34] In subsequent years, there were many dramaturgical reworkings of classical and modern dramas under Alfred Braun's direction, and radio plays started to precede their theatrical counterparts – as was the case with Bertolt Brecht's *Mann ist Mann* (Man's a Man), broadcast on the radio before it was staged in a theatre. Nevertheless, the officials behind the 'radio for all' campaign remained sceptical about the audience's status as potential content producers. In a 1927 prize contest sponsored by the national radio, there were 1,117 submissions of amateur radio dramas; none were deemed worthy of the prize.[35] Still lamenting the state of 'broadcast literature' (*gefunkte Literatur*) in 1927, Otto Alfred Palitzsch proposed shifting from studio-based music, lectures, and recitations towards live reporting on current events, exemplified by Hans Bodenstedt's on-location reportage, in which he interviewed a zookeeper at the zoo, a diver under the sea, and many other workers in their environments.[36] By the end of the decade these debates intersected with the new style of reportage known as New Objectivity, informing speculations on the emergence of a purely auditory type of narrative, though not necessarily the *Hörspiel*.[37]

While some early media thinkers compared radio to print, based on the parallel structures of mass address systems, others compared it to the telephone, based on those of communication devices, and yet communications and mass media increasingly became incompatible models. When asked over mass address systems, communicative questions of identification, disposition, and localisation assume different meanings, since the source(s) and recipient(s) of the 'radiophonic call' are truly unknown. There might not be anyone present to answer the call, and it might not have been made by a human being at all. To address the uncanniness of direct address there were various strategies of speaking on the radio, such as the use of two moderators holding a dialogue for the audience to eavesdrop on, instead of one moderator attempting to hold a dialogue with the absent audience, or the use of meta-discourse markers intended to reflect the broadcast conversation's mediated status.[38] Extending this conception of the radio as telephone, Brecht's 1932 essay on 'Radio as a Communications Apparatus' proposed that

> the radio could be the finest possible communications apparatus in public life, a vast system of channels. That is, it could be so, if it understood how to receive as well as to transmit, how to let the

> listener speak as well as hear, how to bring him into a network instead of isolating him.[39]

At the Baden-Baden Music Festival, Brecht had already attempted to put this theory into practice by using a two-stage platform for *The Flight of the Lindberghs*, with trained performers on the left and the listeners performing Lindbergh's role on the right, singing along to the radio.[40]

Though usually attributed to Brecht, the conception of radio as a multidirectional communication medium, rather than a one-way broadcasting medium, was a common media topos in the 1920s, dating back to at least his associate Eugenie Schwarzwald's description of the radio as 'a gigantic means of communication'.[41] Though cognisant that 'first of all, the invention will be appropriated by business interests', Schwarzwald remained hopeful that 'the cause of radio is too enormous; it must triumph!', and wished that 'many of these waves be viewed with spirit, truth, beauty, and feeling, and may everyone succeed in finding the right one'.[42] Developing the same topos in another direction, the announcer in Bischoff's radio drama assumes the role of a radio station called 'Welle Erdball', calling out to listeners around the world: '"Hello! It's Station Earth! Symphony of time!" / vibrates out of the ether, shrills, and thunders on. / It's not about heaven, hell, and eternity, / it's about you, the listeners.'[43] In the spirit of New Objectivity, Bischoff's radio play eschews the dramatic modes of comedy and tragedy in favour of uncanny direct address. At several points the announcer instructs listeners in the proper mode of reception: 'Please don't look for any connections [. . .] / Please receive this just like a newspaper report'.[44] As Bischoff implicitly recognised, the most difficult task for interactive distribution media is how to prevent the audience from changing the channel or from making paranoid connections between isolated reports. In imitation of radio listeners surfing the airwaves, the announcer reviews the options for them: 'London – football match, Japan – fight in the rainforest, / government crisis, the streets noisy with stomping, / passengers between decks, voyage to America, / the Earth turns without rest'.[45] Attempting to wean radio operators off their normal habit of scanning the airwaves, national broadcasting parroted the motto of the popular NORA radio, also quoted in Bischoff's play: 'Don't search, just tune in and receive' (*Nicht suchen, nur empfangen und wählen*). Incidentally, this was the same model as owned by Viennese coffeehouse wit Alfred Polgar, as documented in his modernist miniature, 'From the Notebooks of a Radio Listener': 'I have a little radio. Its name is Nora, but we call it Kitty [*Mieze*].'[46]

Due to the naturalisation of broadcasting, we tend to take for granted the radio set's affective dimension and the mode's presumed international character, even though they were hardly a foregone conclusion.[47] 'The five continents are drawing ever closer', Siegfried Kracauer once observed, only to conclude that this process would result in a sort of reverse colonisation. 'In truth, it is not we who extend ourselves out toward them; rather, it is their cultures that appropriate us in their boundless imperialism.'[48] Other radio listeners associated the ubiquity of radio voices with imaginative travel, as in Robert Seitz's poem: 'I hear your voices beside me / And I pass with your voices through you, / Walk the boulevards, / And pass the palaces of Granada, / Am in the middle of traffic in port cities / And am alone in the vast plains of a southern continent'.[49] Using similar language, René Schickele suggested that radio allows one to be alone without losing touch with the world, while also acknowledging, unlike Seitz, that crossing medial borders still involves border guards and toll collectors.[50]

Crystallising this cosmopolitan discourse, Rudolf Arnheim belatedly composed one of the first and most influential medium-specific theories, *Radio*, in 1933, 'when its subject seemed to go out of existence', as the wireless transmission of sound seemed about to be eclipsed by the emergent medium of television. For Arnheim, 'the great miracle of wireless' consisted not in any acoustic content but in 'the omnipresence of what people are singing or saying anywhere, the overleaping of frontiers, the conquest of spatial isolation, the importation of culture on the waves of the ether, the same fare for all, sound in silence'.[51] In other words, 'The fact that forty million sets are scattered over the world today appears to be the central problem of broadcasting.'[52] Parroting the official Weimar discourse of 'radio for all', Arnheim assumed that 'wireless programmes [. . .] should give what is important for everyone' and that 'wireless has a detrimental effect only if – with the one-sidedness of its character, which is not to be condemned as negative in itself – it promotes a harmful tendency that already exists'.[53]

Instead of fully determining the medium as the omnidirectional transmission of music, sound, or the human voice to (inter)national audiences according to a regular schedule, early radio can be understood to have remained in an experimental state – much like that of television, only to a lesser extent.[54] In fact, early German radio frequently took advantage of opportunities to conduct experiments on mass audiences that were intended to confirm broadcasters' hypotheses about hypnosis and mass suggestion. In one experiment conducted in 1924, Ernst Rothe delivered what appeared to be a normal radio lecture on the topic of the 'subconscious, suggestion, and hypnosis'. However, this was a carefully staged incident, integrated seamlessly into the programme. At the end of the lecture, it was revealed to have been a test designed to measure listeners' acumen in perceiving auditory details. For Rothe, early 'radio plays' (*Sendespiele*) were, 'for the time being, nothing more than psychological experiments [. . .] One can well prophesy that a new form will emerge in this regard.'[55] In another series of experiments conducted in 1927, Georg von Arco and Alexander Herzberg partnered with the Berlin Funk-Stunde for a para-scientific study of mass telepathy, testing out the audience's ability to recognise the code, colour, and content of an image located in the broadcast studio. Sceptical of errors in the results of similar experiments conducted in Australia and England, Arco and Herzberg subdivided the audience into precise control groups. According to Lily Herzberg, this was the earliest example of such control groups.[56] While c. 4,500 listeners responded, representing different ages and classes, the results were inconclusive, sparking further empirical studies. This was one of the origins of targeted audience research, later exemplified by Arnheim, Adorno, Herta Herzog, Paul Lazarsfeld and others working for the Columbia Office of Radio Research.

Connecting such radiophonic experiments to experiments in psychotechnics, Dominik Schrage's study of *Psychotechnics and Radiophony* highlights parallels between 'electrical-physiological circuitry and authentic-identical experience', which 'makes it possible to conceptualise the radiophonic constellation as a perceptual unit that is at once technically enabled and yet organic'.[57] By the late 1920s this techno-organic power of the spoken word came to dominate Richard Kolb's medium-specific radio theory, which took the 'inner voice' generated while listening to the radio to be the medium's distinctive feature. While acoustic media can transmit anything from sounds to noise, Kolb abstracted the medium's essence from the primacy of the '*spoken* word'.[58] Equating the speaker's voice with the microphone and the listener's ear with the headphone, Kolb took the spoken word to integrate 'the receiving apparatus into our human organism, considering it together with the ear as a single sensory tool'.[59] For Kolb, who was forcibly installed as the superintendent of the Berlin Funk-Stunde in February 1933, the medium of radio blurred the lines between inside and outside to the point that 'the disembodied voice of the radio dramatist [*Hörspieler*] becomes one's own voice'.[60] Kölb's radio theories deeply informed the National Socialist conception of the Führer's voice. Instead of recorded music or experimental sounds, Kolb's radio theory foregrounded the living word connecting the ear of the *Volk* to 'Goebbels'-snout', a popular epithet for the *Volksempfänger*, dissimulating the technical apparatus and making radiophonic commands appear to arise organically in the listener's head. Beyond its legacy for Nazi radio politics, Kolb's concept of the unifying radio voice remained a hallmark of radio theory in West Germany until the 1960s, since it was supposed to restore the perceived ideological chaos and social anomie of modernity.[61]

Such medium-specific theories of radio look different when read through 'radiodetermination', an umbrella term for active radiolocation and passive radionavigation. Originally developed for wireless applications at sea and in the air, these methods involve generating information about an object's spatial and temporal coordinates based on the propagation characteristics of electromagnetic radiation. Though many-to-many connections are often touted as the most emancipatory form of network topology, exemplified by community-driven radio and wireless projects, their implementation in the form of radar renders them problematic. Unlike the asymmetrical broadcasting model, radar makes transmitters identical to receivers: impulses are sent out and reflected from the target object; the temporal interval allows the spatial distance between them to be determined. Following Kittler's analysis, this procedure has been said to have given rise not only to colour television but also to locative media and the digital image.[62] In a 1949 essay on 'The Radar Thinker', which inspired Kittler's speculative theory, Gottfried Benn described a new human being in radically different terms than those of the better-known 'radar type' diagnosed in the contemporaneous American sociology of the 'lonely crowd'. For Benn, 'radar thinking' (*radardenken*) meant receiving signals from every direction, being open for anything, existing between things. It meant '*peilen, loten, horten* – to scan, to sound, to hoard'.[63] Analysing Benn's late lyrics and radio work, Kittler concluded that

> modern philology could only learn from this radar thinker, if only because it would need to formalise the models of the book and the library (still supported by poststructuralism). Whatever its contents may be, literature, in the first place, is data processing: It receives and stores, processes and transmits information.[64]

However, there is a crucial difference between literature and broadcasting. While the materiality of literature consists primarily of surfaces and implements for inscribing and storing perceivable written signs, the materiality of radio and wireless telegraphy consists of apparatuses and infrastructures for transmitting and processing imperceptible electromagnetic signals.

In the unpublished lecture manuscript, 'Playback: A World War History of Radio Drama', Kittler formulated three core principles of the *Hörspiel*, a term whose coinage he provocatively attributed to Friedrich Nietzsche rather than radio broadcasters.[65] First, 'communications technologies can exist without radio drama but [. . .] no radio drama can exist without communications technologies'.[66] Because the new mass medium depended on older communications technologies, these set the limits for any possible play. Second, 'no radio drama can transmit the technical conditions of its possibility', in the twofold sense that radio listeners cannot experience 'wavelength, bandwidth, and silicon chips' and that they lack access to the modern, corporate 'system of power'.[67] Reviewing attempts to answer the 'question [of] what, if any, is the real content of radio drama', Kittler critiqued medium-specific theories from Brecht to Helmut Heißenbüttel for assuming that the answer depends on them and other content programmers rather than the medium's technical conditions of possibility.

> Hence, the third principle of a theory of the radio drama would be to take radio dramas [*Hörspiele*], or *Funkspiele* (which is what the intelligence agencies of World War II called them), for what they are and where they are. Not only in sound and speech archives [. . .] but also in the bandwidths between kilometres and centimetres from which the so-called population has been barred on good strategic grounds.[68]

Studying radio, from this media-philosophical perspective, means studying radio beyond what usually counts as radio. In contrast to the reductive label of 'media ontology' usually affixed to his work, Kittler's archaeological project explicitly involved making speculative connections between historical stories about medium specificity. 'In a more speculative [!] conclusion', Kittler then 'project[ed] these stories into a future that integrates all analogue media as a subset into a universal discrete machine, a.k.a. the computer'.[69] Of wireless futures, Kittler ultimately speculated that 'where there is no wire or silicon fibre, radio will likely once more be tasked with performing its original function: to make connections where and as long as distance and enemies exist'.[70]

The Absent-Minded Audience

'*Achtung, Achtung!*' The famous sign-on for early German radio programmes was an imperative order to pay attention, as one might now expect at the start of a breaking news bulletin. In one respect, the directive took over the function of the wireless telegraph code CQ, adapting this means of 'calling all stations' to the mass address of anonymous radio listeners at unknown coordinates.[71] While the original BBC sign-on famously identified the broadcast station in terms adopted directly from wireless telegraphy ('2LO, Marconi House, London calling'), the German sign-on commanded listeners to pay attention, reiterating officials' central anxiety about unmonitored audiences.[72] When first spoken by announcer Friedrich Georg Knöpfke during the inaugural national broadcast, the imperative was coupled with the following reminder:

> Achtung! Achtung! Here is the Berlin transmitting station at the Vox House on Wave 400m. Ladies and gentlemen, we would like to inform you that the entertainment radio service will start today with the distribution of music performances via wireless telephone [!]. Usage is subject to an official license.[73]

Underscoring these official regulations, the catchphrase lent authority and gravitas to the government's voice and created a fear of missing out on whatever the medium's programmers seemed to spontaneously feed audiences next. While media and modernity studies have long examined the uncanny, otherworldly, and authoritative qualities attributed to the disembodied radio voice, they have tended to downplay corresponding anxieties about the absent-minded audience, the possibility of surveillance, and the banality of broadcasting. '"Achtung! Achtung! We will now hear . . .". And so it goes hour after hour', reflected Kurt Tucholsky on the constant alerts for upcoming programmes.[74] Citing the almost equally famous sign-off for early radio programmes, 'Please don't forget to ground your antenna!' (*Bitte vergessen Sie nicht, die Antenne zu erden!*), Tucholsky ironically concluded that 'the antenna for this disturber of the peace should be grounded, and in the interest of general peace dismantled. Here's to never hearing it again! [*Auf nimmerwiederhören!*]'[75]

'In the beginning of radio was boredom', Hans Flesch reflected in 1930, presenting an alternative origin story to counter the official media hype.[76] Marketed as a remedy for boredom, especially the kind widely attributed to rural and domestic life, 'radio for all' promised to satisfy the urban audience's perceived hunger for culture, spirituality, and enlightenment. However, the affordances of switching the channel produced boredom through the structural principle of repetition. As the artistic director of Southwest German Radio (SÜWRAG) and, before Kolb, superintendent of the Berlin Funk-Stunde, Flesch was responsible not only for putting Brecht, Walter Benjamin, and Theodor W. Adorno on the air, but also for creating an experimental *Hörspiel* only a year after the official public opening of Weimar radio.[77] In retrospect, Flesch reflected that the technical attractions of the new medium blinded its audience to the fact that

> terrible things were being done at the time. The music programme was drawn from decayed concert halls, the literature from the *Gartenlaube*, the lectures placed a premium on the manners and customs of the Minnesänger (under the aegis of 'educating the public'), and legions of cucumbers were pickled ('for the housewife').[78]

Instead of exploring its medium-specific affordances, in other words, early radio programming tended to remediate the bourgeois canon. Flesch countered the official media hype with images of mindless consumption: 'In the beginning was boredom', he reiterated. 'Legions of cucumbers were pickled. It is clear they still have not all been consumed.'[79]

As a programmatic statement of his counter-vision for experimental broadcasting, Flesch's *Zauberei auf dem Sender* (*Magic on the Air*), first broadcast on 24 October 1924, experimented with the medium-specific affordances of sound design and live performance. Recalling the *Funkerspuk*, *Magic on the Air* presents the occupation of a broadcasting studio by various voices who repeatedly interrupt the programme and are unable to be switched off. Interrupting the promised musical concert, a figure named Aunt Fairy Tale (*Märchentante*) starts reading a bedtime story for children; after further interruptions, they try to switch off the station but instead switch on a DUCA player-piano. Unlike Orson Welles, Flesch did not reveal the secret that the chaos was all carefully staged, which led to a mixed reception of the radio play. According to its embedded fairy tale, 'Once upon a time there was a radio subscriber who was content with everything that the radio station offered him – that was long, long ago.'[80] In Lecia Rosenthal's analysis of *Magic on the Air*, as in Kümmel-Schnur's account of the 'debate about radio' and Balbi and Rikitianskaia's call for studying applications of wireless transmission beyond national broadcasting, 'radio emerges not so much as one thing (a technology, device, specific set of texts or programs) but rather a set of debates, conflicts, practices, problems, performances, and utterances'.[81]

In a 1924 essay on 'Boredom', Kracauer presented a different critique of the cacophony of radiophonic voices, asserting that 'radio vaporizes beings, even before they have intercepted a single spark. Since many people feel compelled to broadcast, one finds oneself in a state of permanent receptivity [*Empfängnis*], constantly pregnant with London, the Eiffel Tower, and Berlin.'[82] In contrast to the official discourse of radio as reproductive *Bildung*, Kracauer was concerned about how the medium puts listeners into a 'state of permanent receptivity' associated with 'constant pregnancy'. As Wolf Kittler observes, the verbs *empfangen* (to receive, to conceive) and *verbreiten* (to broadcast, to spread seed) were double entendres in the early days of radio.[83] Furthermore, the potential effeminisation of radio listeners was a constant concern for officials, as Kate Lacey has shown in research on targeted programmes created for women at home.[84] In these respects, Kracauer's image of radio listeners pregnant with international broadcasts registers the feared penetration of technology into domestic spaces, much like earlier concerns about the novel as a new medium. This anxiety resurfaced in discourses about the domestication of radio throughout the 1920s, whether in attempts to black-box the radio apparatus as a form of furniture, or in proposals for the petite bourgeoisie to build a *Rundfunk-Zimmer*, a room modelled on the home library and study but dedicated to contemplative radio listening.[85]

To support his bourgeois critique of the absent-minded audience, Kracauer depicted early radio-listening practices with two striking images of the audience emptied out and put into a state of permanent receptivity. His first image features listeners wearing headphones, which remained the dominant mode of domestic reception despite official plans.[86] Although Bredow and other officials pushed for the use of public assembly-hall radio, most listeners routinely listened to the radio at home. Alone together, an entire family would gather around their shared radio set and plug their own headphones into the apparatus. For Kracauer, the use of headphones isolates listeners from each other, not only making them less communicative but also reinforcing their *Geistesabwesenheit*:

> Silent and lifeless, people sit side by side as if their souls were wandering about far away. But these souls are not wandering according to their own preference; they are badgered by the news hounds, and soon no one can tell anymore who is the hunter and who is the hunted.[87]

Kracauer's second image of radio-listening practices features the loudspeaker, a technology that forces one's participation in a community of listeners but that would not be fully developed until the late 1920s:

> Even in the cafe, where one wants to roll up into a ball like a porcupine and become aware of one's insignificance, an imposing loudspeaker effaces every trace of private existence. The announcements it blares forth dominate the space of the concert intermissions, and

> the waiters (who are listening to it themselves) indignantly refuse the unreasonable requests to get rid of this gramophonic mimicry.[88]

Kracauer's complaints about noisy radio cafés have been taken to indicate his support for the period's noise-abatement campaigns.[89] However, they are better understood as part of a growing unease about perpetual contact – that is, being always reachable and thus forced to participate in the wireless age.

As symbols of broadcasting, the headphone, loudspeaker, and radio dial provided means of conceptualising the other members in an imagined community of radio listeners, be they ideal attentive listers or their distracted foils, both imagined to be white, male, and middle-class.[90] In contrast to Kracauer's ridicule of the 'dainty headphones' that 'entwine themselves around heads all by themselves', other commentators underscored the discomfort caused by unwieldy headsets. Attempting to recall his formative radio-listening experiences, Flesch admitted,

> I cannot remember when I heard the radio for the first time. I only know when I had a pair of headphones on for the first time [. . .] I sat for half an hour in front of the bulky machine housing and felt, due to the weight of the headphones [. . .] and to the senseless, unarticulated noise in my head, considerably intimidated and cramped.[91]

In response to the same opinion poll, Polgar similarly deflated the official media hype:

> At every point in space, the totality of appearances, as far as they are perceptible by ear and eye, would be virtually present! A shattering idea, which must lead anyone who knows how to think philosophically (that is, unfortunately not me) into abysses of speculation.[92]

In retrospect, Viennese radio amateur Karl Flanner recounted a similar experience in more vivid detail, recalling how his uncle

> squeezed the clasp with the earpiece, which looked like the earmuffs one wears in winter, over our heads. From these earpieces resounded a nasty crackle, sputter, and whistling, which my uncle's finger suddenly brought into order, and then the noise suddenly fell silent, and the sound of music rang out and words became comprehensible.[93]

The operator's headband, originally designed for radiotelegraphists who needed to operate the telegraph key with their hands, became a source of irritation for radio listeners who inherited this former design upgrade.

Although popular images suggested that headphones isolate listeners and loudspeakers bring them together, the difference between the two is not technical but linguistic, Polgar observed in his 'Notebooks of a Radio Listener' in 1929. '*Headphones* [. . .] should not be called *phones* but *speakers*', because even when they are not situated over one's ears, they 'emit a sound, admittedly a very thin, faint sound, as though they were dreaming of music or speech'.[94] Like loudspeakers, headphones continuously broadcast regardless of whether anyone is listening. While both media objects command one's attention, the radio listener retains more agency than both the everyday viewer and the everyday listener, due precisely to the intervention of acoustic technology. As Polgar reflected, 'He does not have to listen for one second longer than he wants. At any time, he can take back the sense of hearing that he has borrowed, removing himself in the middle of a sentence, word, or syllable.'[95] Along similar lines, Arnold Zweig described 'the feeling of boredom' as the 'true censor' for the radio, suggesting a possible way-station between Kracauer and Polgar: 'Nobody will listen to what they do not want to hear, if they have the ability to free themselves from unwanted boredom with the simple turn of a dial or the flip of a switch.'[96] While Kracauer considered the radio listener to be unable to switch off, Zweig and Polgar considered the possibilities of at least changing the channel. By pathologising the audience's normal tendency to fidget with devices, programmers restricted the possibilities of surfing the airwaves.

Before the imagined audience for national broadcasting was fully determined, 'radio for all' ended up producing a confusing mixture of programmes addressed to everyone as a whole and as individuals – *omnes et singulatim*. When, in Polgar's 'Notebooks', 'the silence suddenly breaks out in sounds, and, out of the silence, a human being falls into the middle of a mixed choir that persistently demands, "I should and must court you"', the sudden direct address makes him wonder, 'Huh, who is he saying that to?'[97] To introduce chance into the stream of programmed content, Polgar describes an interesting listening practice:

> From time to time, I hold [the headphones] to my ear, without knowing what they're loaded with at the moment, and let myself be surprised. (What's the name, when it comes to the ear, for what we call a 'glance' for the eye? A 'hear'?) From time to time, then, I cast an ephemeral hear into the ether.[98]

Polgar's notion of giving a quick listen to the radio sounds so strange because the act of listening is a time-based activity, and broadcast programming is usually structured to keep listeners glued to one station.

At the end of his 'Notebooks', Polgar describes how, before going on holiday one time, he forgot to turn off his radio set and left the headphones sitting on the tabletop. Polgar imagines the radio broadcasting non-stop while he is away: 'The recipient of dialogues and polemics, humour and stock prices, pretty much anything that moves the human heart, always or only now, was my tabletop.'[99] The classical figure of the author composing silently in his studio for enraptured audiences has been replaced by the low hum of *Bildung* over the radio, and the message of the medium now only gets transmitted from the cold steel of the radio receiver into the lifeless wood of the writer's desk. Upon returning home from his holiday, Polgar is amazed that 'no trace remained, not even such a tiny one as would be left by one's breath. When I think, "What if I had left the water running for two weeks!" It's a good thing spirit [*Geist*] does not have substance.'[100] By alluding to this classic philosophical debate, Polgar's 'Notebooks' championed the contingent materials of radio listening over the universalising abstractions of 'radio for all'.

Just as the topos of *Geistesabwesenheit* was crystallised in headphones and loudspeakers, so the radio dial concretised the period's anxieties about absent-minded audiences. One satirical poem, 'From Wave to Wave', simulated the phenomenon of surfing the airwaves in an almost Dadaistic manner:

> Crrsh! Crrsh! Phwee! Phweee!
> We interrupt the broadcast and continue the concert with gramophone records
> At 7:10 pm, Mussolini will speak
> Potatoes 4.50 Marks
> Achtung! Murder!
> Boom boom!
> Chance of strong ground fog
> Snow White lay in a glass coffin
> Sehr geehrte Damen und Herren, wir sind nicht imstande
> Et nous verrons, messieurs, comment ça passé
> The goalkeeper bravely covers the ball
> And Capablanca pulls C8/D10
> The farmer awaits warm rain
> O Queen, life is beautiful
> I don't have a second one to send
> . . . Dolly the good is in Hollywood . . .
> I'm carrying Elizabeth in my hands . . .
> Phwee! Phwee! Crrsh! Tut![101]

By presenting each line in a different language or linguistic register, the poem attempts to simulate the disorienting experience of channel surfing. However, it also glosses over the static noise that would have been audible between each line, or change of the channel, only presenting it as a framing mechanism.

By the end of the decade, the medium's affordances were celebrated in the lyrics of a popular revue called *I'm Changing the Channel*,[102] while also being pathologised by others through the trope of an 'addiction to channel surfing' (*Drehkrankheit*). According to theologian Johannes Maria Verweyen, radio listeners fidgeting with their devices exhibited a certain intellectual pathology: 'radioitis occurs when the apparatus is not used as a tool of the mind, but as a means "merely to pass the time" [. . .] In our days, the person who literally falls asleep wearing headphones makes it easy to diagnose a case of radioitis.'[103] In 1938 Theodor W. Adorno presented a similar critique of the fetishisation of technology by the amateur radio operator 'who leaves the factory and "occupies" himself with music in the quiet of his bedroom'.[104] For Adorno, the radio amateur exemplified the 'fetishistic listener', insofar as

> it is irrelevant to him what he hears or even how he hears; he is only interested in the fact that he hears and succeeds in inserting himself, with his private equipment, into the public mechanism, without exerting even the slightest influence on it. With the same attitude, countless radio listeners play with the feedback or the sound dial without themselves becoming hams.[105]

While the radio dial is usually understood as mediating between whomever is turning it and whichever stations are being tuned in, media scholar Andreas Fickers argues that the radio dial mediates, in a different sense, between the functional order of allocating broadcast frequencies to various radio stations and the listener's imagined landscape of broadcasting.[106] Generalising this claim, my argument here is that the entire broadcasting apparatus mediated between the official discourse of the airwaves and the vernacular experience of signals and noises.

Critiques of the disappointing contents of 'radio for all' were also registering a sea change from cultural techniques of reading, writing, and counting, which had been integral to radiotelegraphy and -telephony, to technological devices capable of automatic signal processing. Whether praised or blamed, the agency of the channel surfer depends not only on the psychophysical economies of attention and distraction but also on technological affordances. While radio listeners can 'lend an ear' to the airwaves, as Polgar quipped, by putting on or taking off their headphones, wireless operators needed to keep them on to process the signal. If the radiotelegraphist's ear once functioned as a filter, technological devices increasingly took over this function previously performed by the human body. The vacuum tube eliminated the need to isolate a signal out of noise, ultimately transforming the active listener, in Siegert's analysis, into a passive 'message sink' (*Nachrichtensenke*).[107] Automatic tuning devices using vacuum tubes eliminated the need to know how to operate one's radio at all.

Emergent Programmes

Before the institutionalisation of radio, wireless transmissions of time signals, weather forecasts, and emergency distress signals introduced early adopters in elite circles to the experience of broadcasting and its complex modes of address. These kinds of transmissions gradually became standard radio programming content, with many early listeners even citing time signals and weather reports as their favourite programmes, establishing a horizon of expectations for what wireless futures would look like. Following Rikitianskaia, Balbi, and Lobinger, 'these practices can be considered forerunners of radio broadcasting, and the first listeners setting their clocks to information transmitted wirelessly or listening to seismographic reports can be seen as an incipient audience'.[108] These emergent audiences further signalled a change in the 'social value' of information, which moved out of scientific and professional contexts and 'entered many aristocratic and enthusiasts' houses in the unexpected form of family entertainment'.[109] In the process, time came to be seen not only as a private commodity but also as an 'international public good', as national timekeeping and meteorology systems were consolidated into international infrastructures.[110] Despite offering such a productive approach to the pre-history of broadcasting, Rikitianskaia, Balbi, and Lobinger's reliance on a historiographical model that emphasises technological progress and international cooperation downplays the struggles involved in creating (wireless) time signal services. Like the debates over the adoption of the prime meridian, time signals also required the establishment of an absolute zero. To raise the main question addressed at the first International Time Conference: Where should world time be measured and broadcast from?

(Wireless) time signals further impacted modernist understandings of synchronicity and simultaneity. Bypassing gatekeepers who were once the exclusive holders of the 'right time', such as churches, watchmakers, or railway stations, time was now sent directly from governmental or commercial transmitters. As a result, international time was no longer the privilege of exclusive groups but was rather increasingly accessible to unprivileged classes, insofar as a wireless device could be assembled from relatively cheap components. The radiotelegraphic system created for broadcasting time signals was preserved in radio broadcasting, as announcers and moderators provided aural cues for distracted listeners to pay attention, which is why news came to be announced, in the same breath as time signals, 'on the hour'. On the radio, time signals were connected further to station ID practices, corporate branding, and advertising strategies, as evident in the BBC's iconic 'pips'. When the time was read aloud, some announcers would also advertise the brand of clock in an early form of sponsored content: the familiar 'Bulova time signal' of American radio was an overt advertisement for Bulova watches, which, in Alexander Russo's analysis, aimed to redress audience hostility towards radio advertisements and create the misleading sense that advertising, like the radio, provided a public service.[111] In similar fashion, the Kienzle watch manufacturer's 1933 radio ad campaign, *Deutsch die Uhr, Deutsch der Klang* (German clock, German sound), combined a commercial slogan with a nationalist ideology into a package marketed as the perfect Christmas present.

The process of broadcasting time signals was closely tied to that of broadcasting weather reports. As John Durham Peters observes, 'Weather is so fickle that broadcasting it only makes sense when you have a quick and refreshable system of distribution that transcends local horizons; nothing ages so fast as a weather report.'[112] Citing Martin Heidegger's service as a military meteorologist (technically, a *Luftschiffer*) on the Western Front at the end of World War I, Peters suggests that this experience influenced Heidegger's subsequent conception of 'kairological time', which he found formulated in the epistles of Paul.[113] Poignantly, Heidegger's 1919 lectures may even have been written on the back of unused military weather reports, given the scarcity of paper at the time. In Peters' analysis, Heidegger's fascination with *Wachsein* (being vigilant or awake) in Christian theology finds another striking parallel in 'watching the weather', and the philosopher's meteorological work sheds new light on the 'Heideggerian tropes of vigilance, *hüten* (guarding or watching), *kairos*, and observance'.[114]

In Imperial Germany, time signals and weather forecasts had been tied to emergency services from the start. After a heavy storm in the North Sea led to the sinking of eight fishing vessels, the Hydrographic Office created a regular weather service in 1910, combining time signals with storm warnings and daily weather reports distributed by the coastal wireless stations at Norddeich and Cuxhaven.[115] In 1912 Gustav Eichhorn established the world's first dedicated wireless station for receiving weather reports and time signals, broadcast from the Eiffel Tower in Paris to the Central Meteorological Institute in Bern, Switzerland. Using the corresponding Zurich station, where Eichhorn had an official post, these programmes would then be forwarded automatically to every Swiss Telegraph and Telephone office, especially for tourists known for inquiring about the weather.[116] In the 1920s weather forecasts were channelled towards helping aspiring mountain climbers who might get in over their heads – hundreds died in the Bavarian mountains in summer 1923 alone. Because official bulletins printed and posted in local post offices were usually seen too late, and the telephone network was incapable of reaching secluded mountain huts, Ludwig Kapeller created a new wireless forecasting service modelled on maritime weather services. While sensational newspaper reports were depicting self-reliant mountain climbers equipped with pocket wireless devices, these imaginary media, Kapeller observed, remained 'in the realm of technical fable and one can only recommend to these fabulous alpine tourists that they drag along a telephone cable as Ariadne's thread into the labyrinth of high mountain dangers'.[117] Beyond this sardonic recommendation, Kapeller's proposal, leveraging his power as the editor of the official German radio magazine, was to create radio relay stations using the Alpine Clubs' valley stations.

Arnold Fanck's mountain films dramatised both the remoteness of weather services and the vigilance required of meteorologists in the Alps through heavy-handed parables about adventurous explorers and aviators. Exemplarily, *Avalanche* presents the story of a weather station attendant (Sepp Rist), a fledgling astronomer (Leni Riefenstahl), and a local aeroplane pilot (Ernst Udet, a renowned pilot during World War I and Luftwaffe Colonel-General during World War II). Stationed at a remote outpost in the French Alps, the meteorologist's sole task consists in taking readings from meteorological instruments and relaying them in Morse code using a NORA radio set, a vacuum-tube-based device he also exploits to communicate with friends during his ample downtime. The opening sequence juxtaposes close-ups of this wireless technology with spectacular shots of rolling clouds, while also cross-cutting the transmission of storm warning reports about *föhn* conditions with their international reception by other radiotelegraphists in France, Germany, Great Britain, Italy, and Sweden. 'Impressive sound effects supplement the magnificent photography', Kracauer noted in his review of *Avalanche*: 'fragments of Bach and Beethoven from an abandoned radio on Mont Blanc intermittently penetrate the roaring storm, making the dark altitudes seem more aloof and inhuman'.[118] These 'impressive sound effects' included the crackling sounds of Morse code that punctuate the film and culminate, in Fanck's typical idiom of *Sturm und Drang*, with the dramatic transmission of an SOS signal during an unexpected storm. While silent films frequently depicted radiograms visually, by analogy with letters, book pages, and other written documents,[119] early sound films apart from Fanck's tended not to incorporate the noise of radiotelegraphy into musical scores.

Alongside stereotypical romantic comedies about national broadcasting, such as *Funkzauber* (Radio Magic, 1927), Weimar cinema imagined radically different applications of wireless transmission, from interstellar videotelephony in *Wunder der Schöpfung* (Our Heavenly Bodies, 1925) to the radio waves that bring the machines to life in *Metropolis* (1927). The possibility of wireless energy transfer also inspired the oldest surviving SF feature from Germany, a film about an alien from the star Algol. Released in 1920 and long thought to be lost, it is now recognised as one of the aesthetic and conceptual precursors of *Metropolis*.

Energetic Futures

As a cinematic parable about the perils of confusing unlimited energy, inexhaustible vitality, and limitless resources, *Algol: Tragödie der Macht* (Algol: Tragedy of Power, 1920) presents the heavy-handed moral, evident in its subtitle, that the emergence of a worldwide wireless energy system might play out differently than the harmonious comedy predicted by Bredow, Tesla, and others. 'Certainly a tragedy, this work', remarked one film critic, 'even a fated tragedy. Almost. But not quite [. . .] Once again, there's a lack of logic.'[120] Received as a failure, the film remains shrouded in impressions of its convoluted plot, fanciful technology, aesthetic incongruity, and, above all, repetition of the singsong saying: 'A thousand roads lead to the light / Follow one without any fright! / Algol will lead you out of the troubled night / Willpower secures the Earth's might!' Another critic concluded that *Algol*, 'following the tendency of the times, wants to show that the mastery of the world and its natural powers won't make you happy, that happiness is to be found instead in clods of earth, in peaceful work, in the lap of one's family'.[121]

To be fair, *Algol* subtly reconfigures this narrative structure, familiar from the nineteenth-century *Erfinderroman*, in which the young inventor stood in for the hopes of upward social mobility associated with industrialisation 'by winning the dyad "woman and factory"'.[122] In the age of wireless energy transfer, this heroic feat is no longer possible, because electromagnetic radiation exceeds the factory model. *Algol*'s director, Hans Werckmeister, also collaborated on *Amt Zukunft* (Future Office), a now-lost short film scripted by Hans Dominik, and again deployed speculative tropes to critique the present. A generic combination of industrial dystopia and dynasty drama, Hans Brennert and Friedel Köhle's screenplay inflected the Faust legend through the themes of Expressionist drama, such as the father–son conflict, the dangers of new technology, the seductions of power, and the revolt of coal miners, ultimately presenting a parable about the dialectics of Enlightenment with surprising relevance for the Weimar Republic.[123]

Algol's narrative centres on the transformation of earnest, salt-of-the-earth coal miner Robert Herne (Emil Jennings) into an insatiable industrialist, as a result of a Faustian pact he makes with an alien named Algol (John Gottowt).[124] Late one night, the alien shows the miner a prototype of a machine capable of receiving the radiation emitted from his home star and converting it into an unlimited power source. Accepting this Faustian bargain, the protagonist builds a full-scale wireless energy machine, or 'Life-Power-Plant' (*Bios-Werke*), which quickly becomes a new world capital, with Herne being proclaimed the new world leader. By supplying everyone around the world with unlimited energy, the wireless power plant does not revolutionise society but rather makes other countries newly dependent on this centralised resource. A neighbouring agricultural country, which refuses to modernise, mounts a resistance, led by Herne son's Reginald (Ernst Hoffmann), and eventually reaches the plant's stronghold at the end of the film. As they discover, the power source not only supplies wireless electricity but also energises anyone who touches it with a sort of 'living power' (*lebendige Kraft*) and thus increases the elder Herne's 'power of attraction' (*Anziehungskraft*). In an expression of these vital forces, there is an orgiastic dance sequence, one of Sebastian Droste's most remarkable performances.[125] After the anagnorisis, the miner-turned-industrialist destroys the machine and thus saps his own vital energy. 'Woe is me!', the final intertitle proclaims. 'I tried to pass off strength [*Kraft*] for power [*Macht*].' Conflating distinct senses of energy – as a physical force (*Kraft*), a vital force (*Lebenskraft*), the force of gravity or physical attraction (*Anziehungskraft*), and political power (*Macht*) – so *Algol* moralises, leads only to ruin.

Explicitly citing Wilhelm Ostwald's influential theory of cultural energetics, *Algol* implicitly indexes film's relation to thermodynamics and the law of the conservation of energy. Ostwald's 'energetic imperative' associated degrees of civilisation with the efficiency of their energy usage, and thus exhorted, 'Don't waste energy, exploit it!' (*Vergeude keine Energie, verwerte sie!*).[126] Beyond contributing to the genre of early SF feature films, *Algol* can thus also be understood as a 'didactic warning that replacing conventional fuels with renewable energy in a monopolistic market can lead to new dependencies'.[127] The architecture and the shooting locations also made the film topical for German viewers in the years after World War I: the coal miners' revolt and the protagonist's last name, Herne, refer to the Ruhrgebiet, the central energy source for the former German Empire and the site of the revolts of 1919–20. Beyond the problems of familial relations and the corrupting influence of power, *Algol* raises speculative questions about Germany's exploitation of natural resources, its then-uncertain future as an agrarian or industrial society, and its ideal position within global relations. Developing the Faustian dialectics of reason, modernity, and enlightenment, which articulated technology's dual status as a potential force of progress and destruction, *Algol* suggests that the perfection of modern wireless technology will eventually culminate in a return to pre-modern tribalism.

While the vernacular understanding of wireless energy transfer today remains restricted to short-range cases, such as individuals charging their smartphones, the modernist imagination of wireless energy systems played out on a collective and totalising scale. Compared to the alternatives, electrical energy transmitted wirelessly seemed not merely more efficient but more ethical, more just, and somewhat paradoxically, more natural.[128] Since electromagnetic radiation is a naturally occurring resource, infrastructures for harvesting or distributing it wirelessly already seemed long overdue by the late 1920s. 'Whatever happened to making electrical energy available for the general public?' one of Bredow's colleagues wondered in an essay on 'Future Matters' published shortly after Bredow's remarks on wireless futures. 'Old and new prophets have already pointed out these heights. There is no question that we will conquer them.'[129] From Tesla's infamous worldwide wireless system to Bredow's remarks on the coming age of wireless energy, there had been a number of false energy prophecies, including one published in the pre-eminent wireless trade journal in Germany, *Jahrbuch der drahtlosen Telegraphie und Telephonie*, on the eve of the introduction of national radio broadcasting, which were just as quickly debunked.[130] The main obstacles facing the creation of wireless energy infrastructures continue to consist not only in managing power loss over long-distance transmissions but also in measuring energy consumption and therefore making it possible to charge for its use.

'Radio for All'?

Like national broadcasting, the modernist imagination of wireless energy systems alternately promised or threatened to revolutionise society by obviating the need for public utilities and private corporations. Bypassing the existing infrastructure of cables, substations, and central power plants, wireless energy seemed capable of being harvested in less industrial ways and distributed for less capitalistic ends.[131] The energetic futures put forward by the utopian project managers discussed in this chapter serve as a reminder that our existing infrastructure is only one possible system among many for generating, transferring, and accessing energy and information. Despite much attention to national broadcasting in German-speaking countries and even some to the history of wireless telegraphy, the history of wireless energy remains limited to isolated case studies of Tesla's spectacular failures, which are hardly representative of larger trends. Similarly, there have been several studies of the significance of the concept of energy for European modernism, but there have been few studies of the German context, none of which have attempted to read across science and fiction.[132] Reading beyond broadcasting reveals 'energetic modernism' to exceed its purely technical connotations, providing an ethical descriptor of what it meant to be a bourgeois subject in German modernity. Developing the idealist intellectual tradition of *Geistesabwesenheit*, the media economy of attention and distraction was filtered through the politics of presence and absence, surface and depth, and range and coverage. Connecting technical concepts of wireless transmission to their perceived cultural counterparts made the medium into both a technical apparatus and a cultural institution.

The Weimar programme of 'radio *for* all' structurally excluded the possibility of 'radio *by* all'. While amateur radio and national broadcasting share the same historical roots, there was never an amateur radio movement in the Weimar Republic to the extent that there was in the United States, Great Britain, France, Italy, the Netherlands, and many other countries. Although the German wireless industry paralleled or surpassed that of other European countries, the amateur radio movement encountered resistance. Throughout the 1920s its main objective was the reform of the German Empire's draconian telegraph law, which the Weimar Republic's postal ministry, administered by Bredow, transformed into its programme of 'radio for all'. In subsequent years, Brecht's conditional statement that 'the radio could be the finest possible communications apparatus in public, a vast system of channels',[133] continued to provide a rallying call for a leftist politics of wireless transmission, repeated so many times that it would eventually be revised or abandoned by its own authors.[134] Wolf Kittler argues that this critical tradition wanted to exploit the technical fact that every wireless receiver is also potentially a transmitter, thereby making it possible for the audience to participate in the public sphere and political life. However, its proponents overlooked the sociocultural fact that, under capitalism, powerful wireless transmitters are only operated by powerful state institutions, as was the case in Germany, or by powerful corporations, as in the United States.[135] At first glance, the packet-switched networks colloquially known as the Internet might appear to have realised the dream of decentralised, non-hierarchical, many-to-many connections. However, they did so only in a twisted manner, as the control of domain name servers and network backbones today remains the exclusive property of democratic regimes and financially powerful corporations. In a speculative reading, national broadcasting was not the first participatory mass medium, as is often assumed, but rather the first to control or eliminate the possibility of participation – in the name of democracy.

Wireless futures are neither universal nor unbounded. Created in response to specific situations, they have the power, especially when mobilised by powerful officials, to create the very future they promise. In an unpublished typescript, 'Radio – An Antediluvian Invention?', Brecht countered the official media hype by uncovering the old-fashioned aspects of the then-new medium.[136] In 1927, while journalists conducting surveys were already reminiscing with nostalgia about when listeners 'first heard radio', Brecht twisted this formula around to highlight the importance of discourse in establishing horizons of expectation: 'I can remember how I heard *about* the radio for the first time', he wrote. 'There were ironic newspaper accounts about a virtual radio hurricane that was in the process of devastating America. Nonetheless one had the impression that it was not just a craze but something really modern.'[137] Like many of his contemporaries, Brecht read about the radio before he experienced it first-hand, and the anticipation culminated in a sense of disappointment, especially about the medium's content ('a Viennese waltz and a kitchen recipe'). Ridiculing the 'old custom of getting to the bottom of all things, even of the most shallow puddles', Brecht critiqued himself and other bourgeois radio enthusiasts for the tendency to 'let ourselves be led around by the nose for the sake of *possibilities*'.[138] By emphasising future 'possibilities' over present 'results', the bourgeois investment in wireless futures served as a smokescreen for the endless deferral of official promises. Instead of highlighting the medium's two-way communication possibilities, as in his more famous radio essay, Brecht here made a different, highly ironic request for something largely absent from early broadcasting – an archive:

> I strongly wish that after their invention of the radio the bourgeoisie would make a further invention that enables us to fix for all time what the radio communicates. Later generations would then have the opportunity to marvel how a certain caste was able to tell the whole planet what it had to say and at the same time how it enabled the planet to see that it had nothing to say.[139]

In a later poem about 'New Ages', Brecht extended this critique to the fascist glorification of radio technology: 'From the new antennas came the old stupidities. / Wisdom was passed on from one mouth to the next'.[140] As the central media object in wireless systems, the antenna exhibits its own intermedial techno-logics, which will be examined further in the next chapter. The antenna serves as a liminal figure marking the start and end of every wireless transmission.

While the standard sign-on for national German radio broadcasting, '*Achtung! Achtung!*', alerted distracted listeners to an upcoming programme, the obligatory sign-off at the end of each day's regularly scheduled programming gave the absent-minded audience a different nudge: 'Please don't forget to ground your antenna!' This patriarchal reminder to listeners to disconnect and go to sleep without allowing their wireless technology to endanger others came to be remembered as a beloved catchphrase closely associated with the experience of broadcasting.[141] While some early radio listeners recalled falling asleep while listening to the radio, only to be woken up after the end of the day's programmes by these words, other practical jokers revised the phrase into 'Please don't forget to bury your [dead] antenna!' Combining these connotations, radio announcer Max Heye used the phrase as a fitting sign-off to his autobiography.[142] Taken together, these two well-known station identification phrases not only provided a tidy frame for early radio programmes, with the sign-on reminding listeners to tune in and pay attention and the sign-off nudging them to tune out and disconnect. They also provide a reminder of the need to reconfigure the history and theory of wireless from a critical media-philosophical perspective twice removed from the once-dominant model of national radio broadcasting.

Notes

1. Bredow, 'Eure Aufgaben im Rundfunk', 230. On his ambivalent attitude towards the honorific title 'creator of German radio', see Bredow, 'Rückblick und Ausblick'; Bredow, *Im Banne der Ätherwellen*.

2. Bredow, 'Eure Aufgaben im Rundfunk', 230.
3 Bredow, 'Eure Aufgaben im Rundfunk', 230.
4. Bredow, 'Eure Aufgaben im Rundfunk', 230.
5. There is a potential, unstudied connection with the amateur radio movement in the United States; see, for example, Gernsback, *Radio for All*. On the origins of the German slogan *Rundfunk für alle*, and its economic and political motivations, see Lerg, *Die Entstehung des Rundfunks in Deutschland*, 114–22; Kern, 'Radio für alle', 2–10; Schneider, 'Rundfunk "für alle"'; Zielinski, *Variations on Media Thinking*, 207–60.
6. Bredow, 'Eure Aufgaben im Rundfunk', 231.
7. Bredow, 'Eure Aufgaben im Rundfunk', 230.
8. Bredow, *Im Banne der Ätherwellen*, vol. 1, 250–1.
9. On Bredow's programme, see Führer, 'A Medium of Modernity?'; Campbell, *The Radio Hobby*.
10. See, among others, Case, 'Logistical Media'; Rossiter, *Software, Infrastructure, Labor*.
11. Rikitianskaia et al., 'Mediatization of the Air', 769.
12. See Corner, '"Mediatization"'. For case studies of wireless energy, see Thibault, 'Wireless Pasts and Wired Futures'; Lieberman and Kline, 'Dream of an Unfettered Electrical Future'.
13. Rikitianskaia and Balbi, 'Radio Studies beyond Broadcasting'.
14. Rikitianskaia and Balbi, 'Radio Studies beyond Broadcasting', 169.
15. On the *Funkerspuk*, see, among others, Lerg, *Die Entstehung des Rundfunks in Deutschland*, 51–2; Glaubitz et al., *Eine Theorie der Medienumbrüche*, 83–5; Gilfillan, *Pieces of Sound*, 31–2; Hagen, '"Die Stimme als Gast"', 43.
16. Tworek, *News from Germany*, 73–83.
17. Evenius, 'Rundfunk für alle', 2.
18. Evenius, 'Rundfunk für alle', 2.
19. Kümmel, 'Innere Stimmen', 175.
20. Kümmel, 'Innere Stimmen'.
21. Qtd. in Kümmel, 'Innere Stimmen', 176–7.
22. On wireless transmission, see Fürst, *Die Wunder um uns*; Fürst, *Im Bannkreis von Nauen*.
23. Moszkowski, *Die Welt von der Kehrseite*, 310; cf. 100–1.
24. On the 'discourse on discourse channel conditions', see Winthrop-Young, *Kittler and the Media*, 4.
25. Rothe, 'Maritime Fantasien des Frühen Radios'; Rothe, *Katastrophen hören*.
26. Kittler, 'Playback', 94.
27. Kittler, 'Observations on Public Reception', 78–9.
28. Siegert, 'Das Hörspiel als Vergangenheitsbewältigung', 297.
29. Dotzler and Roesler-Keilholz, *Mediengeschichte als Historische Techno-logie*, 132.
30. Natonek, 'Radio', 99.
31. Natonek, 'Radio', 100.
32. Natonek, 'Radio', 100.

33. Brecht, 'Radio as a Communications Apparatus', 41.
34. For the classic source, see Hay, *Literatur und Rundfunk*.
35. See Kaes, *Weimarer Republik*, 200.
36. Palitzsch, 'Broadcast Literature', in Kaes et al., *Weimar Republic Sourcebook*, 600–3.
37. For the classic source, see Hörburger, *Das Hörspiel in der Weimarer Republik*.
38. See Peters, *Speaking into the Air*; Gethmann, *Die Übertragung der Stimme*.
39. Brecht, 'Radio as a Communications Apparatus', 42.
40. See Brecht, 'Radio as a Communications Apparatus', 39.
41. Schwarzwald, 'The Prophesied Ravag', 564–7.
42. Schwarzwald, 'The Prophesied Ravag', 567.
43. Bischoff, 'Hallo! Hier Welle Erdball', excerpt in Schneider, ed., *Radio-Kultur*, 124–5.
44. Bischoff, 'Hallo! Hier Welle Erdball', 124.
45. Bischoff, 'Hallo! Hier Welle Erdball', 125.
46. Polgar, 'Aus Aufzeichnungen eines Radiohörers', 28.
47. See Jaffe, 'Inventing the Radio Cosmopolitan'.
48. Kracauer, 'Boredom', 333.
49. Seitz, 'Überall her aus der Welt', in Schneider, ed., *Radio-Kultur*, 42–3.
50. Schickele, 'Paneuropa der Sender', in Schneider, ed., *Radio-Kultur*, 140–3.
51. Arnheim, *Radio*, 14.
52. Arnheim, *Radio*, 11.
53. Arnheim, *Radio*, 275.
54. Born, 'The Promise of Television'.
55. Rothe, 'Psychologische Experimente im Rundfunk', 319; cf. Borck, *Brainwaves*.
56. See Fuchs, *Georg von Arco*, 245.
57. Schrage, *Psychotechnik und Radiophonie*, 295.
58. Kolb, *Das Horoskop des Hörspiels*, 13.
59. Kolb, *Das Horoskop des Hörspiels*, 53.
60. Kolb, *Das Horoskop des Hörspiels*, 55.
61. Siegert, 'Das Hörspiel als Vergangenheitsbewältigung'.
62. See Kittler, 'Von der optischen Telegrafie zur Photonentechnik'; Geoghegan, 'An Ecology of Operations'.
63. Kittler, 'Benn's Poetry', 11.
64. Kittler, 'Benn's Poetry', 11.
65. Kittler, 'Playback', 94. Kittler's reference is to Nietzsche's *Richard Wagner in Bayreuth*: '[Wagner's] art always leads him into two distinct directions, from the world of the play of sound [*Hörspiel*] to the mysterious and yet related world of visible things [*Schauspiel*], and vice versa'.
66. Kittler, 'Playback', 91.
67. Kittler, 'Playback', 91.
68. Kittler, 'Playback', 92.

69. Kittler, 'Playback', 93.
70. Kittler, 'Playback', 109.
71. Gethmann, *Die Übertragung der Stimme*, 99.
72. On the radio's management of attention and distraction, see Führer, 'A Medium of Modernity'.
73. On the inaugural broadcast, a light musical programme organised by the Berlin Funk-Stunde, see Gilfillan, *Pieces of Sound*, 22; Gethmann, *Die Übertragung der Stimme*, 99; Fischer, *Dokumente zur Geschichte des Deutschen Rundfunks und Fernsehens*, 72–3; Koch and Glaser, *Ganz Ohr*, 10–11.
74. Tucholsky, 'The Loudspeaker', 459 (translation modified). Max Heye and Margarete Wiedecke also composed the humorous radio sketch, '*Achtung! Achtung! Sie hören . . .*', in which the reading of a novel keeps getting interrupted by, 'Attention! You are now listening to . . .'
75. Tucholsky, 'The Loudspeaker', 459 (translation modified).
76. Flesch, 'Rundfunk heute', 246.
77. See Ottmann, *Im Anfang war das Experiment*.
78. Flesch, 'Rundfunk heute', 246.
79. Flesch, 'Rundfunk heute', 247.
80. Flesch, '*Magic on the Air*', 20.
81. See the introduction to Flesch, '*Magic on the Air*', 17.
82. Kracauer, 'Boredom', 332–3. The term Kracauer uses is *zerstäubt* (vaporises, atomises), and not *zerstreut* (distracts, scatters).
83. Kittler, 'Kurt Schwitters', 124.
84. Lacey, *Feminine Frequencies*.
85. On the domestic 'radio room' (*Rundfunk-Zimmer*), see Pater and Schmidt, '"Vom Kellerloch"', 103–16.
86. Koch and Glaser, *Ganz Ohr*, 14; Führer, 'A Medium of Modernity'.
87. Kracauer, 'Boredom', 333.
88. Kracauer, 'Boredom', 333.
89. See Rippey, 'Kracauer and Sound', 185–7.
90. Ehardt, 'Phones, Horns, and "Audio Hoods"', 101–25.
91. Flesch, 'Der Deutsche Rundfunk', qtd. in Ottmann, *Im Anfang war das Experiment*, 9–10. According to Ottmann, it was to this painful and noisy experience that many would later attribute Flesch's preference for broadcasting Neue Musik.
92. Polgar, 'An jedem Raumpunkt – alle Geräusche der Welt', in Schneider, ed., *Radio-Kultur*, 47.
93. Flanner, *Hallo! Hallo! Hier Radio Wien!*, 3–4.
94. Polgar, 'Aus Aufzeichnungen eines Radiohörers', 28.
95. Polgar, 'Aus Aufzeichnungen eines Radiohörers', 29.
96. Zweig, 'Ästhetik des Rundfunks', in Schneider, ed., *Radio-Kultur*, 77–8.
97. Polgar, 'Aus Aufzeichnungen eines Radiohörers', 28. The line he hears, 'Ich soll und muß ein' Buhlen haben', is from the German folk song 'Sollen und Müssen', collected in Achim von Arnim and Clemens Brentano's *Des Knaben Wunderhorn* (1805–08).

98. Polgar, 'Aus Aufzeichnungen eines Radiohörers', 28–9 (parenthesis in original).
99. Polgar, 'Aus Aufzeichnungen eines Radiohörers', 30.
100. Polgar, 'Aus Aufzeichnungen eines Radiohörers', 30–1.
101. 'Von Welle zu Welle', 60.
102. Bibo and Mackeben, 'Aus der Funk-Revue "Ich schalte um . . ."'.
103. Verweyen, 'Radioitis!', 454.
104. Adorno, 'On the Fetish-Character in Music', 292.
105. Adorno, 'On the Fetish-Character in Music', 293. For more sympathetic treatments, see Zielinski, *Variations on Media Thinking*, 207–60; Campbell, *The Radio Hobby*; Douglas, *Listening In*; Haring, *Ham Radio's Technical Culture*.
106. Fickers, 'Visibly Audible'.
107. Siegert, *Passage des Digitalen*, 397.
108. Rikitianskaia et al., 'The Mediatization of the Air', 768.
109. Rikitianskaia et al., 'The Mediatization of the Air', 767.
110. Rikitianskaia et al., 'The Mediatization of the Air', 766.
111. Russo, *Points on the Dial*, 115; Führer, *Wirtschaftsgeschichte des Rundfunks*, 6, 120.
112. Peters, *The Marvelous Clouds*, 249.
113. Peters, *The Marvelous Clouds*, 241–3.
114. Peters, *The Marvelous Clouds*, 241–3.
115. Die Deutsche Seewarte, 'Funkentelegraphische Verbreitung von Wetterberichten und Sturmwarnungen', 650.
116. Eichhorn, *Wetterfunk, Bildfunk, Television*.
117. Kapeller, 'Unfall- und Wetterrundfunk im Hochgebirge', 10–11.
118. Kracauer, *From Caligari to Hitler*, 258.
119. Young, *The Cinema Dreams Its Rivals*, 49–72.
120. Popper, [*Algol*], n.p.
121. Anonymous, [*Algol*], n.p.
122. See Miloradovic-Weber, *Der Erfinderroman*, 12.
123. Neumann, '*Algol*', 72–85.
124. The acting was also described in terms of energy in Anonymous, [*Algol*]: 'Emil Jennings plays Robert Herne, all will and power, unbridled under the trance of power and yet mastered in every movement, a tamed natural power that is not only physically but also mentally superior to all others.'
125. Whitney, 'Etched with the Emulsion', 246–8. The moment Herne destroys the machine, the dancers stop dancing.
126. Ostwald, *Der energetische Imperativ*, 13.
127. Neumann, '*Algol*', 81.
128. Lieberman and Kline, 'Dream of an Unfettered Electrical Future'.
129. Stockmayer, 'Zukünftiges', 296.
130. Vogel, 'Drahtlose Energieübertragung', 197–205; Burstyn, 'Briefe an die Schriftleitung', 445.
131. See Lieberman and Kline, 'Dream of an Unfettered Electrical Future'; Thibault, 'Wireless Pasts and Wired Futures'.

132. See, among others, Asendorf, *Ströme und Strahlen*; Clarke and Henderson, *From Energy to Information*.
133. Brecht, 'Radio as a Communications Apparatus', 42.
134. Enzensberger, 'Constituents of a Theory of the Media', 13–36; cf. Enzensberger, 'Das digitale Evangelium', 92–101.
135. Kittler, 'Kurt Schwitters', 119–43.
136. Brecht, 'Radio – An Antediluvian Invention?', 36–8. Based on its opening formula, as if in response to a question, I suspect that Brecht's unpublished typescript was written in response to a radio survey asking listeners to reminisce about their earliest experiences of the medium.
137. Brecht, 'Radio – An Antediluvian Invention?', 36 (emphasis added).
138. Brecht, 'Radio – An Antediluvian Invention?', 37.
139. Brecht, 'Radio – An Antediluvian Invention?', 37–8.
140. Brecht, 'Die neuen Zeitalter', 856.
141. See Gethmann, *Die Übertragung der Stimme*, 99.
142. Heye, *Lustiges aus dem Reich des Unsichtbaren*, 96.

Chapter 6

The Antenna: At the Limits of Wireless Imaginations

Without antennas, there would be no wireless – only disconnected terminals.[1] Like the bricks once wrapped by dissidents in newspaper and confiscated by the authorities who mistook them for prohibited radios, wireless-enabled devices without antennas would amount to technical objects with social, political, and aesthetic, but not operational, functions.[2] In wireless engineering, thoughtful antenna design relaxes system resources and improves overall performance, as technical antenna handbooks once emphasised, asking readers to reflect on the rapid changes in signal quality that result from adjusting analogue radio and TV antennas.[3] In the standard German-language handbook, Karl Rothammel repeated the amateur operator's motto, 'the best high-frequency amplifier is a good antenna', but then observed: 'Unfortunately, however, there is no such thing as a standard antenna that would obtain optimal results under any condition.'[4] Beyond such specialised technical reference works, the antenna remains a neglected component of media history and theory, despite constituting the most visible and iconic component of any wireless system.[5] Reflecting the structural invisibility of contemporary infrastructure, the antenna's current invisibility is usually attributed to miniaturisation, black-boxing, infrastructural publicity, and the public's perceived lack of media literacy. Antenna towers only receive public attention, on this model, when they are constructed or collapse. Otherwise, they tend to remain inconspicuous.[6]

In the early twentieth century, on the other hand, many modernising cities celebrated their emergent infrastructures, and competing nations constructed new landmarks in the form of monumental transmission towers, as the race to build the wireless station with the greatest transmission range paralleled the competition to build the world's tallest building. The twentieth century witnessed the creation of wireless stations on an increasing scale, starting with wireless telegraph stations in the 1900s–1910s, radio towers in the 1920s–1930s, radar arrays and television towers in the 1940s–1950s, and cellular towers from the 1960s to the present.[7] At first, existing structures were repurposed into wireless stations, as was the case with the Eiffel Tower (constructed 1887–89; telegraph relay station starting in 1906), the Empire State Building (1930–31; NBC broadcasts starting in 1931), and the statue of Christ the Redeemer at Corcovado (1922–31; illuminated wirelessly by Marconi at the opening ceremony in 1931). However, dedicated wireless stations were increasingly constructed in response to technical and market needs and for speculative reasons. Clustering around urban markets, the most iconic wireless stations in the German-speaking world built prior to World War II were the Nauen Transmitter Station (100m, 1906; 200m, 1914) and the Berlin Radio Tower (150m, 1924–26). After World War II, this distinction would pass to multipurpose broadcasting and telecommunications towers, including the Danube Tower in Vienna (252m, 1962–64), the Europa Tower in Frankfurt (337.5m, 1974–79), and the Telemax Tower in Hanover (282m, 1988–92).

What might be gained from revisiting modernist thinking about antennas from our current experience of the 'digital switchover'? Throughout the national broadcasting era, the antenna served primarily as a symbol of mass media, of the one-to-many addressing of a unified audience with the potential to enlighten the masses or mobilise them for violence. Resembling skyscrapers and oil rigs, the iconic upright monopole antenna used throughout this period was another overtly phallic symbol of aerial dominance. During analogue broadcasting's pre- and post-history, on the other hand, the antenna assumed a wide range of forms as an experimental device for producing knowledge about electromagnetic radiation. Because an antenna's shape and size determine the propagation characteristics of electromagnetic radiation, it can be twisted or sculpted into forms including prototypical dipole antennas (for example, TV 'rabbit ears'); monopole antennas (for example, 'whip antennas' used in car radios, or 'rubber ducky' antennas in walkie-talkies); T-, L-, F- and fan-shaped antennas used for radiotelegraphy; loop antennas popular among amateur broadcasters; conical antennas, aperture antennas, 'random wire' antennas, and many others.[8] Before their implementation in wireless telecommunications and national broadcasting, antennas were deployed primarily as 'locative media', or devices for detecting the presence of electromagnetic radiation and determining the positions of wireless stations.[9] As part of their historical transition from experimental devices into communications infrastructures, antennas were hoisted into the air to increase transmission range, inspiring thinking about aeriality and groundedness in modernist art, literature, philosophy, and architecture. This chapter aims to reveal different paths the media object could have taken in the past, along with ones it might take again in the future.

As an artificial phenomenon composed of imperceptible fields and waves, wirelessness challenges the traditional status of the aesthetic object, which had long been equated in European art and architecture with the medium's solid, tangible, perceptible materials. At the same time, antennas greatly inspired modernist architects, insofar as architectural objects were still evaluated based on their degree of success in representing an intangible, hidden world.[10] Given Europe's relatively flat landscape around 1900, the verticality of antennas also became a point of contention, bringing about regulations governing their installation in urban spaces and leading to intense negotiations between the vanguards of modernity and the traditional owners of the highest buildings around. Celebrated as 'landmarks to a new humanity', to borrow the refrain from one occasional poem, antennas were eventually displaced from the public sphere with the decline of this modernist paradigm. While the antenna can be understood as a technical device that mediates between the transmitter and the receiver, it can also be understood as a medium in another sense – namely, mediating between the invisible medium of radio waves and the modern politics of visibility. If the conflation of cultural and political representation tends to make 'being seen' appear to be unquestionably desirable, the invisibility of antennas in the public sphere presents a further incentive for studying the 'politics and poetics of infrastructure' and for reimagining the emancipatory possibilities of 'withdrawal from representation'.[11]

Beautiful Antennas

As a technical object, the antenna is clearly indispensable. But can it have aesthetic value? Gilbert Simondon raises this question near the end of his remarks on 'the genesis of technicity', which resituate the apparent binaries of 'technical thought' and 'aesthetic thought', as well as the 'technical object' and the 'aesthetic object', along the same continuous spectrum.[12] In a digression that keeps returning to 'the beauty of a radio relay [*relais hertzien*] placed on a mountain, and oriented toward another mountain where another relay is placed', Simondon suggests that any aesthetic potential of wireless transmission requires understanding its technical function and that imagination is required to reveal the reality of the technical world. Without technical knowledge, an observer 'only sees a tower of mediocre height, with a parabolic grid in which a very small dipole is placed', and overlooks the structure's technical function in 'emitting and receiving the bundle of directed waves that propagates from one tower to another, through the clouds and the fog'.[13] For Simondon, the question of the object's aesthetic value and its degree of integration into its surroundings depends on imagining its technical function.

> It is with respect to this invisible, imperceptible, and real, actual transmission that the whole [*ensemble*] formed by the mountains and the towers is beautiful, for the towers are placed at the key-points of the two mountains in order to constitute the wireless line [*câble hertzien*]; this type of beauty is as abstract as that of a geometric construction, and the function of the object needs to be understood in order for its structure, and the relation of this structure with the world, to be correctly imagined, and aesthetically felt.[14]

As Simondon specifies, 'technical objects are not inherently beautiful in themselves', but 'in certain cases there is a beauty proper to technical objects', which 'appears when these objects become integrated within a world'.[15] As additional examples of technical objects integrated into their surroundings, Simondon describes the aesthetic experience of a 'line of pylons' traversing a valley and that of a 'radar antenna' placed at a ship's pinnacle. In both cases, the antenna 'is not beautiful in itself and without reference to a universe'.[16]

For an example of the 'true industrial aesthetic' found in 'places of production and emission', Simondon later ruminated on the plateau of Villebon-sur-Yette, south-west of Paris, and 'constituted and structured on its east side by a field of emission antennas'.[17] In this unfinished and unsent letter addressed to Jacques Derrida, 'On Techno-Aesthetics', the antenna once again provided Simondon with an example of the chiastic relation between technics and aesthetics: 'this structure is very remarkable, especially because it cannot be found in nature. It is completely artificial, unless perhaps one would recognize it in the sacred fig tree.'[18] As an example of a complex technical set, the antenna array demonstrates how 'the technicized landscape also takes on the meaning of art'.[19] To Simondon, 'a group of emission antennas is a kind of set, like a forest of metal, and it can remind one of the rigging of a sailboat. This set has intense semantic power', which he also finds expressed in 'the [British] English word [. . .] "aerial", something of the air'.[20] While Simondon's account of the semantics of antennas was correct about the British terminology for 'aerials', which also applies to early German terminology such as the *Luftdraht* or *Luftleiter*, his speculative association of antennas with the 'rigging of a sailboat' rested on a false etymology of *antenna* that was popular in French, English, German, and other languages throughout the twentieth century.

In etymological case studies of the word's history conducted from the 1960s to the 1980s, linguist Jost Trier sought to debunk etymological dictionaries, which had long misattributed the word's derivation to the classical Latin etymology of *antemna* (yard of a ship) and then speculated further on perceived formal resemblances with a ship's rigging.[21] What historical linguists had overlooked, Trier argued, was a crucial intermediary step: the Latin word for a 'ship's rigging' first came to signify insect antennae only through the translation of Aristotle's Greek term for 'insect horns' (*keraioi*); the function, not the form, of these feelers was then compared to the technical object.[22] To a radio tinkerer, Trier explained, insect antennae might appear to be named after wireless antennas, but historical etymology turns out to have proceeded the other way around. The zoological term preceded the technological term and only entered the technological sphere with the growth of amateur broadcasting. Again, it was the 'comparable function' of insect antennae rather than their 'similar form' that gave rise to the technical engineering term.[23] Examining the early history of wireless communication, Trier speculated that Marconi probably introduced the Italian word for insect feelers, *antenna*, into the discourse of technology, because it was already an established part of the Italian vernacular.[24] In the early years of experimentation, 'antenna' was used synonymously in English-language publications with 'aerial' and 'elevated wire system', while German-speaking authors also used words such as *Funkendraht* (wireless line) to describe the space between two wireless stations.[25] Despite attempts at standardisation, the antenna's manifold forms and functions kept generating new names. By 1924 the Reichspost had officially recognised the Germanic terms *Luftdraht* (aerial wire) and *Luftleiter* (aerial line), and further distinctions between the *Dachluftleiter* (roof aerial), *Hochluftleiter* (high aerial), *Rahmenluftleiter* (frame aerial), and *Zimmerluftleiter* (room aerial).[26]

In early German SF, there were also close associations between the vernacular idioms of wireless antennas and insect antennae, as is evident in one of Kurd Lasswitz's short SF stories from 1890. While animal organisation and political systems have long generated comparisons in political theory, Lasswitz's 'Aus dem Tagebuch einer Ameise' (From the diary of an ant) mobilised then cutting-edge entomology to speculate on the ethics of animal research and the durability of human constructions.[27] The fictional frame narrative introduces a human entomologist based loosely on myrmecologist

Erich Wasmann, and fittingly named 'Antenna'. Credited with 'the discovery of the language and script of the ants', Antenna proves that their 'sensory perceptions are based on ether waves of 800- to 2,000-trillion oscillations per second, a speed beyond what is perceptible to our eyes as light'.[28] Using a fluorescent microscope, Antenna converts these vibrations, which the ants use to communicate with an 'ant-loving beetle' in their colony, into perceptible frequencies, demonstrating that the 'ants communicate mutually in a feeler language [*Fühlersprache*] that he calls chemising [*Chemisieren*] or trans-touching [*Übertasten*]'.[29] For further details on the experiment, the fictional editor refers readers to 'Antenna's original work, which was published in Latin under the title *De formicarum lingua et litteris* by the Emswind Brothers in Flausenheim', the publishing house being a satirical reference to Carl Zastrow's humorous novel *Die Bureaukraten von Flausenheim*, and the Latin treatise to scientists debating the 'language and letters of ants'.[30]

The rest of Lasswitz's speculative story adopts the literary form of a series of diary entries composed by one of the ants and dated with unorthodox, non-human times (for example, 'larva's sun', 'worker's sun', 'pupa's sun'). Documenting ethnographic expeditions made by the ants to study the human beings who repeatedly destroy their colony while studying it, the diarist also records the colony's counter-plan of conducting an experiment by nesting in the brain of a living human subject. Lasswitz thus flips the expected observer–observed relation, as the ants studying human beings ask the same questions that Wasmann, August Forel, John Lubbock, and other leading scientists were asking in the years before functionalist and behaviourist explanations claimed to rule out any possibility of animal intelligence: 'What are they saying to each other? Do they have a language, or is everything based on imitation? [. . .] Or is it hereditary instincts?'[31] Presenting a critical non-human perspective on human activity, morality, and intelligence, the diarist observes human beings whose 'feelers are so roughly organised' that 'they only perceive what they direct their senses towards, and how narrowly limited these senses are! [. . .] The multifaceted, the fastest ripples of the ether pass by their coarse nerves without a trace.'[32] From this non-human perspective, the disenchanted ant reflects, in an expression of Lasswitz's neo-Kantian framework, human beings are irrational and insensitive but not entirely irredeemable, assuming that they can still recognise the categorical imperative.[33]

To architecture theorist Mark Wigley, 'the history of the antenna equals the history of the human becoming something "other"'.[34] As is evident from Lasswitz's speculative story, however, this imagined

Other often remains coded in terms of the Same. If aesthetic experience depends on technical education – and, ideally, vice versa – then the antenna always needs to be understood further in relation to its surroundings.

Structure and Infrastructure

When the Eiffel Tower's original twenty-year permit was about to expire, this 'useless and monstrous' construction, as one critic called it, was saved from demolition, thanks, in part, to an antenna.[35] As a collective and celebratory project exemplifying the modernist spirit, the Eiffel Tower once represented the pinnacle of both aesthetics and technology, though it also gave rise to conflicting views. Against the tower's detractors, Gustave Eiffel, who understood himself to be less of an architect than a 'builder of machines', cited not only its design, safety, and beauty, but also its functional value as an aid to scientific research.[36] Its height, Eiffel claimed, made the tower useful for experimental research in meteorology and aerodynamics, as well as for experimental trials in radiotelegraphy. By 1909 the Eiffel Tower's military radiotelegraph station was completed, and over the next two years it would provide a regular wireless time signal service and links to both dirigibles and aeroplanes. The height of the Eiffel Tower's antenna (330m) was even proposed as a standard for defining national airspace, below which would be state property, and above which would be international airspace.[37]

As both an icon of modernity and a functional wireless station, the Eiffel Tower came to serve as the subject of an entire modernist genre of 'wireless poetry', in which 'the subjectivity of the speaker often merges with that attributed to the city, the tower, the machine'.[38] The avant-garde genre's most common refrain – 'I am an antenna' – was fraught with contradictions about the boundaries of the lyrical subject, inflecting the poetic tradition that associated madness with inspiration through the modernist discourses of anthroposophy, *Lebensreform*, psychotechnics, and inner experience.[39] While the main timbre of wireless poetry was initially cosmopolitan, the equation of wireless with poetic subjectivity quickly became a chauvinist competition among the French simultaneists, Italian futurists, Prague poetists, German expressionists, Russian constructivists, and other champions of the European avant-garde.[40] This generic shift, fuelled by the resurgence of nationalism around World War I, ran in parallel with the historical shift from radiotelegraphy to radio, or from a unidirectional mode of international communication into an

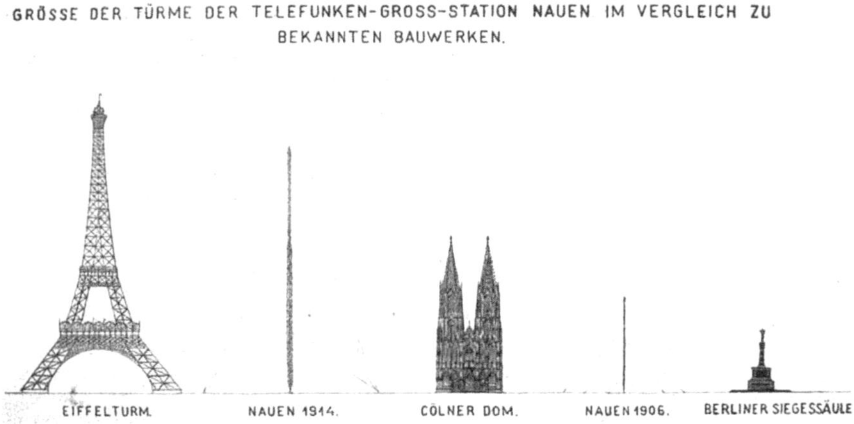

Figure 6.1 'Sizes of the towers of Telefunken's Nauen Large Transmitter Station in comparison to well-known buildings': (from left to right) the Eiffel Tower, Nauen in 1914, Cologne Cathedral, Nauen in 1906, and Berlin's Victory Column. Source: *Telefunken-Zeitung* (August 1919).

omnidirectional mode of national address. With the rapid proliferation of antenna towers, the mid-1920s already saw poets interested in wireless transmission increasingly turn away from international symbols and towards regional and national structures.

Early wireless stations often evoked comparisons with traditional monuments, as evident in an illustration in the August 1919 issue of *Telefunken-Zeitung* (Fig. 6.1) comparing the size of the antenna towers at Nauen (100m, 1906; 200m, 1914) to that of the Eiffel Tower (324m, 1889), Cologne Cathedral (157.4m, 1248–1880), and Berlin's Victory Column (67m, 1864).[41] In addition to demonstrating the relative height of these towers, the illustration reveals the radical thinness and dispersion of the architectural structures at Nauen, which were not repurposed like the other monuments but were designed according to the functional principles of wireless transmission from the outset. Although the size and visibility of many antenna towers made them seem comparable to traditional monuments, they were not as permanent or monolithic. While early antenna towers were patterned to some extent on traditional forms of monumentalism, with the result that the information infrastructure is routinely conflated with the supporting architectural structure, wireless stations differ from most traditional monuments in that they are informed by not only symbolic but technical determinants.

Due to the iconic stature of wireless stations, the infrastructure-making objects (that is, antennas) tend to be equated with their supporting architectural structures (that is, towers or masts). However, there was nothing inevitable about the emergence of infrastructure out of architecture, nor about the combination of antennas and vertical structures into now-recognisable forms of broadcasting houses and communications towers. In fact, the technical object and its structural support were intended to serve two very different functions: antennas were designed to radiate or to detect energy; antenna towers to elevate these wires into an aerial position, increasing transmission range.[42] An antenna need not even transmit or receive meaningful information through radio waves, as Leon Theremin recognised in the late 1920s, and can also function as a proximity sensor. The theremin (aka Aetherophone) creates a circuit between two antennas, which capacitively sense the position of the player's hands like miniature radar systems. Understanding such technical differences can help make better sense of the sociotechnical imaginary of wireless transmission.

Today, the most iconic form of antenna is still the vertical monopole, a simple wire suspended from an upright pole. However, early antennas assumed a wide range of forms, and inspirations for these designs came from many different fields, including physics (Hertz's 'detector'), biology (Galvani's frog's leg; Minchin's 'feeler'), aviation (Jackson's 'wings'), meteorology (Popov's lightning rod), and the circus (Marconi's 'tent pole').[43] What all antennas functionally have in common is that they are primarily for locating people and things. From a media-archaeological perspective, the antenna's family resemblances are less with the mass media of radio and television than with other locative media, such as the divining rod and the lightning rod.[44] Even within the history of mass media, where the antenna would realise its most iconic form, early experiments in radio-based telegraphy were preceded by ones in induction-based telegraphy, hydrotelegraphy, and underground antennas.[45] To put it in terms of German media philosophy, there is no such thing as an antenna. Certain materials only become media technologies through specific cultural techniques performed under the right conditions.

Ever since electromagnetic radiation became the dominant physical medium for wireless transmissions, the materiality of the antenna has remained relatively the same – a wire. Even if a wireless device foregoes connecting wires and can be self-powered by the energy generated from electromagnetic fields, it still relies on wires for its construction. Nothing drives home the point that most modern antennas are only wires more directly than the frame antenna (also known as the 'loop aerial'), a piece of wire wound multiple times around a wooden frame. Although these antennas have long since fallen out of fashion, they were once the favoured small-scale antenna among both amateur operators and the military, since they are easy to assemble and disassemble. Though usually small, frame antennas were used on a massive scale for Telefunken's installations at Nauen near Berlin, Eilvese near Hannover, and Tuckerton near Philadelphia, New York, and other communications hubs on the East Coast.

Due to the nature of their construction, such antennas are highly directional, which means that rotating the supporting frame is necessary to transmit in various directions or to receive signals from multiple stations. Alternately, rather than rotating an antenna – thereby producing spatial differences in electromagnetic fields – a directional antenna can be created by modifying a transmission pattern over time, as Karl Ferdinand Braun did in 1905. For its unique way of exploiting electromagnetic changes over time, Braun's 'phased array antenna' represents a potential precursor to radar, smart antennas, and multiple-input, multiple-output (MIMO) antennas. While communications and broadcasting towers are usually imagined to be immobile structures, directional antennas serve as a reminder of the necessity, even at a fixed location, of some degree of mobility in antenna design.

Just as the upright monopole antenna remains the most iconic antenna form, its most iconic support remains the iron latticework structure used in Eiffel's design for the tower located on the Champ de Mars. Beyond such huge, semi-permanent monuments, early experiments relied on a wide range of light, mobile, temporary, and improvised supports – especially during wartime, as steel shortages limited the availability of construction materials. During World War I, the smokestacks of factories in Germany were transformed into transmitting antennas, and, in the United States, there were similar experiments in transforming trees into receiving antennas.[46] In Germany, many of the radio towers constructed in the early twentieth century were made from wood rather than metal, which not only solved the technical problem of circuit isolation but also made better use of many regions' natural resources. Wooden towers were used for nearly all medium-wave transmitters, as is evident from the dozens constructed under National Socialist radio policies, and the world's tallest wooden lattice tower existed for a decade in Mühlacker (190m, 1934–45). Today, nearly all the wooden antenna towers have been demolished, except for the Gliwice Radio Tower (also known as the 'Silesian Eiffel Tower', 118m, 1934–35), constructed to connect Gliwice to the RRG radio network when the territory was part of Nazi Germany. The trend for finding alternative construction materials and repurposing existing structures as antenna supports demonstrates the contingency of the technical object.

The tower was not necessarily the only available supporting structure for the antenna. Reflecting on the future of wireless architecture in 1912, one commentator claimed that 'it is by no means certain that there will be an increasing development of large stations'. Having observed Telefunken's experiments with 'earth antennas' (*Erdantennen*), the commentator predicted a wireless future of underground transmission, overlooking the period's debate about whether energy and information could be transferred through the ground at significant distances.[47] Before the dominant supporting structure for antennas came to be a latticework mast, various structures were tried out as supports for elevating antenna wires and stabilising them in the air. These included poles and masts, as well as kites and balloons, as in the maniacal mid-nineteenth-century patent, mentioned in a previous chapter, for a so-called wireless system consisting of free-floating air balloons suspending live electrical wires above the ocean.[48] During Marconi's celebrated transatlantic demonstration of wireless telegraphy, the letter S was reportedly received by an antenna attached to a kite. Although the single-wire antenna gradually declined in popularity as more effective antenna designs emerged, it still found use in early aeroplane antennas. Incredibly, these consisted of a long wire, weighted at the bottom with a metal ball, that hung down below the plane and had to be reeled in using a windlass before landing. As is evident in the case of aeroplane antennas and other aerial systems, an antenna's physical length is not necessarily equivalent to its electrical length. Because early long-distance wireless stations used low frequencies (that is, long wavelengths), even the tallest antennas were 'electrically short'. While most antennas are set up in a vertical position, they can also be installed horizontally, leading some modernist observers to conclude that horizontal or underground antennas, and not vertical or aerial ones, were signs of the future.[49]

The architecture of the antenna challenges not only the traditional boundaries between structure and infrastructure but also those defining architecture studies, as John Harwood, Stephan Trüby, and Mark Wigley have argued.[50] While many contemporary architects treat antennas as architectural supplements, like water pipes and electrical wiring, to be handled by engineers, Harwood, Trüby, and Wigley have each argued persuasively for reintegrating infrastructural considerations into architectural practice. At the same time, their progressive call represents a return to the early days of radio and wireless telegraphy, when such considerations routinely cut across then-emergent disciplinary lines. Although the architecture of wireless stations represented a continuation of traditional monumentalism for many bourgeois modernists, it represented a radical departure from traditional aesthetics for some artists and architects, especially for the alliance of the avant-garde known as international constructivism.[51] Emblematically, Vladimir Tatlin's unrealised Monument to the Third International was intended to serve as a combination cultural centre and radio tower, with the spiralling structure topped by an antenna representing the glories of the revolution and Lenin's message 'To All'.[52] In the early Soviet Union, the architecture of the antenna was also central to Ivan Leonidov's Monument to Christopher Columbus, Alexander Vesnin's entry for the Palace of Labour competition, and Alexander Rodchenko's photographs of the Shukhov Radio Tower.[53] In Germany, international constructivists identified a potential counterpart to Soviet architecture in the experimental wireless station constructed by the Telefunken Company at Nauen near Berlin.[54]

Wireless Stations

In contrast to the current invisibility of wireless infrastructure in the public sphere, the early twentieth century celebrated newly created wireless stations with visual spectacles. Just as late nineteenth-century postcards depicted eerie smokestacks and smog-covered destinations as signs of industrial progress, early twentieth-century postcards came to feature antenna towers as signs of a region's modernisation.[55] 'Have you seen *our* wireless towers?' residents of Nauen reportedly boasted about their small town, home of the world's largest wireless stations for the first decades of the twentieth century. 'We Naueners are and will remain proud of our wireless towers. Even if they don't belong to any of us, they will always remain ours.'[56] The wireless equipment then belonged to Telefunken's news service subsidiary, Transradio, whose parent company had acquired the land at a minimal cost in 1906 when it was described as an unremarkable swamp.[57] Quickly developing into a landmark worthy of this sense of ownership, the Nauen Transmitter Station became a tourist attraction in its own right, attracting over 10,000 visitors in its first three years of operation, including residents of the nearby metropolis; participants at the second International Congress on Wireless Telegraphy; and such dignitaries as Emperor Wilhelm II, the Chinese Prince Zaitao, and King Chulalongkorn of Siam.[58] Like Luna parks, wireless stations were vulnerable to the elements. After the first huge antenna tower at Nauen was destroyed in a storm, another tower was erected, then replaced with more efficient models. During the same period, the Nauen Transmitter Station was also made responsible not only for experimental trials but also for long-distance wireless telegraphy. As the site was transformed from an experimental laboratory into part of Telefunken's planned worldwide wireless network, the architecture of the antenna became an increasingly important question.

The original construction at Nauen consisted of a small timber-framed operator's house and a large, 100-metre-high latticework mast attached to an equally long antenna wire. To Telefunken engineer Otto Nairz it seemed like something straight out of early German SF:

> Amazed, the hiker stops at the foot of the tower and his vision gets lost in the tangle of wires hanging almost from the clouds. Is it the station that the Martians in Lasswitz's novel [*On Two Planets*] built at the Earth's North Pole? Not quite, but something hardly less wonderful, it's a giant wireless telegraph station for long-distance traffic.[59]

Used initially for scientific research into the properties of radio waves, the experimental set-up at Nauen quickly developed into a half-kilometre-wide umbrella antenna system with a transmission range of 3,600km.[60]

Next to the massive antenna tower there was a rudimentary wooden radio shack, and the aesthetics of the technical object in its surroundings struck one scientific outreach writer, a recent graduate of Slaby's engineering courses and Bredow's future publicist, as truly remarkable:

> There is suddenly, in the middle of the unspeakably flat Märkisch landscape that sprawls for miles in horrifying silence, a quite thin, very high tower, erected like a harsh exclamation point. It rises a hundred metres, sticking out considerably above many church spires [Fig. 6.2]. Attached to the top of this tower is a web of wires that spreads out in every direction, and that, seen from below, resembles a very delicate spider's web. From above, the web of wires contracts and expands in the most manifold connections and interlacings, until its last branch terminates in a row of low steel masts that are positioned in a circle at 300 metres away from the tower. This web is called an antenna, and it is the true master of the universe [Fig. 6.3].[61]

Against the backdrop of a European landscape still devoid of skylines like those developing in North America, Fürst's most immediate reference points for conveying the sensational height of the Nauen Transmitter Station were nearby 'church spires'. Not only were these the tallest landmarks in Europe built prior to the twentieth century; they were the dominant symbols of power and authority in this primarily Protestant region of Prussia. To explain the operation

Figure 6.2 The Telefunken Station at Nauen, originally captioned: 'In the little telegraphy house, the ether-waves are produced by electrical sparks, and they are then beamed out by the hundreds of wires (the antenna) that are hung from the soaring tower. These ether-waves can already transmit telegrams as far as New York.' Source: Fürst, *Die Wunder um uns*, 10.

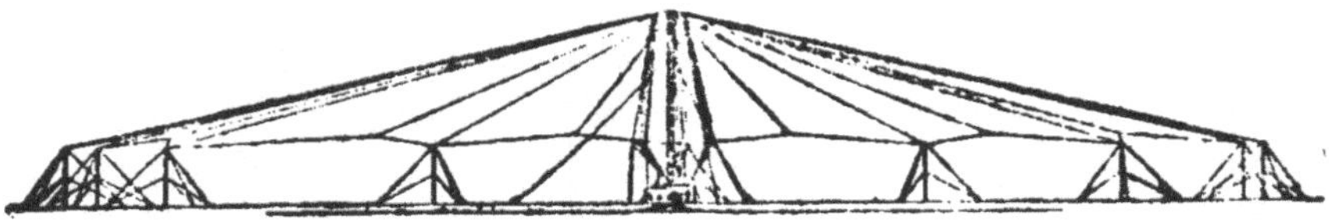

Figure 6.3 The web of wires at Nauen, originally captioned: 'The aerial wires (*Luftdrähte*) of the broadcast station in Nauen. From this equipment, named antenna, that extends across a circle with a 600-metre diameter, electrical waves beam off in every direction into outer space.' Source: Fürst, *Die Wunder um uns*, 13.

of wireless technology in accessible terms, Fürst's report relied on familiar metaphysics, associating wireless transmission with qualities traditionally ascribed to the divine: 'It is almost omniscient: it knows everything that happens in the ether.'[62]

A decade later, the challenge of designing a new central hall to replace the wooden hut at Nauen would fall to Hermann Muthesius, who was tasked with finding an appropriate aesthetic to glorify what had become the largest information transmitter on the continent. The building was dedicated on 29 September 1920 by President Friedrich Ebert with the proclamation of the wireless message, 'CQ [calling all stations] from POZ [Nauen's call sign]', an event accompanied by the publication of a Festschrift. Muthesius's construction represented a form of 'bourgeois modernism' situated between Historicism and New Objectivity.[63] Received favourably, Nauen's new central hall appealed to transcendental affects: visitors reported simultaneously seeing an industrial complex and having a quasi-religious experience. Incidentally, the main building's floor plan resembled a modern cathedral with a large crossing tower, even though its architects argued against this unintended ecclesiastical association.[64] Were it to have been a church, Muthesius insisted, it would have made sense to 'introduce the antenna into the built component raised above the crossing', but technical considerations dictated otherwise.[65] Even before Muthesius's redesign ran into such technical limits around the architectural imagination, the Nauen Transmitter Station provided architects and engineers with an exemplary test case for isolating wireless circuits so as to improve safety and reduce interference. To shield wireless circuits from inductive currents that would reduce system-wide performance, Nauen's isolation system made use of an innovative porcelain foot at the base of the antenna tower. None of this original isolation system remains, but it was what many modernists noticed for the first three decades of the twentieth century.

During one visit to the Nauen Transmitter Station around 1923, El Lissitzky (Lazar Markovich Lissitzky) had the following epiphany about the future of architecture, sparked not by Muthesius's central hall but by the isolated antenna tower (Fig. 6.4):

> *Nauen*: The 250-meter-high antenna tower stands on a single point.
>
> The Egyptian pyramid has been overcome. The flying human being is at the limit. At the limit of the old conceptions, the old form-creation, the old state of society.
>
> A new energy has to be liberated that will give us a new system of movement (e.g., a movement that is not based on friction, that provides an opportunity to hover in space without moving.)[66]

Figure 6.4 Photograph of the foot of the broadcast tower in Nauen, originally captioned: 'The 100-metre-high tower that serves to transmit and to receive radiograms (*Funkentelegrammen*) has a ball-bearing beneath it. On this small movable surface rests the monstrous weight of the tower and the transmission wires hung on it (antenna). To the right in the window of the house you can see one of the four porcelain cross-shaped giant isolators that can generate 100,000 Volts.' Source: Fürst, *Die Wunder um uns*, 9.

To the extent that the history of architecture had been characterised by the slow accumulation of building materials from the ground up, the wireless station suggested a different future for architecture that would proceed from the air down. 'Our form-production is a function of our system of movement', El Lissitzky asserted, mapping the production of new architectural forms on to historical changes in three main systems of movement: the 'wheel, propeller, and what will follow'. For El Lissitzky, the antenna tower belonged not to traditional architecture but to the modern machinery of communication and transportation. El Lissitzky's dream of gliding, floating, and hovering – in a stable manner that, in contrast to the Italian futurist dream of flight, did not require take-off or landing – was as much a social utopia as an architectural one. The suspended antenna appealed to international constructivists' search for equilibrium, the utopian balance of opposing forces needed to overcome friction.[67]

El Lissitzky's search for this kind of frictionless system, inspired by the articulated joint of Nauen's transmitter station, found a counterpart in Frederick Kiesler's utopian blueprints for a 'City in Space'. Significantly, Kiesler's conceptual project was only ever installed as a 'mobile', consisting of wooden planks used to hang artworks in the middle of the gallery room. But it is not too far-fetched to imagine that it and Alexander Calder's famous kinetic sculptures were informed by the equilibrium of floating antennas and electrical wires.[68] Inspired only partly by antenna wires, the modernist desire for aeriality was part of a larger loss of faith in the kind of 'blood-and-soil' ideologies originating in agrarian romanticism and later made into Nazi slogans.[69] To international constructivists, the qualities attributed to wireless transmission – transitory, light, and oriented to the present – reflected the ideal qualities of the new human being envisioned and debated across the political spectrum from fascism to communism. Imagining the new human being as a medial cyborg, Raoul Hausmann's best-known sculpture, *Spirit of the Age: Mechanical Head*, critiqued both the Hegelian concept of Geist and the Zeitgeist after World War I. Emptying out the artist's mind, Hausmann attached objects including a typewriter cylinder and disassembled camera parts to a prefabricated wooden head typically used by wigmakers. Resonating with Hausmann's scientific experiments with a wireless device that he called the 'optophone' because it aimed to convert light into sound, the ruler on his *Mechanical Head* encapsulates the period's speculations about the potential existence of a human sense organ corresponding to wireless antennas and insect antennae.[70]

Based on the suggestive concepts of receptivity, sensitivity, and tuning, which cut across technical and occult discourses of wireless transmission, speculations about human antennas piggybacked on widely cited parallels between telegraph wires and the central nervous system. According to Friedrich Kittler's seminal equation, 'A medium is a medium is a medium. As the sentence says, there is no difference between occult and technological media. Their truth is fatality, their field the unconscious.'[71] While Kittler characterised spiritualist mediums as storage media by analogy with Freud's 'Mystic Writing Pad', Peter Sloterdijk has described 'personal mediums' as wireless stations, or 'people with antennae [*Antennenmenschen*]'.[72] Said to be exemplified by Rudolf Steiner, Hugo Ball, and Martin Buber, Sloterdijk's notion of attuned thinkers suggests the ways in which media technology has informed the discourses of anthroposophy, the *Lebensreform* movement, and inner experience.[73] For Sloterdijk, 'Steiner created a kind of antenna anthropology that we can't simply do without any more, even if we have to rewrite every phrase of this doctrine. Since the dawn of the modern age, people actually have been listening in to the ether and want to know what is to be done.'[74] To spell out one such doctrine in need of revision, the pineal gland – now known to produce melatonin – was regarded by Steiner as a devolved cosmic antenna once capable of receiving biodynamic signals from mythical spirits, fairies, and gnomes.[75] By contrast, Friedrich Nietzsche participated in the same discourse but avoided localising philosophical attunement within a particular region of the brain, attributing his 'sensitiveness' to 'psychological antennae', which let him 'feel and handle every secret'.[76]

In this modernist tradition could be placed not only the 'schizophonic' protagonist of Ernst Toller's play *Hoppla, We're Alive!*, who is haunted by radiotelegraphic commands to commit a political assassination,[77] but also a long line of twentieth-century writers and artists who associated the task of the artist with that of wireless antennas and insect antennae. According to Ezra Pound, 'the artist is the antenna of the human race'.[78] To Joseph Beuys, the artist represents an '"antenna" detecting the fiery energy burning in the earth's core'.[79] Inspired by Wilhelm Reich's orgone accumulator, William S. Burroughs compared radio static to the sounds of ejaculation, and relished the 'Revelation and Prophecy of what I can pick up without FM on my 1920 crystal set with antennae of jissom'.[80] In a rare exception to this phallocentric tradition, Isa Genzken sculpted a series of readymade *World Receivers*, non-functional plaster blocks with metal antennas imitating the shape of shortwave radios. 'My antennas were also meant to be "feelers"', Genzken has commented, 'things you stretch out to feel something, like the sound of the world and its many tones.'[81]

Broadcasting Towers

With the emergence of national broadcasting in the 1920s, the cosmic, paraphysical, and avant-garde associations of wireless stations were also grounded in local, vernacular topics. In an understudied sub-genre of occasional wireless poetry, there were many celebratory poems about regional broadcasting towers, some even composed to be read aloud at station dedication ceremonies. One of Germany's most celebrated monuments to radio broadcasting, as evident from lyrical compositions by Hans Brennert, Karlernst Knatz, Gerhart Hermann Mostar, and Arnold Zweig, was the Berlin Radio Tower. Modelled after the Eiffel Tower (330m x 125m^2), the Berlin Radio

Tower (150m x 20m^2) was affectionately nicknamed *der lange Lulatsch* ('the lanky lad') on account of its even more slender profile, and was known from its location as the Lietzensee Radio Tower. While some authors celebrated the latticework structure while looking up at it from below, others climbed to the observation deck and reflected on the changed look of familiar surroundings from above, with the literary imagination often presenting both views simultaneously. In the poem 'Nature and Spirit', Knatz described the structure as a 'modern wonder without equal / the tower that magically points upwards – / a sign of human labour and yet of the unity of nature and spirit'.[82] For Knatz, the immateriality and ephemerality associated with wireless transmission made the Berlin Radio Tower superior to traditional monuments. 'To their big brother / Berlin's aged towers look up / Defiant, young, not weighed down by history, / creature and symbol of these times, / it spiritualizes itself [*sich vergeistert*] finely in the light, / landmark of a new humanity'.[83]

Although the silhouettes of modern architecture might resemble traditional monuments, Sigfried Giedion observed, the impetus for their construction represented a movement away from the surface – of buildings and of the earth itself – as the focal point of architecture: 'By their design, all buildings today are as open as possible. They blur their arbitrary boundaries. Seek connection and interpenetration.'[84] For Giedion, the modern experience of urban architecture was exemplarily located 'in the air-flooded stairs of the Eiffel Tower, better yet, in the steel limbs of a *pont transbordeur*'. Much like suspended antenna wires, the suspended latticework structure created a new frame for viewing urban modernity: 'Through the delicate iron net suspended in midair stream things, ships, sea, houses, masts, landscape, and harbour. They lose their delimited form: as one descends, they circle into each other and intermingle simultaneously.'[85] In other words, modern passersby no longer looked *at* monumental constructions but right *through* them. The same latticework structures that, according to Giedion, caused the objects of perception to become abstract and merge together provided a productive metaphor in Walter Benjamin's *Arcades Project*. Quoting the above passage from Giedion's architectural study, Benjamin transformed it into a historical-philosophical imperative: 'In the same way, the historian today has only to erect a slender but sturdy scaffolding – a philosophic structure – in order to draw the most vital aspects of the past into his net.'[86] As Benjamin proceeded to explain,

> just as the magnificent vistas of the city provided by the new construction in iron [. . .] for a long time were reserved exclusively for

> the workers and engineers, so too the philosopher who wishes here to garner fresh perspectives must be someone immune to vertigo – an independent and, if need be, solitary worker.[87]

While the visibility of the Berlin Radio Tower made it an emblem of community and cosmopolitanism, the visuals it enabled produced forms of ecstasy and vertigo. In a poetic 1929 essay addressed 'To the Broadcasting Tower, the Neighbour', Arnold Zweig meditated, in the tradition of E. T. A. Hoffmann's 'My Cousin's Corner Window', on the poet's mediated view of the world. In a lyrical apostrophe to this 'magnet of gazes', Zweig compared the tower, rising above the fog, to the evolution of *Homo sapiens*:

> you reveal yourself as humankind's intoxicated rising and staying aloft, as the victorious vertical over the eternal path of the horizontal, and heaving on your two feet like the abstract and thus pure image of the human, who, like you, raised up from the horizontal to the vertical in protest.[88]

Imagining what would have been an invisible antenna at the very top of the tower, Zweig described 'what seems to be only a thin rod, the lance of a ghostly knight, that steel string, the antenna, on which the ether plays music'.[89] For Zweig, the technological condition of building towers needed to be situated within a longer tradition of sacred architecture. As the apex of this lineage, the radio tower epitomised the secular worship of aesthetic objects: 'The fact that you touch the ether, radio tower, that you were erected as a visible conception in order to make our waves pulsate out into the powerful universe, that fact, radio tower, is what makes you so beautiful in the first place.'[90] While Simondon might here emphasise the need for further technical education, Zweig intuited that the radio tower seemed to 'conceal a secret but not so much so that we cannot fumble around at it with both of our primary senses, the mathematical and the religious'.[91]

At the dedication of the Berlin Radio Tower on 3 September 1926, Alfred Braun read a different occasional poem, Hans Brennert's ode 'To the New Roland'. Imitating early radio station IDs, Brennert charged the typical sign-on with cultural capital: 'Achtung! This is the Lietzensee Broadcasting Tower [. . .] Two syllables flash around the world / Achtung! Achtung! The transmitter is on! / Two syllables flash through outer space / always with a bright sound / through every ether symphony / The word BERLIN / The word BERLIN'.[92] By calling the tower the 'iron Roland of the New Berlin', Brennert suggested that it performed a similar function to the statues of the *Nagelmänner* once used to collect war funds in the German

Empire.[93] Implying that donations to the 'new Roland' should be made through subscriptions to public radio, Brennert's poem reiterated a major administrative desideratum for countering what was termed *schwarzhören* (literally, 'black listening', or listening to the radio without a subscription).[94] Underscoring the tower's material construction, the refrain, 'Surrounded by Berlin's heavens of teal / a tower has been built out of steel', would have also reassured those in attendance that the structure was safe to climb as soon as he finished the recitation.[95] In another poem about 'Wireless Towers', Gerhart Hermann Mostar again reversed the conventional imagination of building from the ground up, comparing antennas to 'arrows shot from a string [*Pfeile*] high as a star'.[96] Poetically connecting antenna 'lines' (*Seile*) to both 'musical strings' (*Saite*) and those of a 'bow-and-arrow' (*Sehne*), Mostar combined the mythology of Zeus, Cupid, and Orpheus: 'their tips pierced the field / steeply impale the earth and cause brown calluses, / their feathered ends tremble from the impact / on thin, steel stems / their groaning irons, narrow and tall, / between heaven and the fields / are tensed vibrating, / buzzing, roaring strings'.[97]

The Berlin Radio Tower's observation deck enabled one solitary worker, László Moholy-Nagy – who was not entirely immune to vertigo – to climb up to it and take a famous series of aerial photographs. Together with Rodchenko's celebrated photographs of the Shukhov Radio Tower, Moholy-Nagy's lesser-known series 'From the Radio Tower' (Fig. 6.5) inaugurated a photographic trend that continues to the present.[98] At first glance, Moholy-Nagy's photographs might seem to visualise Giedion's description of urban experience: the aerial gaze on the surrounding landscape through the latticework of the antenna tower might appear to confirm the abstraction of objects and the viewer's alienation from them, suggesting the larger dissolution of the visual field in modernity. If taken from very far away or close up, a photograph ceases to be an index of reality and instead becomes a collection of abstract forms. According to Moholy-Nagy, however, the photographs he took from the Berlin Radio Tower were supposed to provide orientation, and to open a new understanding of architecture. 'For the aeroplane pilot, the bird's eye perspective on the landscape is a possibility for orientation', Moholy-Nagy later stated. 'Soon everyone will have to become familiar with the views from above in nature and in representation.'[99]

One may gain orientation from the top of a tower, though at the expense of vertigo, as is evident in Ludwig Kapeller's description of the Berlin Radio Tower's observation deck: 'You can sip your mocha with the strangely exciting awareness that you are floating with solid

Figure 6.5 Vertiginous view of the urban landscape taken from the observation platform of the Berlin Radio Tower, intended to provide orientation through the cultivation of an aerial gaze. Source: László Moholy-Nagy, 'Vom Funkturm' (From the [Berlin] Radio Tower), 1926–29; National Gallery of Art Archives.

ground under your feet, fifty metres above the earth . . .'[100] In contrast to the avant-garde, Kapeller described the attraction of broadcasting towers as an ephemeral sensation that would inevitably be lost through the normalisation of wireless infrastructure in the public sphere. To Kapeller, the Berlin Radio Tower offered an 'exciting experience today; in a few months perhaps a small sensation, and later still: the ordinariness of a Sunday, which involves climbing a lookout tower, without thoughts of earth, of broadcasting, and of the towering antenna mast'.[101] Likewise, the abstracted view of one's normal surroundings in August Brücher's poem 'View from the Radio Tower' picked up on the classic Romantic trope of the 'overview' (*Überblick*) provided by wandering in the mountains, though the city below no longer seemed sublime, only abstract in a diminutive sense: 'Here you climb up and overlook Berlin: / a toy and the people miniatures'.[102] From Brücher's elevated but abstracted viewpoint, the city's traffic network below took the form of 'open channels' resembling children's paper dolls, as the 'trains creep along like caterpillars'. Reduced to a two-dimensional surface without any depth, the surroundings become 'flat, the naked city skinned'. Thinking of the latticework construction, Brücher simultaneously observed and imagined: 'slowly the moon rises in the metal framework / the elevator falls on its thread like a ball / in the black tower, surrounded by lights / a lattice of stars surrounded by music, / and up above its appearance circles in the universe'.

By the 1930s broadcasting complexes would combine the primary functions of antenna towers, as wireless transmitters, with those of broadcasting studios, as professional workplaces. Taken together, these functions presage a development usually located only in the post-WWII period – networks to be 'lived in'.[103] Completed the year before the BBC's Broadcasting House and inaugurated in 1931, the Haus des Rundfunks in Berlin's Westend district was built to be the seat of the RRG and remains the world's oldest self-contained broadcasting centre. A massive, city-block-wide complex, whose design was awarded to Hans Poelzig through an architectural competition, the Berlin Broadcasting House reflected the rapid institutionalisation of the German radio industry. 'Having started in makeshift accommodations', Siegfried Kracauer commented, 'it is now migrating into gigantic and would-be prestigious buildings.' To Kracauer, the unassuming, functionalist, and allegedly neutral building – whose 'floorplan, like that of any good spatial arrangement, has the charm of a beautiful ornament' – was symptomatic of the same problematic qualities attributed to national broadcasting.[104] Locating the production studios on the inside and the administrative offices on the outside, the floorplan accommodated boardrooms, lecture halls, commissioner offices, and a planned museum, basement bar, rooftop lunchroom, and four hotel rooms. In Kracauer's analysis, this partitioned design 'not only serves to cut the studios off from traffic noise but also ensures convenient access from all the administrative offices',[105] reflecting the medium's separation of producers from consumers. The functional design, which Kracauer found 'forbidding rather than cheering' and compared to the Karstadt Department

Store, made it 'decidedly more reminiscent of a corporate business headquarters than of a place of intellectual and artistic achievement [. . .] The Muses themselves might catch a chill in the administrative corridors.' Ultimately, the form of the Berlin Broadcasting House does not fail to capture its function, as common criticism held, but rather 'involuntarily betrays the true, hidden nature of broadcasting, as a large-scale business that converts the production of scholars, writers, and artists into ready-to-use products'.[106]

With its emphasis on programme contents, radio studies has long tended to overlook the materiality of antennas, radio towers, and broadcasting studios, which is central to media archaeology. Throughout the broadcasting era, the antenna provided a symbol connecting the station to the audience, especially after being showcased at the First German Radio Exhibition and other publicity events. In Vienna, Hermann Leopoldi composed a foxtrot recounting the medium's rapid growth in a series of distasteful double entendres that reflected larger anxieties that associated receptivity with femininity.[107] Sung by Max Kuttner, the suggestive chorus, 'The lovely Adrienna has a large antenna', also registered a legal debate in Red Vienna and the Weimar Republic over rights to install antennas in urban areas. Because it was not yet possible to connect multiple receivers to a single antenna, every listener needed their own, whether installed on the roof or in their domicile, leading to many disputes between landlords and tenants. 'Our antenna is pulled across the room and grounded to the central heating', Austrian satirist and publicist Alexander Roda once admitted. 'We also have a detector – when it is free, I use it as a trouser button.'[108] In light of the radical potential of Hertzian architecture, architecture studies tend to downplay this other side of bourgeois modernism, which equally structures the lived experience of wireless cultures and indicates creative forms of the abuse of army equipment.

In their comedic sketch 'Im Senderaum' (In the broadcast studio), documented as a short sound film, Karl Valentin and Liesl Karlstadt presented a biting satire of this lived experience, ridiculing the rhetoric that blamed the medium's audience for misunderstanding the business of radio.[109] Hoping to obtain a '25-metre-long antenna wire' for a friend, Valentin erroneously attempts to purchase one from the nearest broadcasting station rather than from a radio equipment store. In the studio, Karlstadt plays the bored moderator of a typical Sunday morning concert, who announces a 20-minute 'station break' after which the 'hour of classics' will resume. Downstairs, Valentin tussles with the porter, who phones his boss, Karlstadt, and relays Valentin's misguided demand that they 'wire' the antenna to his friend, as though delivering it via telegram to a particular street address. 'But we transmit everywhere', Karlstadt replies on the phone, informing Valentin that the broadcasters do not sell wires; they are in the business of transmitting 'without wires' (*ohne Draht*). With the station break about to end, Valentin offers to fill in for the sound effects engineer, who still has not returned from his break, in exchange for 5 marks and the 25-metre antenna wire. Given the unenviable task of improvising sound effects for a dramatic recitation of Schiller's 'Song of the Bell', Valentin eventually triggers the siren alarm sound effect, which drowns out everything else and leads the station to be 'switched off', as announced by a flashing sign in the broadcast studio. Behind all the antics, Karlstadt and Valentin reveal the consequences of subverting bourgeois morality: if the audience for national broadcasting refuses to stay out of the studio, then there will be chaos.

For media philosophers Lorenz Engell and John Durham Peters, the tower represents a different model of literacy for media studies than the one traditionally located in the book.[110] Wireless stations, I would add, themselves reconfigured the relation between books and towers, especially through analogies comparing radio broadcasting to the Tower of Babel. While Lasswitz imagined a massive interplanetary wireless communications centre, and Paul Scheerbart once described *Lésabendio* as a novella about an 'anti-Babylonian tower', philosopher and prolific author of speculative fiction Mynona (Salomo Friedlaender) composed the prize-winning story, 'Der antibabylonische Turm' (The anti-Babylonian tower).[111] A provocative contribution to a competition organised by the Weimar Society of Bibliophiles in 1932, Mynona's story was published in 1933 and immediately censored for one critical remark about Nazi race ideologies. 'The Anti-Babylonian Tower' ridiculed the state of bibliophilia in the media age, imagining an invention that made the public sphere superfluous: the titular inversion of the Tower of Babel. 'The Anti-Babylonian Tower' starts off by following the owner of an antiquarian bookstore, obsessed with the materiality of books, who discovers the 'lost work of Socrates', which turns out to have been a prescient formulation of Kant's categorical imperative. He bequeaths the rare book to his adoptive son, Werner, who, being a militant Kantian, sells it to J. Pierpont Morgan, and then invests this 5-million-mark windfall in a financial policy speculating on 'international pacifism'. Aided by the engineer Sucram (an anagram of the name of the neo-Kantian philosopher Ernst Marcus), Werner and Morgan construct anti-Babylonian towers, but ironically name them 'biblioanthropists' (*Biblioanthropen*) in honour of the antiquarian whose discovery provided the project's start-up capital. 'Organic radio' reveals the 'massive impotence' of books – seen as weak transmitters that only reach a small audience and are insufficient to broadcast the categorical imperative – and 'grabs hold of all the body's organs and physiologically transforms them'.[112] In a critique of Nazi radio politics, the walking radio towers, 'skyscrapers in human form', represent a miracle weapon that is said to counter broadcasters controlling people's wills via radio waves. In Kittler's cursory reading, 'media have taken the place of the arts. A "new illiteracy", as Salomo Friedlaender called it long before McLuhan or Ong declared the end (in a celebratory tone) of the "Gutenberg Era", erected "antibabylonian towers".'[113] To nuance Kittler's pseudo-Hegelian reading of the end of art, Mynona's explicit anti-Kantian message was that 'culture began as illiterate. Languages and books went out in a confusing manner from the Tower of Babylon. Until KANT appeared, whom the educated praise for everything but overcome in a flash, overtake and digest disgustingly through the stupid Nietzscheasis.'[114] Under technical conditions of broadcasting, instrumental reason becomes speculative reason.

To the extent that communications towers relied on the open, aerial aesthetics of antennas, broadcasting houses developed a closed, bunker-like aesthetic, which came to be epitomised by another type of wireless tower – the *Flakturm* (anti-aircraft tower). Starting in August 1933, an entire generation known as the *Flakhelfergeneration* came to serve in the Luftwaffe's auxiliary anti-aircraft defence.[115] After the RAF's air raid on Berlin in 1940, Adolf Hitler ordered the construction of massive anti-aircraft complexes to defend the capital from further attacks. Each complex consisted of two towers, a 'combat tower' (aka G-Tower, *Gefechtsturm*) and a 'command tower' (aka L-Tower, *Leitturm*), always constructed in pairs, connected via cable, and intended to work together, with the one targeting an aircraft and the other firing. To locate and identify potential targets, the command tower had a state-of-the-art radar installation with a gigantic UHF dish (the *Würzburg-Riese*) that could be retracted behind a thick concrete and steel dome to prevent damage in the event of an air raid. Designed by architect Friedrich Tamms – with Hitler expressing a personal interest and even making some sketches for their design – the flak towers in Berlin were rapidly constructed over a period of six months. In total, eight such complexes were created in the cities of Berlin, Hamburg, and Vienna. 'It may be the case that wireless represses architecture', Walter Seitter reflects. 'But these "ground stations" were able to increase in terms of their scale, their need for security, and their resemblance to fortresses and bunkers. Their groundedness and their levelness. The more upper levels there are, the more lower levels there are.'[116] In addition to their function as anti-aircraft stations, flak towers served other important functions at the end of World War II, as they became civilian air-raid shelters and storage spaces for artworks, including parts of the Pergamom Altar. Because demolishing the flak towers was not feasible without threatening their surroundings, there were plans in the post-WWII years to convert them into representative objects with decorated facades; most, however, remain intact without any alterations to this day.

While locals now routinely use the parks that have grown back around flak towers and tourists still congregate around the Eiffel Tower, it is usually not to pay tribute to their historical significance as wireless stations. Today, many people still sip coffee on a broadcast tower's observation deck, and some wireless enthusiasts even make pilgrimages to early wireless stations, but these non-functional infrastructures are no longer causes for collective celebration or mourning in the modernist sense.[117]

Crisis, Panic, Futurity

Around 1950, in the years after the air raids but before the satellite crisis, there was already a frisson of terror – a shudder of existential dread – about the worldwide expansion of wireless networks. To Ernst Jünger, the Blitzkrieg-style transmission mobilised during wartime appeared to have eliminated any time for aesthetic contemplation. 'The panic will only intensify', Jünger predicted in a mythopoetic account of the information age, 'wherever automatism increases and approaches a perfect form, as in America.'[118] Where else? For (West) German philosophers of technology coming to terms with National Socialist radio and radar politics, the United States provided ample cannon fodder for ideology critique. According to Jünger, 'panic finds its best feeding grounds there, gets spread through networks that operate at the speed of lightning'.[119] As a symbol of centralised command and control, the antenna tower became a flexible figure for reflecting on the deep time of the media, especially in terms of the exploitation of national broadcasting as a system of mass address.[120] For Jünger, the combination of information overload and omnidirectional wireless transmission spelled angst: 'The need to hear the news several times a day is already a sign of fear; the imagination grows and paralyzes itself in a rising vortex. The myriad antennas rising above our megacities resemble hairs standing on end – they provoke demonic contacts.'[121] In Jünger's imagination, the earth appeared to possess the same evolutionary defence mechanism as members of the animal kingdom: horripilation, the erection of hairs on the skin due to cold, fear, or excitement, provides a tactile image of planetary shock in which the entire globe constitutes a wireless body in a state of distress. The tactility of wireless media, latent for a century in a strain of media pathology that attributed neurasthenia to telegraph wires, would now take on a planetary scale.

Just as radiotelegraphy provided the 'technological unconscious' of Jünger's post-WWI writings on trench warfare, radar informed those of his post-WII philosophy of technology.[122] The 'demonic contacts' in Jünger's description of information overload refer to whatever lies hidden behind the Veil of Isis, a crucial symbol in the philosophy of technology for the concealed secrets of nature; and once the Veil is lifted, their absence from modernity. For Jünger, the first technical object to lift the Veil was the lightning rod. Inaugurating a new age of electric media, this event was 'not only of world-historical but also of earth-historical' significance.[123] Previously held hostage by Zeus's lightning bolts, Jünger explained in mythopoetic language, human beings finally harnessed the anteic forces of the earth mother Gaia, conquering the heavenly gods of Olympus and harnessing the power to communicate through networks that could transport information at the speed of light. For Jünger, the lightning rod was the earliest expression of an anteic unrest that spread over the rest of the earth. With the Veil of Isis having been lifted, one invention after the next followed in its wake, endowing the denuded earth with a new covering. No longer viewed as an adversary to be conquered, the earth was awarded a 'new skin [. . .] of images and thoughts, melodies, signals, and messages'.[124] In the process, according to Jünger, human beings realised their desires to see, hear, and write at a distance, which had previously been associated with magic, in the form of television, telephony, and telegraphy. 'The earth gets spun with a thicker and thicker net of wires and cables; a forest of senders and receivers grows upwards, a forest of antennas that sprout in little points or that, as towers, make cities taller.'[125] In connecting the world, the earth itself appeared to have been transformed into a massive wireless transmitter in search of a receptive audience.

At the height of the Sputnik Age, a similar view of spaceship earth as a wireless station appeared to Marshall McLuhan, partly inspiring his turn from medium-specific theories towards the creation of the field now known as 'media ecology'. Realising that the antenna was not an 'extension of man' in the sense of extending hearing or vision, McLuhan described it as an 'extension of our physical powers' in the creation of different media environments.[126] 'In the age of information, it is information itself that becomes environmental', McLuhan asserted. 'The satellites and antennae projected from our planet, for example, have transformed the planet from being an *environment* into being a *probe*', a term McLuhan also frequently used to describe the form of his own probing soundbites.[127] For McLuhan, modernists' frequent references to antennas and satellites were indications of what he prematurely diagnosed as a shift from consumerism to experimentation: 'Whereas the package belongs to the consumer age, the probe belongs to an age of experimenters' – the very pre- and post-historical period of national broadcasting during which the antenna informs a variety of scientific, aesthetic, and experimental contexts.[128] The architectural and conceptual forms of early antennas, which were not completely determined by functional considerations, are strikingly different from the iconic forms of radio and television towers that would later develop into symbols of national broadcasting. Survival in a technocratic age depended, for McLuhan and Jünger alike, on finding a new space for the imagination, which Jünger termed the 'forest' (*Wald*), a mystical site of rest and contemplation that can exist everywhere, even in a city. Yet if the presence of antennas once functioned as guideposts pointing the way to this heterotopia, then what might play that role in their absence?

Due to black-boxing, digitisation, and miniaturisation, antenna towers are no longer the celebratory monuments they once were, instead fuelling anxiety and paranoia, and yet this need not yield nostalgia for a bygone wireless age. Read critically, the transhistorical imagination of antennas reveals how media technologies inform cultural distinctions, such as (un)receptivity, (in)sensitivity, and (mis) attunement. Though internalised in wireless sensors and processors, the antenna remains visible in the little dot at the end of the waves in the wireless sign. While the wireless sign makes it appear as though so-called users are at the centre of the wireless world, the opposite is often the case. Wi-Fi antennas are not primarily transmitters but receivers that monitor every packet circulated through a network before filtering out the relevant ones for each user's address.[129] Nonetheless, the imagination of wireless connectivity continues to prioritise transmission over reception, imagining connecting rather than being connected. Who or what do we imagine receiving the world's most powerful wireless transmissions with the largest potential audiences? In *Contact*, Carl Sagan imagined the first wireless signal conducted at a high enough frequency to break through the ionosphere, which acts as a planetary filter bubble, preventing radio and television broadcasts from escaping the atmosphere. Instead of a response to the carefully planned interstellar transmissions of the 1970s, some of which Sagan himself helped design, the first message from extraterrestrials in *Contact* retransmits a historical broadcast of Adolf Hitler opening the 1936 Summer Olympics.[130] In a recent essay that twists around this classic colonial topos of first contact in a different manner, Hito Steyerl entertains the idea that, after the requisite time delay, 'in a few hundred thousand years, extraterrestrial forms of intelligence may incredulously sift through our wireless communications. But imagine the perplexity of those creatures when they actually look at the material. Because a huge percentage of the pictures inadvertently sent off into deep space is actually spam.'[131] For Steyerl, 'image spam is our message to the future'. Instead of the Family of Man assumed to represent Spaceship Earth and transmitted by the *Voyager* time capsule, 'our contemporary dispatch to the universe is image spam showing enhanced advertisement mannequins. And this is how the universe will see us; it is perhaps even how it sees us now.'[132] At their radical limits, speculations apply not only to the past and the future but also to the present.

Notes

1. Following current conventions, I use the English plural (*antennas*) for electrical objects, and the Latinate plural (*antennae*) for insect feelers. Historically, there was no standard terminology, as is evident from the use of the hybrid plural form 'antennaes', for example in Marconi, 'Wireless Telegraphic Communication'.
2. See Frohne, 'Radio as a "Minor" Art Practice', 127.
3. Balanis, *Antenna Theory*, 3–4; Balanis, 'Antenna Theory', 7–23; Christodoulou et al., 'Antennas'.
4. Rothammel, *Antennenbuch*, 17.
5. For historical studies, see Ramsay, 'Highlights of Antenna History'; Kraus, 'Antennas Since Hertz and Marconi'; Schulz, *Wireless Antenna History*; Sarkar and Belrose, 'A History of Phased Array Antennas'. For theoretical studies, see the sources cited below in relation to architecture studies, and Parks, 'Around the Antenna Tree'.
6. See Sreevidya and Subramanian, 'Aesthetic Appraisal of Antenna Towers'; Parks, 'Around the Antenna Tree'; Schaefer, 'Dematerialized Infrastructures'; Parks, 'Earth Observation and Signal Territories'; Starosielski, 'Signal Tracks'.
7. See Cerver et al., *Communication Towers / Torres de Comunicación*.
8. See Balanis, 'Antenna Theory', 18–19; cf. Sato and Sato, 'Antenna Development in Japan', 455–72.
9. On 'locative media', see Ingersoll, 'Divining the Network with the Forked Twig'.
10. For the antenna in architecture studies, see Dunne, *Hertzian Tales*; Trüby, *Hertzianismus*, 17–24; Trüby, 'Antenne und Bunker'; Harwood, 'Wires, Walls and Wireless'; Harwood, 'Wires, Wirelessness, and the Morality of Form'; Wigley, *Buckminster Fuller Inc.*, 16–17. Wigley has

also curated the exhibition, *The Human Insect: Antenna Architectures 1887–2017*, and delivered online lectures on 'The Radical Architecture of the Antenna' (2016) and 'The Human Insect' (2021).

11. Larkin, 'The Politics and Poetics of Infrastructure', 327–43; Steyerl, 'The Spam of the Earth'.
12. Simondon, *On the Mode of Existence of Technical Objects*, 191–210.
13. Simondon, *On the Mode of Existence of Technical Objects*, 197.
14. Simondon, *On the Mode of Existence of Technical Objects*, 197.
15. Simondon, *On the Mode of Existence of Technical Objects*, 196.
16. Simondon, *On the Mode of Existence of Technical Objects*, 197.
17. Simondon, 'On Techno-Aesthetics', 5.
18. Simondon, 'On Techno-Aesthetics', 5.
19. Simondon, 'On Techno-Aesthetics', 6.
20. Simondon, 'On Techno-Aesthetics', 6.
21. Trier, 'Antenne'.
22. Trier, 'Antenne', 193–4.
23. Trier, 'Antenne', 194.
24. Trier, 'Antenne', 198–9.
25. Pelosi et al., 'Antennae', 61–3; Slyusar, 'History of Radio Engineering's Term "Antenna"', 83–5.
26. Trier, 'Antenne', 200.
27. Lasswitz, 'Aus dem Tagebuch einer Ameise', 78–118.
28. Lasswitz, 'Aus dem Tagebuch einer Ameise', 78.
29. Lasswitz, 'Aus dem Tagebuch einer Ameise', 78.
30. Lasswitz, 'Aus dem Tagebuch einer Ameise', 79.
31. Lasswitz, 'Aus dem Tagebuch einer Ameise', 81.
32. Lasswitz, 'Aus dem Tagebuch einer Ameise', 81.
33. Lasswitz, 'Aus dem Tagebuch einer Ameise', 118.
34. Wigley, 'We are Living in an Ecology of Antenna'.
35. Maupassant, qtd. in Conley, '"Hive of Words"', 767. On Czech poets' identification with the Eiffel Tower as a wireless station, see Kuhlman, 'Prague Meets Paris'.
36. Eiffel, 'The Eiffel Tower', 735.
37. See Rikitianskaia et al., 'The Mediatization of the Air', 765.
38. Conley, '"Hive of Words"', 767.
39. See Sloterdijk, 'A Plug for Higher Energies', 232–9; cf. Peters, 'Broadcasting and Schizophrenia'.
40. The classics in the genre include Guillaume Apollinaire's 'Zone' and Blaise Cendrars's 'La Tour', which in turn inspired a poem by Alfred Richard Meyer as well as Ywan Goll's collection, *Der Eiffelturm*.
41. 'Grösse der Türme der Telefunken-Gross-Station Nauen', 51.
42. See Phillips, *Early Radio Wave Detectors*.
43. See, among others, Hong, *Wireless*, 23. Interestingly, the Hertz dipole served as the model for the elliptical construction of the reading room of the Warburg Library of Cultural Studies (Kulturwissenschaftliche Bibliothek Warburg).
44. See Ingersoll, 'Divining the Network with the Forked Twig'.

45. See Herbst, *Erdantennen und Untergrundantennen.*
46. Moeller, Untitled, in Herbst, *Erdantennen und Untergrundantennen*, 96.
47. 'Drahtlose Telegraphie', in Herbst, *Erdantennen und Untergrundantennen*, 15.
48. Goedicke, The Suspending of the Lines of Electric Telegraphs in the Air.
49. Kiebitz, 'Neuere Versuche über gerichtete drahtlose Telegraphie', in Herbst, *Erdantennen und Untergrundantennen*, 24.
50. Harwood, 'Wires, Walls and Wireless'; Trüby, 'Antenne und Bunker'; Wigley, *Buckminster Fuller Inc.*
51. Umbach, *German Cities and Bourgeois Modernism.*
52. Milutis, *Ether*, 96.
53. See Wigley, 'The Radical Architecture of the Antenna'; Thurmann-Jajes et al., *Radio as Art*; Augaitis and Lander, *Radio Rethink.*
54. On the history of Nauen, see Telefunken and Transradio, *Festschrift zur Einweihung der Grossfunkstelle Nauen*; Fürst, *Im Bannkreis von Nauen*; Böhm, 'Unsere Großstationstechnik'; Bollé, *Die Grossfunkstation Nauen.*
55. The DokuFunk Archiv in Vienna contains one of the world's largest collections of QSL cards. See Harranth, *Aus den Schätzen der QSL-Collection.*
56. Eckler, 'Die Stadt Nauen', 94.
57. Bollé, *Die Grossfunkstation Nauen*, 13–14.
58. Bollé, *Die Grossfunkstation Nauen.*
59. Nairz, 'Die Riesenstation der Gesellschaft für drahtlose Telegraphie in Nauen', 97.
60. See Bollé, *Die Grossfunkstation Nauen*, 13–14.
61. Fürst, *Die Wunder um uns*, 12–13 (the original figure numbers have been amended).
62. Fürst, *Die Wunder um uns*, 20.
63. Umbach, *German Cities and Bourgeois Modernism*, 60–1.
64. See Bollé, *Die Grossfunkstation Nauen*, 23–4.
65. Hermann Muthesius, qtd. in Bollé, *Die Grossfunkstation Nauen*, 24.
66. El Lissitzky, 'Wheel – Propeller – and What Will Follow', 106.
67. See further Asendorf, *Ströme und Strahlen*, 127.
68. Kiesler, 'The City in Space', 192.
69. On the crucial architectural concept of *Bodenständigkeit*, an environmental term for being rooted in the soil, see Cupers, 'Bodenständigkeit'.
70. See Niebisch, 'Ether Machines'.
71. Kittler, *Discourse Networks*, 229.
72. Sloterdijk, 'A Plug for Higher Energies', 234. On the notion of human media, see Schüttpelz, 'Trance-Medien/Personale Medien', 227–33; cf. Geoghegan, 'Mind the Gap'.
73. For period usage of *Antennenmenschen*, primarily in occult discourses, see Schiffmann, 'Der Mensch als Antenne'; 'Antenne Mensch'.
74. Sloterdijk, 'A Plug for Higher Energies', 236.

75. See, for example, Steiner's lecture on 'Involution and Evolution', part of a lecture series on 'Esoteric Cosmology' delivered in Paris from 25 May to 14 June 1906.
76. Nietzsche, *Ecce Homo*, §8 ('Why I am so wise'), 83.
77. Toller, *Hoppla, wir leben!*
78. Pound, *ABC of Reading*, 73, 81–3. Pound's analogy was to insect antennae and not electrical antennas.
79. Qtd. in Richter, 'Joseph Beuys', n.p. Beuys served as a radio operator and aerial gunner during World War II, performed with antennae in the action artwork 'Mainstream', and described his multiples as 'antennas'.
80. See Kahn, 'Three Receivers', 73–80.
81. Farquharson, 'Diedrich Diederichsen in Conversation with Isa Genzken', 140.
82. Knatz, 'Natur und Geist', 41. Knatz composed another poem, 'Gute Antenne!', a New Year's greeting addressed to radio.
83. Knatz, 'Natur und Geist', 41.
84. Giedion, *Building in France*, 91.
85. Giedion, *Building in France*, 91.
86. Benjamin, *The Arcades Project*, 459.
87. Benjamin, *The Arcades Project*, 459.
88. Zweig, 'An den Funkturm, den Nachbarn', 209–10.
89. Zweig, 'An den Funkturm, den Nachbarn', 210.
90. Zweig, 'An den Funkturm, den Nachbarn', 209.
91. Zweig, 'An den Funkturm, den Nachbarn', 210.
92. Brennert, 'Dem neuen Roland', 38–40.
93. Part of a WWI propaganda campaign, the *Nagelmänner* were iron statues that citizens would pay to hammer iron nails into, the proceeds going to the war campaign.
94. On *schwarzhören*, see Führer, 'A Medium of Modernity?', 731; Gilfillan, *Pieces of Sound*, 79.
95. Brennert, 'Dem neuen Roland', 38–40.
96. Mostar, 'Funktürme', in Seitz and Zucker, eds, *Um uns die Stadt*, 40–1.
97. Mostar, 'Funktürme', 41.
98. For a later photographic series, see, for example, Spencer J. Harding's photographs of derelict microwave relay stations in his exhibition *The Long Lines* (2017).
99. Moholy-Nagy, *Von Material zu Architektur*, 201; cf. 222–3.
100. Kapeller, 'Ein Blick aus der Höhe', 137.
101. Kapeller, 'Ein Blick aus der Höhe', 138.
102. Brücher, 'Blick vom Funkturm', in Seitz and Zucker, eds, *Um uns die Stadt*, 41–2.
103. See Treue, 'Das Haus des Rundfunks'. Long before the 'smart city', city planners Ludwig Hoffmann and Martin Wagner dreamed of the 'wireless city Witzleben'.
104. Kracauer, 'Radio Station', 540–4.

105. Kracauer, 'Radio Station', 541.
106. Kracauer, 'Radio Station', 543.
107. See Ehardt, *Radiobilder*, 58–9.
108. Roda Roda, 'Radio', 77–8.
109. The sketch, also known as 'Rundfunk' and 'Der Antennendraht', is titled 'Im Senderaum' in Valentin, *Karl Valentin*, 498–507. I am grateful to Anton Kaes for this reference.
110. Engell, 'Sinn und Sichlichkeit'; Peters, 'Calendar, Clock, Tower'.
111. Mynona, 'Der antibabylonische Turm'. The story's original title was 'Biblioanthropists' (*Biblioanthropen*). For context and close reading, see Wedemeyer, 'Ningún libro es también una escalera', 378–88.
112. Mynona, 'Der antibabylonische Turm', 197.
113. Kittler, 'Signal-to-Noise Ratio', 172.
114. Mynona, 'Der antibabylonische Turm' (capitalisation in original).
115. Prominent members of the Flakhelfergeneration (born c. 1926–29) include Joseph Ratzinger (Pope Benedict XVI), sociologists Jürgen Habermas and Niklas Luhmann, historian Wilhelm Volkert, and literary authors Günter Grass, Martin Walser, and Günter de Bruyn.
116. Seitter, *Physik der Medien*, 374.
117. Mitchell, *Me++*.
118. Jünger, *The Forest Passage*, 29 (translation modified).
119. Jünger, *The Forest Passage*, 29 (translation modified).
120. See Benn, 'The Radar Thinker', 45–57.
121. Jünger, *The Forest Passage*, 29 (translation modified).
122. On this concept, without reference to Jünger's work, see Powell, *The Technological Unconscious*.
123. Jünger, *An der Zeitmauer*, 124.
124. Jünger, *An der Zeitmauer*, 124.
125. Jünger, *An der Zeitmauer*, 124.
126. This conception of the tower as an 'extension of Man' can be found in Peters, 'Calendar, Clock, Tower'; cf. Peters, *The Marvelous Clouds*, 233–9.
127. McLuhan, 'The Relation of Environment to Anti-Environment', 118 (emphasis added).
128. McLuhan, 'The Relation of Environment to Anti-Environment', 118.
129. Chun and Friedland, 'Habits of Leaking'.
130. Sagan, *Contact*, 86.
131. Steyerl, 'The Spam of the Earth'.
132. Steyerl, 'The Spam of the Earth'.

Conclusion

Wireless Futures, 2000/2100

The future is wireless. At least, this much seemed certain to anyone speculating on media change at the turn of the century.[1]

According to this undifferentiated vision of wireless futures, new media make old media obsolete, and the reasons for 'going wireless' are natural or self-evident. At the turn of the century, 1900/2000, the wire was considered an unsightly material artefact of an emergent medium, a technical difficulty to be solved through inevitable progress. And yet even in the so-called wireless age, there are only more wires than ever before. If wireless futures have long seemed imminent, why do they keep disappearing somewhere in the offing? According to systems engineering and critical infrastructure studies alike, it remains improbable that distinct modes of transmission will fully converge in a unified wireless architecture, due primarily to the scarcity of desirable frequencies in the radio spectrum.[2] But what if wireless futures depend not only on markets and technical limits but on fundamentally reimagining media change?

At first glance, the structural parallels between the rise of wireless telegraphy in the 1890s and that of local area networks in the 1990s may appear to be a case of historical cycles. However, the recursive approach of German media philosophy emphasises how the past returns with a twist. Around 1900/2000, the two most direct parallels can be seen in the later period's resuscitation of the former's wireless terminology and its updating of modernist stories about the promises and perils of the so-called wireless age. When it comes to terminology, media studies can avoid perpetuating assumptions about the uniform experience of 'wirelessness' by using the term 'wireless' in the adjectival rather than the nominal form, primarily to describe a mode and not a medium, and yet there will always be terminological slippage as media change. In a 1991 article predicting an impending 'Wireless Revolution', for instance, Theodore S. Rappaport modified and limited the title's slogan to 'wireless personal communications revolutions', but then referred broadly to 'cellular radio systems', 'paging service[s]', 'new wireless communication services called PCS (personal communications services)', 'citizens band (CB) radio', and the 'cordless telephone'.[3] Whether in the case of wired and wireless telegraphy, landline and cellular telephone networks, or wireline and wireless computer networks, the latter supplements the former, revealing its perceived flaws and latent potentialities. Like the adjective 'post' and the notion of a 'postal principle', the prospects of 'going wireless' thus remain framed as a response to whatever came before it, endlessly deferring the question of the 'post-wireless'.[4] As a result, the concept of wireless invariably remains a supplement to other familiar modes of transmission. In both cases, the discursive relation between the new and the old was conceived first in terms of extension, replacement, or supplementation, and only later in its own terms.

'Going wireless' suggests a certain trajectory for media change, whereby a new mode of transmission is taken to supersede an old one and render it obsolete. Reinforcing the vernacular assumption that wires are a thing of the past and wireless a sign of the future, the marketing slogan reduces the complex process of media change to a linear, unidirectional, and irreversible model of inevitable progress. At the same time, the teleological process of going wireless remains framed in retrospective terms, and wireless functions as a relational concept. To establish parallels across modes and genres of wireless technology, the narrative of a wireless revolution suppresses the historical points of convergence and disjuncture between wired and wireless systems and instead mobilises the central modernist understanding of media overcoming space and time. By this modernist logic, the ubiquity of electromagnetic radiation makes wireless signals available, at least in theory, to anyone, anywhere, at any time. Hence, any imaginable wireless application can be taken to realise the communicative dream of universal accessibility, the realities of mass migration, or the capitalistic ideal of unlimited circulation. However, it can also fuel concerns about surveillance, the impossibility of disconnection, and the health and safety implications of 'electrosmog'. By emphasising device ownership over infrastructure improvements, the narrative of a wireless revolution promises a particular form of social change with a sense of belonging that can only be obtained through access to symbols of wealth, status, and power.

Wilhelmine wireless was supposed to solve the social, political, and economic problems inherent in wired systems, but many of them resurfaced in different forms. Although wireless telegraphy offered obvious economic advantages over wired telegraphy in terms of producing, laying, and maintaining cables, collecting payments for wireless services proved more difficult than it had been for wired services, where information producers and receivers are directly connected. Wireless infrastructures might have also presented an initial improvement on the vulnerability of wired infrastructures, evident when undersea telegraph cables were cut at the onset of the Spanish-American War and again during World War I. However, wireless transmissions are themselves vulnerable to interception, which required the creation of encryption techniques. Similarly, wireless networks might have seemed to represent a more efficient medium for European empires to monitor their colonies, though remote stations were more difficult to maintain in times of crisis. In laboratory experiments and scientific lectures, the study of wireless phenomena was a way of resolving debates about the speed of light and experimentally vindicating speculations about the existence of a continuous electromagnetic spectrum. However, wireless research had to move out of the laboratory to become practical, because of the size restrictions of wavelengths and the corresponding apparatus. While wireless telegraphy was initially framed as a direct response to wired telegraphy, other applications of radio waves responded to different problematics, and the overall emergence of wireless transmission defies the traditional problem–solution logic of media history and theory. The four main explanations for the growth of wireless technology cited above appeal to economic, military, imperial, and scientific forces.[5] As this study has shown, however, wireless cannot be understood as the monocausal solution to any single problem in the past, but only as contingent negotiations of an array of recurrent, future-oriented questions.

Another crucial parallel between the discourse of wireless futures, 1900/2000, can be found in an apparent divergence in the scale of wireless technology relative to its human operators. 'While the notion of wireless networks implies that there are fewer wires', Adrian Mackenzie observed in his study of *Wirelessness*,

> it could easily be argued that actually there are more wires. Rather than wireless cities or wireless networks, it might be more accurate to speak of the rewiring of cities through the highly reconfigurable paths of chipsets. Billions of chipsets means trillions of wires or conductors on a microscopic scale.[6]

On an 'electronic pilgrimage' to a Marconi station 'to honour an approaching centenary', William J. Mitchell observed a similar divergence between wireless data and telegraph networks: while 'the network had scaled up', 'the transmission and reception apparatus had dramatically scaled down'.[7] In Mitchell's analysis, the sensation of ubiquitous connectivity depends on seamless connections across multiple scales, from microtransmitters though Bluetooth, Wi-Fi, and other local networks, to municipal projects, national broadcasting, and global satellite systems.[8] To describe the 'complex logic of wireless coverage', Mitchell imagined 'wireless infrastructure "shells" encircling the earth at successively greater altitudes, like the layers of a rather messy and incomplete onion'.[9] Colloquially sorted according to increasing transmission range, contemporary wireless infrastructure consists of many overlapping systems, including nanonetworks and near-field communications (NFC), personal area networks (PAN), wireless local area networks (WLAN), metropolitan area networks (MAN), and wide area networks (WAN). As the spatial scope increases, in Mitchell's analysis, so does the required amount of power, the possibility of interference, and the necessity of regulation and licensing.

What would it take to reimagine wirelessness through a flattened ontology, which neither measures technology around a human scale, nor presumes a godlike perspective from which the totality of wireless systems could be observed? 'Electromagnetic waves may be everywhere', Bruno Latour observes while outlining the flattened approach known as *actor-network theory*, 'but I still have to have an antenna, a subscription and a decoder if I am to get CNN (Cable News Network).'[10] For Latour, our everyday experience with these kinds of inputs and outputs reveals seams within the rhetoric of seamless connectivity:

> Technological networks, as the name indicates, are nets thrown over spaces, and they retain only a few scattered elements of those spaces [. . .] They are by no means comprehensive, global or systematic, even though they embrace surfaces without covering them, and extend a very long way.[11]

While we can comprehend the local dimension of technological networks immediately, we struggle to understand the translocal operations of actor-networks. Building on Latour's argument, Florian Sprenger and Daniel Gethmann emphasise that wireless does not merely globalise the local coordinates of the social; it radically reconfigures them.[12] Wireless might signal a return to the deeper historical past in the form of 'global nomads', as Joshua Meyrowitz has speculated, and yet this creative rewriting of McLuhan's 'global village' remains eerily close to the industry's preferred equation of technological mobility with social mobility.[13]

Once a rarefied sign of modernity, wireless signals are now commonplace, and the wireless sign is a 'common place' (in the sense of any media topos), a reminder of the rapid normalisation of devices, networks, and practices over the past two decades. If 'going wireless' once suggested a revolutionary, future-oriented trajectory, it is equally important today to account for the evolutionary and less glamorous-sounding phenomenon of having 'gone wireless'. According to user-submitted data, there are around 15 million cellular towers, 350 million unique Bluetooth devices, and 700 million unique Wi-Fi networks worldwide. Based on different metrics, ranging from device ownership to usage time, mobile devices and wireless networks have been predicted to overtake the number of wired networks by the year 2000, the 2010s, or the 2020s. One reason for the continuous deferral of such targets is that the wireless world remains entangled with the wired world. When media gurus envision megaprojects for 'connecting the world', the slogan usually turns out not to mean increasing the density of networks in the Global South but rather connecting them to centres of financial capital in the Global North, as was the case with Wilhelmine wireless a century ago.

Although wireless signals are indifferent to national borders, wireless infrastructures are not, and the largest wireless networks have tended to reproduce the established colonial hierarchies of communications and transportation networks. Wireless connectivity continues to cluster around urban areas in the Global North, with c. 290 million of the 700 million unique Wi-Fi networks cited above being in the United States, followed by c. 48 million in Germany. While some countries are witnessing the rollout of next-generation 5G cellular networks, many others are still relying on decades-old 2G networks, a contrast that usually feeds into the industry's narrative of expanding into untapped markets and finding its 'next billion users'. For rural areas and emerging markets, wireless systems based on light waves (Li-Fi), millimetre waves (5G), and microwaves (WiMax) are frequently presented as future solutions to what can be described from the service provider's point of view as the 'last-mile problem', and, less commonly, from the customer's point of view, as the 'first-mile problem'.[14] While wireless systems circumvent the need to physically install cables across long distances, allegedly further mitigating against cable theft, vandalism, and maintenance issues, most last-mile solutions involve mixed networks, such as connecting a stationary terminal to a wireline network to create the impression of fixed wireless access and spatial mobility. If wireless telegraphy and telephony were once considered to be luxuries, wireless Internet access now appears to be a necessity.

'Media that have reached their saturation points are difficult to write about', as Friedrich Kittler once observed.[15] It is worth repeating Kittler's dictum, not because media philosophers lack critical distance from our objects of study but because contemporary media are such big businesses that it can be difficult to imagine any viable alternatives. Writing at a crucial turning point, Kittler's 'Observations on Public Reception' primarily referenced radio and television broadcasting, still more ubiquitous than personal computers in 1991. For Heidi Grundmann, the organiser of the symposium where Kittler spoke, 'the medium of radio, like many other communications media, is still a hybrid of analogue and digital technologies'.[16] This remains the case today, despite the so-called digital transition in the Global North, as analogue and hybrid radio remains a crucial medium not only in the Global South but also, as Kittler once predicted, in any strategic military operation. Like Kittler, Grundmann recognised that 'radio itself can by no means be reduced to the institution of radio as we mainly know it as public service broadcasting'.[17] Especially with our knowledge of wartime media manipulation, Grundmann concluded, 'artistic attempts to remain critical end up affirming the medium itself', as 'the art market, business, history, and museums' appropriate avant-garde shock tactics, disempower once-revolutionary strategies, and twist everything around to the point that provocation and disruption seem like 'a matter of course in everyday life [*Alltäglichkeit*]'.[18]

At present, wireless futures may look particularly bleak. Rather than creating a sense of wonder, electromagnetic radiation gives rise to anxiety and paranoia. No longer a cause for collective celebration, wireless stations polarise municipal councils and inspire conspiracy theorists to violent action. Though promising freedom and mobility, wireless networks often turn out to reinforce historical inequalities, as well as giving rise to a wide range of biopolitical concerns about control, surveillance, and public health. In recent years, the promises and perils of wireless connectivity have erupted alternately in factual revelations about the American tech industry's complicity in government surveillance of its citizens, and in baseless conspiracy theories attributing the spread of COVID-19 to the rollout of 5G cellular networks.

In the age of 'surveillance capitalism', it is clear that 'free Wi-Fi' always comes at a price. In exchange for short-term network access, organisations extract location-based data not only to directly analyse and monitor customer behaviours but also to exert indirect control over their employees in the form of 'refractive surveillance'.[19] Terms of service (TOS) agreements exacerbate the situation, as was made apparent in a recent publicity stunt in which a London-based security firm included a 'Herod clause' in the End-User License Agreement (EULA) for a free Wi-Fi hotspot, providing short-term wireless Internet access in exchange for the user's 'first-born child'.[20] Even if customers are circumspect, their mobile phones and wireless networks are still subject to constant surveillance and location-based tracking, as evident in Google's 'Spy-Fi' scandal and subsequent revelations about location services on the company's Android smartphones. Although it may sound speculative, if not conspiratorial, one might consider the reasons why Google, Apple, Microsoft, and Amazon invested so heavily in designing their own proprietary wireless routers. As Wendy Hui Kyong Chun and Sarah Friedland observe, 'wireless networks call into question the distinction between the personal and the network, the directed and the broadcast'. If operating in the suggestively named 'promiscuous' mode, a network interface card (NIC) forwards all network traffic to its central processing unit (CPU). 'Without this necessary vulnerability/openness, there would be no Internet, no communications', Chun and Friedland deduce. 'Our network cards only appear "promiscuous" if we envision our machines as personal.'[21]

In response to the spread of 'free Wi-Fi', many locations have started creating 'Wi-Fi free zones', a trend evident not only in coffee shops and city centres but across entire regions, as with the highly publicised National Radio Quiet Zone (NRQZ) in West Virginia and part of Maryland. Due to the restrictions on radio transmissions, this area has become a refuge for those who report having electromagnetic hypersensitivity. While most English-language journalistic accounts attribute the NRQZ's prohibitions against wireless signals to protections for the Green Bank Observatory's radioastronomy telescopes, other accounts point out that the policy also serves to protect the US Navy's largest wireless station, which was revealed to be part of the international 'Five Eyes' intelligence programme. In Germany, where the critical discourse of 'data capitalism' was catalysed much earlier and more strongly around the NSA surveillance revelations than in the United States,[22] artists Christoph Wachter and Mathias Jud developed the award-winning experimental installation 'Can You Hear Me?', which allowed passersby to send anonymous talk-back to NSA and GCHQ operatives.

In spring 2020 the diffuse anxiety about the emergent COVID-19 pandemic connected well-founded concerns about global surveillance technology to unfounded conspiracy theories about the physiological effects of electromagnetic radiation, resulting in violent outbursts against the rollout of 5G cellular networks. According to the constantly changing conspiracy theory, the social distancing necessitated by the global pandemic was a thinly veiled cover for pushing through the installation of next-generation antennas in contested locations. Instead of marching to the factories where the devices were being manufactured, isolated groups violated stay-at-home orders to vent their aggression on nearby antenna towers, which had once provided a powerful modernist symbol of collective progress. In June 2020 the Federal Communications Commission (FCC) took advantage of the confusion to declare the Chinese wireless company Huawei to be a national security threat, reinforcing the administration's jingoism, chauvinism, and trade war politics. If Huawei's rapid growth appears to signal the start of another Sputnik Age, it is worth recalling that '5G is not the atomic bomb'.[23] Contemporary information networks are not only the condition of possibility for the circulation of paranoia. As Urs Stäheli observes in a critique of our inability to imagine disconnection, 'a certain pathological logic is now inscribed directly into networks – the logic of suspicion, distrust, and uncontrollable intensification, which is simultaneously that of creativity, pattern identification, and making surprising connections'.[24]

There were two main strands of the 5G conspiracy theory. Significantly, both were articulated before the spread of the novel coronavirus and both conflated energy with information in a manner familiar from over a century ago. One strand asserted that SARS-CoV-2 was being broadcast at the frequencies used by 5G networks and could be spread over the airwaves. To be clear, electromagnetic channels transmit immaterial information and not matter itself; images, sounds, and numbers are transported in a fundamentally different manner than goods, things, and passengers. Over a century ago, the similar misconception that telephone lines and radio waves could transmit diseases was already the subject of as many fears as jokes. Debunking the conflation of energy and information, Ludwig Wittgenstein quipped that pragmatist 'philosophers who think that one can as it were use thought to make an extension of experience, should think about the fact that one can transmit talk, but not measles, by telephone'.[25] In 'A Stimulus to Make the Most Productive Use of the Radio', Kurt Schwitters put to bed fears about contagion over the airwaves with a short fairy tale about a fictitious broadcast 'by the strongest man in the world'.[26] While the broadcast was supposed to contain a sermon on sexually transmitted infections, a printing error results satirically in the simultaneous impregnation of women listeners nationwide. If wireless signals could actually transmit respiratory droplets, it would follow that they should be able to transmit the entire range of bodily fluids.

Alongside the misconception that the coronavirus could be broadcast and caught 'over the airwaves', the other strand of the

5G conspiracy theory speculated that the electromagnetic radiation used in next-generation wireless transmissions suppresses the human immune system, making individuals vulnerable to infection. While some ionising forms of electromagnetic radiation can indeed affect one's physiology on a cellular level (for example, UV rays, X-rays, gamma rays), they occur far away on the electromagnetic spectrum from non-ionising radiation (for example, radio waves, microwaves), the two categories being separated by the relatively harmless phenomenon of visible light. In a report for the Global Disinformation Index published before the COVID-19 pandemic, Ben Decker had already traced this version of the 5G conspiracy theory back to the reception of two speeches made by former FCC chairman Tom Wheeler in June and July 2016, which quickly sparked an 'adversarial narrative' known under the hashtag 'stop5g'.[27] Over the next two years, the adversarial narrative snowballed into larger concerns about health, the economy, the environment, national security, and big government. Once incorporated into the news cycle in early 2019, the media created a global discourse around the conspiracy theory by connecting previously isolated echo chambers. 'Adversarial narratives like "Stop 5G" are effective because they inflame social tensions by exploiting and amplifying perceived grievances of individuals, groups, and institutions', Decker concluded. 'The payload is agnostic to the truth. Rather, the end game is to foster an adversarial narrative conflict, which has become key to the networked disinformation landscape.'[28]

Paranoid networks know only the logic of limitless growth. Even after being refuted, the 5G conspiracy continues to circulate on social media, thanks to one viral video of an anthroposophical healer presenting an adversarial narrative that combined pathos and pathology. To support his grand narrative that every historical pandemic has coincided with a 'quantum leap in the electrification of the earth', the pseudo-lecturer paraphrased the dubious historical research of one controversial anti-cellular activist-cum-advocate for the medical recognition of electromagnetic hypersensitivity. Mobilising the rhetoric of anthroposophy, which played no role in the pseudo-historian's project, the pseudo-lecturer presented quotations from one of anthroposophy's founding figures, Austrian philosopher Rudolf Steiner. As with the misuse of quotations from Steiner by anthroposophical doctors in the anti-vaccination movement, Steiner's unmistakably esoteric vocabulary gets twisted into the semblance of secular rationality through a pseudo-academic idiom, characterised by a 'scholarly' style, citing 'research', appealing to 'authorities', and deploying technical 'terminology'.[29] Taken out of context, Steiner's remarks quoted by conspiracy theorists may sound relevant to the proposed correlation between historical pandemics and the advent of new media technologies: 'In times when there were no electrical currents, when the air was not swarming with electrical influences, it was easier to be human. For this reason, to be human at all today, it is necessary to expend much stronger spiritual capacities than it was a century ago.'

In their original context, however, Steiner's comments were clearly a reactionary statement about the perceived ills of modernity:

> Compare the world today with that a hundred years ago. You will say that if one compares the world today with that a hundred years ago, there is, on the whole, a difference between today and the time a hundred years ago. But one of the most powerful differences, which is not usually identified, is that we have made telegraph wires, telephone wires, and so on pass through our atmosphere. Now, the growth of wires in Europe still seems like child's play compared to America. That's why there's a trace of insight in that location into what this means for humankind. People there finally sense that human beings are not uninfluenced by what is alive in the telegraph wires and buzzing through the air, that human beings will become real induction apparatuses. Remember that there is an opposite current in your nerves and a parallel current in your bloodstream. Humankind carries all this within itself today, but people hardly talk about it. These are Ahrimanic forces, in the most eminent sense, which make people today absorb their external cultures, which they cannot possibly reject. People worry about the possible and the impossible but what people today think about the least are precisely the strongest realities. For instance, people should talk about the extent to which the difference between Goethe and people today consists in the fact that Goethe was not yet surrounded by telegraph wires. You see what kind of desolation the human soul is in today, that is essentially connected with all of this.[30]

In the same lecture, Steiner did present some elementary science about the effects of wired – and not wireless – telegraphy on the human body, but his anxiety about invisible forces was not directed towards electromagnetic but rather 'Ahrimanic forces'. Rather than exhorting his original followers to break the machine or to abandon modern technology, Steiner advised them to find a new balance for modern human beings between science and spirituality.

For the prospects of wireless futures at present, there is still reason for hope, even if only in knowing that contemporary trends mirror, resurrect, or recursively process discourses and topoi about wireless transmission from over a century ago. Our still-changing present media environment can be particularly stimulating for the study of bygone media futures, providing an incentive to reconfigure media theory, and opening new perspectives on literary, intellectual, and cultural history. Even if wireless futures may seem to represent one deferred promise after the next, they also create a space for revisionist interpretations of once-dominant media practices.

While speculation is often imagined to be an idle activity, media philosophy models counter-forms of critical speculation, and yet the project of thinking through media need not become the exclusive domain of philosophy. As part of a global tradition, critical media practice in the European model that Hans-Jörg Rheinberger calls 'artistic research' aims at generating medial knowledge through hands-on, collaborative, cross-disciplinary experimentation with media objects.[31] In an essay on 'Artists as Researchers in Wireless Communication', Stephen Wilson provided one of the first English-language surveys of these experiments conducted c. 1992–2004 and exhibited at Cuxhaven, Germany, in 2004 to celebrate the centenary of its wireless station.[32] To denaturalise new media, artistic researchers have adopted the framework of media archaeology and the recursive processing of old media. For his 2011 project 'Föhnseher', whose title is a portmanteau of the German words for 'television' (*Fernseher*) and the *föhn* wind, Julian Oliver hacked and modified an analogue TV so that it could capture, filter, and display digital images transmitted from nearby mobile phones. The aim of Oliver's experiment was not only to increase user awareness of surveillance and data leakage, but also to challenge cherished assumptions about the analogue–digital divide. Inspired by further artistic research into wireless technology, Jussi Parikka has proposed that a 'critical engineering' attitude towards 'evil media' differentiates media archaeology from the non-critical attitude that takes concepts such as information, communication, and accessibility to be unassailable goods.[33] By exploring the 'secrecy and paranoia' around wireless transmission, critical engineering 'exposes how infrastructure is in most cases less stable than it seems. It also leaks data on many fronts, intervening in negotiations of public and private, also more broadly in wireless infrastructures across cities.'[34] What Parikka calls 'critically engineered wireless politics' exposes the invisible operations of network infrastructures, much as critical theory exposes the invisible operations of culture, society, history, and ideology.

Just as practising archaeologists excavate sites and examine material artefacts, media archaeologists dig through layers of media history to uncover surprising media objects. By unearthing and remixing nearly two hundred archival film clips, Manu Luksch, Martin Reinhart, and Thomas Tode developed a filmic argument about the structural parallels between electric media, c. 1900, and social media, c. 2000, aptly titled *Mobilisierung der Träume* (Dreams Rewired, 2015).[35] Every generation, according to the essay film's central thesis, tends to think of itself as the modern age. In contrast to the uncritical nostalgia of retrofuturism, where the past serves primarily to remind the present of broken promises, *Dreams Rewired* aims to create 'a double exposure of past (archive footage) and present (contemporary voiceover) to bring historical context to current dilemmas'. Around 1900/2000, an impending wireless revolution promised 'an era of total communication, annihilation of distance and the end of war', while also engendering 'fears over the erosion of privacy, security, morality'. In one striking sequence on 'Transmission', the narrative voiceover (Tilda Swinton) poetically describes 'an instant, open communication channel – without wires. Antennae, our extended feelers, reach into the sky.' To make the channel perceptible, the editors superimpose images of electricity and the crackling sounds of Morse code over archival footage from a variety of filmic sources. To make the once-silent footage resonate with the present, they even imagine a dialogue for *Eve's Wireless*, an archival clip from 1922 that was recently made into a conspiratorial meme because it appears to show a young woman chatting on a mobile phone years before its invention. The central risk of media archaeology, in reading the past through the present, consists in claiming to have discovered an ancient artefact that merely fell out of one's own pocket. This is probably what happened with the memes of time-travelling mobile phones, as the viral video probably shows a one-way radio, not a two-way phone, or, most likely, a hearing aid. Today, it is easier for conspiracy theorists to imagine a world where time travel is an everyday occurrence, and where governments conspire to conceal important inventions from the public, than it is to confront the banal reality of a world in which bodies fall along a spectrum of identities and abilities, and technologies are not concealed from individuals but imposed upon them.

1G, 2G, 3G, 4G, 5G, and any future label for the next 'generation' of mobile devices and cellular networks create the impression of a linear, progressive sequence, and thus make it difficult to imagine alternatives to the status quo.[36] Apart from microprocessors, most consumer-grade technology is said to develop incrementally according to evolutionary trends, and yet mobile devices and cellular networks are said to develop only in revolutionary jumps, which nevertheless occur predictably enough to warrant the designation of discrete generations. A designation used for cellular networks since the mid-1980s and for Wi-Fi networks since the mid-2010s, 'wireless generations' are usually defined by an exponential increase in data transmission speed and a corresponding decrease in latency, making the possibilities of interaction increasingly approach what the military-industrial complex defines as 'real time'. Like any notion of generations, those of wireless transmission provide a powerful fiction that imposes a certain narrative on a particular group of people and things. As a narrative form, generations create a clear beginning, middle, and end, giving meaning to a procession of historical events. While cyclical concepts have been crucial for many cultures, the current sense of generations only took off after World War II, when the emerging fields of cybernetics and futurology mobilised the concept to claim that models and simulations are sufficient to predict the future. In the case of wireless transmission, the first generation of wireless technology was defined only retrospectively with the advent of the second, and thus the wireless futures described in this book would be part of wireless generation zero. By pitting each generation of technology against a previous one, the designation of generations negotiates the risks of speculative investments in untested technologies. However, the wireless industry's ongoing struggle to think of previous generations together with the current ones speaks to a larger sea change in the widely diagnosed collapse of our ability to imagine radically different futures.[37]

While wireless cultures continue to be the subject of extensive empirical research in communications and mass media studies, media-philosophical studies remain few and far between, and historical studies tend to take the field's core concepts, such as access, networking, and mobility, to be unassailable goods. Seeing as the most influential theories of wireless transmission came about during the heady days of 'free Wi-Fi', many already seem naïve or short-sighted, as is evident in their omission of wireless energy transfer and their apparent obliviousness to the flip side of free Wi-Fi in forms of surveillance capitalism. Likewise, the promises-and-perils methodology that remains dominant in historical studies of communications and mass media no longer appears adequate to capture the dynamics of media change. From the critical, recursive perspective developed in this book, we might critique the promises and perils of the promises-and-perils methodology, especially regarding the purported neutrality and objectivity associated with considering both sides of an issue. One of the classic strategies of the simultaneously critical and speculative tradition in which I would like to place this book is to problematise the very act of questioning. Instead of asking about the origins of wireless connectivity, *Wireless Futures* has interrogated the origins of questions about the origins of wireless connectivity, in addition to the contents of wireless futures, their aesthetic forms and functions. In both cases, these recursive gestures are intended to open a new space for imaginative critiques connecting the past, present, and future.

The imagination of wireless futures takes on a certain urgency during periods of media-in-transition, when various possibilities for future development still seem, if not entirely wide open, then at least subject to negotiation. The mutual entanglement of past, present, and future is precisely what prevents the time-critical mode of wireless transmission from becoming the object of baseless conjecture and makes it one of critical media-philosophical speculation.

Notes

1. See, for instance, Williamson, 'Forget about Wired, the Future is Wireless', 18; Gleick, 'The Wireless Age'.
2. See Lehr and Chapin, 'On the Convergence of Wired and Wireless', 33–41.
3. Rappaport, 'The Wireless Revolution', 52.
4. On the post(al), see Siegert, *Relays*; Winthrop-Young, 'Going Postal to Deliver Subjects'; Krämer, *Medium, Messenger, Transmission.*
5. Castells, *Rise of the Network Society*; Kittler, 'Rock Music'; Innis, *Empire and Communications*; Hagen, *Das Radio*.
6. Mackenzie, *Wirelessness*, 64.
7. Mitchell, *Me++*, 2.
8. Mitchell, *Me++*, 49–54.
9. Mitchell, *Me++*, 49.
10. Latour, *We Have Never Been Modern*, 117–18.
11. Latour, *We Have Never Been Modern*, 118.
12. Gethmann and Sprenger, *Die Enden des Kabels*, 23.
13. Meyrowitz, 'Global Nomads in the Digital Veldt', 91–102; Meyrowitz, 'The Rise of Glocality', 21–30.
14. See Lambrechts and Sinha, *Last Mile Internet Access*, 101–8.
15. Kittler, 'Observations on Public Reception', 75.
16. Grundmann, 'Die Geometrie des Schweigens', n.p.
17. Grundmann, 'Die Geometrie des Schweigens', n.p.
18. Grundmann, 'Die Geometrie des Schweigens', n.p.
19. See Levy and Barocas, 'Refractive Surveillance'.
20. Fox-Brewster, 'Londoners Give Up Eldest Children'.
21. See Chun and Friedland, 'Habits of Leaking', 5.
22. See Gabriel, 'Die offene Gesellschaft und ihre digitalen Feinde'.
23. Ren Pengfei, qtd. in Inkster, 'Huawei and the Great Decoupling', n.p.
24. Stäheli, 'Undoing Networks', 12.
25. Wittgenstein, *Zettel*, Number 256.
26. Schwitters, 'Stimulus to Make the Most Productive Use of Radio', 18–19; cf. Kittler, 'Kurt Schwitters', 119–43.

27. Decker, 'Adversarial Narratives', 9.
28. Decker, 'Adversarial Narratives', 19.
29. On this use of Steiner in the anti-vaccination movement, see Dyrendal, 'Hidden Knowledge, Hidden Powers', 204–6, 222–3.
30. Steiner, *Vom Wesen des Wirkenden Wortes*, 14.
31. See Rheinberger, 'Experiment, Forschung, Kunst'.
32. Wilson, 'Artists as Researchers in Wireless Communication', 80–101. For overviews of earlier critical media practice, see, for the German-speaking world, Weibel and Decker, *Vom Verschwinden der Ferne*.
33. Parikka, 'Critically Engineered Wireless Politics', 3.
34. Parikka, 'Critically Engineered Wireless Politics', 12–13, 15.
35. *Dreams Rewired* presents footage of wireless transmission from a wide range of sources, including feature films, for example, *Aelita* (Yakov Protazanov, 1924) and *Stürme über dem Montblanc* (Arnold Fanck, 1930); science films, for example, *50 Jahre Fernsprechen in Deutschland* (1933) and *Weltumspannende Funkwellen* (Bernhard Huth, 1934); avant-garde advertising shorts, for example, *Der Rundfunk auf dem Lande* (Julius Pinschewer, 1928) and *Europa Radio* (Hans Richter, 1931); and company films, for example, *Die Grossstadt Nauen im Weltverkehr* (1921), *Die Geburt des Reichsrundfunks in Berlin im Jahre 1923* (1923), and *Achtung! Achtung! Ein Film vom Deutschen Rundfunk* (1928–29).
36. See, among others, Webb, *The 5G Myth*.
37. On the change 'from a past-directed recording platform to a data-driven anticipation of the future', see Hansen, *Feed-Forward*, 4.

Bibliography

50 Jahre Telefunken: Festschrift zum 50-jährigen Jubiläum der Telefunken Gesellschaft für Drahtlose Telegraphie MbH. Special issue, *Telefunken-Zeitung* 100 (May 1953).

'About Ourselves'. *The Wireless Age* (October 1913): 4–5.

Adelson, Leslie A. 'Futurity Now: An Introduction'. *The Germanic Review: Literature, Culture, Theory* 88, no. 3 (2013): 213–18.

Adorno, Theodor W. *Current of Music: Elements of a Radio Theory*, edited by Robert Hullot-Kentor. Polity, 2009.

Adorno, Theodor W. 'On the Fetish-Character in Music and the Regression of Listening'. In *The Essential Frankfurt School Reader*, edited by Andrew Arato and Eike Gebhardt. Continuum, 1977.

Agamben, Giorgio. *What is an Apparatus? And Other Essays*. Translated by David Kishik and Stefan Pedatella. Stanford University Press, 2009.

Aitken, Hugh G. J. *Syntony and Spark: The Origins of Radio*. Princeton University Press, 1985.

Almog, Yael, Caroline Sauter, and Sigrid Weigel. 'Ursprung/Urszene'. *Trajekte* 30 (2015): 4–15.

Andriopoulos, Stefan. 'Psychic Television'. *Critical Inquiry* 31, no. 3 (2005): 618–37.

Anduaga, Aitor. *Wireless and Empire: Geopolitics, Radio Industry, and Ionosphere in the British Empire, 1918–1939*. Oxford University Press, 2009.

Anonymous. [*Algol*]. *Der Kinematograph* 713 (12 September 1920). https://www.filmportal.de/en/node/1057/material/604480 (accessed 11 August 2025).

'Antenne Mensch: Zehn merkwürdige und rätselhafte Geschehnisse, die Vernunft und Wissenschaft nicht erklären können'. *Uhu* 9, no. 13 (1932): 74–8.

Apollinaire, Guillaume. 'The False Amphion, or the Stories and Adventures of Baron D'Ormesan'. In *The Heresiarch and Co*. Translated by Rémy Inglis Hall. Doubleday, 1965.

Appadurai, Arjun, and Neta Alexander. *Failure*. Polity, 2019.

Arapostathis, Stathis, and Graeme Gooday. *Patently Contestable: Electrical Technologies and Inventor Identities on Trial in Britain*. MIT Press, 2013.

Arco, Georg von. 'Wünsche und Wege im Rundfunk'. *Funk* 36 (1925): 429–31.

Arnheim, Rudolf. *Radio*. Translated by Margaret Ludwig and Herbert Read. Faber & Faber, 1936.

Aschoff, Volker. *Geschichte der Nachrichtentechnik*. 2 vols. Springer, 1995.

Asendorf, Christoph. *Ströme und Strahlen: Das langsame Verschwinden der Materie um 1900*. Anabas, 1989.

Asserate, Asfa-Wossen. *Deutsche Tugenden: Von Anmut bis Weltschmerz*. Beck, 2013.

Augaitis, Daina, and Dan Lander, eds. *Radio Rethink: Art, Sound, and Transmission*. Walter Phillips Gallery, 1994.

Ayrton, William Edward. 'Sixty Years of Submarine Telegraphy'. *The Electrician* 38, no. 17 (19 February 1897): 545–8.

Balanis, Constantine A. *Antenna Theory: Analysis and Design*. 4th edn. Wiley, 2016.

Balanis, Constantine A. 'Antenna Theory: A Review', *Proceedings of the IEEE* 80, no. 1 (1992): 7–23.

Balbi, Gabriele. 'Wireless's "Critical Flaw": The Marconi Company, Corporation Mentalities, and the Broadcasting Option'. *Journalism & Mass Communication Quarterly* 94, no. 4 (2017): 1239–60.

Balbi, Gabriele, and Simone Natale. 'The Double Birth of Wireless: Italian Radio Amateurs and the Interpretative Flexibility of New Media'. *Journal of Radio & Audio Media* 22, no. 1 (2015): 26–41.

Barker, Timothy. *Against Transmission: Media Philosophy and the Engineering of Time*. Bloomsbury Academic, 2018.

Barton, Ruth. *Hedy Lamarr*. University Press of Kentucky, 2010.

Beals, Kurt. *Wireless Dada: Telegraphic Poetics in the Avant Garde*. Northwestern University Press, 2020.

Beer, Gillian. 'Wave Theory and the Rise of Literary Modernism.' In *Open Fields: Science in Cultural Encounter*. Oxford University Press, 1996.

Benjamin, Walter. *The Arcades Project*. Translated by Howard Eiland and Kevin McLaughlin. Belknap Press of Harvard University Press, 2002.

Benjamin, Walter. 'On the Minute'. In *The Work of Art in the Age of Its Technological Reproducibility and Other Writings on Media*, edited by Michael W. Jennings et al. Translated by Thomas Y. Levin. Harvard University Press, 2008.

Benjamin, Walter. *Radio Benjamin*. Edited by Lecia Rosenthal. Translated by Jonathan Lutes, Lisa Harries Schumann, and Diana K. Reese. Verso, 2014.

Benn, Gottfried. 'The Radar Thinker'. In *Ptolemy's Disciple*, edited and translated by Simona Draghici. Plutarch, 2005.

Bergmann, Kerstin, and Siegfried Zielinski. '"Sehende Maschinen": Einige Miniaturen zur Archäologie des Fernsehens'. In *Televisionen*, edited by Stefan Münker. Suhrkamp, 1999.

Bessire, Lucas, and Daniel Fisher. 'The Anthropology of Radio Fields'. *Annual Review of Anthropology* 42 (2013): 363–78.

Beverage, Harold H., and William C. Crowswell. 'Some Notes on the History of Antenna Developments: 1913 through 1937'. *IEEE Antennas and Propagation Society Newsletter* (1989): 13–18.

Bexte, Peter. 'Kabel im Denkraum'. In *Updates: Visuelle Medienkompetenz*, edited by Arthur Engelbert and Manja Herlt. Königshausen & Neumann, 2002.

Bibo, Günther, and Theo Mackeben. 'Aus der Funk-Revue "Ich schalte um . . ."'. *Scherl's Magazin* 8 (August 1930): 856–7.

Bloom, Emily C. *The Wireless Past: Anglo-Irish Writers and the BBC, 1931–1968*. Oxford University Press, 2016.

Bollé, Michael. *Die Grossfunkstation Nauen und ihre Bauten von Hermann Muthesius*. Willmuth Arenhövel, 1996.

Borck, Cornelius. *Brainwaves: A Cultural History of Electroencephalography*. Translated by Ann M. Hentschel. Routledge, 2018.

Böhm, Otto. 'Unsere Großstationstechnik'. In *25 Jahre Telefunken: Festschrift der Telefunken-Gesellschaft, 1903–1928*, edited by Fritz Schröter, Ernst Zechel, and Otto Nairz. Simon, 1928.

Born, Erik. 'German Media Studies: A Critical Update'. *New German Critique*, no. 150 (2023): 5–24.

Born, Erik. 'Going Wireless in the Belle Époque: A Photo Essay'. *Continent* 7, no. 1 (2018): 5–15.

Born, Erik. 'A Little History of the Wireless Icon'. Palais des Beaux Arts Wien, 2015. https://www.palaisdesbeauxarts.at/collection-view/eric-born/ (accessed 11 August 2025).

Born, Erik. 'Media Archaeology, Cultural Techniques, and the Middle Ages: An Approach to the Study of Media before the Media'. *Seminar* 52, no. 2 (2016): 107–33.

Born, Erik. 'The Promise of Television'. *The Promise of Cinema: German Film Theory, 1907–1933* (October 2017). https://www.thepromiseofcinema.com/index.php/the-promise-of-television/index.html (accessed 11 August 2025).

Born, Erik. 'Sparks to Signals: Literature, Science, and Wireless Technology, 1800–1930'. PhD dissertation, University of California, Berkeley, 2016.

Born, Erik. 'What was Time Axis Manipulation?' In *Friedrich Kittler: Neue Lektüren*, edited by Jens Schröter and Till A. Heilmann. Springer, 2022.

Born, Erik. 'Wi-Fi Signal Icon', The Academic Minute: A WAMC National Production, 2020. https://academicminute.org/erik-born-cornell-university-wifi-signal-icon/ (accessed 11 August 2025).

Born, Erik, and Richard Lambert. 'Newspapers and Radio'. In *The Red Vienna Sourcebook*, edited by Rob McFarland, Georg Spitaler, and Ingo Zechner. Camden House, 2020.

Bose, Jagadish Chandra. 'Runaway Cyclone'. Translated by Bodhisattva Chattopadhyay. In *Science Fiction in Colonial India, 1835–1905: Five Tales of Speculation, Resistance, and Rebellion*, edited by Mary Ellis Gibson. Anthem, 2019.

Braun, Karl Ferdinand. *Drahtlose Telegraphie durch Wasser und Luft: Nach Vorträgen gehalten im Winter 1900*. Veit, 1901.

Braun, Karl Ferdinand. 'Electrical Oscillations and Wireless Telegraphy'. In *Nobel Lectures, Physics 1901–1921*, Vol. 1. Elsevier, 1967.

Braun, Karl Ferdinand. Schaltungsweise des mit einer Luftleitung verbundenen Gebers für Funkentelegraphie. Kaiserliches Patentamt 111,578, filed 14 October 1898, and issued 7 July 1900.

Braun, Karl Ferdinand. Schaltung für elektrische Funkentelegraphie. Kaiserliches Patentamt 142,792, filed 1 January 1901, and issued 16 July 1903.

Braun, Karl Ferdinand. Telegraphirsystem [*sic*] ohne fortlaufende Leitung. Kaiserliches Patentamt 115,081, filed 13 July 1898, and issued 7 November 1900.

Brecht, Bertolt. 'Die neuen Zeitalter'. In *Werke*. Vol. 10. Edited by Werner Hecht et al. Suhrkamp, 1993.

Brecht, Bertolt. 'Radio – An Antediluvian Invention?' In *Bertolt Brecht on Film & Radio*. Edited and translated by Marc Silberman. Bloomsbury, 2000.

Brecht, Bertolt. 'The Radio as a Communications Apparatus'. In *Bertolt Brecht on Film & Radio*. Edited and translated by Marc Silberman. Bloomsbury, 2000.

Brecht, Bertolt. 'Texts on Radio Broadcasting (1926–1932)'. In *Bertolt Brecht on Film & Radio*. Edited and translated by Marc Silberman. Bloomsbury, 2000.

Bredow, Hans. 'Eure Aufgaben im Rundfunk'. In *Medientheorie 1888–1933: Texte und Kommentare*, edited by Albert Kümmel and Petra Löffler. Suhrkamp, 2002.

Bredow, Hans. *Im Banne der Ätherwellen*. 2 vols. Mundus, 1954–56.

Bredow, Hans. 'Rückblick und Ausblick'. *Funk* 27 (1924): 381–4.

Brehmer, Arthur, ed. *Die Welt in hundert Jahren*. Buntdruck, 1910.

Briggs, Asa. 'Prediction and Control: Historical Perspectives'. *The Sociological Review* 13 (1965): 39–52.

Briggs, Asa, and Daniel Snowman, eds. *Fins de Siècle: How Centuries End, 1400–2000*. Yale University Press, 1996.

Bromley, Anna. 'On the Air: Clandestine Radiophonic Protest Groups in Italy, Switzerland, and Germany, 1976–77'. In *A Companion to Sound in German-Speaking Cultures*, edited by Rolf J. Goebel. Boydell & Brewer, 2023.

Brunngraber, Rudolf. *Der tönende Erdkreis: Roman der Funktechnik*. Rowohlt, 1951.

Brunngraber, Rudolf. *Was zu kommen hat: Von Nietzsche zur Technokratie*. 'Neues Österreich' Zeitungs- und Verlagsgesellschaft, 1947.

Brunngraber, Rudolf. *Wie es kam: Psychologie des Dritten Reichs*. 'Neues Österreich' Zeitungs- und Verlagsgesellschaft, 1946.

Burstyn, W. 'Briefe an die Schriftleitung: "Drahtlose Energieübertragung."' *Jahrbuch der drahtlosen Telegraphie und Telephonie* 19 (1922): 445.

Busch, Christopher. 'Strategische Zitate: Zu Friedrich Kittlers Heidegger-Lektüre'. *Zeitschrift für Literaturwissenschaft und Linguistik*, no. 175 (2014): 161–9.

Buschauer, Regine. *Mobile Räume: Medien- und diskursgeschichtliche Studien zur Tele- Kommunikation*. Transcript, 2010.

Campbell, Bruce. *The Radio Hobby, Private Associations, and the Challenge of Modernity in Germany*. Palgrave Macmillan, 2019.

Campbell, Timothy C. 'Marinetti, *Marconista*: The Futurist Manifestos and the Emergence of Wireless Writing'. In *Broadcasting Modernism*, edited by Debra Rae Cohen, Michael Coyle, and Jane A. Lewty. University Press of Florida, 2009.

Campbell, Timothy C. *Wireless Writing in the Age of Marconi*. University of Minnesota Press, 2006.

Canales, Jimena. 'The Media of Relativity: Einstein and Telecommunications Technologies'. *Technology and Culture* 56, no. 3 (2015): 611–12.

Canales, Jimena. *The Physicist and the Philosopher*. Princeton University Press, 2015.

Carey, James W. 'Technology and Ideology: The Case of the Telegraph'. In *Communication as Culture: Essays on Media and Society*. Rev. edn. Routledge, 2009.

Case, Judd A. 'Logistical Media: Fragments from Radar's Prehistory'. *Canadian Journal of Communication* 38, no. 3 (2013): 379–95.

Castells, Manuel. *The Rise of the Network Society*. Blackwell, 1996.

Castells, Manuel, ed. *Mobile Communication and Society: A Global Perspective. A Project of the Annenberg Research Network on International Communication*. MIT Press, 2007.

Cerver, Francisco Asensio, et al., *Communication Towers / Torres de Comunicación*. Actor, 1992.

Christodoulou, Christos, Parveen F. Wahid, and Michael T. Chryssomallis. 'Antennas'. In *Wiley Encyclopedia of Electrical and Electronics Engineering*, edited by John G. Webster. Wiley, 2015.

Chun, Wendy Hui Kyong. *Control and Freedom: Power and Paranoia in the Age of Fiber Optics*. MIT Press, 2008.

Chun, Wendy Hui Kyong, and Sarah Friedland. 'Habits of Leaking: Of Sluts and Network Cards'. *Differences* 26, no. 2 (2015): 1–28.

Clarke, Arthur C. *1984, Spring: A Choice of Futures*. Ballantine Books, 1984.

Clarke, Bruce, and Linda Dalrymple Henderson, eds. *From Energy to Information: Representation in Science and Technology, Art, and Literature*. Stanford University Press, 2002.

Cohen, Debra Rae. 'Wireless Imaginations'. In *Sound and Literature*, edited by Anna Snaith. Cambridge University Press, 2020.

Cohen, Debra Rae, Michael Coyle, and Jane A. Lewty, eds. *Broadcasting Modernism*. University Press of Florida, 2009.

Collins, A. Frederick. 'The Effect of Electric Waves on the Human Brain'. *Electrical World and Engineer*, 22 February 1902: 335–8.

Collins, A. Frederick. 'Spark, Space, Wireless, Etheric, Hertzian Wave or Cableless Telegraphy – Which?' *Western Electrician* 29 (24 August 1901): 119.

Conley, Tim. '"Hive of Words": The Transnational Poetics of the Eiffel Tower'. *Modernism/Modernity* 17, no. 4 (2010): 765–7.

Connor, Steven. ‘Atmospherics’. In *Sonic Mediations: Body, Sound, Technology*, edited by Carolyn Birdsall and Anthony Enns. Cambridge Scholars Publishing, 2008.

Corner, John. ‘“Mediatization”: Media Theory’s Word of the Decade’. *Media Theory* 2, no. 2 (2018): 79–90.

Crookes, William. ‘Some Possibilities of Electricity’. *Fortnightly Review* 51 (February 1892): 13504–5.

Cupers, Kenny. ‘Bodenständigkeit: The Environmental Epistemology of Modernism’. *The Journal of Architecture* 21, no. 8 (2016): 1226–52.

Dammann, Clas. *Stimme aus dem Äther, Fenster zur Welt: Die Anfänge von Radio und Fernsehen in Deutschland*. Böhlau, 2005.

Daniels, Dieter. *Kunst als Sendung: Von der Telegrafie zum Internet*. Beck, 2002.

Decker, Ben. ‘Adversarial Narratives: A New Model for Disinformation’. Global Disinformation Index, August 2019. https://www.disinformationindex.org/wp-content/uploads/2019/08/GDI_Adverserial-Narratives_Report_V6.pdf (accessed 31 July 2020).

Decker, Edith, and Peter Weibel. *Vom Verschwinden der Ferne: Telekommunikation und Kunst*. Dumont, 1990.

Dessauer, Friedrich. ‘Die Drahtlose Telegraphie, ihre Grundlage und Bedeutung’. *Neues Hochland* (1905): 205–16.

De Vries, Imar O. ‘Mobile Telephony: Realising the Dream of Ideal Communication?’ In *Mobile World: Past, Present, Future*, edited by Lynne Hamill and Amparo Lasen. Amsterdam University Press, 2012.

De Vries, Imar O. *Tantalisingly Close: An Archaeology of Communication Desires in Discourses of Mobile Wireless Media*. Amsterdam University Press, 2012.

Die Deutsche Seewarte. ‘Funkentelegraphische Verbreitung von Wetterberichten und Sturmwarnungen über Nordsee und Ostsee’. *Annalen für Hydrographie* (1910): 650.

Dienel, Hans-Liudger. *Der Optimismus der Ingenieure: Triumph der Technik in der Krise der Moderne um 1900*. Steiner, 1998.

Dietz, G. C. ‘What Shall We Call It?’ *Electrical Review* 39, no. 22 (1901): 670.

Dominik, Hans. ‘Ätherwellen’. In *Technische Märchen*. Hugo Steinitz, 1903.

Dominik, Hans. ‘Ätherwellen: Technische Plauderei’. *Berliner Tageblatt*, 9 February 1902.

Dominik, Hans. ‘Ein Experiment’. In *Eine Erfindung und andere unbekannte Zukunftserzählungen von Hans Dominik aus den Jahren 1902–1919*. Edited by Detlef Münch. Synergen, 2007.

Dominik, Hans. ‘Stimmen im Äther’. In *Im Wunderland der Technik: Meisterstücke und neue Errungenschaften*. Bong, 1922.

Dominik, Hans. *Technische Märchen*. Steinitz, 1903.

Dominik, Hans. *Wissenschaftliche Plaudereien*. Steinitz, 1903.

Dotzler, Bernhard J., and Silke Roesler-Keilholz. *Mediengeschichte als historische Techno-logie*. Nomos, 2017.

Douglas, Susan. *Listening In: Radio and the American Imagination*. University of Minnesota Press, 2004.
Döblin, Alfred. *Berlin Alexanderplatz: The Story of Franz Biberkopf*. Translated by Eugene Jolas. Continuum, 2004.
Döblin, Alfred. 'Plus- und Minusempfindungen eines Hörers'. In *Kleine Schriften*. Vol. 3. Edited by Anthony W. Riley. Walter, 1999.
Dreams Rewired. Directed by Manu Luksch, Martin Reinhart, and Thomas Tode. Icarus Films, 2015.
Dunne, Anthony. *Hertzian Tales: Electronic Products, Aesthetic Experience, and Critical Design*. MIT Press, 2008.
Dussel, Konrad. *Deutsche Rundfunkgeschichte*. UVK, 2010.
Dyrendal, Asbjørn. 'Hidden Knowledge, Hidden Powers: Esotericism and Conspiracy Culture'. In *Contemporary Esotericism*, edited by Egil Asprem and Kennet Granholm. Acumen, 2012.
Eckler, G. 'Die Stadt Nauen'. *Telefunken-Zeitung* 17, Nauen-Nummer (August 1919): 94.
Eichhorn, Gustav. *Wetterfunk, Bildfunk, Television (Drahtloses Fernsehen)*. Teubner, 1926.
Ein Humanist. 'Fremdwörter in der Technik'. *Funk* 36 (1925): 452.
Einstein, Albert. 'Rede zur Eröffnung der Siebten Großen Deutschen Funkausstellung in Berlin, 1930'. *Rundfunk-Jahrbuch* (1931): 240.
Ehardt, Christine. 'Phones, Horns, and "Audio Hoods" as Media of Attraction'. In *Sounds of Modern History: Auditory Cultures in 19th- and 20th-Century Europe*, edited by Daniel Morat. Berghahn, 2014.
Ehardt, Christine. *Radiobilder: Eine Kulturgeschichte des Radios in Österreich*. Vienna University Press, 2020.
Eiffel, Gustave. 'The Eiffel Tower'. *Annual Report of the Board of Regents of the Smithsonian Institution* (1890): 729–35.
'Eine Sensation der Wissenschaft: Die drahtlose Telegraphie in der Rocktasche'. *Wiener Tagblatt*, 11 February 1919.
El Lissitzky. 'Wheel – Propeller – and What Will Follow'. Translated by Steven Lindberg and Margareta Ingrid Christian. In *G: An Avant-Garde Journal of Art, Architecture, Design, and Film, 1923–1926*, edited by Detlef Mertins and Michael W. Jennings. Getty, 2010.
Engell, Lorenz. 'Ontogenetic Machinery'. *Radical Philosophy* 169, no. 5 (2011): 10–12.
Engell, Lorenz. 'Sinn und Sinnlichkeit (Turm und Taste): Über Fern- und Nahmedien'. In *Ausfahrt nach Babylon: Essais und Vorträge zur Kritik der Medienkultur*. VDG Weimar, 2000.
Engell, Lorenz, and Bernhard Siegert, eds. 'Schwerpunkt Medienphilosophie'. Special issue of *Zeitschrift für Medien- und Kulturforschung*, vol. 2. Meiner, 2010.
Enns, Anthony, and Shelley Trower, eds. *Vibratory Modernism*. Palgrave Macmillan, 2013.
Enzensberger, Hans Magnus. 'Constituents of a Theory of the Media'. *New Left Review* 64 (1970): 13–36.

Enzensberger, Hans Magnus. 'Das digitale Evangelium'. *Der Spiegel* 2 (10 January 2000): 92–101.
Ernst, Christoph, Petra Gropp, and Karl Anton Sprengard, eds. *Perspektiven interdisziplinärer Medienphilosophie*. Transcript, 2003.
Ernst, Christoph, and Jens Schröter. *Media Futures: Theory and Aesthetics*. Palgrave Macmillan, 2021.
Ernst, Wolfgang. 'Das Radiotier'. In *Zoologicon: Ein kulturhistorisches Wörterbuch der Tiere*, edited by Christian Kassung, Jasmin Mersmann, and Olaf B. Rader. Fink, 2012.
Ernst, Wolfgang. *Digital Memory and the Archive*. Edited by Jussi Parikka. Translated by Dawn Michelle d'Atri. University of Minnesota Press, 2013.
Ernst, Wolfgang. 'Distory: One Hundred Years of Electron Tubes, Media-Archaeologically Interpreted, Vis-à-Vis One Hundred Years of Radio'. In Ernst, *Digital Memory and the Archive*.
Ernst, Wolfgang. 'Experimenting with Media Temporality: Pythagoras, Hertz, Turing'. In Ernst, *Digital Memory and the Archive*.
Ernst, Wolfgang. *Gleichursprünglichkeit: Zeitwesen und Zeitgegebenheit technischer Medien*. Kadmos, 2012.
Espenschied, Lloyd. 'Radio Broadcast Coverage of City Areas'. *Bell System Technical Journal* 6, no. 1 (1927): 117.
Evenius, G. W. 'Rundfunk für alle'. *Berliner Börsen-Courier* 459 (21 October 1923).
F. H. 'Die Radio-Polizist-Maschine'. In *Medientheorie 1888–1933: Texte und Kommentare*, edited by Albert Kümmel and Petra Löffler. Suhrkamp, 2002.
Fahie, John Joseph. *A History of Wireless Telegraphy, 1838–1899*. Dodd, 1899.
Farquharson, Alex, ed. 'Diedrich Diederichsen in Conversation with Isa Genzken'. In Alex Farquharson et al., *Isa Genzken*, 7–29. Phaidon, 2006.
Feldhaus, Franz Maria, and Walther H. Fitze. *Geschichtszahlen der drahtlosen Telegraphie und Telephonie*. Rothgiesser & Diesing, 1925.
Ferraris, Maurizio. *Where Are You? An Ontology of the Cell Phone*. Fordham University Press, 2014.
Fiala, A. K. 'Elektrophysiologische Zukunftsprobleme'. In *Medientheorie 1888–1933: Texte und Kommentare*, edited by Albert Kümmel and Petra Löffler. Suhrkamp, 2002.
Fickers, Andreas. 'Visibly Audible: The Radio Dial as Mediating Interface'. In *The Oxford Handbook of Sound Studies*, edited by Trevor Pinch and Karin Bijsterveld. Oxford University Press, 2012.
Filk, Christian. 'Medienphilosophie des Radios'. In *Systematische Medienphilosophie*, edited by Mike Sandbothe and Ludwig Nagl. Akademie, 2005.
Filk, Christian. 'Medientheorie des Radios – Überlegungen zu einer systematischen Rekonstruktion'. *Medienwissenschaft* 3 (2005): 280–94.
Fischer, Eugen Kurt. *Dokumente zur Geschichte des Deutschen Rundfunks und Fernsehens*. Musterschmidt, 1957.

Fischer, William B. *The Empire Strikes Out: Kurd Lasswitz, Hans Dominik, and the Development of German Science Fiction*. Bowling Green State University Popular Press, 1984.

Fisher, Daniel. 'Radio'. In *Keywords in Sound*, edited by David Novak and Matt Sakakeeny. Duke University Press, 2015.

Fisher, Margaret. 'Futurism and Radio'. In *Futurism and the Technological Imagination*, edited by Günter Berghaus. Brill, 2009.

Flanner, Karl. *Hallo! Hallo! Hier Radio Wien!* Verein Museum und Archiv im Viertel unter dem Wienerwald, 2007.

Flesch, Hans. '*Magic on the Air: Attempt at a Radio Grotesque*', edited by Lecia Rosenthal. Translated by Lisa Harries Schumann. *Cultural Critique* 91 (2015): 14–31.

Flesch, Hans. 'Rundfunk heute'. *Der Querschnitt* 10, no. 4 (1930): 246.

Flessner, Bernd. 'Cyberspace im Kaiserreich'. In *Bild, Rede, Schrift: Kleriker, Adel, Stadt und ausserchristliche Kulturen in der Vormoderne – Wissenschaften und Literatur seit der Renaissance*, edited by Jean Marie Valentin and Jean-François Candoni. Lang, 2007.

Flichy, Patrice. *Dynamics of Modern Communication: The Shaping and Impact of New Communication Technologies*. Translated by Liz Libbrecht. SAGE, 1995.

Flichy, Patrice. *The Internet Imaginaire*. MIT Press, 2008.

Forster, Kathrin. '"Die Welt in 100 Jahren" – wissenschaftliche Prognosen in der Literatur um 1900'. PhD thesis, University of Vienna, 2010.

Fox-Brewster, Tom. 'Londoners Give Up Eldest Children in Public Wi-Fi Security Horror Show'. *The Guardian*, 29 September 2014.

Föllmer, Golo, and Hans-Ulrich Wagner. 'Radio'. In *Handbuch Medienwissenschaft*, edited by Jens Schröter, Simon Ruschmeyer and Elisabeth Walke. Metzler, 2014.

Fraunholz, Uwe, Thomas Hänseroth, and Anke Woschech. 'Hochmoderne Visionen und Utopien: Zur Transzendenz technisierter Fortschrittserwartungen'. In *Technology Fiction: Technische Visionen und Utopien in der Hochmoderne*, edited by Uwe Fraunholz and Anke Woschech. Transcript, 2014.

Frerichs, O. 'Hier Mars, Hier Erde'. *Telefunken-Zeitung* 3, no. 17 (1919): 84–9.

Frey, Hans. *Fortschritt und Fiasko: Die ersten 100 Jahre der deutschen Science Fiction*. Memoranda, 2018

Friedel, Walter. *Elektrisches Fernsehen, Fernkinematographie und Bildfernübertragung*. Meusser, 1925.

Friedewald, Michael. 'The Beginnings of Radio Communication in Germany, 1897–1918'. *Journal of Radio Studies* 7, no. 2 (2000): 441–63.

Friedewald, Michael. *Die 'Tönenden Funken': Geschichte eines frühen drahtlosen Kommunikationssystems 1905–1914*. Verlag für Geschichte der Naturwissenschaften und Technik, 1999.

Friedewald, Michael. 'Telefunken vs. Marconi, or the Race for Wireless Telegraphy at Sea, 1896–1914'. Social Science Research Network (SSRN) Scholarly Paper, 2012.

Frohne, Ursula. 'Radio as a "Minor" Art Practice'. In *Radio as Art: Concepts, Spaces, Practices*, edited by Anne Thurmann-Jajes et al. Transcript, 2019.
Fuchs, Margot. 'Anfänge der drahtlosen Telegraphie im Deutschen Reich, 1897–1918'. In *Vom Flügeltelegraphen zum Internet: Geschichte der modernen Telekommunikation*, edited by Hans Jürgen Teuteberg and Cornelius Neutsch. Steiner, 1998.
Fuchs, Margot. *Georg von Arco (1869–1940) – Ingenieur, Pazifist, Technischer Direktor von Telefunken: Eine Erfinderbiographie*. Diepholz, 2004.
Fullerton, John, and Jan Olsson. *Allegories of Communication: Intermedial Concerns from Cinema to the Digital*. John Libbey, 2005.
'Funkentelegraphische Weltprojekte'. *Telefunken-Zeitung* 12 (June 1913): 134–40.
Führer, Karl Christian. 'A Medium of Modernity? Broadcasting in Weimar Germany, 1923–1932'. *The Journal of Modern History* 69, no. 4 (1997): 722–53.
Führer, Karl Christian. *Wirtschaftsgeschichte des Rundfunks in der Weimarer Republik*. Verlag für Berlin-Brandenburg, 1997.
Fürst, Artur. 'Das drahtlose Telephon in Nauen'. *Berliner Tageblatt*, 12 July 1913.
Fürst, Artur. *Die Wunder um uns: Neue Einblicke in Natur und Technik*. Vita, 1911.
Fürst, Artur. *Im Bannkreis von Nauen: Die Eroberung der Erde durch die drahtlose Telegraphie*. Deutsche Verlag-Anstalt, 1922.
Fürst, Artur. 'Rundfunks Zukunft'. *Funk: Die Wochenschrift des Funkwesens* 2 (1924): 1–3.
Gabriel, Sigmar. 'Die offene Gesellschaft und ihre digitalen Feinde'. *Frankfurter Allgemeine Zeitung*, 2 July 2013. www.faz.net/aktuell/feuilleton/debatten/gastbeitragvon-sigmar-gabriel-die-offene-gesellschaft-und-ihre-digitalen-feinde-12267309.html (accessed 11 August 2025).
Geisler, Michael, and Michelle Mattson, eds. 'Special Issue on German Media Studies'. *New German Critique* 78 (1999).
Geoghegan, Bernard Dionysius. 'After Kittler: On the Cultural Techniques of Recent German Media Theory'. *Theory, Culture & Society* 30, no. 6 (2013): 66–82.
Geoghegan, Bernard Dionysius. 'An Ecology of Operations: Vigilance, Radar, and the Birth of the Computer Screen'. *Representations* 147, no. 1 (2019): 59–95.
Geoghegan, Bernard Dionysius. 'Mind the Gap: Spiritualism and the Infrastructural Uncanny'. *Critical Inquiry* 42 (2016): 899–922.
Geoghegan, Bernard Dionysius. 'Untimely Mediations: On Two Recent Contributions to "German Media Theory"'. *Paragraph* 37, no. 3 (2014): 419–25.
Germanicus. '"Fremdwörter" in der Technik'. *Funk* 32 (1925): 393.
Gernsback, Hugo. *Radio for All*. Lippincott, 1922.

Gernsback, Hugo. 'Radio Police Automaton'. *Science and Invention* (May 1924): 14.

Gerstmann, H. 'Elektrische Wellen'. *Die Nation* 7, no. 19 (1890): 283–5.

Gesellschaft für drahtlose Telegraphie mBH. *Telefunken-Stationen und -Geräte: Zusammenstellung der modernsten tönenden und ungedämpften Radio-Stationen und Geräte*. Exhibition catalogue, 1919.

Gesellschaft für Drahtlose Telegraphie mbH. Empfangseinrichtung für drahtlose Telegraphie und Telephonie. Kaiserliches Patentamt 271,059, filed 3 September 1911, and issued 3 March 1914.

Gesellschaft für Drahtlose Telegraphie mbH. Einrichtung zur Erzeugung elektrischer Schwingungen. Kaiserliches Patentamt 291,604, filed 10 April 1913, and issued 23 June 1919.

Gethmann, Daniel. *Die Übertragung der Stimme: Vor- und Frühgeschichte des Sprechens im Radio*. Diaphanes, 2006.

Gethmann, Daniel. *Feld: Modelle, Begriffe und Architektonische Raumkonzepte*. Diaphanes, 2020.

Gethmann, Daniel. 'Innere Scheinbilder: Von der Ästhetik der Elektrizität zur Bild-Konzeption der Erkenntnis'. In *Evidenz – '. . . das sieht man doch!'*, edited by Rolf F. Nohr. LIT, 2004.

Gethmann, Daniel, and Florian Sprenger. *Die Enden des Kabels: Kleine Mediengeschichte der Übertragung*. Kadmos, 2014.

Gibson, Charles R. *Wireless Telegraphy and Telephony Without Wires*. Seeley, 1914.

Giedion, Sigfried. *Building in France, Building in Iron, Building in Ferroconcrete*. Translated by J. Duncan Berry. Getty Center, 1995.

Gilfillan, Daniel. *Pieces of Sound: German Experimental Radio*. University of Minnesota Press, 2009.

Gitelman, Lisa. *Always Already New: Media, History, and the Data of Culture*. MIT Press, 2008.

Glaubitz, Nicola, et al. *Eine Theorie der Medienumbrüche 1900/2000*. Universi, 2011.

Goedicke, Reinhold. The Suspending of the Lines of Electric Telegraphs in the Air by Means of Gas Balloons, Across Water and Land, or the Atmospheric Telegraph. British Patent No. 2907, issued 19 November 1857.

Gradenwitz, Alfred. 'Frogs' Muscles as Wireless Detectors'. *Electrical Review* 71 (1912): 830.

Gradenwitz, Alfred. 'A German Police Telephone: Scientific Aids for Patrol Service'. *Scientific American* 75 (25 January 1913): Supplement, 61.

Greenspan, Anna. *China and the Wireless Undertow: Media as Wave Philosophy*. Edinburgh University Press, 2023.

Grimm, Thomas. 'Das Taschentelephon. (Wiener Monolog aus dem Jahre 1925)'. *Fremden-Blatt* 85 (27 March 1910): 33–4.

Gropp, Petra. 'Literaturwissenschaft'. In Christoph Ernst, Petra Gropp, and Karl Anton Sprengard. *Perspektiven interdisziplinärer Medienphilosophie*. Transcript, 2003.

Groys, Boris. 'What Is German Media Philosophy? Subjectivity as Medium of the Media'. *Radical Philosophy* 169, no. 5 (2011): 7–9.

'Grösse der Türme der Telefunken-Gross-Station Nauen im Vergleich zu bekannten Bauwerken'. *Telefunken-Zeitung* 17, no. 3 (1919): 51.

Grundmann, Heidi. 'Die Geometrie des Schweigens'. Interferenzen IV. Vienna, Austria: Museum Moderner Kunst, Stiftung Ludwig, 1991. https://kunstradio.at/THEORIE/geo_d.html (accessed 11 August 2025).

Grunert, Carl. 'Auf den Schwingungen des Weltäthers'. In *Im Königreich Nirgendwo: Sämtliche Zukunfts-Novellen und Gedichte (1887–1914)*, edited by Dieter von Reeken. Reeken, 2019.

Grunert, Carl. 'Der Ätherseelenmensch'. In *Die Liebe der Zukunft vor 100 Jahren: 20 utopisch-erotische Novellen, 1871–1914*, edited by Detlef Münch. Synergen, 2006.

Grunert, Carl. 'Die Fernehe'. In *Die Liebe der Zukunft vor 100 Jahren: 20 utopisch-erotische Novellen, 1871–1914*, edited by Detlef Münch. Synergen, 2006.

Grunert, Carl. 'Enemies in Space'. Translated by Willy Ley. In *Invaders of Earth*, edited by Groff Conklin. Vanguard, 1952.

Grunert, Carl. *Feinde im Weltall? und andere Novellen*. Franck, 1907.

Gumbrecht, Hans Ulrich. *In 1926: Living at the Edge of Time*. Harvard University Press, 1997.

Gumbrecht, Hans Ulrich, and Karl Ludwig Pfeiffer, eds. *Materialities of Communication*. Stanford University Press, 1988.

Günther, Hanns. *Fünfsprachenwörterbuch für Radioamateure: Ein Hilfsbuch zum Studium der fremdsprachlichen Radioliteratur*. Franck, 1924.

Günther, Hanns, and Heinz Richter. *Lexikon der Funktechnik und ihrer Grenzgebiete*. Franck, 1938.

Hacking, Ian. 'Genres of Communication, Genres of Information'. In *Mobile Understanding: The Epistemology of Ubiquitous Communication*, edited by János Kristóf Nyíri. Passagen, 2006.

Hagen, Wolfgang. 'Alternating Currents and Ether: Two Paradigms of Radio Development – U.S. vs. Europe'. In *Re-Inventing Radio: Aspects of Radio as Art*, edited by Heidi Grundmann. Verein Werks and Boltzmann Institute, 2008.

Hagen, Wolfgang. *Das Radio: Zur Geschichte und Theorie des Hörfunks – Deutschland/USA*. Fink, 2005.

Hagen, Wolfgang. '"Die Stimme als Gast": Benjamins Sendungen'. In *Sendungen: Mediale Konturen zwischen Botschaft und Fernsicht*, edited by Wladimir Velminski. Transcript, 2009.

Hagen, Wolfgang. 'Medienäther – Äthermedien: Eine epistemologische Halluzination des Stillstands'. Lecture at University of Weimar, 29 April 2006.

Hagen, Wolfgang. *Radio Schreber*. VDG Weimar, 2001.

Hagen, Wolfgang. '"Stürmische Plötzlichkeiten": Zur medialen Genealogie des elektrischen Funkens'. In *Blitzlicht*, edited by Katja Müller-Helle and Florian Sprenger. Diaphanes, 2012.

Hansen, Mark B. N. *Feed-Forward: On the Future of Twenty-First-Century Media*. University of Chicago Press, 2015.

Hansen, Miriam. 'The Mass Production of the Senses: Classical Cinema as Vernacular Modernism'. *Modernism/Modernity* 6, no. 2 (1999): 59–77.

Haring, Kristen. *Ham Radio's Technical Culture*. MIT Press, 2007.

Harman, Graham. 'Speculation'. In *The Oxford Encyclopedia of Literary Theory*, edited by John Frow. Oxford University Press, 2022.

Harranth, Wolf. *Aus den Schätzen der QSL-Collection*. Theuberger, 1996.

Hartenau, W. [Walther Rathenau]. 'Die Resurrection Co'. Excerpt translated by Louis Kaplan. *New German Critique* 62 (1994): 63–9.

Harwood, John. 'Wires, Walls and Wireless: Notes Toward an Investigation of Radio Architecture'. *Media-N: Journal of the New Media Caucus* 10, no. 1 (2015).

Harwood, John. 'Wires, Wirelessness, and the Morality of Form in "The New Machine Art"'. In *Architecture / Machine*, edited by Moritz Gleich and Laurent Stalder. gta, 2017.

Haupt, Sabine. 'Strahlenmagie: Texte des späten 19. und frühen 20. Jahrhunderts zwischen Okkultismus und Sciencefiction – Ein diskursanalytisch-komparatistischer Überblick'. In *Gespenster: Erscheinungen – Medien – Theorien*, edited by Moritz Baßler, Bettina Gruber and Martina Wagner-Egelhaaf. Königshausen & Neumann, 2005.

Haus, Adrian. 'Radiogerede – Worte rund um "Funk"'. In *Radio Radio: Studien zum Verhältnis von Literatur und Rundfunk*, edited by Heiner Boehncke and Michael Crone. Lang, 2005.

Hausmann, Raoul. *Scharfrichter der bürgerlichen Seele: Raoul Hausmann in Berlin 1900–1933*, edited by Eva Züchner. Hatje, 1998.

Hay, Gerhard, ed. *Literatur und Rundfunk 1923–1933*. Gerstenberg, 1975.

Headrick, Daniel R. *The Tentacles of Progress: Technology Transfer in the Age of Imperialism, 1850–1940*. Oxford University Press, 1988.

Heidegger, Martin. 'The Age of the World Picture'. Translated by William Lovitt. In *Science and the Quest for Reality*, edited by Alfred I. Tauber. NYU Press, 1997.

Heidegger, Martin. *Being and Time: A Translation of* Sein und Zeit. Translated by Joan Stambaugh. State University of New York Press, 1996.

Henderson, Linda Dalrymple. 'Cubism, Futurism, and Ether Physics in the Early Twentieth Century'. *Science in Context* 17 (winter 2004): 451–2.

Herbert, A. P. 'Modern Nuisances'. *The Living Age*, 7 August 1920.

Herbst, Wilhelm, ed. *Erdantennen und Untergrundantennen: Eine Dokumentation*. Herbst, 2015.

Hertz, Heinrich. 'On the Action of a Rectilinear Electrical Oscillation on a Neighbouring Circuit'. In *Electric Waves*. Translated by D. E. Jones. MacMillan, 1900.

Hertz, Heinrich. 'On the Relations Between Light and Electricity'. In *Miscellaneous Papers*, edited by Philipp Lenard. Translated by D. E. Jones and G. A. Schott. Macmillan, 1896.

Hertz, Heinrich. *The Principles of Mechanics Presented in a New Form*, edited by Hermann von Helmholtz. Translated by D. E. Jones and J. T. Walley. Macmillan, 1899.

Hertz, Heinrich. 'Ueber einen Einfluss des ultravioletten Lichtes auf die electrische Entladung'. *Annalen der Physik* 267, no. 8 (1887): 983–1000.

Hesse, Hermann. *The Steppenwolf*. Translated by Kurt Beals. Norton, 2023.

Heye, Max. *Lustiges aus dem Reich des Unsichtbaren: Erlebnisse eines Rundfunksprechers*. Seidinger, 1924.

Hong, Sungook. 'Unfaithful Offspring? Technologies and Their Trajectories'. *Perspectives on Science* 6, no. 3 (1998): 259–87.

Hong, Sungook. *Wireless: From Marconi's Black-Box to the Audion*. MIT Press, 2001.

Horn, Eva. 'Editor's Introduction: "There Are No Media"'. *Grey Room* 29 (autumn 2007): 6–13.

Hörburger, Christian. *Das Hörspiel in der Weimarer Republik: Versuch einer Kritischen Analyse*. Akademischer Verlag, 1975.

Hughes, Jon. 'Facts and Fiction: Rudolf Brunngraber, Otto Neurath, and Viennese Neue Sachlichkeit'. In *Interwar Vienna: Culture Between Tradition and Modernity*, edited by Deborah Holmes and Lisa Silverman. Camden House, 2009.

Hughes, Michael, and Katherine Bosworth, eds. *Titanic Calling: Wireless Communications during the Great Disaster*. Bodleian Library, 2012.

Huhtamo, Erkki. 'Dismantling the Fairy Engine: Media Archaeology as Topos Study'. In *Media Archaeology: Approaches, Applications, and Implications*, edited by Erkki Huhtamo and Jussi Parikka. University of California Press, 2011.

Huhtamo, Erkki. 'Magic Spectacles and Portable Boxes: Notes toward a Media Archaeology of Mobile Media'. In *The Routledge Companion to Mobile Media Art*, edited by Larissa Hjorth, Adriana de Souza e Silva and Klare Lanson. Routledge, 2020.

Huhtamo, Erkki. 'Pockets of Plenty: An Archaeology of Mobile Media'. In *The Mobile Audience: Media Art and Mobile Technologies*, edited by Martin Rieser. Rodopi, 2011.

Huhtamo, Erkki, and Jussi Parikka. 'Introduction: An Archaeology of Media Archaeology'. In *Media Archaeology: Approaches, Applications, and Implications*, edited by Erkki Huhtamo and Jussi Parikka. University of California Press, 2011.

Huurdeman, Anton A. *The Worldwide History of Telecommunications*. Wiley, 2003.

'In Our Opinion'. *The Wireless Age* (November 1913): 89.

Ingersoll, Alex. 'Divining the Network with the Forked Twig'. *Amodern* 2, special issue: *Network Archaeology* (2013) edited by Nicole Starosielski, Braxton Soderman and Cris Cheek. https://amodern.net/article/divining-the-network-with-the-forked-twig/ (accessed 11 August 2025).

Inkster, Nigel. 'Huawei and the Great Decoupling'. *The Institute of Art and Ideas*, 5 August 2020.

Innerhofer, Roland. *Deutsche Science Fiction 1870–1914: Rekonstruktion und Analyse der Anfänge einer Gattung*. Böhlau, 1996.

Jaffe, Aaron. 'Inventing the Radio Cosmopolitan: Vernacular Modernism at a Standstill'. In *Broadcasting Modernism*, edited by Debra Rae Cohen, Michael Coyle and Jane A. Lewty. University Press of Florida, 2009.

Jäckel, Michael. 'Ein Ausblick in die Medienzukunft – Prognosen und Überraschungen'. In Michael Jäckel, Gerrit Fröhlich and Daniel Röder, *Medienwirkungen kompakt: Einführung in ein dynamisches Forschungsfeld*. Springer, 2012.

Jameson, Fredric. 'Progress versus Utopia; Or, Can We Imagine the Future?' *Science Fiction Studies* 9, no. 2 (1982): 147–58.

Jellinek, E. H. 'Stefan Jellinek (1871–1968): The Only Professor of Electro-Pathology'. *Journal of Medical Biography* 24, no. 3 (2016): 319–23.

Jellinek, Stefan. *Elektro-Pathologie: Die Erkrankungen durch Blizschlag und elektrischischen Starkstrom in klinischer und forensischer Darstellung*. Ferdinand Enke, 1903.

Jentsch, Otto. *Telegraphie und Telephonie ohne Draht*. Springer, 1904.

Jünger, Ernst. *An der Zeitmauer*. Klett-Cotta, 2002.

Jünger, Ernst. *The Forest Passage*. Translated by Thomas Friese. Telos, 2013.

Kaes, Anton. 'The Debate about Cinema: Charting a Controversy (1909–1929)'. *New German Critique*, no. 40 (1987): 7–33.

Kaes, Anton. *Weimarer Republik: Manifeste und Dokumente zur deutschen Literatur 1918–1933*. Metzler, 1995.

Kaes, Anton, Martin Jay, and Edward Dimendberg. 'New Mass Media: Radio and Gramophone'. In *The Weimar Republic Sourcebook*, edited by Anton Kaes, Martin Jay, and Edward Dimendberg. University of California Press, 1994.

Kahn, Douglas. *Earth Sound, Earth Signal: Energies and Earth Magnitude in the Arts*. University of California Press, 2013.

Kahn, Douglas. 'Introduction: Histories of Sound Twice Removed'. In *Wireless Imagination: Sound, Radio, and the Avant-Garde*, edited by Douglas Kahn and Gregory Whitehead. MIT Press, 1992.

Kahn, Douglas. 'Three Receivers'. In *Experimental Sound and Radio*, edited by Allen S. Weiss. MIT Press, 2001.

Kahn, Douglas, and Gregory Whitehead, eds. *Wireless Imagination: Sound, Radio, and the Avant-Garde*. MIT Press, 1992.

Kant, Immanuel. 'Meditationum quarundam de igne succincta delineatio' (Concise Outline of Some Reflections on Fire). Edited by Kurd Lasswitz. In *Kants gesammelte Schriften* [Akademie Ausgabe], ed. Preußische Akademie der Wissenschaften, vol. 1 (*Vorkritische Schriften I. 1747–1756*). Georg Reimer, 1902.

Kapeller, Ludwig. 'Ein Blick aus der Höhe: Empfindsame Betrachtung von der Plattform des Witzlebener Funkturms'. *Funk* 18 (1926): 137–8.

Kapeller, Ludwig. 'Unfall- und Wetterrundfunk im Hochgebirge'. *Funk* 1 (1924): 10–11.

Kaplan, Louis. 'Walter Rathenau's Media Technological Turn as Mediated through W. Hartenau's "Die Resurrection Co.": An Essay at Resurrection'. *New German Critique* 62 (1994): 39–62.

Katz, James Everett, and Mark A. Aakhus, eds. *Perpetual Contact: Mobile Communication, Private Talk, Public Performance*. Cambridge University Press, 2002.
Kern, Stephen. *The Culture of Time and Space: 1880–1918*. Harvard University Press, 2003.
Kern, Ulrich. 'Radio für alle: Funk und Rundfunk in den 20er Jahren'. In *Radio für Alle*, edited by Horst Steffens and Ulrich Kern. Landesmuseum für Technik und Arbeit, 1994.
Ketelsen, Uwe K. 'Der Rundfunk: Ein Medium des kollektivierenden Anrufs – Arnolt Bronnen / A. H. Schelle-Noetzels *Kampf im Aether oder die Unsichtbaren* (1935) als "rechter" Rundfunkroman'. *Zeitschrift für Genozidforschung* 12, no. 1 (2011): 36–64.
Kiesler, Friedrich J. 'The City in Space'. In *G: An Avant-Garde Journal of Art, Architecture, Design, and Film, 1923–1926*, edited by Detlef Mertins and Michael W. Jennings. Getty, 2010.
Kipling, Rudyard. 'Wireless'. *Scribner's Magazine* 32, no. 2 (1902): 129–43.
Kirschenbaum, Matthew G. *Mechanisms: New Media and the Forensic Imagination*. MIT Press, 2008.
Kittler, Friedrich. 'Anmerkungen zum Volksempfang'. In *Die Geometrie des Schweigens: Ein Symposium zur Theorie und Praxis einer Kunst im elektronischen Raum – Am Beispiel der Radiokunst*, edited by Heidi Grundmann and Robert Reitbauer. Ludwig, 1991. https://www.kunstradio.at/SILENCE/ (accessed 11 August 2025).
Kittler, Friedrich. 'Benn's Poetry – "A Hit in the Charts": Song Under Conditions of Media Technologies'. *SubStance* 19, no. 61 (1990): 5–20.
Kittler, Friedrich. *Discourse Networks, 1800/1900*. Translated by Michael Metteer and Chris Cullens. Stanford University Press, 1992.
Kittler, Friedrich. *Gramophone, Film, Typewriter*. Translated by Geoffrey Winthrop-Young and Michael Wutz. Stanford University Press, 1999.
Kittler, Friedrich. 'The History of Communication Media'. *CTHEORY*, 30 July 1996. https://journals.uvic.ca/index.php/ctheory/article/view/14325/ (accessed 11 August 2025).
Kittler, Friedrich. 'Im Telegrammstil'. In *Stil*, edited by Hans Ulrich Gumbrecht and K. Ludwig Pfeiffer. Suhrkamp, 1986.
Kittler, Friedrich. 'The Last Radio Broadcast'. In *Re-Inventing Radio: Aspects of Radio as Art*, edited by Heidi Grundmann et al. Revolver, 1994.
Kittler, Friedrich. 'Medien der Philosophie, Philosophie der Medien'. In *Handbuch der Medienphilosophie*, edited by Gerhard Schweppenhäuser. WBG, 2018.
Kittler, Friedrich. *Musik und Mathematik*. 2 vols. Fink, 2009.
Kittler, Friedrich. 'Observations on Public Reception'. Translated by Anna Lausch. In *Radio Rethink: Art, Sound and Transmission*, edited by Daina Augaitis and Dan Lander. Walter Phillips Gallery, 1994.
Kittler, Friedrich. *Optical Media: Berlin Lectures 1999*. Translated by Anthony Enns. Polity, 2009.
Kittler, Friedrich. 'Playback: A World War History of Radio Drama'. In *Operation Valhalla: Writings on War, Weapons, and Media*, edited by

Geoffrey Winthrop-Young, Michael Wutz and Ilinca Iurascu. Duke University Press, 2021.
Kittler, Friedrich. 'Rock Music: A Misuse of Military Equipment'. In Kittler, *The Truth of the Technological World.*
Kittler, Friedrich. 'Signal-to-Noise Ratio'. In Kittler, *The Truth of the Technological World.*
Kittler, Friedrich. 'Towards an Ontology of Media'. *Theory, Culture & Society* 26, no. 2–3 (2009): 23–31.
Kittler, Friedrich. *The Truth of the Technological World: Essays on the Genealogy of Presence*, edited by Hans Ulrich Gumbrecht. Translated by Erik Butler. Stanford University Press, 2013.
Kittler, Friedrich. 'Universities: Wet, Hard, Soft, and Harder'. *Critical Inquiry* 31 (2004): 244–55.
Kittler, Friedrich. 'Von der optischen Telegrafie zur Photonentechnik'. In *The Moderns: Wie sich das 20. Jahrhundert in Kunst und Wissenschaft erfunden hat*, edited by Cathrin Pichler and Susanne Neuburger. Ambra, 2012.
Kittler, Wolf. 'Abstimmung: Kiplings Erzählung Wireless als Lektüre von Marconis Patent 7777'. In *Die Werkstatt des Dichters: Imaginationsräume literarischer Produktion*, edited by Klaus Kastberger and Stefan Maurer. De Gruyter, 2017.
Kittler, Wolf. 'Grabenkrieg – Nervenkrieg – Medienkrieg: Franz Kafka und der 1. Weltkrieg'. In *Armaturen der Sinne: Literarische und technische Medien 1870 bis 1920*, edited by Jochen Hörisch and Michael Wetzel. Fink, 1990.
Kittler, Wolf. 'Kurt Schwitters'. In *Praktizierte Intermedialität: Deutsch-französische Porträts von Schiller bis Goscinny/Uderzo*, edited by Fernand Hörner, Harald Neumeyer and Bernd Stiegler. Transcript, 2010.
Klein-Arendt, Reinhard. *Kamina ruft Nauen! Die Funkstellen in den deutschen Kolonien 1904–1918*. Herbst, 1996.
Kluitenberg, Eric. 'Connection Machines'. In *Book of Imaginary Media: Excavating the Dream of the Ultimate Communication Medium*, edited by Eric Kluitenberg. Debalie, 2006.
Kluitenberg, Eric. 'On the Archaeology of Imaginary Media'. In *Media Archaeology: Approaches, Applications, and Implications*, edited by Erkki Huhtamo and Jussi Parikka. University of California Press, 2011.
Kluitenberg, Eric, ed. *Book of Imaginary Media: Excavating the Dream of the Ultimate Communication Medium*. Debalie, 2006.
Knorr – Cetina, Karin D. *The Manufacture of Knowledge: An Essay on the Constructivist and Contextual Nature of Science*. Pergamon, 1991.
Knörr, Kai. *Funken: Eine Medienkulturgeschichte*. Kadmos, 2023.
Knörr, Kai. 'Funken'. In *Historisches Worterbuch des Mediengebrauchs*, edited by Matthias Bickenbach, Heiko Christians and Nikolaus Wegmann. Böhlau, 2014.
Koch, Hans Jürgen, and Hermann Glaser. *Ganz Ohr: Eine Kulturgeschichte des Radios in Deutschland*. Böhlau, 2005.

Koch, Werner. *Erfindergeist auf Abwegen: Über Patentschriften merkwürdigen Inhalts*. Econ, 1964.

Kolb, Richard. *Das Horoskop des Hörspiels*. Max Hesses, 1932.

Korn, Arthur. *Elektrisches Fernsehen*. Salle, 1930.

Korn, Arthur. 'Why We Still Do Not Have Television: Possibilities of Electric Television'. Translated by Alex H. Bush. In *The Promise of Cinema: German Film Theory, 1907–1933*, edited by Anton Kaes, Nicholas Baer, and Michael Cowan. University of California Press, 2016.

König, Wolfgang. 'Telegraphie, Telefonie, Funk: Kommunikation und Technik im 19. Jahrhundert'. In *Die Medien und ihre Technik: Theorien, Modelle, Geschichte*, edited by Harro Segeberg. Schüren, 2004.

Kracauer, Siegfried. 'Boredom'. In *The Mass Ornament: Weimar Essays*. Translated by Thomas Y. Levin. Harvard University Press, 1995.

Kracauer, Siegfried. *From Caligari to Hitler: A Psychological History of the German Film*. Princeton University Press, 2004.

Kracauer, Siegfried. 'Radio Station'. Translated by David Britt. In *Metropolis Berlin: 1880–1940*, edited by Iain Boyd Whyte and David Frisby. University of California Press, 2012.

Krajewski, Markus. *World Projects: Global Information before World War I*. Translated by Charles Marcrum II. University of Minnesota Press, 2015.

Kraus, John D. 'Antennas Since Hertz and Marconi'. *IEEE Transactions on Antennas and Propagation* 33, no. 2 (1985): 132.

Krämer, Sybille. *Medium, Messenger, Transmission: An Approach to Media Philosophy*. Translated by Anthony Enns. Amsterdam University Press, 2015.

Kuhlman, Martha. 'Prague Meets Paris: The Reception and Representation of the "Eiffelka"'. *Modernism/Modernity* 14, no. 2 (2007): 291–308.

Kümmel, Albert. 'Innere Stimmen – Die deutsche Radiodebatte'. In *Einführung in die Geschichte der Medien*, edited by Albert Kümmel, Leander Scholz and Eckhard Schumacher. Fink, 2004.

Kümmel, Albert, and Petra Löffler, eds. *Medientheorie 1888–1933: Texte und Kommentare*. Suhrkamp, 2002.

Kümmel-Schnur, Albert. 'Patente als Agenten von Mediengeschichte'. In *Bildtelegraphie: Eine Mediengeschichte in Patenten (1840–1930)*, edited by Albert Kümmel-Schnur and Christian Kassung. Transcript, 2014.

Kümmel-Schnur, Albert, and Jens Schröter. *Äther: Ein Medium der Moderne*. Transcript, 2007.

Lacey, Kate. *Feminine Frequencies: Gender, German Radio, and the Public Sphere, 1923–1945*. University of Michigan Press, 2000.

Lacey, Kate. 'Up in the Air? The Matter of Radio Studies'. *Radio Journal: International Studies in Broadcast & Audio Media* 16, no. 2 (2018): 109–26.

Lambrechts, Wynand, and Saurabh Sinha. *Last Mile Internet Access for Emerging Economies*. Springer, 2019.

Lampl. 'Der radiotelegrafische Empfangsapparat in der Westentasche'. *Deutsche Uhrmacher-Zeitung* 12 (1914): 185

Larkin, Brian. 'The Politics and Poetics of Infrastructure'. *Annual Review of Anthropology* 42, no. 1 (2013): 327–43.

Lasswitz, Kurd. *Auf zwei Planeten: Roman in zwei Büchern*. Elischer, 1897.

Lasswitz, Kurd. 'Aus dem Tagebuch einer Ameise'. In *Seifenblasen: Moderne Märchen*. Universitäts- und Landesbibliothek, 1890.

Lasswitz, Kurd. *Gedichte und Erzählungen: Gedichte, Scherzlieder, Humoresken und sonstige Erzählungen aus dem Jahren 1869–1910*, edited by Dieter von Reeken. 2nd rev. edn. Reeken, 2013.

Lasswitz, Kurd. *Geschichte der Atomistik vom Mittelalter bis Newton*. 2 vols. Voss, 1890.

Lasswitz, Kurd. 'Marsphantasien'. In *Kollektion Lasswitz: Sachbücher, Vorträge, Aufsätze*, edited by Dieter von Reeken. Reeken, 2009.

Lasswitz, Kurd. 'Nach Chicago (Eine Preiskonkurrenz)'. In *Gedichte und Erzählungen*, edited by Dieter von Reeken. 2nd rev. edn. Reeken, 2013.

[Lasswitz, Kurd.] 'Nach Chicago (Eine Preiskonkurrenz)'. *Unsere Zeit: Scherers Familienblatt (Salon-Ausgabe)*, 8, no. 1 (1892/93): 101–6.

Lasswitz, Kurd. 'Newton und die Fernwirkung'. *Die Nation* 33 (1890): 490–2.

Lasswitz, Kurd. 'Telelyt'. In *Telelyt – sämtliche Science Fiction Erzählungen 1871–1910*, edited by Detlef Münch. Synergen, 2018.

[Lasswitz, Kurd.] 'Was soll sie thun?' *Das Echo* 11, no. 523 (8 September 1892): 1139–42.

Latour, Bruno. *Pandora's Hope: Essays on the Reality of Science Studies*. Harvard University Press, 1999.

Latour, Bruno. 'Trains of Thought: Piaget, Formalism and the Fifth Dimension'. *Common Knowledge* 6, no. 3 (1997): 170–91.

Latour, Bruno. *We Have Never Been Modern*. Translated by Catherine Porter. Harvard University Press, 1993.

Lee, Thomas H. *The Design of CMOS Radio-Frequency Integrated Circuits*. Cambridge University Press, 2003.

Lemstra, Wolter, Vic Hayes, and John Groenewegen, eds. *The Innovation Journey of Wi-Fi: The Road to Global Success*. Cambridge University Press, 2010.

Lerg, Winfried B. *Die Entstehung des Rundfunks in Deutschland: Herkunft und Entwicklung eines publizistischen Mittels*. J. Knecht, 1965.

Lertes, Peter. *Fernbildtechnik und elektrisches Fernsehen*. Bechhold, 1926.

Lethen, Helmut. 'Amsterdam 1964: The Magic Transgression of the Single "Twist and Shout"'. Translated by Erik Born. In *The Legacy of Transgressive Objects*, edited by Katja Müller-Helle. Walther König, 2019.

Levy, Karen, and Solon Barocas. 'Refractive Surveillance: Monitoring Customers to Manage Workers'. *International Journal of Communication* 12 (2018): 1166–88.

Lewty, Jane. 'Syntonic Desire: Unheard Tales of Transmission in Radio's Wake'. In *Mind Factory*, edited by Louis Armand. Litteraria Pragensia, 2005.

Lieben, Robert von. Kathodenstrahlenrelais. Kaiserliches Patentamt 179,807, filed 4 March 1906, and issued 19 November 1906.

Lieberman, Jennifer L., and Ronald R. Kline. 'Dream of an Unfettered Electrical Future: Nikola Tesla, the Electrical Utopian Novel, and an Alternative American Sociotechnical Imaginary'. *Configurations* 25, no. 1 (2017): 1–27.

Lodemann, Karlsruhe. 'Drahtlose Telephonie'. *Technik und Naturwissenschaft: Beiblatt zum Kosmos, Handweiser für Naturfreunde* 11 (1908): 345–7.

Loos, Victor. 'Der drahtlose Impresario'. *Die Fackel* 3, no. 99 (8 April 1902): 11–14.

Loos, Victor. 'Der technische Impresario'. *Die Fackel* 3, no. 93 (4 February 1902): 12–14.

Lopez, John S. 'The Wireless Future: The Bewildering Discoveries of Twentieth Century Scientists and Inventors Eclipsing the Wildest Dreams of the Romanticist of a Score of Years Ago'. *Van Norden: The World Mirror* 5, no. 4 (1909): 424–30.

Lovink, Geert. 'Discipline Design: The Rise of Media Philosophy – An Email Exchange with Frank Hartmann'. https://networkcultures.org/geertlovink-archive/interviews/interview-with-frank-hartmann-2/ (accessed 11 August 2025).

Lovink, Geert. 'Essay on Speculative Media Theory (1996)'. In *Dark Fiber: Tracking Critical Internet Culture*. MIT Press, 2002.

Lovink, Geert. 'From Speculative Media to Net Criticism'. Lecture at the NTT InterCommunication Center (ICC), Tokyo, Japan, 12 December 1996. https://www.nettime.org/Lists-Archives/nettime-l-9701/msg00032.html (accessed 11 August 2025).

Lovink, Geert, and Ned Rossiter, *Organization After Social Media*. Minor Compositions, 2018.

Lux, Heinrich. 'Rundschau – Kultur Technik: Telephonie ohne Draht'. *Sozialistische Monatshefte* 3 (6 February 1908): 197–8.

Lyall, Francis. *International Communications: The International Telecommunication Union and the Universal Postal Union*. Ashgate, 2011.

Ma, Shaoling. *The Stone and the Wireless: Mediating China, 1896–1906*. Duke University Press, 2021.

Mackenzie, Adrian. *Wirelessness: Radical Empiricism in Network Cultures*. MIT Press, 2010.

Malanowski, Gregory. *Race for Wireless: How Radio Was Invented (or Discovered)*. AuthorHouse, 2011.

Mantei, Sebastian. *Von der Sandbüchse zum Post-und Telegraphenland: Der Aufbau des Kommunikationsnetzwerks in Deutsch-Südwestafrika (1884–1915)*. Namibia Wissenschaftliche Gesellschaft, 2007.

Marconi, Guglielmo. Improvements in Transmitting Electrical Impulses and Signals, and in Apparatus Therefor. British Patent No. 12039, filed 2 June 1896, and issued 2 July 1897.

Marconi, Guglielmo. 'Wireless Telegraphic Communication'. In *Nobel Lectures in Physics*. Vol. 1. Elsevier, 1967.

Marinetti, F. T. 'Destruction of Syntax – Wireless Imagination – Words-in-Freedom'. In *Futurist Manifestos*, translated by Robert Brain, R. W. Flint et al. Viking, 1970.

Marvin, Carolyn. *When Old Technologies Were New: Thinking About Electric Communication in the Late Nineteenth Century*. Oxford University Press, 1988.

Mattern, Friedemann. *Die Informatisierung des Alltags: Leben in smarten Umgebungen*. Springer, 2007.

Maxwell, James Clerk. 'A Dynamic Theory of the Electric Field'. *Philosophical Transactions of the Royal Society of London* 155 (1865): 459–512.

McIntosh, D., and J. Graham-Willmore. 'The Effect of Electric Waves on the Human Brain'. *Electrical World and Engineer*, 31 May 1902: 952–4.

McLuhan, Marshall. 'Radio: The Tribal Drum'. *AV Communication Review* 12, no. 2 (1964): 133–45.

McLuhan, Marshall. 'The Relation of Environment to Anti-Environment'. In *Media Research: Technology, Art and Communication*, edited by Michel Moos. Routledge, 2014.

McLuhan, Marshall. *Take Today: The Executive as Dropout*. Harcourt, 1972.

McLuhan, Marshall. *Understanding Media: The Extensions of Man*. MIT Press, 1994.

McLuhan, Marshall, and Quentin Fiore. *The Medium is the Massage: An Inventory of Effects*. Touchstone, 1989.

Meier, Helmut. 'Drahtlose Telegraphie im Schützengraben? Die "Tafunk" und ihre Wissenschaftler im Ersten Weltkrieg'. In *Geschichte der elektrischen Kommunikation bis zum Smartphone*, edited by Anja Titze. Klartext, 2019.

Meier zu Eissen, Hans. *Telegraphie des Deutschen Reichs 1848–1945: Telegraphische Dokumente und Korrespondenzen von Königen, Kaisern und Diktatoren*. Meier zu Eissen, 2013.

Menke, Richard. *Telegraphic Realism: Victorian Fiction and Other Information Systems*. Stanford University Press, 2008.

Merleau-Ponty, Maurice. *Phenomenology of Perception*. Translated by Colin Smith. Routledge and Kegan Paul, 1978.

Mertins, Detlef, and Michael W. Jennings, eds. *G: An Avant-Garde Journal of Art, Architecture, Design, and Film, 1923–1926*. Getty, 2010.

Meyers Grosses Konversations-Lexikon. 1905. https://www.zeno.org/Meyers-1905/A/Wasserleitungen.

Meyrowitz, Joshua. 'Global Nomads in the Digital Veldt'. In *Mobile Democracy: Essays on Society, Self and Politics*, edited by Kristóf Nyíri. Passagen, 2003.

Meyrowitz, Joshua. 'The Rise of Glocality: New Senses of Place and Identity in the Global Village'. In *A Sense of Place: The Global and the Local in Mobile Communication*, edited by János Kristóf Nyíri. Passagen, 2005.

Miloradovic-Weber, Christa. *Der Erfinderroman, 1850–1950: Zur literarischen Verarbeitung der technischen Zivilisation – Konstituierung eines literarischen Genres*. Lang, 1989.
Milutis, Joe. *Ether: The Nothing That Connects Everything*. University of Minnesota Press, 2006.
Mitcham, Carl. *Thinking through Technology: The Path between Engineering and Philosophy*. University of Chicago Press, 1994.
Mitchell, William J. *Me++: The Cyborg Self and the Networked City*. MIT Press, 2003.
Moholy-Nagy, László. *Von Material zu Architektur*. Kupferberg, 1968.
Moszkowski, Alexander. *Die Welt von der Kehrseite: Eine Philosophie der reinen Galle*. Fontane, 1922.
Mowitt, John. *Radio: Essays in Bad Reception*. University of California Press, 2011.
Mulligan, Joseph F. 'The Aether and Heinrich Hertz's *The Principles of Mechanics Presented in a New Form*'. *Physics in Perspective* 3 (2001): 136–64.
Musil, Robert. *Diaries 1899–1941*. Translated by Philip Payne. Basic Books, 1999.
Müller, Simone M., and Heidi J. S. Tworek. 'Imagined Use as a Category of Analysis: New Approaches to the History of Technology'. *History and Technology* 32, no. 2 (2016): 105–19.
Münch, Detlef, ed. *Die Liebe der Zukunft vor 100 Jahren: 20 utopisch-erotische Novellen, 1871–1914*. Synergen, 2006.
Münker, Stefan, Alexander Roesler, and Mike Sandbothe, eds. *Medienphilosophie: Beiträge zur Klärung eines Begriffs*. Fischer, 2003.
Mynona [Salomo Friedlaender]. 'Der antibabylonische Turm: Utopie'. In *Prosa*. Edited by Hartmut Geerken, vol. 2. Text + Kritik, 1980.
Mynona [Salomo Friedlaender]. 'Idee vom Ferntaster'. *Der Sturm* 4, no. 170–71 (July 1913): 66–7.
Mynona [Salomo Friedlaender]. 'Goethe spricht in den Phonographen: Eine Liebesgeschichte'. In *Gesammelte Schriften*, edited by Hartmut Geerken and Detlef Thiel, vol. 7. Waitawhile, 2008.
Nairz, Otto. 'Die Riesenstation der Gesellschaft für drahtlose Telegraphie in Nauen'. *Prometheus* 18, no. 891 (14 November 1906): 97–101.
Natale, Simone. 'A Cosmology of Invisible Fluids: Wireless, X-Rays, and Psychical Research Around 1900'. *Canadian Journal of Communication* 36, no. 2 (2011): 263–75.
Natale, Simone, and Gabriele Balbi. 'Media and the Imaginary in History: The Role of the Fantastic in Different Stages of Media Change'. *Media History* 20, no. 2 (2014): 203–18.
Natonek, Hans. 'Radio'. *Medienwissenschaft: Rezensionen* 1 (1984): 99–100.
Navarro, Jaume, ed. *Ether and Modernity: The Recalcitrance of an Epistemic Object in the Early Twentieth Century*. Oxford University Press, 2018.
Nesper, Eugen. *Die drahtlose Telegraphie und ihr Einfluss auf den Wirtschaftsverkehr unter besonderer Berücksichtigung des Systems 'Telefunken'*. Springer, 1905.

'Neueste Nachrichten aus beiden Hemisphären'. *Kladderadatsch*, 16 June 1879: 110.

Neumann, Dietrich. '*Algol*: Eine Deutsche Parabel'. In *Walter Reimann: Maler und Filmarchitekt*. Deutsches Filmmuseum, 1997.

Nianci, Xu. 'New Tales of Mr. Braggadocio'. Translated by Nathaniel Isaacson. *Renditions* 77–8 (2012): 15–38.

Niebisch, Arndt. 'Close Writing: Friedrich Kittler und die Digital Humanities'. *Metaphora*, no. 1 (2015): IV-1–IV-15.

Niebisch, Arndt. 'Ether Machines: Raoul Hausmann's Optophonetic Media'. In *Vibratory Modernism*, edited by Anthony Enns and Shelley Trower. Palgrave Macmillan, 2013.

Nietzsche, Friedrich. *Ecce Homo*. In *The Anti-Christ, Ecce Homo, Twilight of the Idols, and Other Writings*. Translated by Judith Norman. Cambridge University Press, 2005.

Nietzsche, Friedrich. *The Gay Science, With a Prelude in German Rhymes and an Appendix of Songs*, edited by Bernard Williams. Translated by Josefine Nauckhoff. Cambridge University Press, 2001.

Nipkow, Paul. Elektrisches Teleskop. Kaiserliches Patentamt 30,105, filed 6 January 1884, and issued 15 January 1885.

Nyíri, János Kristóf, ed. *Mobile Understanding: The Epistemology of Ubiquitous Communication*. Passagen, 2006.

Ofak, Ana. '"Where voices and currents flow . . ." Nikola Tesla und Telekommunikation'. In *Sendungen – Mediale Konturen zwischen Botschaft und Fernsicht*, edited by Wladimir Velminski. De Gruyter, 2009.

Ofak, Ana, and Philipp von Hilgers, eds. *Rekursionen: Von Faltungen des Wissens*. Fink, 2010.

Ofak, Ana, and Friedrich A. Kittler, eds. *Medien vor den Medien*. Fink, 2007.

Ohlsberg, Otto. *Handbuch für Funkentelegraphisten: Lehr- und Übungsbuch auch für den Selbstunterricht*. 2nd edn. Decker, 1918.

Ostwald, Wilhelm. *Der energetische Imperativ*. Akademische Verlagsgesellschaft, 1912.

Ottmann, Solveig. *Im Anfang war das Experiment: Das Weimarer Radio bei Hans Flesch und Ernst Schoen*. Kadmos, 2013.

Palitzsch, Otto Alfred. 'Broadcast Literature (1927)'. In *The Weimar Republic Sourcebook*, edited by Anton Kaes, Martin Jay, and Edward Dimendberg. University of California Press, 1994.

Parikka, Jussi. 'Critically Engineered Wireless Politics'. *Culture Machine* 14 (2013): 1–26.

Parikka, Jussi. 'Friedrich Kittler – a Media Anthropology Without the Man?' *European Association of Social Anthropologists* e-seminar (2012). https://easaonline.org/event/39-friedrich-kittler-a-media-anthropology-without-the-man/ (accessed 31 May 2024).

Parikka, Jussi. 'To Media Study: Media Studies and Beyond'. *MAST: The Journal of Media Art Study and Theory* 1, no. 1 (2020): 59–63.

Parikka, Jussi. *What is Media Archaeology*? Polity, 2013.

Parikka, Jussi, and Erkki Huhtamo. *Media Archaeology: Approaches, Applications, and Implications*. University of California Press, 2011.

Parks, Lisa. 'Around the Antenna Tree: The Politics of Infrastructural Visibility'. *Flow* 9, no. 8 (2009).

Parks, Lisa. 'Earth Observation and Signal Territories: Studying US Broadcast Infrastructure through Historical Network Maps, Google Earth, and Fieldwork'. *Canadian Journal of Communication* 38, no. 3 (2013): 1–24.

Pater, Monika, and Uta C. Schmidt. '"Vom Kellerloch bis hoch zur Mansard ist alles drin vernarrt" – zur Veralltäglichung des Radios im Deutschland der 1930er Jahre'. In *MedienAlltag: Domestizierungsprozesse Alter und Neuer Medien*, edited by Jutta Röser. Verlag für Sozialwissenschaften, 2007.

Patnode, Randall. 'Path Not Taken: Wired Wireless and Broadcasting in the 1920s'. *Journal of Broadcasting & Electronic Media* 49, no. 4 (2005): 383–401.

Pelosi, Giuseppe, Stefano Selleri, and Barbara Valotti. 'Antennae'. *IEEE Antennas and Propagation Magazine* 42, no. 1 (2000): 61–3.

Peters, Carl. 'Die Kolonien in 100 Jahren'. In *Die Welt in hundert Jahren*, edited by Arthur Brehmer. Buntdruck, 1910.

Peters, John Durham. 'Broadcasting and Schizophrenia'. *Media, Culture and Society* 32 (2010): 123–40.

Peters, John Durham. 'Calendar, Clock, Tower'. In *Deus in Machina: Religion and Technology in Historical Perspective*, edited by Jeremy Stolow. Fordham University Press, 2013.

Peters, John Durham. *The Marvelous Clouds: Toward a Philosophy of Elemental Media*. University of Chicago Press, 2015.

Peters, John Durham. *Speaking Into the Air: A History of the Idea of Communication*. University of Chicago Press, 1999.

Peters, John Durham. '"You Mean My Whole Fallacy Is Wrong": On Technological Determinism'. *Representations*, special issue: *Fallacies* (autumn 2017): 10–26.

Peters, John Durham, Florian Sprenger, and Christina Vagt. *Action at a Distance*. University of Minnesota Press, 2020.

Phillips, Vivian J. *Early Radio Wave Detectors*. Peregrinus, 1980.

Pias, Claus. 'Friedrich Kittler und der "Mißbrauch von Heeresgerät": Zur Situation Eines Denkbildes 1964 –1984 – 2014'. *Merkur*, no. 791 (2015): 31–44.

Pias, Claus. 'What's German about German Media Theory'. In *Media Transatlantic: Developments in Media and Communication Studies between North American and German-Speaking Europe*, edited by Norm Friesen. Springer, 2016.

Plessner, Helmuth. 'Die Utopie der Maschinen'. In *Gesammelte Schriften*, edited by Günter Dux. Suhrkamp, 1980.

'The Pocket Telephone in Germany'. *Telephony* 62, no. 9 (2 March 1912): 280.

Polgar, Alfred. 'Aus Aufzeichnungen eines Radiohörers'. In *Kleine Schriften*, edited by Marcel Reich-Ranicki and Ulrich Weinzierl. Rowohlt, 1982.

Popper, Georg. [*Algol*]. *Hamburger Theaterzeitung* 39, no. 1 (1 October 1920). https://www.filmportal.de/en/node/1057/material/604482 (accessed 11 August 2025).

Pornschlegel, Clemens. 'Verkehrter Volksempfang: Heideggers Radio-Logik'. In *HardWar/SoftWar: Krieg und Medien 1914–1945*, edited by Wolfgang Scherer and Martin Stingelin. Fink, 1991.

Potter, Simon J., David Clayton, Friederike Kind-Kovács, Vincent Kuitenbrouwer, Nelson Ribeiro, Rebecca Scales, and Andrea L. Stanton. *The Wireless World: Global Histories of International Radio Broadcasting*. Oxford University Press, 2022.

Pound, Ezra. *ABC of Reading*. New Directions, 1960.

Powell, Larson. *The Technological Unconscious in German Modernist Literature: Nature in Rilke, Benn, Brecht, and Döblin*. Camden House, 2008.

Preece, William Henry. 'Electric Signalling without Wires'. *Journal Society of Arts*, 23 February 1894.

Preece, William Henry. 'Signalling Through Space Without Wires', *Science* 6, no. 155 (17 December 1897): 889–96.

Ramsay, Jack. 'Highlights of Antenna History'. *IEEE Communications Magazine* (September 1981): 4–16.

Rappaport, Theodore S. 'The Wireless Revolution', *IEEE Communications Magazine* (November 1991): 52–71.

Reichenbach, Hans, and Fritz Noack. *Was ist Radio*?. 2nd edn. Schmidt, 1929.

Rheinberger, Hans-Jörg. 'Experiment, Forschung, Kunst'. Lecture for Annual Conference of the Dramaturgischen Gesellschaft, Oldenburg, Germany, 26–29 April 2012.

Rheinberger, Hans-Jörg. 'Forming and Being Informed: Hans-Jörg Rheinberger in Conversation with Michael Schwab'. In *Experimental Systems: Future Knowledge in Artistic Research*, edited by Michael Schwab. Leuven University Press, 2013.

Rheinberger, Hans-Jörg, and Gerhard Herrgott. *Experimentalsysteme und epistemische Dinge: Eine Geschichte der Proteinsynthese im Reagenzglas*. Wallstein, 2001.

Richardson, Alan W. 'Hans Reichenbach, Radio Philosopher: A Preliminary Report'. *Synthese*, no. 199 (2021): 12625–41.

Richter, Petra. 'Joseph Beuys: An Earthquake in People's Minds'. *Tate Papers*, no. 31 (spring 2019). https://www.tate.org.uk/research/tate-papers/31/joseph-beuys-earthquake-in-peoples-minds/ (accessed 11 August 2025).

Riedel, Heide. *Fernsehen – Von der Vision zum Programm: 50 Jahre Programdienst in Deutschland*. Deutsches Rundfunk-Museum, 1985.

Rieger, Stefan. 'Psychopaths Electrified – Die Wahnwege des Wissens im Nothschrei eines Magnetisch-Vergifteten'. In *Grenzgänge zwischen Wahn und Wissen: Zur Koevolution von Experiment und Paranoia 1850–1930*, edited by Torsten Hahn, Jutta Person, and Nico Pethes. Campus, 2002.

Riepl, Wolfgang. *Das Nachrichtenwesen des Altertums*. Teubner, 1913.

Rikitianskaia, Maria. *The Global Wireless: Transnational Radiotelegraphy and Its Disruption in World War I*. De Gruyter, 2024.

Rikitianskaia, Maria, and Gabriele Balbi. 'Radio Studies beyond Broadcasting: Towards an Intermedia and Inter-Technological Radio History'. *Radio Journal: International Studies in Broadcast & Audio Media* 18, no. 2 (2020): 159–73.

Rikitianskaia, Maria, Gabriele Balbi, and Katharina Lobinger. 'The Mediatization of the Air: Wireless Telegraphy and the Origins of a Transnational Space of Communication, 1900–1910s'. *Journal of Communication* 68, no. 4 (2018): 758–79.

Rilke, Rainer Maria. 'The Sonnets to Orpheus'. In *Duino Elegies and the Sonnets to Orpheus*. Translated by A. Poulin Jr. Mariner, 2005.

Rippey, Theodore F. 'Kracauer and Sound: Reading with an Anxious Ear'. In *Culture in the Anteroom: The Legacies of Siegfried Kracauer*, edited by Gerd Gemünden and Johannes von Moltke. University of Michigan Press, 2012.

Ritter, Claus. *Anno Utopia, oder so war die Zukunft*. Das Neue Berlin, 1982.

Robida, Alfred. *The Twentieth Century*, edited by Arthur B. Evans. Translated by Philippe Willems. Wesleyan University Press, 2004.

Robinson, Cedric J. *Cedric J. Robinson: On Racial Capitalism, Black Internationalism, and Cultures of Resistance*, edited by H. L. T. Quan. Pluto Press, 2019.

Roda Roda, Alexander. 'Radio'. *Medienwissenschaft: Rezensionen* 5, no. 4 (1988): 77–8.

Roellinghoff, Charlie K. 'Radio im Humor: Ein paar Drahtlosigkeiten'. *Uhu* 3 (December 1924): 80–7.

Ronell, Avital. *The Telephone Book: Technology, Schizophrenia, Electric Speech*. University of Nebraska Press, 1989.

Rosenkrantz, Linda. *Telegram! Modern History as Told through More than 400 Witty, Poignant, and Revealing Telegrams*. Henry Holt, 2003.

Rossiter, Ned. *Software, Infrastructure, Labor: A Media Theory of Logistical Nightmares*. Routledge, 2016.

Roth, Joseph. 'Radiophon'. In *Berliner Saisonbericht: Unbekannte Reportagen und journalistische Arbeiten 1920–39*, edited by Klaus Westermann. Kiepenhauer & Witsch, 1984.

Rothe, Ernst. 'Psychologische Experimente im Rundfunk: Der Hörer als Versuchsobjekt'. *Funk* 22 (1924): 317–19.

Rothe, Katja. *Katastrophen hören: Experimente im frühen europäischen Radio*. Kadmos, 2009.

Rothe, Katja. 'Maritime Fantasien des frühen Radios'. In *Grenzflächen des Meeres*, edited by Thomas Brandstetter, Karin Harasser and Günther Friesinger. Turia + Kant, 2009.

Rothammel, Karl. *Antennenbuch*. 7th edn. Deutscher Militärververlag, 1969.

Rothman, Tony. 'Random Paths to Frequency Hopping'. *American Scientist*, no. 107 (2019): 46–54.

Ruhmer, Ernst Walter. *Drahtlose Telephonie*. Ruhmer, 1907.

Ruhmer, Ernst Walter. *Wireless Telephony, in Theory and Practice*. Translated by James Erskine-Murray. Van Nostrand, 1908.

Russo, Alexander. *Points on the Dial: Golden Age Radio Beyond the Networks*. Duke University Press, 2010.

Sagan, Carl. *Contact*. Simon and Schuster, 1997.

Sandbothe, Mike, and Marcus Burkhardt. 'Medienphilosophie'. In *Handbuch Medienwissenschaft*, edited by Jens Schröter, Simon Ruschmeyer and Elisabeth Walke. Metzler, 2014.

Sandbothe, Mike, and Ludwig Nagl, eds. *Systematische Medienphilosophie*. Akademie, 2005.

Sarkar, Tapan K., et al., eds. *History of Wireless*. Wiley, 2006.

Sarkar, Tapan K., and John S. Belrose. 'A History of Phased Array Antennas'. In *History of Wireless*, edited by Tapan K. Sarkar et al. Wiley, 2006.

Sarrazin, Otto. 'Sprachliches zur "Drahtlosen Telegraphie"'. *Zeitschrift des Allgemeinen Deutschen Sprachvereins* 29, no. 6 (1914): 194–9.

Sato, Gentei, and Motoyuki Sato. 'The Antenna Development in Japan: Past and Present'. In *History of Wireless*, edited by Tapan K. Sarkar et al. Wiley, 2006.

Schaal, Dirk. 'Bild und Ikonographie der Elektrizität: Über den Wahrnehmungs- und Bedeutungswandel einer Energieform seit dem Industriellen Zeitalter – Überlegungen für eine Ikonographie der Wirtschaft'. In *Energie in der Modernen Gesellschaft*, edited by Thomas Kroll. Vandenhoeck & Ruprecht, 2012.

Schaefer, Peter. 'Dematerialized Infrastructures: On the Ethereal Origins of Local Area Networks'. *Amodern* 2, special issue: *Network Archaeology* (2013), edited by Nicole Starosielski, Braxton Soderman, and Cris Cheek. https://amodern.net/article/dematerialized-infrastructures-and-the-ethereal-origins-of-local-area-networks/ (accessed 11 August 2025).

Schaffner, Kenneth F. *Nineteenth-Century Aether Theories*. Pergamon, 1972.

Schapira, Carl. 'Die Zukunft des deutschen Rundfunks'. *Funk: Die Wochenschrift des Funkwesens* 27 (1924): 417.

Schäfer, Hanns. 'Das Abhorchen von Ferngesprächen und die Erdtelegraphie im Felde'. *Polytechnisches Journal* 334 (1919): 93–7.

Schätzlein, Frank. 'Theorien'. In *Radio: Eine Einführung*, edited by Hans J. Kleinsteuber. VS Verlag für Sozialwissenschaften, 2012.

Schelle-Noetzel, A. H. [Arnolt Bronnen]. *Kampf im Aether oder die Unsichtbaren*. Rowohlt, 1935.

Schiffmann, Chr. 'Der Mensch als Antenne'. *Zentralblatt für Okkultismus* 20 (1927): 405–8.

Schirrmacher, Arne. 'Lenard's Ether and Its Vortex of Emotions: Between Accomodating and Fighting Modern Physics with *Äther* and *Uräther* in the German Political Context'. In *Ether and Modernity: The Recalcitrance of an Epistemic Object in the Early Twentieth Century*, edited by Jaume Navarro. Oxford University Press, 2018.

Schlobinski, Peter, and Oliver Siebold. *Wörterbuch der Science-Fiction*. Lang, 2008.

Schneider, Irmela. 'Rundfunk "für alle": Verbreitungsmedien und Paradoxien der All-Inklusion'. In *Medien – Diversität – Ungleichheit: Zur medialen*

Konstruktion sozialer Differenz, edited by Ulla Wischermann and Tanja Thomas. Verlag für Sozialwissenschaften, 2008.

Schneider, Irmela, ed. *Radio-Kultur in der Weimarer Republik: Eine Dokumentation*. Narr, 1984.

Schneider, Ursula. 'Rudolf Brunngraber: Eine Monographie'. PhD thesis, University of Vienna, 1990.

Scholl, Lars U. 'Marconi versus Telefunken: Drahtlose Telegraphie und ihre Bedeutung für die Schiffahrt'. In *Sozialgeschichte der Technik: Ulrich Troitzsch zum 60. Geburtstag*, edited by Günter Bayerl and Wolfhard Weber. Waxmann, 1998.

Scholz, Leander, et al. 'Rhetorik des Neuen: Mediendiskurse zwischen Buchdruck, Zeitung, Film, Radio, Hypertext und Internet'. In *Die Kommunikation der Medien*, edited by Jürgen Fohrmann and Erhard Schüttpelz. De Gruyter, 2004.

Schrage, Dominik. *Psychotechnik und Radiophonie: Subjektkonstruktionen in artifiziellen Wirklichkeiten 1918–1932*. Fink, 2001.

Schreber, Daniel Paul. *Memoirs of My Nervous Illness*. Edited and translated by Ida Macalpine and Richard A. Hunter. NYRB, 2000.

Schreier, Wolfgang, *Die Entstehung der Funktechnik*. Deutsches Museum, 1995.

Schröter, Fritz, Ernst Zechel, and Otto Nairz, eds. *25 Jahre Telefunken: Festschrift der Telefunken-Gesellschaft, 1903–1928*. Simon, 1928.

Schröter, Jens, and Till Heilmann. *Friedrich Kittler: Neue Lektüren*. Springer, 2022.

Schulz, Walter J. *Wireless Antenna History: A Vertical Design Primer*. Herbst, 1988.

Schüttpelz, Erhard. 'Trance-Medien/Personale Medien'. In *Handbuch Medienwissenschaft*, edited by Jens Schröter. Metzler, 2014.

Schwarzwald, Eugenie. 'The Prophesied Ravag (1934)'. In *The Red Vienna Sourcebook*, edited by Rob McFarland, Georg Spitaler and Ingo Zechner. Camden House, 2020.

Schweppenhäuser, Gerhard, ed. *Handbuch der Medienphilosophie*. WBG, 2018.

Schwitters, Kurt. 'A Stimulus to Make the Most Productive Use of Radio'. Translated by Louis P. Kaplan. In *Radiotext(e)*, edited by Neil Strauss and Dave Mandl. Semiotext(e), 1993.

Seel, Martin. 'Eine vorübergehende Sache'. In *Medienphilosophie: Beiträge zur Klärung eines Begriffs*, edited by Stefan Münker, Alexander Roesler, and Mike Sandbothe. Fischer, 2003.

Segeberg, Harro. 'Technische Konkurrenzen: Film und Tele-Medien im Blick der Literatur'. In *Hansers Sozialgeschichte der deutschen Literatur vom 16. Jahrhundert bis zur Gegenwart*, edited by Rolf Grimminger. Hanser, 1980.

Seitter, Walter. 'The Meta-Physics of Media'. In *Media Matter: The Materiality of Media, Matter as Medium*, edited by Bernd Herzogenrath. Bloomsbury, 2015.

Seitter, Walter. *Physik der Medien: Materialien, Apparate, Präsentierungen*. VDG Weimar, 2002.

Seitz, Robert, and Heinz Zucker, eds. *Um uns die Stadt: Eine Anthologie neuer Großstadtdichtung*. Vieweg & Sohn, 1931.

Seydel, Albert, ed. *'Made in Germany': Technisch-humoristisches, Beschauliches und Erbauliches Allerlei in Poesie und Prosa*. Polytechnische Buchhandlung A. Seydel, 1896.

Siegert, Bernhard. 'Cacography or Communication? Cultural Techniques in German Media Studies'. *Grey Room* 29, no. 1 (2007): 26–47.

Siegert, Bernhard. 'Das Hörspiel als Vergangenheitsbewältigung'. In *Medienkultur der 50er Jahre: Diskursgeschichte der Medien nach 1945*, edited by Irmela Schneider and Peter M. Spangenberg. Vol. 1. Westdeutscher Verlag, 2002.

Siegert, Bernhard. 'Eskalation eines Mediums: Die Lichtung des Radiohörens im Hochfrequenzkrieg'. In *On the Air: Kunst im öffentlichen Raum*, edited by Heidi Grundmann et al. Transit, 1993.

Siegert, Bernhard. 'The Map *Is* the Territory'. *Radical Philosophy* 169 (2011): 13–16.

Siegert, Bernhard. *Passage des Digitalen: Zeichenpraktiken der neuzeitlichen Wissenschaften 1500–1900*. Brinkmann + Bose, 2003.

Siegert, Bernhard. *Relays: Literature as an Epoch of the Postal System*. Translated by Kevin Repp. Stanford University Press, 1999.

Siemens, Georg. *History of the House of Siemens*. 3 vols. Karl Alber, 1957.

Simmel, Georg. 'The Metropolis and Mental Life'. In *The Sociology of Georg Simmel*. Translated and edited by Kurt H. Wolff. The Free Press, 1950.

Simondon, Gilbert. *On the Mode of Existence of Technical Objects*. Translated by Cécile Malaspina and John Rogove. Univocal, 2016.

Simondon, Gilbert. 'On Techno-Aesthetics'. Translated by Arne De Boever. *Parrhesia* 14 (2012): 1–8.

Sinclair, Upton. *Mental Radio*. Thomas, 1930.

Slaby, Adolf. *Die Funkentelegraphie: Gemeinverständliche Vorträge*. Simion, 1901.

Slaby, Adolf. 'Die neuesten Fortschritte auf dem Gebiete der Funkentelegraphie'. In *Die Funkentelegraphie: Gemeinverständliche Vorträge*. Simion, 1901.

Slaby, Adolf. 'The New Telegraphy: Recent Experiments in Telegraphy with Sparks'. *The Century Magazine* 55 (1898): 867–74.

Slaby, Adolf, and Georg von Arco. Eine durch Kondensator geschlossene, an Erde liegende Sendeschleife für Funkentelegraphie. Kaiserliches Patentamt 133,718, filed 4 November 1899, and issued 26 August 1902.

Slaby, Adolf, and Georg von Arco. Empfangsapparat für Funkentelegraphie. Kaiserliches Patentamt 116,071, filed 9 February 1900, and issued 3 December 1900.

Slaby, Adolf, and Georg von Arco. Empfangsapparat für Funkentelegraphie mit gemeinsamer Stromquelle im Morse- und Fritterstromkreise. Kaiserliches Patentamt 124,645, filed 9 February 1900, and issued 26 October 1901.

Slaby, Adolf, and Georg von Arco. Schaltung am Empfänger für Funkentelegraphie. Kaiserliches Patentamt 113,285, filed 25 April 1899, and issued 11 September 1900.

Slaby, Adolf, and Georg von Arco. Schaltungsweise der Gebe- und Empfangsstation für Funkentelegraphie mit vertikalen Luftleitungen. Kaiserliches Patentamt 124,154, filed 23 December 1898, and issued 18 October 1901.

Sloss, Robert. 'Das drahtlose Jahrhundert'. In *Die Welt in hundert Jahren*, edited by Arthur Brehmer. Buntdruck, 1910.

Sloss, Robert. 'Sight Magic and Sound Magic in the Wireless Age'. *New Broadway Magazine* 21, no. 3 (1908): 300–8.

Sloterdijk, Peter. 'A Plug for Higher Energies'. In *Selected Exaggerations: Conversations and Interviews*. Polity, 2016.

Slyusar, V. I. 'To History of Radio Engineering's Term "Antenna"'. In *VIII International Conference on Antenna Theory and Techniques*. Kyiv, 2011.

Snickars, Pelle, and Patrick Vonderau, *Moving Data: The iPhone and the Future of Media*. Columbia University Press, 2013.

Sprenger, Florian. 'Between the Ends of a Wire: Electricity, Instantaneity and the Globe of Telegraphy'. In *Global Communication Electric: Actors of a Globalizing World*, edited by Michaela Hampf and Simone Müller-Pohl. Campus, 2013.

Sreevidya, S., and N. Subramanian. 'Aesthetic Appraisal of Antenna Towers'. *Journal of Architectural Engineering* 3 (2003): 102–8.

Sroka, Otto. 'Die Fernseh-Zeitung. Rezept nach Palmström-Korff'. *Medienwissenschaft: Rezensionen* 7, no. 1–2 (1990): 188–9.

Stäheli, Urs. 'Undoing Networks'. Translated by Erik Born. In *Undoing Networks*, edited by Tero Karppi, Urs Stäheli, Clara Wieghorst and Lea Zierott. University of Minnesota Press, 2020.

Standage, Tom. *The Victorian Internet: The Remarkable Story of the Telegraph and the Nineteenth Century's Online Pioneers*. Bloomsbury, 2014.

Star, Susan Leigh. 'Cooperation Without Consensus in Scientific Problem Solving: Dynamics of Closure in Open Systems'. In *CSCW: Cooperation or Conflict?*, edited by Steve Easterbrook. Spring, 1993.

Starosielski, Nicole. 'The Ends of Media Studies'. *Public Culture* 33, no. 3 (2021): 305–11.

Starosielski, Nicole. 'Signal Tracks'. *Media-N: Journal of the New Media Caucus* 10, no. 1 (2014).

Steiner, Rudolf. *Vom Wesen des Wirkenden Wortes: Vier Vorträge mit Fragenbeantwortungen, gehalten in Stuttgart vom 11. Bis 14. Juli 1923*. Rudolf-Steiner-Verlag, 1994.

Sterne, Carus. 'Alte Ahnungen der drahtlosen Telegraphie'. *Prometheus* 12 [618], no. 46 (1901): 721–5.

Sterne, Jonathan. *MP3: The Meaning of a Format*. Duke University Press, 2012.

Sterne, Jonathan. '"What Do We Want?" "Materiality!" "When Do We Want It?" "Now!"' In *Media Technologies: Essays on Communication,*

Materiality, and Society, edited by Tarleton Gillespie, Pablo J. Boczkowski and Kirsten A. Foot. MIT Press, 2014.
Steyerl, Hito. 'The Spam of the Earth: Withdrawal from Representation'. *e-flux Journal* 32 (February 2012). https://www.e-flux.com/journal/32/68260/the-spam-of-the-earth-withdrawal-from-representation (accessed 11 August 2025).
Stockmayer, Ludwig von. 'Zukünftiges'. *Funk* 36 (1926): 296.
Strauven, Wanda. 'The Imagination of Wireless Distribution'. In *Networks of Entertainment: Early Film Distribution 1895–1915*, edited by Frank Kessler and Nanna Verhoeff. Indiana University Press, 2007.
Strauven, Wanda. 'The Observer's Dilemma: To Touch or Not to Touch'. In *Media Archaeology: Approaches, Applications, and Implications*, edited by Erkki Huhtamo and Jussi Parikka. University of California Press, 2011.
Süsskind, Charles. 'Hertz and the Technological Significance of Electromagnetic Waves'. *Isis* 56, no. 3 (1965): 342–5.
Telefunken and Transradio. *Festschrift zur Einweihung der Grossfunkstelle Nauen am 29.9.20*. Simon, 1920.
Tesla, Nikola. *My Inventions* [1919]. Barnes and Noble, 1995.
Tesla, Nikola. 'Talking with Planets'. *Collier's Weekly*, 19 February 1901: 4–5.
Tesla, Nikola. 'When Woman is a Boss'. *Colliers*, 30 January 1926, 17, 34.
Thibault, Ghislain. 'Bolts and Waves: Representing Radio Signals'. *Early Popular Visual Culture* 16, no. 1 (2018): 39–56.
Thibault, Ghislain. 'Streaming: A Media Hydrography of Televisual Flows'. *VIEW: Journal of European Television History and Culture* 4, no. 7 (2015): 110.
Thibault, Ghislain. 'Wireless Pasts and Wired Futures'. In *Theories of the Mobile Internet: Materialities and Imaginaries*, edited by Andrew Herman, Jan Hadlaw and Thom Swiss. Routledge, 2015.
Thiele, Erdmann, ed. *Telefunken nach 100 Jahren: das Erbe einer deutschen Weltmarke*. 2nd edn. Nicolai, 2003.
Thiele, Martin. *Zur Geschichte der Nachrichten-Truppe 1899–1924*, vol. 1. J.S. Preuß, 1925.
Thieme, Friedrich. 'Das Warenhaus der Zukunft: Humoristische Skizze'. In *Die Liebe der Zukunft vor 100 Jahren: 20 utopisch-erotische Novellen, 1871–1914*, edited by Detlef Münch. Synergen, 2006.
Thomson, Elihu. 'Curious Effects of Hertzian Waves'. *Electrical Engineer*, 4 July 1894.
Thomson, J. J. 'Address to the British Association Meeting at Winnipeg'. *The Electrical Review* 65, no. 1657 (27 August 1909): 335.
Thon, Luise. *Die Sprache des deutschen Impressionismus: Ein Beitrag zur Sprach- und Literaturgeschichte*. Max Hueber, 1928.
Thurmann-Jajes, Anne, et al., eds. *Radio as Art: Concepts, Spaces, Practices*. Transcript, 2019.
Tismar, Jens. *Das deutsche Kunstmärchen des zwanzigsten Jahrhunderts*. Metzler, 1981.

Toller, Ernst. *Hoppla, wir leben!*. In *Gesammelte Werke*. Vol. 3. Edited by Wolfgang Frühwald and John M. Spalek. Hanser, 1996.

Toscano, Aaron Antonio. *Marconi's Wireless and the Rhetoric of a New Technology*. Springer, 2012.

Treue, Wilhelm. 'Das Haus des Rundfunks'. *Rundfunk und Geschichte* 11, no. 2 (1985): 136–48.

Trier, Jost. 'Antenne'. In *Festschrift für Hugo Moser – zum 60. Geburtstag am 19. Juni 1969*, edited by Ulrich Engel, Paul Grebe, and Heinz Rupp. Schwann, 1969.

Trithemius, Johannes. *Steganographia*. Matthias Becker, 1606.

Trüby, Stephan. 'Antenne und Bunker'. In *Ästhetik der Materialität*, edited by Christiane Heibach and Carsten Rohde. Fink, 2015.

Trüby, Stephan. *Hertzianismus: Elektromagnetismus in Architektur, Design und Kunst*. Fink, 2009.

Tucholsky, Kurt [Peter Panter]. 'The Loudspeaker'. Translated by Iain Boyd White. In *Metropolis Berlin, 1880–1940*, edited by Iain Boyd White and David Frisby. University of California Press, 2012.

Turkle, Sherry. 'Always-On/Always-On-You: The Tethered Self'. In *Handbook of Mobile Communication Studies*, edited by James Everett Katz. MIT Press, 2008.

Tworek, Heidi J. S. 'How Not to Build a World Wireless Network: German–British Rivalry and Visions of Global Communications in the Early Twentieth Century'. *History and Technology* 32, no. 2 (2016): 178–200.

Tworek, Heidi. *News from Germany: The Competition to Control World Communications, 1900–1945*. Harvard University Press, 2019.

Umbach, Maiken. *German Cities and Bourgeois Modernism, 1890–1924*. Oxford University Press, 2009.

Umbach, Maiken. 'Made in Germany'. In *Deutsche Erinnerungsorte*, edited by Etienne François and Hagen Schulze. Vol. 2. Beck, 2001.

Updike, John. 'Telephone Poles'. In *Telephone Poles and Other Poems*. Knopf, 1963.

Uricchio, William. 'Storage, Simultaneity, and the Media Technologies of Modernity'. In *Allegories of Communication: Intermedial Concerns from Cinema to the Digital*, edited by John Fullerton and Jan Olsson. John Libbey, 2004.

Vagt, Christina. 'Physics and Aesthetics: Simulation as Action at a Distance'. In John Durham Peters, Florian Sprenger, and Christina Vagt. *Action at a Distance*. University of Minnesota Press, 2020.

Valentin, Karl, and Liesl Karlstadt. 'Im Senderaum'. In *Karl Valentin: Gesammelte Werke in einem Band*. Edited by Michael Schulte. Piper, 1985.

Verweyen, Johannes Maria. 'Radioitis! Gedanken zum Radiohören'. In *Medientheorie 1888–1933: Texte und Kommentare*, edited by Albert Kümmel and Petra Löffler. Suhrkamp, 2002.

Vogel, Fritz von. 'Drahtlose Energieübertragung'. *Jahrbuch der drahtlosen Telegraphie und Telephonie* 19 (1922): 197–205.

Vogel, Juliane. 'Verstrickungskünste – Lösungskünste: Zur Geschichte des dramatischen Knotens'. *Poetica* 40, no. 3/4 (2008): 269–88.

Volmar, Axel, ed. *Zeitkritische Medien*. Kadmos, 2009.

'Von Welle zu Welle'. *Fliegende Blättern*, 31 March 1931: 60.

Völker, Clara. *Mobile Medien: Zur Genealogie des Mobilfunks und zur Ideengeschichte von Virtualität*. Transcript, 2010.

Warburg, Aby. 'A Lecture on Serpent Ritual'. *Journal of the Warburg Institute* 2, no. 4 (1939): 277–92.

Wark, McKenzie. 'Telegram from Nowhere'. In *Mutations*, edited by Rem Koolhaas et al. Actor, 2000.

Webb, William. *The 5G Myth: When Vision Decoupled from Reality*. De Gruyter, 2019.

Wedemeyer, Arnd. 'Ningún libro es también una escalera'. In *Babel: Festschrift für Werner Hamacher*, edited by Aris Fioretos. Urs Engeler, 2009.

Weiher, Siegfried von. *Männer der Funktechnik: Eine Sammlung von 70 Lebenswerken deutscher Pioniere der Funktechnik (drahtlose Telegrafie, Radar, Rundfunk und Fernsehen)*. VDE, 1983.

Weilenmann, August. *Die elektrischen Wellen und ihre Anwendung zur drahtlosen Strahlentelegraphie nach Marconi*. Fäsi & Beer, 1903.

Wells, H. G. *The First Men in the Moon*. George Newnes, 1901.

Wells-Barnett, Ida B. *The Red Record: Tabulated Statistics and Alleged Causes of Lynching in the United States*. Donohue & Henneberry, 1895.

Whitney, Allison. 'Etched with the Emulsion: Weimar Dance and Body Culture in German Expressionist Cinema'. *Seminar: A Journal of Germanic Studies* 46, no. 3 (2010): 246–8.

Whyte, Iain Boyd, and David Frisby, eds. *Metropolis Berlin, 1880–1940*. University of California Press, 2012.

Wigley, Mark. *Buckminster Fuller Inc.: Architecture in the Age of Radio*. Lars Müller, 2016.

Wigley, Mark. 'We are Living in an Ecology of Antenna'. Interview by Ruben Baart. *Next Nature*, 17 March 2018.

Williamson, Debra Aho. 'Forget about Wired, the Future is Wireless'. *Advertising Age* 71, no. 10 (2000): 18.

Willmann, Françoise. 'Leibniz's Metaphysics as an Epistemological Obstacle to the Mathematization of Nature: The View of a Late 19th Century Neo-Kantian, Kurd Lasswitz'. In *New Essays on Leibniz Reception: In Science and Philosophy of Science, 1800–2000*, edited by Ral Krömer and Yannick Chin-Drian. Springer, 2012.

Wilson, Stephen. 'Artists as Researchers in Wireless Communication'. In *Ohne Schnur: Kunst und drahtlose Kommunikation*, edited by Katja Kwastek. Revolver, 2004.

Winkler, Hartmut. 'Tauschen, Austauschen, Kommunizeren: Netzbildung in Ökonomie und Medien'. In *Netzwerke: Eine Kulturtechnik der Moderne*, edited by Jürgen Barkhoff, Hartmut Böhme, and Jeanne Riou. Böhlau, 2004.

Winn, J. Emmett, and Susan Lorene Brinson, eds. *Transmitting the Past: Historical and Cultural Perspectives on Broadcasting*. University of Alabama Press, 2005.

Winseck, Dwayne R., and Robert M. Pike, *Communication and Empire: Media, Markets, and Globalization, 1860–1930*. Duke University Press, 2007.

Winthrop-Young, Geoffrey. 'Going Postal to Deliver Subjects: Remarks on a German Postal a Priori'. *Angelaki* 7, no. 3 (2002): 143–58.

Winthrop-Young, Geoffrey. 'The Kittler Effect'. *New German Critique*, no. 132 (2017): 205–24.

Winthrop-Young, Geoffrey. *Kittler and the Media*. Polity, 2011.

Winthrop-Young, Geoffrey. 'Recursive Innovation'. In *The Technological Introject: Friedrich Kittler between Implementation and the Incalculable*, edited by Jeffrey Champlin and Antje Pfannkuchen. Fordham University Press, 2018.

Winthrop-Young, Geoffrey. 'Siren Recursions'. In *Kittler Now: Current Perspectives in Kittler Studies*, edited by Stephen Sale and Laura Salisbury. Polity, 2015.

'The Wireless 'Phone Will Get You'. *The Electrical Experimenter* (January 1916): 487.

Wittgenstein, Ludwig. *Zettel*. Translated by G. E. M. Anscombe. University of California Press, 2007.

Wythoff, Grant. 'The Invention of Wireless Cryptography'. *The Appendix*, 8 July 2014.

Wythoff, Grant. 'Pocket Wireless and the Shape of Media to Come, 1899–1922'. *Grey Room* 51 (April 2013): 54–6.

Wythoff, Grant, ed. *The Perversity of Things: Hugo Gernsback on Media, Tinkering, and Scientifiction*. University of Minnesota Press, 2016.

Young, Liam Cole. 'Imagination and Literary Media Theory'. *Media Theory* 1, no. 1 (2017): 17–33.

Young, Paul. *The Cinema Dreams Its Rivals: Media Fantasy Films from Radio to the Internet*. University of Minnesota Press, 2006.

Zielinski, Siegfried. *Deep Time of the Media: Toward an Archaeology of Hearing and Seeing by Technical Means*. Translated by Gloria Custance. MIT Press, 2006.

Zielinski, Siegfried. 'Modelling Media for Ignatius Loyola: A Case Study on Athanasius Kircher's World of Apparatus between the Imaginary and the Real'. In *Book of Imaginary Media: Excavating the Dream of the Ultimate Communication Medium*, edited by Eric Kluitenberg. Debalie, 2006.

Zielinski, Siegfried. *Variations on Media Thinking*. University of Minnesota Press, 2019.

Zweig, Stefan. 'An den Funkturm, den Nachbarn'. In *Literatur und Rundfunk 1923–1933*, edited by Gerhard Hay. Gerstenberg, 1975.

Index

Note: Figures are shown by a page reference in *italics*.

EU Authorised Representative:
Easy Access System Europe Mustamäe tee 50, 10621 Tallinn, Estonia
gpsr.requests@easproject.com

Printed and bound by CPI Group (UK) Ltd, Croydon, CR0 4YY
18/04/2026
02092619-0008